Kaplan Publishing are constantly fi̱ ··
ways to make a difference to your s
exciting online resources really do
different to students looking for ex

C000185970

This book comes with free EN-gage online resources so that you can study anytime, anywhere.

Having purchased this book, you have access to the following online study materials:

CONTENT	ACCA (including FFA,FAB,FMA)		AAT		FIA (excluding FFA,FAB,FMA)	
	Text	Kit	Text	Kit	Text	Kit
iPaper version of the book	✓	✓	✓	✓	✓	✓
Interactive electronic version of the book	✓					
Fixed tests / progress tests with instant answers	✓		✓			
Mock assessments online			✓	✓		
Material updates	✓	✓	✓	✓	✓	✓
Latest official ACCA exam questions		✓				
Extra question assistance using the signpost icon*		✓				
Timed questions with an online tutor debrief using the clock icon*		✓				
Interim assessment including questions and answers		✓			✓	
Technical articles	✓	✓			✓	✓

* Excludes F1, F2, F3, FFA, FAB, FMA

How to access your online resources

Kaplan Financial students will already have a Kaplan EN-gage account and these extra resources will be available to you online. You do not need to register again, as this process was completed when you enrolled. If you are having problems accessing online materials, please ask your course administrator.

If you are already a registered Kaplan EN-gage user go to www.EN-gage.co.uk and log in. Select the 'add a book' feature and enter the ISBN number of this book and the unique pass key at the bottom of this card. Then click 'finished' or 'add another book'. You may add as many books as you have purchased from this screen.

If you purchased through Kaplan Flexible Learning or via the Kaplan Publishing website you will automatically receive an e-mail invitation to Kaplan EN·gage online. Please register your details using this email to gain access to your content. If you do not receive the e-mail or book content, please contact Kaplan Flexible Learning.

If you are a new Kaplan EN-gage user register at www.EN-gage.co.uk and click on the link contained in the email we sent you to activate your account. Then select the 'add a book' feature, enter the ISBN number of this book and the unique pass key at the bottom of this card. Then click 'finished' or 'add another book'.

Your Code and Information

This code can only be used once for the registration of one book online. This registration and your online content will expire when the final sittings for the examinations covered by this book have taken place. Please allow one hour from the time you submit your book details for us to process your request.

Please scratch the film to access your EN-gage code.

Please be aware that this code is case-sensitive and you will need to include the dashes within the passcode, but not when entering the ISBN. For further technical support, please visit www.EN-gage.co.uk

Paper F9

Financial Management

EXAM KIT

British Library Cataloguing-in-Publication Data

A catalogue record for this book is available from the British Library.

Published by:

Kaplan Publishing UK

Unit 2 The Business Centre

Molly Millar's Lane

Wokingham

Berkshire

RG41 2QZ

ISBN: 978 0 85732 683 6

© Kaplan Financial Limited, 2013

Printed and bound in Great Britain.

Acknowledgements

The past ACCA examination questions are the copyright of the Association of Chartered Certified Accountants. The original answers to the questions from June 1994 onwards were produced by the examiners themselves and have been adapted by Kaplan Publishing.

We are grateful to the Chartered Institute of Management Accountants and the Institute of Chartered Accountants in England and Wales for permission to reproduce past examination questions. The answers have been prepared by Kaplan Publishing.

CONTENTS

	Page
Index to questions and answers	v
Analysis of past exam papers	xi
Exam Technique	xiii
Paper specific information	xv
Kaplan's recommended revision approach	xvii
Kaplan's detailed revision plan	xix
Mathematical tables and formulae sheet	xxv

Section

1	Practice questions	1
2	Answers to practice questions	69

Key features in this edition

In addition to providing a wide ranging bank of real past exam questions, we have also included in this edition:

- An analysis of all of the recent examination papers.

- Paper specific information and advice on exam technique.

- Our recommended approach to make your revision for this particular subject as effective as possible.

   This includes step by step guidance on how best to use our Kaplan material (Complete text, pocket notes and exam kit) at this stage in your studies.

- Enhanced tutorial answers packed with specific key answer tips, technical tutorial notes and exam technique tips from our experienced tutors.

- Complementary online resources including full tutor debriefs and question assistance to point you in the right direction when you get stuck.

Recent real examination questions with enhanced tutorial answers

The real June and December 2011, and June and December 2012 exam questions with enhanced "walk through answers", updated in line with legislation relevant to your exam sitting, is available on Kaplan EN-gage at:

www.EN-gage.co.uk

You will find a wealth of other resources to help you with your studies on the following sites:

www.EN-gage.co.uk

www.accaglobal.com/students/

INDEX TO QUESTIONS AND ANSWERS

INTRODUCTION

Past exam questions have been modified (sometimes extensively) to reflect the current F9 syllabus.

KEY TO THE INDEX

PAPER ENHANCEMENTS

We have added the following enhancements to the answers in this exam kit:

Key answer tips

All answers include key answer tips to help your understanding of each question.

Tutorial note

Many answers include more tutorial notes to explain some of the technical points in more detail.

Top tutor tips

For selected questions, we "walk through the answer" giving guidance on how to approach the questions with helpful 'tips from a top tutor', together with technical tutor notes.

These answers are indicated with the "footsteps" icon in the index.

ONLINE ENHANCEMENTS

 Timed question with Online tutor debrief

For selected questions, we recommend that they are to be completed in full exam conditions (i.e. properly timed in a closed book environment).

In addition to the examiner's technical answer, enhanced with key answer tips and tutorial notes in this exam kit, online you can find an answer debrief by a top tutor that:

- works through the question in full

- points out how to approach the question

- shows how to ensure that the easy marks are obtained as quickly as possible, and

- emphasises how to tackle exam questions and exam technique.

These questions are indicated with the "clock" icon in the index.

 Online question assistance

Have you ever looked at a question and not known where to start, or got stuck part way through?

For selected questions, we have produced "Online question assistance" offering different levels of guidance, such as:

- ensuring that you understand the question requirements fully, highlighting key terms and the meaning of the verbs used

- how to read the question proactively, with knowledge of the requirements, to identify the topic areas covered

- assessing the detailed content of the question body, pointing out key information and explaining why it is important

- help in devising a plan of attack

With this assistance, you should then be able to attempt your answer confident that you know what is expected of you.

These questions are indicated with the "signpost" icon in the index.

Online question enhancements and answer debriefs will be available on Kaplan EN-gage at:

www.EN-gage.co.uk

FINANCIAL MANAGEMENT FUNCTION AND ENVIRONMENT

			Page number		
			Question	Answer	Past exam
1	UUL		1	69	–
2	CCC		2	71	–
3	Neighbouring countries		3	74	–
4	RZP Co		4	76	–
5	JJG Co	🕐	5	79	June 09
6	Dartig Co	🔳	6	84	Dec 08
7	News for you		7	88	–
8	CC Co		8	91	–
9	RWF		9	94	–

WORKING CAPITAL MANAGEMENT

10	Gorwa Co		10	96	Dec 08
11	FLG Co		11	101	June 08
12	PKA Co	🔳	12	104	Dec 07
13	Ulnad		13	110	–
14	APX Co		13	113	Dec 09
15	HGR Co	🕐	15	119	June 09
16	Anjo		16	124	–
17	ZSE Co		18	126	June 10
18	PNP plc	◪	18	131	June 07
19	WQZ		19	136	Dec 10

INVESTMENT APPRAISAL

20	Armcliff Co		20	140	–
21	Dairy Co		22	144	–
22	Investment appraisal		23	147	–
23	PV Co	🕐	23	151	June 09
24	BFD Co		24	156	–
25	Trecor		25	158	–
26	Charm Inc		26	161	–
27	Play Co		26	164	–
28	Duo Co	🔳	27	168	Dec 07

			Page number		
			Question	*Answer*	*Past exam*
29	OKM Co		28	174	*June 10*
30	Umunat Inc		29	179	–
31	Victory		30	181	–
32	Springbank Inc	🔖	31	184	–
33	CJ Co		32	188	*Dec 10*
34	Basril		33	194	–
35	ASOP Co		33	197	*Dec 09*
36	Cavic		34	202	–

BUSINESS FINANCE

37	FMY		35	205	–
38	Nugfer		36	209	*Dec 10*
39	Echo Co	🎲	37	214	*Dec 07*
40	Pavlon		38	221	–
41	Arwin		39	223	–
42	Spender Construction Inc		41	227	–
43	Associated International Supplies Co		43	232	–
44	GTK Inc	🎲	44	236	*June 07*
45	TFR		45	239	*June 07*

COST OF CAPITAL

46	Droxfol		46	243	–
47	Ill colleague		48	247	–
48	KFP Co	🕐	49	249	*June 09*
49	Burse Co	🎲	50	253	*June 08*
50	YGV Co		51	258	*June 10*
51	GM Co		52	263	–
52	IRQ Co		53	265	–
53	DD Co		54	268	*Dec 09*

BUSINESS VALUATIONS

			Question	Answer	Past exam
			Page number		
54	QSX Co		55	272	*June 10*
55	OCT		55	276	–
56	Hendil (Part II)		56	280	–
57	NN Co		58	283	*Dec 10*
58	MAT Co		60	287	–
59	THP Co		61	290	*June 08*
60	Phobis		62	296	*Dec 07*

RISK MANAGEMENT

61	NG Co		63	300	*Dec 09*
62	Nedwen		64	304	–
63	Lagrag Co		65	307	–
64	Boluje Co		65	309	*Dec 08*
65	Exporters plc		66	313	–
66	Elect Co		67	316	–

ANALYSIS OF PAST PAPERS

The table below summarises the key topics that have been tested in the new syllabus examinations to date.

	J08	D08	J09	D09	J10	D10	J11	D11	J12
Financial management function									
Nature and purpose of financial management					✓				
Financial objectives and corporate strategy			✓		✓				
Stakeholders and their impact on corporate strategy		✓							✓
Not for profits								✓	
Financial management environment									
Economic environment									
Financial markets and institutions				✓					
Working capital management									
Elements and importance (including cash operating cycle)		✓		✓				✓	✓
Inventories	✓					✓	✓		
Receivables	✓	✓			✓	✓		✓	
Payables							✓		
Cash			✓		✓				✓
Working capital needs and funding strategies	✓		✓	✓	✓		✓		✓
Investment appraisal									
Appraisal process	✓		✓			✓			
Non-discounted techniques			✓						
NPV with tax							✓	✓	
NPV with tax and inflation	✓	✓	✓	✓	✓	✓	✓		✓
IRR	✓		✓		✓				
Risk and uncertainty					✓		✓	✓	✓
Lease or buy				✓					
Asset replacement				✓	✓				✓
Capital rationing				✓				✓	

	J08	D08	J09	D09	J10	D10	J11	D11	J12
Business finance									
Sources of short term finance									
Sources of long term finance		✓	✓	✓	✓	✓	✓	✓	✓
Internal sources and dividend policy				✓		✓	✓		
Gearing and capital structure		✓		✓	✓	✓	✓		
Small & medium enterprises									
Islamic financing									✓
Cost of capital									
Sources and relative costs	✓		✓						✓
Estimating cost of equity	✓								
CAPM	✓	✓		✓	✓	✓			
Cost of debt	✓			✓	✓	✓			
Overall cost of capital	✓	✓	✓	✓	✓	✓	✓	✓	✓
Gearing theories			✓				✓		
Impact of cost of capital on investments					✓				
Business valuations									
Nature and purpose of valuation									
Models for valuing shares	✓		✓	✓	✓	✓		✓	✓
Valuing debt and other financial assets		✓					✓		
Efficient markets hypothesis						✓			
Risk management									
Foreign exchange risk		✓		✓			✓		✓
Interest rate risk		✓				✓			
Forward contracts				✓			✓		✓
Money market hedge		✓		✓			✓		✓
Futures									
Hedging for interest rate risk									

EXAM TECHNIQUE

- Use the allocated **15 minutes reading and planning time** at the beginning of the exam:
  - read the questions and examination requirements carefully, and
  - begin planning your answers.

  See the Paper Specific Information for advice on how to use this time for this paper.

- **Divide the time** you spend on questions in proportion to the marks on offer:
  - there are 1.8 minutes available per mark in the examination
  - within that, try to allow time at the end of each question to review your answer and address any obvious issues

  Whatever happens, always keep your eye on the clock and **do not over run on any part of any question!**

- Spend the last **five minutes** of the examination:
  - reading through your answers, and
  - **making any additions or corrections**.

- If you **get completely stuck** with a question:
  - leave space in your answer book, and
  - **return to it later.**

- Stick to the question and **tailor your answer** to what you are asked.
  - pay particular attention to the verbs in the question.

- If you do not understand what a question is asking, **state your assumptions**.

  Even if you do not answer in precisely the way the examiner hoped, you should be given some credit, if your assumptions are reasonable.

- You should do everything you can to make things easy for the marker.

  The marker will find it easier to identify the points you have made if your **answers are legible**.

- **Written elements of questions**:

  Your answer should have a clear structure

  Be concise.

  It is better to write a little about a lot of different points than a great deal about one or two points.

- **Computations**:

  It is essential to include all your workings in your answers.

  Many computational questions require the use of a standard format:

  e.g. net present values, writing down allowances and cash budgets.

  Be sure you know these formats thoroughly before the exam and use the layouts that you see in the answers given in this book and in model answers.

- **Reports, memos and other documents**:

  Some questions ask you to present your answer in the form of a report, a memo, a letter or other document.

  Make sure that you use the correct format – there could be easy marks to gain here.

PAPER SPECIFIC INFORMATION

THE EXAM

FORMAT OF THE EXAM

4 compulsory questions each of 25 marks which will be **a mixture of computations and discussion**:

Total time allowed: 3 hours plus 15 minutes reading and planning time.

Questions will be drawn evenly from across the whole syllabus.

PASS MARK

The pass mark for all ACCA Qualification examination papers is 50%.

READING AND PLANNING TIME

Remember that all three hour paper based examinations have an additional 15 minutes reading and planning time.

ACCA GUIDANCE

ACCA guidance on the use of this time is as follows:

This additional time is allowed at the beginning of the examination to allow candidates to read the questions and to begin planning their answers before they start to write in their answer books.

This time should be used to ensure that all the information and, in particular, the exam requirements are properly read and understood.

During this time, candidates may only annotate their question paper. They may not write anything in their answer booklets until told to do so by the invigilator.

KAPLAN GUIDANCE

As all questions are compulsory, there are no decisions to be made about choice of questions, other than in which order you would like to tackle them.

Therefore, in relation to F9, we recommend that you take the following approach with your reading and planning time:

- **Skim through the whole paper**, assessing the level of difficulty of each question.

- **Write down** on the question paper next to the mark allocation **the amount of time you should spend on each part.** Do this for each part of every question.

- **Decide the order** in which you think you will attempt each question:

  This is a personal choice and you have time on the revision phase to try out different approaches, for example, if you sit mock exams.

A common approach is to tackle the question you think is the easiest and you are most comfortable with first. Others may prefer to tackle the longest questions first, or conversely leave them to the last.

Psychologists believe that you usually perform at your best on the second and third question you attempt, once you have settled into the exam, so not tackling the hardest question first may be advisable.

It is usual however that student tackle their least favourite topic and/or the most difficult question in their opinion last.

Whatever you approach, you must make sure that you leave enough time to attempt all questions fully and be very strict with yourself in timing each question.

- **For each question** in turn, read the requirements and then the detail of the question carefully.

  Always read the requirement first as this enables you to **focus on the detail of the question with the specific task in mind**.

  For computational questions:

  Highlight key numbers / information and key words in the question, scribble notes to yourself on the question paper to remember key points in your answer.

  Jot down proformas required if applicable.

  For written questions:

  Plan the key areas to be addressed and your use of titles and sub-titles to enhance your answer.

  For all questions:

  Spot the easy marks to be gained in a question and parts which can be performed independently of the rest of the question. For example, laying out basic proformas correctly, entering discount factors or calculating writing down allowances or attempting the more discussional part of the question. Make sure that you do these parts first when you tackle the question.

  Don't go overboard in terms of planning time on any one question – you need a good measure of the whole paper and a plan for all of the questions at the end of the 15 minutes.

  By covering all questions you can often help yourself as you may find that facts in one question may remind you of things you should put into your answer relating to a different question.

- With your plan of attack in mind, **start answering your chosen question** with your plan to hand, as soon as you are allowed to start.

 Always keep your eye on the clock and do not over run on any part of any question!

DETAILED SYLLABUS

The detailed syllabus and study guide written by the ACCA can be found at:

www.accaglobal.com/students/

KAPLAN'S RECOMMENDED REVISION APPROACH

QUESTION PRACTICE IS THE KEY TO SUCCESS

Success in professional examinations relies upon you acquiring a firm grasp of the required knowledge at the tuition phase. In order to be able to do the questions, knowledge is essential.

However, the difference between success and failure often hinges on your exam technique on the day and making the most of the revision phase of your studies.

The **Kaplan complete text** is the starting point, designed to provide the underpinning knowledge to tackle all questions. However, in the revision phase, pouring over text books is not the answer.

Kaplan Online fixed tests help you consolidate your knowledge and understanding and are a useful tool to check whether you can remember key topic areas.

Kaplan pocket notes are designed to help you quickly revise a topic area, however you then need to practise questions. There is a need to progress to full exam standard questions as soon as possible, and to tie your exam technique and technical knowledge together.

The importance of question practice cannot be over-emphasised.

The recommended approach below is designed by expert tutors in the field, in conjunction with their knowledge of the examiner and their recent real exams.

The approach taken for the fundamental papers is to revise by topic area. However, with the professional stage papers, a multi topic approach is required to answer the scenario based questions.

You need to practice as many questions as possible in the time you have left.

OUR AIM

Our aim is to get you to the stage where you can attempt exam standard questions confidently, to time, in a closed book environment, with no supplementary help (i.e. to simulate the real examination experience).

Practising your exam technique on real past examination questions, in timed conditions, is also vitally important for you to assess your progress and identify areas of weakness that may need more attention in the final run up to the examination.

In order to achieve this we recognise that initially you may feel the need to practise some questions with open book help and exceed the required time.

The approach below shows you which questions you should use to build up to coping with exam standard question practice, and references to the sources of information available should you need to revisit a topic area in more detail.

Remember that in the real examination, all you have to do is:

- attempt all questions required by the exam

- only spend the allotted time on each question, and

- get them at least 50% right!

Try and practice this approach on every question you attempt from now to the real exam.

EXAMINER COMMENTS

We have included the examiner's comments to the specific new syllabus examination questions in this kit for you to see the main pitfalls that students fall into with regard to technical content.

However, too many times in the general section of the report, the examiner comments that students had failed due to:

- "misallocation of time"

- "running out of time" and

- showing signs of "spending too much time on an earlier questions and clearly rushing the answer to a subsequent question".

Good exam technique is vital.

THE KAPLAN PAPER F9 REVISION PLAN

Stage 1: Assess areas of strengths and weaknesses

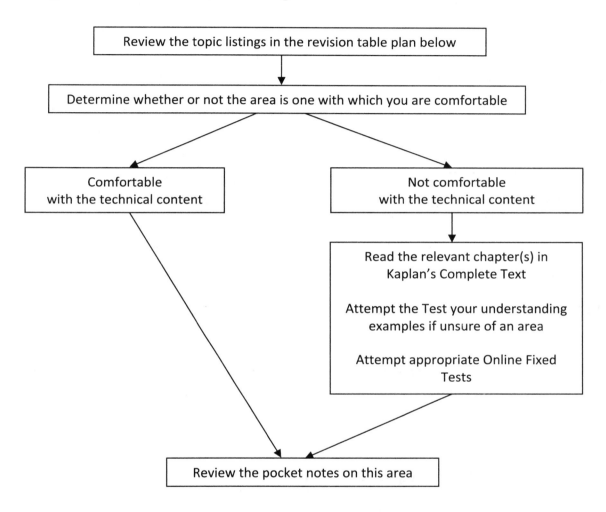

Stage 2: Practice questions

Follow the order of revision of topics as recommended in the revision table plan below and attempt the questions in the order suggested.

Try to avoid referring to text books and notes and the model answer until you have completed your attempt.

Try to answer the question in the allotted time.

Review your attempt with the model answer and assess how much of the answer you achieved in the allocated exam time.

Fill in the self-assessment box below and decide on your best course of action.

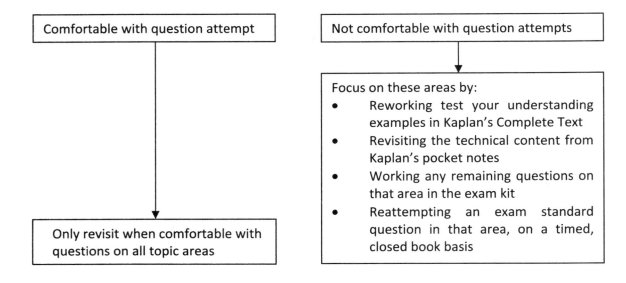

Note that:

 The "footsteps questions" give guidance on exam techniques and how you should have approached the question.

 The "clock questions" have an online debrief where a tutor talks you through the exam technique and approach to that question and works the question in full.

Stage 3:   Final pre-exam revision

We recommend that you **attempt at least one three hour mock examination** containing a set of previously unseen exam standard questions.

It is important that you get a feel for the breadth of coverage of a real exam without advanced knowledge of the topic areas covered – just as you will expect to see on the real exam day.

Ideally this mock should be sat in timed, closed book, real exam conditions and could be:

- a mock examination offered by your tuition provider, and/or
- the pilot paper in the back of this exam kit, and/or
- the last real examination paper (available shortly afterwards on Kaplan EN-gage with "enhanced walk through answers" and a full "tutor debrief").

THE DETAILED REVISION PLAN

Topic	Complete Text Chapter	Pocket note Chapter	Questions to attempt	Tutor guidance	Date attempted	Self assessment
Investment appraisal	2 & 3	2 & 3	22 23	Start with the basics - remind yourself of the four techniques and ensure you can compare and contrast between them. Start with question 22 before attempting question 23 as an example of a recent past exam question in this area.		
– Further aspects of discounted cash flows	4	4	21 29 25 27	A popular exam topic, guaranteed to form part of the exam. There are many questions on this area. Start with questions 21 and 29 which are basic warm up questions covering both inflation and tax. Build up to questions 25 and 27 which are slightly more complex questions on this area.		
– Risk and uncertainty	6	6	30 28	This is an aspect that is often examined alongside the more complex areas of discounted cash flow techniques. Question 28 is a good example of how this topic can be examined.		
– Asset investment decisions and capital rationing	5	5	34 35	This is an area that has not been widely examined within the recent exam diets. Despite this, it is worth having a quick recap of the techniques using these two questions.		

Topic	Complete Text Chapter	Pocket note Chapter	Questions to attempt	Tutor guidance	Date attempted	Self assessment
Working capital management	7	7	–	Begin by recapping on the key ratio calculations relating to working capital management and the calculation of the cash operating cycle.		
– Receivables and payables	9	9	16	Questions on working capital management will often draw upon several different elements. Question 16 gives a good general introduction to the cash operating cycle before linking in to the management of receivables.		
– Inventory	8	8	12 11	Both of these questions cover many aspects of working capital management and are good illustrations of the way the examiner tends to tackle this topic. You may want to leave part (d) of question 12 until later in your revision.		
– Cash and funding strategies	10	10	13 15	Question 13 contains good coverage of this chapter. Question 15 covers an area that has not been widely examined under the new syllabus.		
Financial management function	1	1	1 (c)	Now is a good point to visit some of the less widely examined areas of the syllabus. Question 1 (c) is a good example of how these more discursive elements are examined.		

KAPLAN PUBLISHING

Topic	Complete Text Chapter	Pocket note Chapter	Questions to attempt	Tutor guidance	Date attempted	Self assessment
The economic environment for business	11	11	8 (c)	Again, Question 8 (c) reflects how this topic could be examined. You may want to leave completing this question in full until you've covered the risk management area of the syllabus.		
Financial markets and the treasury function	12	12	–	This is a fairly new area to the syllabus but it's worth covering this before you start reviewing the topics of business finance and risk management.		
Sources of finance	15	15	5	Question 5, taken from the June 09 exam, is an excellent illustration of the way the examiner will often pull from more than one syllabus area within his questions.		
Financial ratios	19	19	45 4	Questions involving the calculation and interpretation of financial ratios are very common. You must be able to calculate each of the key ratios as well as appreciate how they interrelate with each other. Both of these questions are good examples.		
The cost of capital	17	17	49 52	This is another popular exam topic. As well as reviewing the complete text and the pocket notes, ensure you download and review the examiner's series of articles relating to CAPM.		

Topic	Complete Text Chapter	Pocket note Chapter	Questions to attempt	Tutor guidance	Date attempted	Self assessment
Capital structure	18	18	40 45 51	This is a tricky topic. Be sure to work carefully through the pocket notes, perhaps attempting the test your understandings within the complete text before attempting the exam standard questions.		
Business valuations and market efficiency	20	20	48 59 6 60	This is another popular exam topic and one which can be easily linked with other areas of the syllabus. You must be able to apply each of the main methods of business valuation and consider the impact that financing may have on a company's valuation.		
Dividend policy	16	16	39	This small topic is often examined alongside business valuations or sources of finance. Question 39 is an excellent illustration.		
Foreign exchange risk	13	13	62 12 (d)	Another topic that students often find difficult. Review the illustrations within the complete text but don't neglect the more discursive aspects, which are examined more frequently.		
Interest rate risk	14	14	63 10	This topic has not been extensively tested within recent exams. Question 10 is a good illustration of the examiner's style.		

Note that not all of the questions are referred to in the programme above. We have recommended an approach to build up from the basic to exam standard questions.

The remaining questions are available in the kit for extra practice for those who require more questions on some areas.

MATHEMATICAL TABLES AND FORMULAE SHEET

Economic order quantity

$$= \sqrt{\frac{2C_oD}{C_H}}$$

Miller-Orr Model

$$\text{Return point} = \text{Lower limit} + (\frac{1}{3} \times \text{spread})$$

$$\text{Spread} = 3\left[\frac{\frac{3}{4} \times \text{Transaction cost} \times \text{Variance of cash flows}}{\text{Interest rate}}\right]^{\frac{1}{3}}$$

The Capital Asset Pricing Model

$$E(r)_j = R_f + \beta_j (E(r_m) - R_f)$$

The asset beta formula

$$\beta_a = \left(\frac{V_e}{(V_e + V_d(1-T))} \; \beta_e\right) + \left(\frac{V_d(1-T)}{(V_e + V_d(1-T))} \; \beta_d\right)$$

The Growth Model

$$P_0 = \frac{Do(1+g)}{(r_e - g)}$$

Gordon's growth approximation

$$g = br_e$$

The weighted average cost of capital

$$\text{WACC} = \left(\frac{V_e}{V_e + V_d}\right)k_e + \left(\frac{V_d}{V_e + V_d}\right)k_d(1-T)$$

The Fisher formula

$$(1 + i) = (1 + r)(1 + h)$$

Purchasing power parity and interest rate parity

$$S_1 = S_0 \times \frac{(1+h_c)}{(1+h_b)} \qquad F_0 = S_0 \times \frac{(1+i_c)}{(1+i_b)}$$

Present Value Table

Present value of 1 i.e. $(1 + r)^{-n}$

Where   r = discount rate
                n = number of periods until payment

Periods (n)	1%	2%	3%	4%	5%	6%	7%	8%	9%	10%	
1	0.990	0.980	0.971	0.962	0.952	0.943	0.935	0.926	0.917	0.909	1
2	0.980	0.961	0.943	0.925	0.907	0.890	0.873	0.857	0.842	0.826	2
3	0.971	0.942	0.915	0.889	0.864	0.840	0.816	0.794	0.772	0.751	3
4	0.961	0.924	0.888	0.855	0.823	0.792	0.763	0.735	0.708	0.683	4
5	0.951	0.906	0.863	0.822	0.784	0.747	0.713	0.681	0.650	0.621	5
6	0.942	0.888	0.837	0.790	0.746	0.705	0.666	0.630	0.596	0.564	6
7	0.933	0.871	0.813	0.760	0.711	0.665	0.623	0.583	0.547	0.513	7
8	0.923	0.853	0.789	0.731	0.677	0.627	0.582	0.540	0.502	0.467	8
9	0.914	0.837	0.766	0.703	0.645	0.592	0.544	0.500	0.460	0.424	9
10	0.905	0.820	0.744	0.676	0.614	0.558	0.508	0.463	0.422	0.386	10
11	0.896	0.804	0.722	0.650	0.585	0.527	0.475	0.429	0.388	0.350	11
12	0.887	0.788	0.701	0.625	0.557	0.497	0.444	0.397	0.356	0.319	12
13	0.879	0.773	0.681	0.601	0.530	0.469	0.415	0.368	0.326	0.290	13
14	0.870	0.758	0.661	0.577	0.505	0.442	0.388	0.340	0.299	0.263	14
15	0.861	0.743	0.642	0.555	0.481	0.417	0.362	0.315	0.275	0.239	15

(n)	11%	12%	13%	14%	15%	16%	17%	18%	19%	20%	
1	0.901	0.893	0.885	0.877	0.870	0.862	0.855	0.847	0.840	0.833	1
2	0.812	0.797	0.783	0.769	0.756	0.743	0.731	0.718	0.706	0.694	2
3	0.731	0.712	0.693	0.675	0.658	0.641	0.624	0.609	0.593	0.579	3
4	0.659	0.636	0.613	0.592	0.572	0.552	0.534	0.516	0.499	0.482	4
5	0.593	0.567	0.543	0.519	0.497	0.476	0.456	0.437	0.419	0.402	5
6	0.535	0.507	0.480	0.456	0.432	0.410	0.390	0.370	0.352	0.335	6
7	0.482	0.452	0.425	0.400	0.376	0.354	0.333	0.314	0.296	0.279	7
8	0.434	0.404	0.376	0.351	0.327	0.305	0.285	0.266	0.249	0.233	8
9	0.391	0.361	0.333	0.308	0.284	0.263	0.243	0.225	0.209	0.194	9
10	0.352	0.322	0.295	0.270	0.247	0.227	0.208	0.191	0.176	0.162	10
11	0.317	0.287	0.261	0.237	0.215	0.195	0.178	0.162	0.148	0.135	11
12	0.286	0.257	0.231	0.208	0.187	0.168	0.152	0.137	0.124	0.112	12
13	0.258	0.229	0.204	0.182	0.163	0.145	0.130	0.116	0.104	0.093	13
14	0.232	0.205	0.181	0.160	0.141	0.125	0.111	0.099	0.088	0.078	14
15	0.209	0.183	0.160	0.140	0.123	0.108	0.095	0.084	0.074	0.065	15

Annuity Table

Present value of an annuity of 1 i.e. $\dfrac{1-(1+r)^{-n}}{r}$

Where   r = discount rate
           n = number of periods

Periods (n)	1%	2%	3%	4%	5%	6%	7%	8%	9%	10%	
1	0.990	0.980	0.971	0.962	0.952	0.943	0.935	0.926	0.917	0.909	1
2	1.970	1.942	1.913	1.886	1.859	1.833	1.808	1.783	1.759	1.736	2
3	2.941	2.884	2.829	2.775	2.723	2.673	2.624	2.577	2.531	2.487	3
4	3.902	3.808	3.717	3.630	3.546	3.465	3.387	3.312	3.240	3.170	4
5	4.853	4.713	4.580	4.452	4.329	4.212	4.100	3.993	3.890	3.791	5
6	5.795	5.601	5.417	5.242	5.076	4.917	4.767	4.623	4.486	4.355	6
7	6.728	6.472	6.230	6.002	5.786	5.582	5.389	5.206	5.033	4.868	7
8	7.652	7.325	7.020	6.733	6.463	6.210	5.971	5.747	5.535	5.335	8
9	8.566	8.162	7.786	7.435	7.108	6.802	6.515	6.247	5.995	5.759	9
10	9.471	8.983	8.530	8.111	7.722	7.360	7.024	6.710	6.418	6.145	10
11	10.37	9.787	9.253	8.760	8.306	7.887	7.499	7.139	6.805	6.495	11
12	11.26	10.58	9.954	9.385	8.863	8.384	7.943	7.536	7.161	6.814	12
13	12.13	11.35	10.63	9.986	9.394	8.853	8.358	7.904	7.487	7.103	13
14	13.00	12.11	11.30	10.56	9.899	9.295	8.745	8.244	7.786	7.367	14
15	13.87	12.85	11.94	11.12	10.38	9.712	9.108	8.559	8.061	7.606	15

(n)	11%	12%	13%	14%	15%	16%	17%	18%	19%	20%	
1	0.901	0.893	0.885	0.877	0.870	0.862	0.855	0.847	0.840	0.833	1
2	1.713	1.690	1.668	1.647	1.626	1.605	1.585	1.566	1.547	1.528	2
3	2.444	2.402	2.361	2.322	2.283	2.246	2.210	2.174	2.140	2.106	3
4	3.102	3.037	2.974	2.914	2.855	2.798	2.743	2.690	2.639	2.589	4
5	3.696	3.605	3.517	3.433	3.352	3.274	3.199	3.127	3.058	2.991	5
6	4.231	4.111	3.998	3.889	3.784	3.685	3.589	3.498	3.410	3.326	6
7	4.712	4.564	4.423	4.288	4.160	4.039	3.922	3.812	3.706	3.605	7
8	5.146	4.968	4.799	4.639	4.487	4.344	4.207	4.078	3.954	3.837	8
9	5.537	5.328	5.132	4.946	4.772	4.607	4.451	4.303	4.163	4.031	9
10	5.889	5.650	5.426	5.216	5.019	4.833	4.659	4.494	4.339	4.192	10
11	6.207	5.938	5.687	5.453	5.234	5.029	4.836	4.656	4.486	4.327	11
12	6.492	6.194	5.918	5.660	5.421	5.197	4.988	4.793	4.611	4.439	12
13	6.750	6.424	6.122	5.842	5.583	5.342	5.118	4.910	4.715	4.533	13
14	6.982	6.628	6.302	6.002	5.724	5.468	5.229	5.008	4.802	4.611	14
15	7.191	6.811	6.462	6.142	5.847	5.575	5.324	5.092	4.876	4.675	15

Section 1

PRACTICE QUESTIONS

FINANCIAL MANAGEMENT FUNCTION AND ENVIRONMENT

1   UUL

UUL Co is a public water supply company which was privatised a number of years ago. As the deputy Finance Director you are reviewing the draft financial statements which contain the following statement by the chairman:

'This company has delivered above average performance in fulfilment of our objective of maximising shareholder wealth. Earnings, dividends and the share price have all shown good growth. It is our intention to continue to deliver strong performance in the future'.

The following information has been extracted from the draft financial statements:

Year	20X6	20X2
Dividend per share	7.1c	4.2c
Earnings per share	41.3c	31.6c
Price/earnings ratio	22.0	17.0

You have obtained the following information regarding the water industry for the last 5 years:

Dividend growth	11% annually
Earnings growth	12% annually
Share price growth	18% annually

General inflation in the economy has averaged 2% per annum.

The number of shares in issue has remained unchanged over the last 5 years and the price/earnings ratios are calculated using year end share prices.

Required:

(a)   **Calculate the equivalent annual growth in:**

   (i)   **Dividends per share**

   (ii)   **Earnings per share**

   (iii)   **Share price**

   Critically comment on the views expressed by the chairman.   **(8 marks)**

(b)   Assuming a share price of $9.12 at the end of 20X5 calculate and comment on the total shareholder return (dividend yield plus capital growth) for 20X6.   **(3 marks)**

(c)   Identify three other key stakeholders in a company such as UUL Co. Identify what financial and other objectives the company should aim to follow in order to satisfy each of these stakeholders.   **(7 marks)**

(d)   Identify what government intervention and other regulation UUL Co may suffer and how this will impact upon the company.   **(7 marks)**

(Total: 25 marks)

2   CCC

(a)   CCC is a local government entity. It is financed almost equally by a combination of central government funding and local taxation. The funding from central government is determined largely on a per capita (per head of population) basis, adjusted to reflect the scale of deprivation (or special needs) deemed to exist in CCC's region. A small percentage of its finance comes from the private sector, for example from renting out City Hall for private functions.

CCC's main objectives are:

- to make the region economically prosperous and an attractive place to live and work

- to provide service excellence in health and education for the local community.

DDD is a large listed entity with widespread commercial and geographical interests. For historic reasons, its headquarters are in CCC's region. This is something of an anomaly as most entities of DDD's size would have their HQ in a capital city, or at least a city much larger than where it is.

DDD has one financial objective: To increase shareholder wealth by an average 10% per annum. It also has a series of non-financial objectives that deal with how the entity treats other stakeholders, including the local communities where it operates.

DDD has total net assets of $1.5 billion and a gearing ratio of 45% (debt to debt plus equity), which is typical for its industry. It is currently considering raising a substantial amount of capital to finance an acquisition.

Required:

Discuss the criteria that the two very different entities described above have to consider when setting objectives, recognising the needs of each of their main stakeholder groups. Make some reference in your answer to the consequences of each of them failing to meet its declared objectives.   **(13 marks)**

(b)   MS is a private entity in a computer-related industry. It has been trading for six years and is managed by its main shareholders, the original founders of the entity. Most of the employees are also shareholders, having been given shares as bonuses. None of the shareholders has attempted to sell shares in the entity, so the problem of placing a value on them has not arisen. Dividends have been paid every year at the rate of 60 cents per share, irrespective of profits. So far, profits have always been sufficient to cover the dividend at least once but never more than twice.

MS is all-equity financed at present although $15 million new finance is likely to be required in the near future to finance expansion. Total net assets as at the last balance sheet date were $45 million.

Required:

Discuss and compare the relationship between dividend policy, investment policy and financing policy in the context of the small entity described above, MS, and DDD, the large listed entity described in part (a). **(12 marks)**

(Total: 25 marks)

3 NEIGHBOURING COUNTRIES

(a) Two neighbouring countries have chosen to organise their electricity supply industries in different ways.

In Country A, electricity supplies are provided by a nationalised industry. In Country B, electricity supplies are provided by a number of private sector companies.

Required:

Explain how the objectives of the nationalised industry in Country A might differ from those of the private sector companies in Country B.

Briefly discuss whether investment planning and appraisal techniques are likely to differ in the nationalised industry and private sector companies. **(10 marks)**

(b) Whilst the financial plans of a business are based on a single objective, it can face a number of constraints that put pressure on the company to address more than one objective simultaneously.

Required:

What types of constraints might a company face when assessing its long-term plans? Specifically refer in your answer to:

(i) **responding to various stakeholder groups, and** **(4 marks)**

(ii) **the difficulties associated with managing organisations with multiple objectives.** **(5 marks)**

(c) Financial intermediaries bring together investors and borrowers of funds.

Required:

Explain briefly the role of financial intermediaries. **(6 marks)**

(Total: 25 marks)

4 RZP CO

As assistant to the Finance Director of RZP Co, a company that has been listed on the London Stock Market for several years, you are reviewing the draft Annual Report of the company, which contains the following statement made by the chairman:

'This company has consistently delivered above-average performance in fulfilment of our declared objective of creating value for our shareholders. Apart from 20X2, when our overall performance was hampered by a general market downturn, this company has delivered growth in dividends, earnings and ordinary share price. Our shareholders can rest assured that my directors and I will continue to deliver this performance in the future'.

The five-year summary in the draft Annual Report contains the following information:

Year	20X4	20X3	20X2	20X1	20X0
Dividend per share	2.8¢	2.3¢	2.2¢	2.2¢	1.7¢
Earnings per share	19.04¢	14.95¢	11.22¢	15.84¢	13.43¢
Price/earnings ratio	22.0	33.5	25.5	17.2	15.2
General price index	117	113	110	105	100

A recent article in the financial press reported the following information for the last five years for the business sector within which RZP Co operates:

Share price growth	average increase per year of 20%
Earnings growth	average increase per year of 10%
Nominal dividend growth	average increase per year of 10%
Real dividend growth	average increase per year of 9%

You may assume that the number of shares issued by RZP Co has been constant over the five-year period. All price/earnings ratios are based on end-of-year share prices.

Required:

(a) **Analyse the information provided and comment on the views expressed by the chairman in terms of:**

    (i) **growth in dividends per share;**

    (ii) **share price growth;**

    (iii) **growth in earnings per share.**

    Your analysis should consider both arithmetic mean and equivalent annual growth rates. **(13 marks)**

(b) **Calculate the total shareholder return (dividend yield plus capital growth) for 20X4 and comment on your findings.** **(3 marks)**

(c) **Discuss the factors that should be considered when deciding on a management remuneration package that will encourage the directors of RZP Co to maximise the wealth of shareholders, giving examples of management remuneration packages that might be appropriate for RZP Co.** **(9 marks)**

(Total: 25 marks)

5   JJG CO (JUNE 09)

 Timed question with Online tutor debrief

JJG Co is planning to raise $15 million of new finance for a major expansion of existing business and is considering a rights issue, a placing or an issue of bonds. The corporate objectives of JJG Co, as stated in its Annual Report, are to maximise the wealth of its shareholders and to achieve continuous growth in earnings per share. Recent financial information on JJG Co is as follows

	2008	2007	2006	2005
Turnover ($m)	28.0	24.0	19.1	16.8
Profit before interest and tax ($m)	9.8	8.5	7.5	6.8
Earnings ($m)	5.5	4.7	4.1	3.6
Dividends ($m)	2.2	1.9	1.6	1.6
Ordinary shares ($m)	5.5	5.5	5.5	5.5
Reserves ($m)	13.7	10.4	7.6	5.1
8% Bonds, redeemable 2015 ($m)	20.0	20.0	20.0	20.0
Share price ($)	8.64	5.74	3.35	2.67

The par value of the shares of JJG Co is $1.00 per share. The general level of inflation has averaged 4% per year in the period under consideration. The bonds of JJG Co are currently trading at their par value of $100. The following values for the business sector of JJG Co are available:

Average return on capital employed	25%
Average return on shareholders' funds	20%
Average interest coverage ratio	20 times
Average debt/equity ratio (market value basis)	50%
Return predicted by the capital asset pricing model	14%

Required:

(a)   **Evaluate the financial performance of JJG Co, and analyse and discuss the extent to which the company has achieved its stated corporate objectives of:**

    (i)   **Maximising the wealth of its shareholders;**

    (ii)   **Achieving continuous growth in earnings per share.**

    Note: up to 7 marks are available for financial analysis   **(12 marks)**

(b)   **If the new finance is raised via a rights issue at $7.50 per share and the major expansion of business has not yet begun, calculate and comment on the effect of the rights issue on:**

    (i)   **The share price of JJG Co;**

    (ii)   **The earnings per share of the company; and**

    (iii)   **The debt/equity ratio**   **(6 marks)**

(c)   **Analyse and discuss the relative merits of a rights issue, a placing and an issue of bonds as ways of raising the finance for the expansion**   **(7 marks)**

                                                  (Total: 25 marks)

 Calculate your allowed time, allocate the time to the separate parts

6 DARTIG CO (DEC 08) *Walk in the footsteps of a top tutor*

Dartig Co is a stock-market listed company that manufactures consumer products and it is planning to expand its existing business. The investment cost of $5 million will be met by a 1 for 4 rights issue. The current share price of Dartig Co is $2.50 per share and the rights issue price will be at a 20% discount to this. The finance director of Dartig Co expects that the expansion of existing business will allow the average growth rate of earnings per share over the last four years to be maintained into the foreseeable future.

The earnings per share and dividends paid by Dartig over the last four years are as follows:

	2003	2004	2005	2006	2007
Earnings per share (cents)	27.7	29.0	29.0	30.2	32.4
Dividend per share (cents)	12.8	13.5	13.5	14.5	15.0

Dartig Co has a cost of equity of 10%. The price/earnings ratio of Dartig Co has been approximately constant in recent years. Ignore issue costs.

Required:

(a) Calculate the theoretical ex rights price per share prior to investing in the proposed business expansion. ` **(3 marks)**

(b) Calculate the expected share price following the proposed business expansion using the price/earnings ratio method. **(3 marks)**

(c) Discuss whether the proposed business expansion is an acceptable use of the finance raised by the rights issue, and evaluate the expected effect on the wealth of the shareholders of Dartig Co. **(5 marks)**

(d) Using the information provided, calculate the ex div share price predicted by the dividend growth model and discuss briefly why this share price differs from the current market price of Dartig Co. **(6 marks)**

(e) At a recent board meeting of Dartig Co, a non-executive director suggested that the company's remuneration committee should consider scrapping the company's current share option scheme, since executive directors could be rewarded by the scheme even when they did not perform well. A second non-executive director disagreed, saying the problem was that even when directors acted in ways which decreased the agency problem, they might not be rewarded by the share option scheme if the stock market were in decline.

Required:

Explain the nature of the agency problem and discuss the use of share option schemes as a way of reducing the agency problem in a stock-market listed company such as Dartig Co. **(8 marks)**

(Total: 25 marks)

7 NEWS FOR YOU

News For You operates a chain of newsagents and confectioner's shops in the south of a Northern European country, and are considering the possibility of expanding their business across a wider geographical area. The business was started in 20X2 and annual turnover grew to $10 million by the end of 20X6. Between 20X6 and 20X9 turnover grew at an average rate of 2% per year.

The business still remains under family control, but the high cost of expansion via the purchase or building of new outlets would mean that the family would need to raise at least $2 million in equity or debt finance. One of the possible risks of expansion lies in the fact that both tobacco and newspaper sales are falling. New income is being generated by expanding the product range stocked by the stores, to include basic foodstuffs such as bread and milk. News For You purchases all of its products from a large wholesale distributor which is convenient, but the wholesale prices leave News For You with a relatively small gross margin. The key to profit growth for News For You lies in the ability to generate sales growth, but the company recognises that it faces stiff competition from large food retailers in respect of the prices that it charges for several of its products.

In planning its future, News For You was advised to look carefully at a number of external factors which may affect the business, including government economic policy and, in recent months, the following information has been published in respect of key economic data:

(i)   Bank base rate has been reduced from 5% to 4.5%, and the forecast is for a further 0.5% reduction within six months.

(ii)   The annual rate of inflation is now 1.2%, down from 1.3% in the previous quarter, and 1.7% 12 months ago. The rate is now at its lowest for 25 years, and no further falls in the rate are expected over the medium/long term.

(iii) Personal and corporation tax rates are expected to remain unchanged for at least 12 months.

(iv)   Taxes on tobacco have been increased by 10% over the last 12 months, although no further increases are anticipated.

(v)   The government has initiated an investigation into the food retail sector focusing on the problems of 'excessive' profits on certain foodstuffs created by the high prices being charged for these goods by the large retail food stores.

Required:

(a)   **Explain the relevance of each of the items of economic data listed above to News For You.**   **(13 marks)**

(b)   **Explain whether News For You should continue with their expansion plans. Clearly justify your arguments for or against the expansion.**   **(12 marks)**

(Total: 25 marks)

8   CC CO

CC Co is considering launching a new product. Relevant financial information includes:

Selling price (current price terms)	$12 per unit
Variable costs (current price terms)	$7 per unit
Incremental fixed overhead costs	$250,000 per year

General price inflation is expected to average 4.7% per year over the period. However, the selling price is expected to inflate at 5% per annum, the variable costs to inflate by just 4% per annum, and the fixed costs by 6% per year.

Production and sales are expected to be at the following levels:

Year	1	2	3	4
Units	250,000	500,000	400,000	200,000

To manufacture the new product CC Co will need to purchase a new machine. The only suppliers of this machine are located overseas. If the machine was ordered immediately it would cost €1.5m. Payment must be made in Euros and would be due upon delivery of the machine in three month's time.

CC Co will be able to claim capital allowances on the investment on a straight line basis over the estimated four-year life of the asset. The company pays tax one year in arrears at a rate of 30% and the asset is not expected to have any scrap value at the end of the project.

The real weighted average cost of capital of CC Co is 5.1%.

The spot exchange rate is 0.70 €/$ and the three-month forward exchange rate is 0.698 €/$. CC Co can earn 2.9% per year on short-term euro deposits and can borrow short term in dollars at 5.5%.

Required:

(a)   **Calculate the expected dollar payment in three months' time using both a forward market hedge and a money market hedge and recommend whether a forward market hedge or a money market hedge should be used to mitigate the exchange risk on the potential purchase of the machine.**   **(6 marks)**

(b)   **Based on your recommendation in part (b,) calculate the net present value of the proposed investment in three months' time and comment on the project's acceptability.**   **(11 marks)**

(c)   **Discuss the effect inflation has on the level of profits and the cash flow position of a company. Your answer should include a discussion of the impact inflation has on exchange rates.**   **(8 marks)**

(Total: 25 marks)

9 RWF

RWF Co has stated the following corporate objectives:

- — Maintain gearing (debt/equity) at or below 60%
- — Provide real growth in earnings per share

RWF Co is considering a potential project which should expand sales and automate production but is unsure how to fund the $9 million required. It can either carry out a rights issue at $6 per share or issue additional debt at a pre-tax cost of 10%.

The most recent income statement and forecasts which include the impact of the project and financing alternatives are shown below:

Income statements:	$000	$000	$000
	Current	Forecast Debt issue	Forecast Rights issue
Sales	70,000	85,000	85,000
Variable cost of sales	32,000	34,000	34,000
Fixed cost of sales	9,000	16,000	16,000
Gross profit	29,000	35,000	35,000
Administration costs	16,000	17,000	17,000
Profit before interest and tax	13,000	18,000	18,000
Interest	4,000	4,900	4,000
Profit before tax	9,000	13,100	14,000
Taxation	2,700	3,930	4,200
Profit after tax	6,300	9,170	9,800
Dividends	2,000	2,500	3,000
Retained earnings	4,300	6,670	6,800

At the end of the most recent year RWF Co had 12 million shares, share capital and reserves totalling $90 million and $50 million of 8% debentures. General inflation is currently 5%.

Required:

(a)   Evaluate the two finance options being considered and recommend which option RWF Co should accept. You should consider the impact each finance option will have on the ability of the company to achieve its stated objectives. The impact on three other key ratios of the business (including operating gearing) should also be considered. **(17 marks)**

(b)   Provide a critical discussion of the corporate objectives which have been stated by RWF Co and recommend how the company could improve its corporate objectives. **(5 marks)**

(c)   State the key factors a company should consider when taking the three key financial management decisions and give examples of how those factors could impact on the decisions made. **(3 marks)**

(Total: 25 marks)

WORKING CAPITAL MANAGEMENT

10 GORWA CO (DEC 08)

The following financial information related to Gorwa Co:

	2007 $000	2006 $000
Sales (all on credit)	37,400	26,720
Cost of sales	34,408	23,781
Operating profit	2,992	2,939
Finance costs (interest payments)	355	274
Profit before taxation	2,637	2,665

	2007 $000	2007 $000	2006 $000	2006 $000
Non-current assets		13,632		12,750
Current assets				
Inventory	4,600		2,400	
Trade receivables	4,600		2,200	
	9,200		4,600	
Current liabilities				
Trade payables	4,750		2,000	
Overdraft	3,225		1,600	
	7,975		3,600	
Net current assets		1,225		1,000
		14,857		13,750
8% Bonds		2,425		2,425
		12,432		11,325
Capital and reserves				
Share capital		6,000		6,000
Reserves		6,432		5,325
		12,432		11,325

The average variable overdraft interest rate in each year was 5%. The 8% bonds are redeemable in ten years' time.

A factor has offered to take over the administration of trade receivables on a non-recourse basis for an annual fee of 3% of credit sales. The factor will maintain a trade receivables collection period of 30 days and Gorwa Co will save $100,000 per year in administration costs and $350,000 per year in bad debts. A condition of the factoring agreement is that the factor would advance 80% of the face value of receivables at an annual interest rate of 7%.

Required:

(a) Discuss, with supporting calculations, the possible effects on Gorwa Co of an increase in interest rates and advise the company of steps it can take to protect itself against interest rate risk. **(7 marks)**

(b) Use the above financial information to discuss, with supporting calculations, whether or not Gorwa Co is overtrading. **(10 marks)**

(c) Evaluate whether the proposal to factor trade receivables is financially acceptable. Assume an average cost of short-term finance in this part of the question only. **(8 marks)**

(Total: 25 marks)

11 FLG CO (JUNE 08)

FLG Co has annual credit sales of $4.2 million and cost of sales of $1.89 million. Current assets consist of inventory and accounts receivable. Current liabilities consist of accounts payable and an overdraft with an average interest rate of 7% per year. The company gives two months' credit to its customers and is allowed, on average, one month's credit by trade suppliers. It has an operating cycle of three months.

Other relevant information:

Current ratio of FLG Co	1.4
Cost of long-term finance of FLG Co	11%

Required:

(a) Discuss the key factors which determine the level of investment in current assets. **(6 marks)**

(b) Discuss the ways in which factoring and invoice discounting can assist in the management of accounts receivable. **(6 marks)**

(c) Calculate the size of the overdraft of FLG Co, the net working capital of the company and the total cost of financing its current assets. **(6 marks)**

(d) FLG Co wishes to minimise its inventory costs. Annual demand for a raw material costing $12 per unit is 60,000 units per year. Inventory management costs for this raw material are as follows:

Ordering cost:	$6 per order
Holding cost:	$0.5 per unit per year

The supplier of this raw material has offered a bulk purchase discount of 1% for orders of 10,000 units or more. If bulk purchase orders are made regularly, it is expected that annual holding cost for this raw material will increase to $2 per unit per year.

Required:

(i) Calculate the total cost of inventory for the raw material when using the economic order quantity. **(4 marks)**

(ii) Determine whether accepting the discount offered by the supplier will minimise the total cost of inventory for the raw material. **(3 marks)**

(Total: 25 marks)

12 PKA CO (DEC 07) *Walk in the footsteps of a top tutor*

PKA Co is a European company that sells goods solely within Europe. The recently-appointed financial manager of PKA Co has been investigating the working capital management of the company and has gathered the following information:

Inventory management

The current policy is to order 100,000 units when the inventory level falls to 35,000 units. Forecast demand to meet production requirements during the next year is 625,000 units. The cost of placing and processing an order is €250, while the cost of holding a unit in stores is €0.50 per unit per year. Both costs are expected to be constant during the next year. Orders are received two weeks after being placed with the supplier. You should assume a 50-week year and that demand is constant throughout the year.

Accounts receivable management

Domestic customers are allowed 30 days' credit, but the financial statements of PKA Co show that the average accounts receivable period in the last financial year was 75 days. The financial manager also noted that bad debts as a percentage of sales, which are all on credit, increased in the last financial year from 5% to 8%.

Accounts payable management

PKA Co has used a foreign supplier for the first time and must pay $250,000 to the supplier in six months' time. The financial manager is concerned that the cost of these supplies may rise in euro terms and has decided to hedge the currency risk of this account payable. The following information has been provided by the company's bank:

Spot rate ($ per €):   1.998 ± 0.002

Six months forward rate ($ per €):   1.979 ± 0.004

Money market rates available to PKA Co:

	Borrowing	Deposit
One year euro interest rates:	6.1%	5.4%
One year dollar interest rates:	4.0%	3.5%

Assume that it is now 1 December and that PKA Co has no surplus cash at the present time.

Required:

(a)   Identify the objectives of working capital management and discuss the conflict that may arise between them.   **(3 marks)**

(b)   Calculate the cost of the current ordering policy and determine the saving that could be made by using the economic order quantity model.   **(7 marks)**

(c)   Discuss ways in which PKA Co could improve the management of domestic accounts receivable.   **(7 marks)**

(d)   Evaluate whether a money market hedge, a forward market hedge or a lead payment should be used to hedge the foreign account payable.   **(8 marks)**

(Total: 25 marks)

13   ULNAD

Ulnad Co has annual sales revenue of $6 million and all sales are on 30 days' credit, although customers on average take ten days more than this to pay. Contribution represents 60% of sales and the company currently has no bad debts. Accounts receivable are financed by an overdraft at an annual interest rate of 7%.

Ulnad Co plans to offer an early settlement discount of 1.5% for payment within 15 days and to extend the maximum credit offered to 60 days. The company expects that these changes will increase annual credit sales by 5%, while also leading to additional incremental costs equal to 0.5% of sales revenue. The discount is expected to be taken by 30% of customers, with the remaining customers taking an average of 60 days to pay.

Required:

(a)   Evaluate whether the proposed changes in credit policy will increase the profitability of Ulnad Co.   **(6 marks)**

(b)   **Renpec Co, a subsidiary of Ulnad Co, has set a minimum cash account balance of $7,500. The average cost to the company of making deposits or selling investments is $18 per transaction and the standard deviation of its cash flows was $1,000 per day during the last year. The average interest rate on investments is 5.11%.**

   Determine the spread, the upper limit and the return point for the cash account of Renpec Co using the Miller-Orr model and explain the relevance of these values for the cash management of the company.   **(6 marks)**

(c)   **Identify and explain the key areas of accounts receivable management.**   **(6 marks)**

(d)   **Discuss the key factors to be considered when formulating a working capital funding policy.**   **(7 marks)**

(Total: 25 marks)

14   APX CO (DEC 09)

APX Co achieved a turnover of $16 million in the year that has just ended and expects turnover growth of 8.4% in the next year. Cost of sales in the year that has just ended was $10.88 million and other expenses were $1.44 million.

The financial statements of APX Co for the year that has just ended contain the following statement of financial position:

	$m	$m
Non-current assets		22.0
Current assets		
Inventory	2.4	
Trade receivables	2.2	
	——	
		4.6
		——
Total assets		26.6
		——

Equity finance:

	$m	$m
Ordinary shares	5.0	
Reserves	7.5	
		12.5
Long-term bank loan		10.0
		22.5
Current liabilities		
Trade payables	1.9	
Overdraft	2.2	
		4.1
Total liabilities		26.6

The long-term bank loan has a fixed annual interest rate of 8% per year. APX Co pays taxation at an annual rate of 30% per year.

The following accounting ratios have been forecast for the next year:

Gross profit margin:	30%
Operating profit margin:	20%
Dividend payout ratio:	50%
Inventory turnover period:	110 days
Trade receivables period:	65 days
Trade payables period:	75 days

Overdraft interest in the next year is forecast to be $140,000. No change is expected in the level of non-current assets and depreciation should be ignored.

Required:

(a) Discuss the role of financial intermediaries in providing short-term finance for use by business organisations. **(4 marks)**

(b) Prepare the following forecast financial statements for APX Co using the information provided:

    (i)   an income statement for the next year; and

    (ii)   a statement of financial position at the end of the next year. **(9 marks)**

(c) Analyse and discuss the working capital financing policy of APX Co. **(6 marks)**

(d) Analyse and discuss the forecast financial performance of APX Co in terms of working capital management. **(6 marks)**

(Total: 25 marks)

15   HGR CO (JUNE 09)

> 🕐 *Timed question with Online tutor debrief*

The following financial information relates to HGR Co:

Statement of financial position at the current date (extracts)

	$000	$000	$000
Non-current assets			48,965
Current assets			
Inventory		8,160	
Accounts receivable		8,775	
		———	
		16,935	
Current liabilities			
Overdraft	3,800		
Accounts payable	10,200		
	———		
		14,000	
		———	
Net current assets			2,935
			———
Total assets less current liabilities			51,900
			———

Cash flow forecasts from the current date are as follows:

	Month 1	*Month 2*	*Month 3*
Cash operating receipts ($000)	4,220	4,350	3,808
Cash operating payments ($000)	3,950	4,100	3,750
Six-monthly interest on traded bonds ($000)		200	
Capital investment ($000)			2,000

The finance director has completed a review of accounts receivable management and has proposed staff training and operating procedure improvements, which he believes will reduce accounts receivable days to the average sector value of 53 days. This reduction would take six months to achieve from the current date, with an equal reduction in each month. He has also proposed changes to inventory management methods, which he hopes will reduce inventory days by two days per month each month over a three-month period from the current date. He does not expect any change in the current level of accounts payable.

HGR Co has an overdraft limit of $4,000,000. Overdraft interest is payable at an annual rate of 6.17% per year, with payments being made each month based on the opening balance at the start of that month. Credit sales for the year to the current date were $49,275,000 and cost of sales was $37,230,000. These levels of credit sales and cost of sales are expected to be maintained in the coming year. Assume that there are 365 working days in each year.

Required:

(a) Discuss the working capital financing strategy of HGR Co.   **(7 marks)**

(b) For HGR Co, calculate:

    (i)   the bank balance in three months' time if no action is taken; and

    (ii)   the bank balance in three months' time if the finance director's proposals are implemented

    Comment on the forecast cash flow position of HGR Co and recommend a suitable course of action.   **(10 marks)**

(c) Discuss how risks arising from granting credit to foreign customers can be managed and reduced.   **(8 marks)**

                                                                 (Total: 25 marks)

 Calculate your allowed time, allocate the time to the separate parts

16 ANJO

Extracts from the recent financial statements of Anjo Inc are as follows:

Income statements

	20X6	20X5
	$000	$000
Sales revenue	15,600	11,100
Cost of sales	9,300	6,600
Gross profit	6,300	4,500
Administration expenses	1,000	750
Profit before interest and tax	5,300	3,750
Interest	100	15
Profit before tax	5,200	3,735

Statements of financial position

	20X6		20X5	
	$000	$000	$000	$000
Non-current assets		5,750		5,400
Current assets				
Inventory	3,000		1,300	
Receivables	3,800		1,850	
Cash	120		900	
		6,920		4,050
Total assets		8,800		7,700

	$000	20X6 $000	$000	20X5 $000
Total equity		4,930		5,950
Current liabilities				
Trade payables	2,870		1,600	
Overdraft	1,000		150	
		3,870		1,750
Total equity and liabilities		8,800		7,700

All sales were on credit. Anjo Inc has no long-term debt. Credit purchases in each year were 95% of cost of sales. Anjo Inc pays interest on its overdraft at an annual rate of 8%. Current sector averages are as follows:

Inventory days: 90 days

Receivables days: 60 days

Payables days: 80 days

Required:

(a)   Calculate the following ratios for each year and comment on your findings.

      (i)   **Inventory days**

      (ii)   **Receivables days**

      (iii) **Payables days**   **(6 marks)**

(b)   Calculate the length of the cash operating cycle (working capital cycle) for each year and explain its significance.   **(4 marks)**

(c)   Discuss the advantages and disadvantages of using just-in-time inventory management methods.   **(7 marks)**

(d)   A factor has offered to take over sales ledger administration and debt collection for an annual fee of 0.5% of credit sales. A condition of the offer is that the factor will advance Anjo Inc 80% of the face value of its receivables at an interest rate 1% above the current overdraft rate. The factor claims that it would reduce outstanding receivables by 30% and reduce administration expenses by 2% per year if its offer were accepted.

      Evaluate whether the factor's offer is financially acceptable, basing your answer on the financial information relating to 20X6.   **(8 marks)**

                                                                 (Total: 25 marks)

17   ZSE CO (JUNE 10)

ZSE Co is concerned about exceeding its overdraft limit of $2 million in the next two periods. It has been experiencing considerable volatility in cash flows in recent periods because of trading difficulties experienced by its customers, who have often settled their accounts after the agreed credit period of 60 days. ZSE has also experienced an increase in bad debts due to a small number of customers going into liquidation.

The company has prepared the following forecasts of net cash flows for the next two periods, together with their associated probabilities, in an attempt to anticipate liquidity and financing problems. These probabilities have been produced by a computer model which simulates a number of possible future economic scenarios. The computer model has been built with the aid of a firm of financial consultants.

Period 1 cash flow	Probability	Period 2 cash flow	Probability
$000		$000	
8,000	10%	7,000	30%
4,000	60%	3,000	50%
(2,000)	30%	(9,000)	20%

ZSE Co expects to be overdrawn at the start of period 1 by $500,000.

Required:

(a)   **Calculate the following values:**

(i)   **the expected value of the period 1 closing balance;**

(ii)   **the expected value of the period 2 closing balance;**

(iii)   **the probability of a negative cash balance at the end of period 2;**

(iv)   **the probability of exceeding the overdraft limit at the end of period 2.**

Discuss whether the above analysis can assist the company in managing its cash flows.   **(13 marks)**

(b)   **Identify and discuss the factors to be considered in formulating a trade receivables management policy for ZSE Co.**   **(8 marks)**

(c)   **Discuss whether profitability or liquidity is the primary objective of working capital management.**   **(4 marks)**

(Total: 25 marks)

18   PNP PLC (JUNE 07)

The following financial information relates to PNP plc, a UK-based firm, for the year just ended.

	£000
Sales revenue	5,242.0
Variable cost of sales	3,145.0
Inventory	603.0
Receivables	744.5
Payables	574.5

Segmental analysis of receivables

	Balance	Average payment period	Discount	Irrecoverable
Class 1	£200,000	30 days	1.0%	None
Class 2	£252,000	60 days	Nil	£12,600
Class 3	£110,000	75 days	Nil	£11,000
Overseas	£182,500	90 days	Nil	£21,900
	£744,500			£45,500

The receivables balances given are before taking account of irrecoverable debts. All sales are on credit. Production and sales take place evenly throughout the year. Current sales for each class of receivables are in proportion to their relative year-end balances before irrecoverable debts. The overseas receivables arise from regular export sales by PNP to the USA. The current spot rate is $1.7348/£ and the three-month forward rate is $1.7367/£.

It has been proposed that the discount for early payment be increased from 1.0% to 1.5% for settlement within 30 days. It is expected that this will lead to 50% of existing Class 2 receivables becoming Class 1 receivables, as well as attracting new business worth £500,000 in turnover. The new business would be divided equally between Class 1 and Class 2 receivables. Fixed costs would not increase as a result of introducing the discount or by attracting new business. PNP finances receivables from an overdraft at an annual interest rate of 8%.

Required:

(a) Calculate the net benefit or cost of increasing the discount for early payment and comment on the acceptability of the proposal. **(9 marks)**

(b) Calculate the current cash operating cycle and the revised cash operating cycle caused by increasing the discount for early payment. **(4 marks)**

(c) Determine the effect of using a forward market hedge to manage the exchange rate risk of the outstanding overseas receivables. **(2 marks)**

(d) Identify and explain the key elements of a receivables management system suitable for PNP plc. **(10 marks)**

(Total: 25 marks)

 Online question assistance

19 **WQZ CO (DEC 10)**

WQZ Co is considering making the following changes in the area of working capital management:

Inventory management

It has been suggested that the order size for Product KN5 should be determined using the economic order quantity model (EOQ).

WQZ Co forecasts that demand for Product KN5 will be 160,000 units in the coming year and it has traditionally ordered 10% of annual demand per order. The ordering cost is expected to be $400 per order while the holding cost is expected to be $5.12 per unit per year. A buffer inventory of 5,000 units of Product KN5 will be maintained, whether orders are made by the traditional method or using the economic ordering quantity model.

Q = 16000

Co

D

C_H

Buffer

Receivables management

WQZ Co could introduce an early settlement discount of 1% for customers who pay within 30 days and at the same time, through improved operational procedures, maintain a maximum average payment period of 60 days for credit customers who do not take the discount. It is expected that 25% of credit customers will take the discount if it were offered.

It is expected that administration and operating cost savings of $753,000 per year will be made after improving operational procedures and introducing the early settlement discount.

Credit sales of WQZ Co are currently $87.6 million per year and trade receivables are currently $18 million. Credit sales are not expected to change as a result of the changes in receivables management. The company has a cost of short-term finance of 5.5% per year.

Required:

(a) Calculate the cost of the current ordering policy and the change in the costs of inventory management that will arise if the economic order quantity is used to determine the optimum order size for Product KN5. (6 marks)

(b) Briefly describe the benefits of a just-in-time (JIT) procurement policy. (5 marks)

(c) Calculate and comment on whether the proposed changes in receivables management will be acceptable. Assuming that only 25% of customers take the early settlement discount, what is the maximum early settlement discount that could be offered? (6 marks)

(d) Discuss the factors that should be considered in formulating working capital policy on the management of trade receivables. (8 marks)

(Total: 25 marks)

INVESTMENT APPRAISAL

20 ARMCLIFF CO

Armcliff Co is a division of Shevin Inc which requires each of its divisions to achieve a rate of return on capital employed of at least 10% pa. For this purpose, capital employed is defined as fixed capital and investment in inventories. This rate of return is also applied as a hurdle rate for new investment projects. Divisions have limited borrowing powers and all capital projects are centrally funded.

The following is an extract from Armcliff's divisional accounts:

Income statement for the year ended 31 December 20X4

	$m
Sales revenue	120
Cost of sales	(100)
Operating profit	20

Assets employed as at 31 December 20X4

	$m	$m
Non-current assets (NBV)		75
Current assets (including inventories $25m)	45	
Current liabilities	(32)	
		13
Net capital employed		88

Armcliff's production engineers wish to invest in a new computer-controlled press. The equipment cost is $14m. The residual value is expected to be $2m after four years operation, when the equipment will be shipped to a customer in South America.

The new machine is capable of improving the quality of the existing product and also of producing a higher volume. The firm's marketing team is confident of selling the increased volume by extending the credit period.

The expected additional sales are:

Year 1	2,000,000 units
Year 2	1,800,000 units
Year 3	1,600,000 units
Year 4	1,600,000 units

Sales volume is expected to fall over time due to emerging competitive pressures. Competition will also necessitate a reduction in price by $0.50 each year from the $5 per unit proposed in the first year. Operating costs are expected to be steady at $1 per unit, and allocation of overheads (none of which are affected by the new project) by the central finance department is set at $0.75 per unit.

Higher production levels will require additional investment in inventories of $0.5m, which would be held at this level until the final stages of operation of the project. Customers at present settle accounts after 90 days on average.

Required:

(a) **Determine whether the proposed capital investment is attractive to Armcliff, using the average rate of return on capital method, as defined as average profit-to-average capital employed, ignoring receivables and payables.**

Note: Ignore taxes. **(10 marks)**

(b) (i) **Suggest three problems which arise with the use of the average return method for appraising new investment.** **(3 marks)**

(ii) **In view of the problems associated with the ARR method, why do companies continue to use it in project appraisal?** **(3 marks)**

(c) **Briefly discuss the dangers of offering more generous credit, and suggest ways of assessing customers' creditworthiness.** **(9 marks)**

(Total: 25 marks)

21 DAIRY CO

After securing an extension to an existing contract, the directors of Dairy Co are reviewing the options relating to a machine that is a key part of the company's production process.

Option 1 – Replace the machine

The cost of a new machine would be $450,000, payable immediately.

Maintenance costs would be payable at the end of each year of the project. The first maintenance payment for the new machine is $25,000 although this is expected to rise by 7.5% per year.

Option 2 – Overhaul the existing machine

The alternative to replacement is a complete overhaul of an existing machine, the cost of which would be $275,000, also payable immediately. This would be classified as capital expenditure.

However, under this option, the annual maintenance costs will be higher at $40,000 in year 1 with expected annual increases of 10.5%.

As the new machine is likely to reduce the variable cost, the contribution will be different depending on which machine is used. The contribution from each machine (excluding maintenance costs) is tabulated as follows, with the inflow of funds assumed to be at the end of each year:

Year	Year 1	Year 2	Year 3	Year 4	Year 5
Contribution with new machine ($)	150,000	170,000	190,000	210,000	220,000
Contribution with overhauled machine ($)	130,000	145,000	155,000	160,000	160,000

The financial manager is unsure of the cost of capital, but expects it is around 12%. Taxation can be ignored.

Required:

(a) Calculate the net present value of each option.   (7 marks)

(b) Calculate the discounted payback period for each alternative.   (4 marks)

(c) Estimate the internal rate of return of each plan.   (5 marks)

(d) Interpret the results that you have obtained in parts (a), (b), and (c) above, and recommend which alternative should be chosen.   (4 marks)

(e) Explain the different roles of a treasury department and a finance department in the context of a new investment, and discuss the need for close liaison between the two departments.   (5 marks)

(Total: 25 marks)

22 INVESTMENT APPRAISAL

(a) Explain and illustrate (using simple numerical examples) the Accounting Rate of Return and Payback approaches to investment appraisal, paying particular attention to the limitations of each approach. **(8 marks)**

(b) (i) Explain the differences between NPV and IRR as methods of Discounted Cash Flow analysis. **(7 marks)**

(ii) A company with a cost of capital of 14% is trying to determine the optimal replacement cycle for the laptop computers used by its sales team. The following information is relevant to the decision:

The cost of each laptop is $2,400. Maintenance costs are payable at the end of *each full year* of ownership, but not in the year of replacement, e.g. if the laptop is owned for two years, then the maintenance cost is payable at the end of year 1.

Interval between replacement (years)	Trade-in value ($)	Maintenance cost
1	1,200	Zero
2	800	$75 (payable at end of Year 1)
3	300	$150 (payable at end of Year 2)

Required:

Ignoring taxation, calculate the equivalent annual cost of the three different replacement cycles, and recommend which should be adopted. What other factors should the company take into account when determining the optimal cycle? **(10 marks)**

(Total: 25 marks)

23 PV CO (JUNE 09)

 Timed question with Online tutor debrief

PV Co is evaluating an investment proposal to manufacture Product W33, which has performed well in test marketing trials conducted recently by the company's research and development division. The following information relating to this investment proposal has now been prepared

Initial investment	$2 million
Selling price (current price terms)	$20 per unit
Expected selling price inflation	3% per year
Variable operating costs (current price terms)	$8 per unit
Fixed operating costs (current price terms)	$170,000 per year
Expected operating cost inflation	4% per year

The research and development division has prepared the following demand forecast as a result of its test marketing trials. The forecast reflects expected technological change and its effect on the anticipated life-cycle of Product W33

Year	1	2	3	4
Demand (units)	60,000	70,000	120,000	45,000

It is expected that all units of Product W33 produced will be sold, in line with the company's policy of keeping no inventory of finished goods. No terminal value or machinery scrap value is expected at the end of four years, when production of Product W33 is planned to end. For investment appraisal purposes, PV Co uses a nominal (money) discount rate of 10% per year and a target return on capital employed of 30% per year. Ignore taxation.

Required:

(a) **Identify and explain the key stages in the capital investment decision-making process, and the role of investment appraisal in this process.** **(7 marks)**

(b) **Calculate the following values for the investment proposal:**

    (i)   **net present value;**

    (ii)   **internal rate of return;**

    (iii) **return on capital employed (accounting rate of return) based on average investment; and.**

    (iv) **discounted payback period** **(13 marks)**

(c) **Discuss your findings in each section of (b) above and advise whether the investment proposal is financially acceptable.** **(5 marks)**

(Total: 25 marks)

 Calculate your allowed time, allocate the time to the separate parts

24 BFD CO

BFD Co is a private company formed three years ago by four brothers who, as directors, retain sole ownership of its ordinary share capital. One quarter of the initial share capital was provided by each brother.

The directors are delighted with the rapid growth of BFD Co and are considering further expansion through buying new premises and machinery to manufacture Product FT7. This new product has only just been developed and patented by BFD Co. Test marketing has indicated considerable demand for the product, as shown by the following research data.

Year of operation	1	2	3	4
Accounting year	20X5/6	20X6/7	20X7/8	20X8/9
Sales volume (units)	100,000	120,000	130,000	140,000

Sales after 20X8/9 (the fourth year of operation) are expected to continue at the 20X8/9 level in perpetuity.

Initial investment of $3,000,000 would be required in new premises and machinery, as well as an additional $200,000 of working capital. The directors have no further financial resources to offer and are considering approaching their bank for a loan to meet their investment needs. Selling price and standard cost data for Product FT7, based on an annual budgeted volume of 100,000 units, are as follows:

	$ per unit
Selling price	18.00
Direct material	7.00
Direct labour	1.50
Fixed production overhead	4.50

The fixed production overhead is incurred exclusively in the production of Product FT7 and excludes depreciation. Selling price and standard unit variable cost data for Product FT7 are expected to remain constant.

BFD Co expects to be able to claim writing down allowances on the initial investment of $3,000,000 on a straight line basis over 10 years. The company pays tax on profit at an annual rate of 25% in the year in which the liability arises and has an after-tax cost of capital of 12%.

Required:

(a) Calculate the net present value of the proposed investment in Product FT7. Assume that it is now 1 December 20X5. **(18 marks)**

(b) Comment on the acceptability of the proposed investment in Product FT7 and discuss what additional information might improve the decision-making process. **(7 marks)**

(Total: 25 marks)

25 TRECOR

Trecor Co plans to buy a new machine to meet expected demand for a new product, Product T. This machine will cost $250,000 and last for four years, at the end of which time it will be sold for $5,000. Trecor Co expects demand for Product T to be as follows:

Year	1	2	3	4
Demand (units)	35,000	40,000	50,000	25,000

The selling price for Product T is expected to be $12.00 per unit and the variable cost of production is expected to be $7.80 per unit. Incremental annual fixed production overheads of $25,000 per year will be incurred. Selling price and costs are all in current price terms.

Selling price and costs are expected to increase as follows:

	Increase
Selling price of Product T:	3% per year
Variable cost of production:	4% per year
Fixed production overheads:	6% per year

Other information

Trecor Co has a real cost of capital of 5.7% and pays tax at an annual rate of 30% one year in arrears. It can claim capital allowances on a 25% reducing balance basis. General inflation is expected to be 5% per year.

Trecor Co has a target return on capital employed of 20%. Depreciation is charged on a straight-line basis over the life of an asset.

Required:

(a) Calculate the net present value of buying the new machine and comment on your findings (work to the nearest $1,000). **(13 marks)**

(b) Calculate the before-tax return on capital employed (accounting rate of return) based on the average investment and comment on your findings. **(5 marks)**

(c) Discuss the strengths and weaknesses of internal rate of return in appraising capital investments. **(7 marks)**

(Total: 25 marks)

26 CHARM INC

Charm Inc, a software company, has developed a new game, 'Fingo', which it plans to launch in the near future. Sales of the new game are expected to be very strong, following a favourable review by a popular PC magazine. Charm Inc has been informed that the review will give the game a 'Best Buy' recommendation. Sales volumes, production volumes and selling prices for 'Fingo' over its four-year life are expected to be as follows:

Year	1	2	3	4
Sales and production (units)	150,000	70,000	60,000	60,000
Selling price ($ per game)	$25	$24	$23	$22

Financial information on 'Fingo' for the first year of production is as follows:

Direct material cost	$5.40 per game
Other variable production cost	$6.00 per game
Fixed costs	$4.00 per game

Advertising costs to stimulate demand are expected to be $650,000 in the first year of production and $100,000 in the second year of production. No advertising costs are expected in the third and fourth years of production. Fixed costs represent incremental cash fixed production overheads. 'Fingo' will be produced on a new production machine costing $800,000. Capital allowances will be claimed on a reducing balance basis at a rate of 25%. The machine will have a useful life of four years at the end of which no scrap value is expected.

Charm Inc pays tax on profit at a rate of 30% per year and tax liabilities are settled in the year in which they arise. Charm Inc uses an after-tax discount rate of 10% when appraising new capital investments. Ignore inflation.

Required:

(a)   **Calculate the net present value of the proposed investment and comment on your findings.** **(11 marks)**

(b)   **Calculate the internal rate of return of the proposed investment and comment on your findings.** **(5 marks)**

(c)   **Discuss the reasons why the net present value investment appraisal method is preferred to other investment appraisal methods such as payback, return on capital employed and internal rate of return.** **(9 marks)**

(Total: 25 marks)

27 PLAY CO

Play Co manufactures safety surfacing for children's playgrounds. The main raw material required is rubber particles and these are currently purchased from an outside supplier for $3.50 per tonne. This price is contractually guaranteed for the next four years. If the contract is terminated within the next two years, Play Co will be charged an immediate termination penalty of $150,000 which will not be allowed as a tax deductible expense.

The directors are considering investing in equipment that would allow Play Co to manufacture these particles in house by using recycled tyres.

The machine required to process the tyres will cost $400,000, and it is estimated that at the end of year four the machine will have a second-hand value of $50,000.

The costs associated with the new venture are as follows:

Variable costs (per tonne produced) $0.80

Fixed costs (per annum) $192,500

The additional fixed costs include maintenance costs of $40,000 and the additional depreciation charge (calculated on a straight-line basis over the life of the asset) relating to the machine.

All of the above are quoted in current price terms. Inflationary increases are expected as follows:

Variable costs: 3% per annum

Maintenance costs: 5% per annum

Other fixed costs: 2% per annum

The annual demand for the particles (based on the sales forecasts of the company) is:

	Year 1	Year 2	Year 3	Year 4
Demand (in tonnes)	100,000	110,000	130,000	160,000

Profit tax of 30% per year will be payable one year in arrears. Capital allowances (tax allowable depreciation) on a 25% reducing balance basis could be claimed on the cost of the equipment, with a balancing allowance being claimed in the fourth year of operation when the machine is disposed of.

Required:

(a)   **Using 15% as the after-tax discount rate, advise Play Co on the desirability of purchasing the equipment. (Your workings should be shown to the nearest $000)**

(12 marks)

(b)   **Identify and discuss the limitations of Net Present Value techniques when applied to investment appraisal.**   **(8 marks)**

(c)   **Comment on how the project would affect the different stakeholders of Play Co.**

(5 marks)

(Total: 25 marks)

28   **DUO CO (DEC 07)** *Walk in the footsteps of a top tutor*

Duo Co needs to increase production capacity to meet increasing demand for an existing product, 'Quago', which is used in food processing. A new machine, with a useful life of four years and a maximum output of 600,000 kg of Quago per year, could be bought for $800,000, payable immediately. The scrap value of the machine after four years would be $30,000. Forecast demand and production of Quago over the next four years is as follows:

Year	1	2	3	4
Demand (kg)	1.4 million	1.5 million	1.6 million	1.7 million

Existing production capacity for Quago is limited to one million kilograms per year and the new machine would only be used for demand additional to this.

The current selling price of Quago is $8.00 per kilogram and the variable cost of materials is $5.00 per kilogram. Other variable costs of production are $1.90 per kilogram. Fixed costs of production associated with the new machine would be $240,000 in the first year of production, increasing by $20,000 per year in each subsequent year of operation.

Duo Co pays tax one year in arrears at an annual rate of 30% and can claim capital allowances (tax-allowable depreciation) on a 25% reducing balance basis. A balancing allowance is claimed in the final year of operation.

Duo Co uses its after-tax weighted average cost of capital when appraising investment projects. It has a cost of equity of 11% and a before-tax cost of debt of 8.6%. The long-term finance of the company, on a market-value basis, consists of 80% equity and 20% debt.

Required:

(a) Calculate the net present value of buying the new machine and advise on the acceptability of the proposed purchase (work to the nearest $1,000). **(13 marks)**

(b) Calculate the internal rate of return of buying the new machine and advise on the acceptability of the proposed purchase (work to the nearest $1,000). **(4 marks)**

(c) Explain the difference between risk and uncertainty in the context of investment appraisal, and describe how sensitivity analysis and probability analysis can be used to incorporate risk into the investment appraisal process. **(8 marks)**

(Total: 25 marks)

29 OKM CO (JUNE 10)

The following draft appraisal of a proposed investment project has been prepared for the finance director of OKM Co by a trainee accountant. The project is consistent with the current business operations of OKM Co.

Year	1	2	3	4	5
Sales (units/yr)	250,000	400,000	500,000	250,000	
	$000	$000	$000	$000	$000
Contribution	1,330	2,128	2,660	1,330	
Fixed costs	(530)	(562)	(596)	(631)	
Depreciation	(438)	(438)	(437)	(437)	
Interest payments	(200)	(200)	(200)	(200)	
Taxable profit	162	928	1,427	62	
Taxation		(49)	(278)	(428)	(19)
Profit after tax	162	879	1,149	(366)	(19)
Scrap value				250	
After-tax cash flows	162	879	1,149	(116)	(19)
Discount at 10%	0.909	0.826	0.751	0.683	0.621
Present values	147	726	863	(79)	(12)

Net present value = 1,645,000 – 2,000,000 = ($355,000) so reject the project. The following information was included with the draft investment appraisal:

(1)   The initial investment is $2 million

(2)   Selling price: $12/unit (current price terms), selling price inflation is 5% per year

(3)   Variable cost: $7/unit (current price terms), variable cost inflation is 4% per year

(4)   Fixed overhead costs: $500,000/year (current price terms), fixed cost inflation is 6% per year

Incremental Mental 300,000 per year

Sunk costs

(5) $200,000/year of the fixed costs are development costs that have already been incurred and are being recovered by an annual charge to the project → *Income statement*

(6)   Investment financing is by a $2 million loan at a fixed interest rate of 10% per year

(7)   OKM Co can claim 25% reducing balance capital allowances on this investment and pays taxation one year in arrears at a rate of 30% per year

(8)   The scrap value of machinery at the end of the four-year project is $250,000 9. The real weighted average cost of capital of OKM Co is 7% per year $(1+7) = (1+R)(1+H)$

(10)   The general rate of inflation is expected to be 4.7% per year

Required:

do first →

(a)   Identify and comment on any errors in the investment appraisal prepared by the trainee accountant.   (5 marks)

(b)   Prepare a revised calculation of the net present value of the proposed investment project and comment on the project's acceptability.   (12 marks)

(c)   Discuss the problems faced when undertaking investment appraisal in the following areas and comment on how these problems can be overcome:

(i)   assets with replacement cycles of different lengths;

(ii)   an investment project has several internal rates of return;

(iii)   the business risk of an investment project is significantly different from the business risk of current operations.   (8 marks)

(Total: 25 marks)

30   UMUNAT INC

Umunat Inc is considering investing $50,000 in a new machine with an expected life of five years. The machine will have no scrap value at the end of five years. It is expected that 20,000 units will be sold each year at a selling price of $3.00 per unit. Variable production costs are expected to be $1.65 per unit, while incremental fixed costs, mainly the wages of a maintenance engineer, are expected to be $10,000 per year. Umunat Inc uses a discount rate of 12% for investment appraisal purposes and expects investment projects to recover their initial investment within two years.

Required:

(a)   Explain why risk and uncertainty should be considered in the investment appraisal process.   (5 marks)

(b)   Calculate and comment on the payback period of the project.   (4 marks)

(c) Evaluate the sensitivity of the project's net present value to a change in the following project variables:

(i) sales volume;

(ii) sales price;

(iii) variable cost;

and discuss the use of sensitivity analysis as a way of evaluating project risk.

(10 marks)

(d) Upon further investigation it is found that there is a significant chance that the expected sales volume of 20,000 units per year will not be achieved. The sales manager of Umunat Inc suggests that sales volumes could depend on expected economic states that could be assigned the following probabilities:

Economic state	Poor	Normal	Good
Probability	0.3	0.6	0.1
Annual sale volume (units)	17,500	20,000	22,500

Required:

Calculate and comment on the expected net present value of the project. **(6 marks)**

(Total: 25 marks)

31 VICTORY

Victory Co is considering the purchase of new equipment which would enable the company to expand its operations. The equipment will cost $1.2 million and have a three-year life, at the end of which it will have a scrap value of $600,000.

The equipment will mean Victory requires further factory space at an annual rental of $80,000, payable in advance, with the first payment being made on the day the equipment is purchased.

Further annual fixed costs charged to the project will be $715,000 in total. Amongst other things, this includes:

- $86,000 of bank interest payable on the loan to cover the cost of the equipment.

- $74,000 of costs allocated out of head office overheads.

- A depreciation charge for the new machinery that has been calculated using the straight-line method over the life of the machine.

Additional annual sales are expected to be 60,000 units per annum in each of the three years. Each unit will sell for $40 and has a variable production cost of $25.

A further investment of $340,000 will be required for working capital. This will need to be in place at the start of the year. This will increase to $400,000 in the following year and $450,000 in the year after that. This working capital investment will be fully recovered at the end of the project.

If Victory Co buys the new equipment it can claim capital allowances on the investment on a 25% reducing balance basis. The company pays taxation in the year to which it relates at an annual rate of 30%. Victory Co uses a cost of capital of 10% per annum for appraising its investments.

Required:

(a)   Prepare a forecast of the annual after-tax cash flows of the investment and calculate and comment on its net present value   **(11 marks)**

(b)   Calculate the sensitivity of your answer to part (a) to changes in:

   (i)   the expected annual sales (in units)

   (ii)   the estimated sales proceeds of the equipment

   Discuss the implications of your findings to Victory Co   **(8 marks)**

(c)   Explain the difference between risk and uncertainty and describe two other methods (excluding sensitivity analysis) that a company can use to incorporate either risk or uncertainty when appraising investments   **(6 marks)**

(Total: 25 marks)

32   SPRINGBANK INC

Springbank Inc is a medium-sized manufacturing company that plans to increase capacity by purchasing new machinery at an initial cost of $3 million. The new machine will also require a further investment in working capital of $400,000. The investment is expected to increase annual sales by 5,500 units. Investment in replacement machinery would be needed after five years. Financial data on the additional units to be sold is as follows:

	$
Selling price per unit	500
Production costs per unit	200

Variable administration and distribution expenses are expected to increase by $220,000 per year as a result of the increase in capacity. The full amount of the initial investment in new machinery of $3 million will give rise to capital allowances on a 25% per year reducing balance basis. The scrap value of the machinery after five years is expected to be negligible. Tax liabilities are paid in the year in which they arise and Springbank Inc pays tax at 30% of annual profits.

The Finance Director of Springbank Inc has proposed that the $3.4 million investment should be financed by an issue of loan stock at a fixed rate of 8% per year.

Springbank Inc uses an after tax discount rate of 12% to evaluate investment proposals. In preparing its financial statements, Springbank Inc uses straight-line depreciation over the expected life of non-current assets.

Required:

(a)   Calculate the net present value of the proposed investment in increased capacity of Springbank Inc, clearly stating any assumptions that you make in your calculations.   **(11 marks)**

(b)   Calculate the increase in sales (in units) that would produce a zero net present value for the proposed investment.   **(8 marks)**

(c)   On the basis of your previous calculations and analysis, comment on the acceptability of the proposed investment and discuss whether the proposed method of financing can be recommended.   **(6 marks)**

(Total: 25 marks)

 Online question assistance

33   CJ CO (DEC 10)

CJ Co is a profitable company which is financed by equity with a market value of $180 million and by debt with a market value of $45 million. The company is considering two investment projects, as follows.

Project A

This project is an expansion of existing business costing $3.5 million, payable at the start of the project, which will increase annual sales by 750,000 units. Information on unit selling price and costs is as follows:

Selling price: $2.00 per unit (current price terms)
Selling costs: $0.04 per unit (current price terms)
Variable costs: $0.80 per unit (current price terms)

Selling price inflation and selling cost inflation are expected to be 5% per year and variable cost inflation is expected to be 4% per year. Additional initial investment in working capital of $250,000 will also be needed and this is expected to increase in line with general inflation.

Project B

This project is a diversification into a new business area that will cost $4 million. A company that already operates in the new business area, GZ Co, has an equity beta of 1.5. GZ Co is financed 75% by equity with a market value of $90 million and 25% by debt with a market value of $30 million.

Other information

CJ Co has a nominal weighted average after-tax cost of capital of 10% and pays profit tax one year in arrears at an annual rate of 30%. The company can claim capital allowances (tax-allowable depreciation) on a 25% reducing balance basis on the initial investment in both projects.

Risk-free rate of return: 4%
Equity risk premium: 6%
General rate of inflation: 4.5% per year

Directors' views on investment appraisal

The directors of CJ Co require that all investment projects should be evaluated using either payback period or return on capital employed (accounting rate of return). The target payback period of the company is two years and the target return on capital employed is 20%, which is the current return on capital employed of CJ Co. A project is accepted if it satisfies either of these investment criteria.

The directors also require all investment projects to be evaluated over a four-year planning period, ignoring any scrap value or working capital recovery, with a balancing allowance (if any) being claimed at the end of the fourth year of operation.

Required:

(a)   Calculate the net present value of Project A and advise on its acceptability if the project were to be appraised using this method.   **(12 marks)**

(b)   Critically discuss the directors' views on investment appraisal.   **(7 marks)**

(c)   Calculate a project-specific cost of equity for Project B and explain the stages of your calculation.   **(6 marks)**

(Total: 25 marks)

34   BASRIL

Basril Inc is reviewing investment proposals that have been submitted by divisional managers. The investment funds of the company are limited to $800,000 in the current year. Details of three possible investments, none of which can be delayed, are given below.

Project 1

An investment of $300,000 in work station assessments. Each assessment would be on an individual employee basis and would lead to savings in labour costs from increased efficiency and from reduced absenteeism due to work-related illness. Savings in labour costs from these assessments in money terms are expected to be as follows:

Year	1	2	3	4	5
Cash flows (£000)	85	90	95	100	95

Project 2

An investment of $450,000 in individual workstations for staff that is expected to reduce administration costs by $140,800 per annum in money terms for the next five years.

Project 3

An investment of $400,000 in new ticket machines. Net cash savings of $120,000 per annum are expected in current price terms and these are expected to increase by 3.6% per annum due to inflation during the five-year life of the machines.

Basril Inc has a money cost of capital of 12% and taxation should be ignored.

Required:

(a)   Determine the best way for Basril Inc to invest the available funds and calculate the resultant NPV:

(i)   on the assumption that each of the three projects is divisible;

(ii)   on the assumption that none of the projects are divisible.   (10 marks)

(b)   Explain how the NPV investment appraisal method is applied in situations where capital is rationed.   (3 marks)

(c)   Discuss the reasons why capital rationing may arise.   (7 marks)

(d)   Discuss the meaning of the term 'relevant cash flows' in the context of investment appraisal, giving examples to illustrate your discussion.   (5 marks)

(Total: 25 marks)

35   ASOP CO (DEC 09)

ASOP Co is considering an investment in new technology that will reduce operating costs through increasing energy efficiency and decreasing pollution. The new technology will cost $1 million and have a four-year life, at the end of which it will have a scrap value of $100,000.

A licence fee of $104,000 is payable at the end of the first year. This licence fee will increase by 4% per year in each subsequent year.

The new technology is expected to reduce operating costs by $5.80 per unit in current price terms. This reduction in operating costs is before taking account of expected inflation of 5% per year.

Forecast production volumes over the life of the new technology are expected to be as follows:

Year	1	2	3	4
Production (units per year)	60,000	75,000	95,000	80,000

If ASOP Co bought the new technology, it would finance the purchase through a four-year loan paying interest at an annual before-tax rate of 8.6% per year.

Alternatively, ASOP Co could lease the new technology. The company would pay four annual lease rentals of $380,000 per year, payable in advance at the start of each year. The annual lease rentals include the cost of the licence fee.

If ASOP Co buys the new technology it can claim capital allowances on the investment on a 25% reducing balance basis. The company pays taxation one year in arrears at an annual rate of 30%. ASOP Co has an after-tax weighted average cost of capital of 11% per year.

Required:

(a) **Based on financing cash flows only, calculate and determine whether ASOP Co should lease or buy the new technology.** **(11 marks)**

(b) **Using a nominal terms approach, calculate the net present value of buying the new technology and advise whether ASOP Co should undertake the proposed investment.** **(6 marks)**

(c) **Discuss and illustrate how ASOP Co can use equivalent annual cost or equivalent annual benefit to choose between new technologies with different expected lives.** **(3 marks)**

(d) **Discuss how an optimal investment schedule can be formulated when capital is rationed and investment projects are either:**

    (i) **divisible; or**

    (ii) **non-divisible.** **(5 marks)**

(Total: 25 marks)

36 CAVIC

Cavic Co services custom cars and provides its clients with a courtesy car while servicing is taking place. It has a fleet of 10 courtesy cars which it plans to replace in the near future. Each new courtesy car will cost $15,000. The trade-in value of each new car declines over time as follows:

Age of courtesy car (years)	1	2	3
Trade-in value ($/car)	11,250	9,000	6,200

Servicing and parts will cost $1,000 per courtesy car in the first year and this cost is expected to increase by 40% per year as each vehicle grows older. Cleaning the interior and exterior of each courtesy car to keep it up to the standard required by Cavic's clients will cost $500 per car in the first year and this cost is expected to increase by 25% per year.

Cavic Co has a cost of capital of 10%. Ignore taxation and inflation.

Required:

(a)   Using the equivalent annual cost method, calculate whether Cavic Co should replace its fleet after one year, two years, or three years.   **(12 marks)**

(b)   Discuss the causes of capital rationing for investment purposes.   **(4 marks)**

(c)   Explain how an organisation can determine the best way to invest available capital under capital rationing. Your answer should refer to the following issues:

      (i)   single-period capital rationing;

      (ii)   multi-period capital rationing;

      (iii)   project divisibility;

      (iv)   the investment of surplus funds.   **(9 marks)**

(Total: 25 marks)

BUSINESS FINANCE

37   FMY

FMY Co manufactures glass bottles for the drinks industry. It has been trading for 15 years. The company at present has no long-term debt although it does have an overdraft facility that is used for short-term financing needs.

The company is forecasting post-tax earnings of $4.5 million on revenue of $32 million for the current year. These sales and earnings levels are expected to continue unless new investment is undertaken. The Managing Director (MD), who is also a significant shareholder, is planning a major expansion programme that will require raising $5 million of new finance for capital investment. This investment yields a positive net present value of $1.2 million when evaluated at the company's post-tax cost of capital of 12%, and is expected to increase post-tax earnings by $1m per annum (before considering the method of financing the expansion).

The Board is considering two alternative methods of financing this expansion:

(1)   A 1 for 4 rights issue to existing shareholders. There are currently 10 million shares in issue, each of which is trading at $2.20.

(2)   Medium-term (five years) debt, interest rate fixed at 8.6%, secured on the company's non-current assets, mainly land and buildings.

The company pays tax one year in arrears at 30%.

Required:

(a)   Comment on the effect of each suggested method of financing on the valuation of the company. Your answer should refer to capital structure theories amongst other things.   **(12 marks)**

(b)   Identify and discuss any additional factors that need to be considered by the Board when deciding whether to raise new equity through a rights issue.   **(5 marks)**

(c)   Explain the major differences between Islamic finance and other conventional forms of finance such as those being considered by FMY Co. Identify, and briefly discuss, two Islamic financial instruments that would be of use to FMY Co in the above situation.   **(8 marks)**

(Total: 25 marks)

38   NUGFER (DEC 10)

The following financial position statement as at 30 November 2010 refers to Nugfer Co, a stock exchange-listed company, which wishes to raise $200m in cash in order to acquire a competitor.

	$m	$m	$m
Assets			
Non-current assets			300
Current assets			211
Total assets			511
Equity and liabilities			
Share capital		100	
Retained earnings		121	
Total equity			221
Non-current liabilities			
Long-term borrowings		100	
Current liabilities			
Trade payables	30		
Short-term borrowings	160		
Total current liabilities		190	
Total liabilities			290
Total equity and liabilities			511

The recent performance of Nugfer Co in profitability terms is as follows:

Year ending 30 November	2007	2008	2009	2010
	$m	$m	$m	$m
Revenue	122.6	127.3	156.6	189.3
Operating profit	41.7	43.3	50.1	56.7
Finance charges (interest)	6.0	6.2	12.5	18.8
Profit before tax	35.7	37.1	37.6	37.9
Profit after tax	25.0	26.0	26.3	26.5

Notes:

(1)   The long-term borrowings are 6% bonds that are repayable in 2012

(2)   The short-term borrowings consist of an overdraft at an annual interest rate of 8% 3. The current assets do not include any cash deposits

(4)   Nugfer Co has not paid any dividends in the last four years

(5)   The number of ordinary shares issued by the company has not changed in recent years

(6)   The target company has no debt finance and its forecast profit before interest and tax for 2011 is $28 million

Required:

(a)   Evaluate suitable methods of raising the $200 million required by Nugfer Co, supporting your evaluation with both analysis and critical discussion.   (15 marks)

(b)   Briefly explain the factors that will influence the rate of interest charged on a new issue of bonds.   (4 marks)

(c)   Identify and describe the three forms of efficiency that may be found in a capital market.   (6 marks)

(Total: 25 marks)

39   ECHO CO (DEC 07)   *Walk in the footsteps of a top tutor*

The following financial information relates to Echo Co:

Income statement information for the last year

	$m
Profit before interest and tax	12
Interest	3
Profit before tax	9
Income tax expense	3
Profit for the period	6
Dividends	2
Retained profit for the period	4

Statement of financial position information as at the end of the last year

	$m	$m
Ordinary shares, par value 50c	5	
Retained earnings	15	
Total equity		20
8% loan notes, redeemable in three years' time		30
Total equity and non-current liabilities		50

Average data on companies similar to Echo Co:

Interest coverage ratio   8 times

Long-term debt/equity (book value basis)   80%

The board of Echo Co is considering several proposals that have been made by its finance director. Each proposal is independent of any other proposal.

Proposal A

The current dividend per share should be increased by 20% in order to make the company more attractive to equity investors.

Proposal B

A bond issue should be made in order to raise $15 million of new debt capital. Although there are no investment opportunities currently available, the cash raised would be invested on a short-term basis until a suitable investment opportunity arose. The loan notes would pay interest at a rate of 10% per year and be redeemable in eight years time at par.

Proposal C

A 1 for 4 rights issue should be made at a 20% discount to the current share price of $2.30 per share in order to reduce gearing and the financial risk of the company.

Required:

(a)   **Analyse and discuss Proposal A.**   **(5 marks)**

(b)   **Evaluate and discuss Proposal B.**   **(7 marks)**

(c)   **Calculate the theoretical ex rights price per share and the amount of finance that would be raised under Proposal C. Evaluate and discuss the proposal to use these funds to reduce gearing and financial risk.**   **(7 marks)**

(d)   **Discuss the attractions of operating leasing as a source of finance.**   **(6 marks)**

                                                              (Total: 25 marks)

40   PAVLON

(a)   Pavlon Inc has recently obtained a listing on the Stock Exchange. 90% of the company's shares were previously owned by members of one family but, since the listing, approximately 60% of the issued shares have been owned by other investors.

Pavlon's earnings and dividends for the five years prior to the listing are detailed below:

Years prior to listing	Profit after tax ($)	Dividend per share (cents)
5	1,800,000	3.6
4	2,400,000	4.8
3	3,850,000	6.16
2	4,100,000	6.56
1	4,450,000	7.12
Current year	5,500,000(estimate)	

The number of issued ordinary shares was increased by 25% three years prior to the listing and by 50% at the time of the listing. The company's authorised capital is currently $25,000,000 in 25¢ ordinary shares, of which 40,000,000 shares have been issued. The market value of the company's equity is $78,000,000.

The board of directors is discussing future dividend policy. An interim dividend of 3.16 cents per share was paid immediately prior to the listing and the finance director has suggested a final dividend of 2.34 cents per share.

The company's declared objective is to maximise shareholder wealth.

Required:

(i)   **Comment upon the nature of the company's dividend policy prior to the listing and discuss whether such a policy is likely to be suitable for a company listed on the Stock Exchange.**   **(6 marks)**

(ii) **Discuss whether the proposed final dividend of 2.34 cents is likely to be an appropriate dividend:**

   –   **If the majority of shares are owned by wealthy private individuals; and**

   –   **If the majority of shares are owned by institutional investors.**

                                                                                (10 marks)

(b)   The company's profit after tax is generally expected to increase by 15% per year for three years, and 8% per year after that. Pavlon's cost of equity capital is estimated to be 12% per year. Dividends may be assumed to grow at the same rate as profits.

Required:

(i)   **Use the dividend valuation model to give calculations to indicate whether Pavlon's shares are currently under- or over-valued.**   **(6 marks)**

(ii) **Briefly outline the weaknesses of the dividend valuation model.**   **(3 marks)**

                                                                        (Total: 25 marks)

41   ARWIN

Arwin plans to raise $5m in order to expand its existing chain of retail outlets. It can raise the finance by issuing 10% loan stock redeemable in ten years' time, or by a rights issue at $4.00 per share. The current financial statements of Arwin are as follows:

Income statement for the last year

	$000
Sales revenue	50,000
Cost of sales	30,000
Gross profit	20,000
Administration costs	14,000
Profit before interest and tax	6,000
Interest	300
Profit before tax	5,700
Taxation at 30%	1,710
Profit after tax	3,990

Changes in equity

	$000
Dividends	2,394
Net change in equity (retained profits)	1,596

Statement of financial position

	$000
Net non-current assets	20,100
Net current assets	4,960
	———
	25,060
	———
Ordinary shares, par value 25¢	2,500
Retained profit	20,060
12% loan stock (redeemable in six years)	2,500
	———
	25,060
	———

The expansion of business is expected to increase sales revenue by 12% in the first year. Variable cost of sales makes up 85% of cost of sales. Administration costs will increase by 5% due to new staff appointments. Arwin has a policy of paying out 60% of profit after tax as dividends and has no overdraft.

Required:

(a) For each financing proposal, prepare the forecast income statement after one additional year of operation. **(5 marks)**

(b) Evaluate and comment on the effects of each financing proposal on the following:

    (i) Financial gearing;

    (ii) Operational gearing;

    (iii) Interest cover;

    (iv) Earnings per share. **(12 marks)**

(c) Discuss the dangers to a company of a high level of gearing, including in your answer an explanation of the following terms:

    (i) Business risk;

    (ii) Financial risk. **(8 marks)**

(Total: 25 marks)

42   SPENDER CONSTRUCTION INC

Assume that 'now' is the end of December 20X7.

Spender Construction Inc is an expanding building company wishing to raise funds to invest in building a new headquarters and IT centre with upgraded facilities for its logistics and project management business. The total investment required is estimated to be $7 million. The financial justification for the investment is based upon estimates that the new centre will cut fixed administration costs by approximately $500,000 per annum, and reduce the cost of sales by 2%. Sales for the year to 31 December 20X8 are forecast to rise 15% above 20X7 levels (regardless of the investment decision), and so the company anticipates a need for higher working capital funding, in addition to finance for the capital expenditure.

Spender's finance director has commented that in raising funds the Board need to be conscious of the fact that the company operates in a sector which is notorious for its volatility of demand, and also that the company has relatively high levels of fixed operating costs. The industry average is for fixed operating costs to equal 7% of sales revenue. Summarised financial statements for Spender Construction Inc are shown below:

Income statement, year ending 31 December 20X7

	$000
Sales revenue	55,258
Cost of sales	41,827
Gross profit	13,431
Selling and distribution costs	348
Administration costs	8,250
Operating profit	4,833
Interest charges	327
Profit before tax	4,506
Corporation tax payable	1,352
Profit after tax	3,154

Note:

	$000
Dividends	1,520
Net change in equity (retained profits)	1,634

Statement of financial position as at 31 December 20X7

	$000
Non-current assets	5,800
Current assets	27,928
	———
Total assets	33,728
	———
Equity and liabilities	
Ordinary share capital	4,000
Share premium account	800
Retained profit	7,652
	———
Total equity	12,452
10% loan stock 20X6	1,200
Current liabilities	20,076
	———
Total equity and liabilities	33,728
	———

Additional information

(1)   The nominal value of ordinary share capital is 50 cents per share.

(2)   Costs are classified as fixed or variable as follows:

Cost of sales: 100% variable.

Selling and distribution: $100,000 per annum fixed, balance variable.

Administration costs: $7 million per annum fixed, balance variable.

(3)   The current rate of corporation tax is 30%.

(4)   Current liabilities as at 31 December 20X7 includes a $2 million overdraft, and a $450,000 sales tax bill.

(5)   The current market price of ordinary shares in Spender Inc is $6.50.

(6)   Working capital needs are expected to rise in line with sales.

(7)   The dividend forecast for year ending 31 December 20X8 is 25 cents per share.

(8)   Bank interest charges for the year to 31 December 20X8 are forecast to be $280,000. Interest is charged at 12.5% per annum.

(9)   Depreciation charges on non-current assets for the year to 31 December 20X7 are $435,000.

(10)   Assume that payments totalling $2.5 million were made during 20X7 in respect of trade payables outstanding at the end of the previous year.

(11)   Working capital requirements for 20X7 were the same as those for the previous year.

Required:

(a) Explain and illustrate, using the above data, each of the following terms and comment upon the implications of these two forms of gearing for the equity investors in Spender Construction Inc:

    (i) operational gearing

    (ii) financial gearing. **(12 marks)**

(b) Evaluate (by comparison of shareholder risks and returns, including EPS) the relative merits of raising the $7 million required for the capital investment via a 1 for 6 rights issue priced at $5.25, or 10% loan stock issue redeemable in 20 years time. Ignore issue costs. **(10 marks)**

(c) Explain the meaning of the term dividend cover and, using the forecast figures for the year ending 31 December 20X8, calculate the dividend cover for Spender Construction Inc assuming the loan stock issue is made. **(3 marks)**

(Total: 25 marks)

43 ASSOCIATED INTERNATIONAL SUPPLIES CO

The following are summary financial statements for Associated International Supplies Co.

	20X4	20X9
	$000	$000
Non-current assets	115	410
Current assets	650	1,000
Total assets	765	1,410
Capital and reserves	210	270
Non-current liabilities	42	158
Current liabilities	513	982
	765	1,410
Sales revenue	1,200	3,010
Cost of sales, expenses and interest	1,102	2,860
Profit before tax	98	150
Tax and distributions	33	133
Retained earnings	65	17

Notes: Cost of sales was $530,000 for 20X4 and $1,330,000 for 20X9.

Trade receivables are 50% of current assets; trade payables 25% of current liabilities for both years.

Required:

(a) You are a consultant advising Associated International Supplies Co. Using suitable financial ratios, and paying particular attention to growth and liquidity, write a report on the significant changes faced by the company since 20X4. The report should also comment on the capacity of the company to continue trading, together with any other factors considered appropriate. An appendix to the report should be used to outline your calculations. **(17 marks)**

(b) Explain and evaluate the sources of finance available to small businesses for non-current assets. **(8 marks)**

(Total: 25 marks)

44 **GTK INC (JUNE 07)** *Walk in the footsteps of a top tutor*

The finance director of GTK Inc is preparing its capital budget for the forthcoming period and is examining a number of capital investment proposals that have been received from its subsidiaries. Details of these proposals are as follows:

Proposal 1

Division A has requested that it be allowed to invest $500,000 in solar panels, which would be fitted to the roof of its production facility, in order to reduce its dependency on oil as an energy source. The solar panels would save energy costs of $700 per day but only on sunny days. The Division has estimated the following probabilities of sunny days in each year.

	Number of sunny days	Probability
Scenario 1	100	0.3
Scenario 2	125	0.6
Scenario 3	150	0.1

Each scenario is expected to persist indefinitely, i.e. if there are 100 sunny days in the first year, there will be 100 sunny days in every subsequent year. Maintenance costs for the solar panels are expected to be $2,000 per month for labour and replacement parts, irrespective of the number of sunny days per year. The solar panels are expected to be used indefinitely.

Proposal 2

Division C has requested approval and funding for a new product which it has been secretly developing, Product RPG. Product development and market research costs of $350,000 have already been incurred and are now due for payment. $300,000 is needed for new machinery, which will be a full scale version of the current pilot plant. Advertising takes place in the first year only and would cost $100,000. Annual cash inflow of $100,000, net of all production costs but before taking account of advertising costs, is expected to be generated for a five-year period. After five years Product RPG would be retired and replaced with a more technologically advanced model. The machinery used for producing Product RPG would be sold for $30,000 at that time.

Other information

GTK Inc is a profitable, listed company with several million dollars of shareholders' funds, a small overdraft and no long-term debt. For profit calculation purposes, GTK Inc depreciates assets on a straight-line basis over their useful economic life. The company can claim writing down allowances on machinery on a 25% reducing balance basis and pays tax on profit at an annual rate of 30% in the year in which the liability arises. GTK Inc has a before-tax cost of capital of 10%, an after-tax cost of capital of 8% and a target return on capital employed of 15%.

Required:

(a)   For the proposed investment in solar panels (Proposal 1), calculate:

      (i)   the net present value for each expected number of sunny days

      (ii)   the overall expected net present value of the proposal

      Comment on your findings. Ignore taxation in this part of the question.   **(9 marks)**

(b)   Calculate the before-tax return on capital employed (accounting rate of return) of the proposed investment in Product RPG (Proposal 2), using the average investment method, and advise on its acceptability.   **(6 marks)**

(c)   Assuming GTK Inc wishes to raise $1.1 million, discuss how equity finance or traded debt (bonds) might be raised, clearly indicating which source of finance you recommend and the reasons for your recommendation.   **(10 marks)**

(Total: 25 marks)

45   TFR (JUNE 07)

TFR is a small, profitable, owner-managed company which is seeking finance for a planned expansion. A local bank has indicated that it may be prepared to offer a loan of $100,000 at a fixed annual rate of 9%. TFR would repay $25,000 of the capital each year for the next four years. Annual interest would be calculated on the opening balance at the start of each year. Current financial information on TFR is as follows:

Current turnover:	$210,000
Net profit margin:	20%
Annual taxation rate:	25%
Average overdraft:	$20,000
Average interest on overdraft:	10% per year
Dividend payout ratio:	50%
Shareholders funds:	$200,000
Market value of non-current assets	$180,000

As a result of the expansion, turnover would increase by $45,000 per year for each of the next four years, while net profit margin would remain unchanged. No capital allowances would arise from investment of the amount borrowed.

TFR currently has no other debt than the existing and continuing overdraft and has no cash or near-cash investments. The non-current assets consist largely of the building from which the company conducts its business. The current dividend payout ratio has been maintained for several years.

Required:

(a) Assuming that TFR is granted the loan, calculate the following ratios for TFR for each of the next four years:

    (i)   interest cover

    (ii)   medium to long-term debt/equity ratio

    (iii) return on equity

    (iv) return on capital employed.   **(10 marks)**

(b) Comment on the financial implications for TFR of accepting the bank loan on the terms indicated above.   **(8 marks)**

(c) Discuss the difficulties commonly faced by small firms such as TFR when seeking additional finance.   **(7 marks)**

(Total: 25 marks)

COST OF CAPITAL

46 DROXFOL

Droxfol Co is a listed company that plans to spend $10m on expanding its existing business. It has been suggested that the money could be raised by issuing 9% loan notes redeemable in ten years' time. Current financial information on Droxfol Co is as follows.

Income statement information for the last year

	$000
Profit before interest and tax	7,000
Interest	(500)
Profit before tax	6,500
Tax	(1,950)
Profit for the period	4,550

Statement of Financial Position for the last year

	$000	$000
Non-current assets		20,000
Current assets		20,000
Total assets		40,000

Equity and liabilities

Ordinary shares, par value $1 $K_e = \dfrac{D_0(1+g)}{P_0} + g$ 5,000

Retained earnings   22,500

Total equity   27,500

10% loan notes   5,000

9% preference shares, par value $1 $K_p = \dfrac{D}{P_0}$ 2,500

Total non-current liabilities   7,500

Current liabilities   5,000

Total equity and liabilities   40,000

The current ex div ordinary share price is $4.50 per share. An ordinary dividend of 35 cents per share has just been paid and dividends are expected to increase by 4% per year for the foreseeable future. The current ex div preference share price is 76.2 cents. The loan notes are secured on the existing non-current assets of Droxfol Co and are redeemable at par in eight years' time. They have a current ex interest market price of $105 per $100 loan note. Droxfol Co pays tax on profits at an annual rate of 30%.

The expansion of business is expected to increase profit before interest and tax by 12% in the first year. Droxfol Co has no overdraft.

Average sector ratios:

Financial gearing: 45% (prior charge capital divided by equity share capital on a book value basis)

Interest coverage ratio: 12 times

Required:

(a) Calculate the current weighted average cost of capital of Droxfol Co.   (9 marks)

(b) Discuss whether financial management theory suggests that Droxfol Co can reduce its weighted average cost of capital to a minimum level.   (8 marks)

(c) Evaluate and comment on the effects, after one year, of the loan note issue and the expansion of business on the following ratios:

    (i) interest coverage ratio;

    (ii) financial gearing;

    (iii) earnings per share.

Assume that the dividend growth rate of 4% is unchanged.   (8 marks)

(Total: 25 marks)

47 ILL COLLEAGUE

A colleague has been taken ill. Your managing director has asked you to take over from the colleague and to provide urgently needed estimates of the discount rate to be used in appraising a large new capital investment. You have been given your colleague's working notes, which you believe to be numerically accurate.

Working notes

Estimates for the next five years (annual averages)

Stock market total return on equity	16%
Own company dividend yield	7%
Own company share price rise	14%
Own company equity Beta	1.4
Growth rate of own company earnings	12%
Growth rate of own company dividends	11%
Growth rate of own company sales	13%
Treasury bill yield	12%

The company's gearing level (by market values) is 1:2 debt to equity, and after-tax earnings available to ordinary shareholders in the most recent year were $5,400,000, of which $2,140,000 was distributed as ordinary dividends. The company has 10 million issued ordinary shares, which are currently trading on the Stock Exchange at 321 cents. Corporate debt may be assumed to be risk-free. The company pays tax at 35% and personal taxation may be ignored.

Required:

(a) Estimate the company's weighted average cost of capital using:

   (i)   the dividend valuation model;

   (ii) the capital asset pricing model.

   State clearly any assumptions that you make.

   Under what circumstances would these models be expected to produce similar values for the weighted average cost of capital?   (9 marks)

(b) You are now informed that the proposed investment is a major diversification into a new industry, and are provided with the following information about the new industry:

Average industry gearing level (by market value)	1:3 debt to equity
Average β equity	1.50

   Using any relevant information from parts (a) and (b), recommend which discount rate should be used for the investment. Any relevant calculations not included in your answer to part (a) should form part of your answer.   (6 marks)

(c) Discuss the practical problems of using the capital asset pricing model in investment appraisal.   (10 marks)

(Total: 25 marks)

48   KFP CO (JUNE 09)

 Timed question with Online tutor debrief

KFP Co, a company listed on a major stock market, is looking at its cost of capital as it prepares to make a bid to buy a rival unlisted company, NGN. Both companies are in the same business sector. Financial information on KFP Co and NGN is as follows:

	KFP Co		NGN	
	$m	$m	$m	$m
Non-current assets		36		25
Current assets	7		7	
Current liabilities	3		4	
Net current assets		4		3
Total assets less current liabilities		40		28

	KFP Co		NGN	
	$m	$m	$m	$m
Ordinary shares, par value 50c	15		5	
Retained earnings	10		3	
Total equity		25		8
7% bonds, redeemable at par in seven years' time		15		
9% bonds, redeemable at par in two years' time				20
Total equity and non-current liabilities		40		28

Other relevant financial information:

Risk-free rate of return	4.0%
Average return on the market	10.5%
Taxation rate	30%

NGN has a cost of equity of 12% per year and has maintained a dividend payout ratio of 45% for several years. The current earnings per share of the company is 80c per share and its earnings have grown at an average rate of 4.5% per year in recent years.

The ex div share price of KFP Co is $4.20 per share and it has an equity beta of 1.2. The 7% bonds of the company are trading on an ex interest basis at $94.74 per $100 bond. The price/earnings ratio of KFP Co is eight times.

The directors of KFP Co believe a cash offer for the shares of NGN would have the best chance of success. It has been suggested that a cash offer could be financed by debt.

Required:

(a) Calculate the weighted average cost of capital of KFP Co on a market value weighted basis. **(10 marks)**

(b) Calculate the total value of the target company, NGN, using the following valuation methods:

   (i) Price/earnings ratio method, using the price/earnings ratio of KFP Co; and

   (ii) Dividend growth model. **(6 marks)**

(c) Discuss the relationship between capital structure and weighted average cost of capital, and comment on the suggestion that debt could be used to finance a cash offer for NGN. **(9 marks)**

(25 marks)

 Calculate your allowed time, allocate the time to the separate parts

---

49 BURSE CO (JUNE 08) *Walk in the footsteps of a top tutor*

Burse Co wishes to calculate its weighted average cost of capital and the following information relates to the company at the current time:

Number of ordinary shares	20 million
Book value of 7% convertible debt	$29 million
Book value of 8% bank loan	$2 million
Market price of ordinary shares	$5.50 per share
Market value of convertible debt	$107.11 per $100 bond
Equity beta of Burse Co	1.2
Risk-free rate of return	4.7%
Equity risk premium	6.5%
Rate of taxation	30%

Burse Co expects share prices to rise in the future at an average rate of 6% per year. The convertible debt can be redeemed at par in eight years' time, or converted in six years' time into 15 shares of Burse Co per $100 bond.

Required:

(a) Calculate the market value weighted average cost of capital of Burse Co. State clearly any assumptions that you make. **(12 marks)**

(b) Discuss the circumstances under which the weighted average cost of capital can be used in investment appraisal. **(6 marks)**

(c) Discuss whether the dividend growth model or the capital asset pricing model offers the better estimate of the cost of equity of a company. **(7 marks)**

(Total: 25 marks)

---

50   YGV CO (JUNE 10)

YGV Co is a listed company selling computer software. Its profit before interest and tax has fallen from $5 million to $1 million in the last year and its current financial position is as follows:

	$000	$000
Non-current assets		
Tangible assets	3,000	
Intangible assets	8,500	11,500
Current assets		
Inventory	4,100	
Trade receivables	11,100	15,200
Total assets		26,700
Current liabilities		
Trade payables	5,200	
Overdraft	4,500	9,700
Equity		
Ordinary shares	10,000	
Reserves	7,000	17,000
		26,700

YGV Co has been advised by its bank that the current overdraft limit of $4.5 million will be reduced to $500,000 in two months' time. The finance director of YGV Co has been unable to find another bank willing to offer alternative overdraft facilities and is planning to issue bonds on the stock market in order to finance the reduction of the overdraft. The bonds would be issued at their par value of $100 per bond and would pay interest of 9% per year, payable at the end of each year. The bonds would be redeemable at a 10% premium to their par value after 10 years. The finance director hopes to raise $4 million from the bond issue.

The ordinary shares of YGV Co have a par value of $1.00 per share and a current market value of $4.10 per share. The cost of equity of YGV Co is 12% per year and the current interest rate on the overdraft is 5% per year. Taxation is at an annual rate of 30%.

Other financial information:

Average gearing of sector (debt/equity, market value basis):   10%

Average interest coverage ratio of sector: 8 times

Required:

(a) Calculate the after-tax cost of debt of the 9% bonds. (4 marks)

(b) Calculate and comment on the effect of the bond issue on the weighted average cost of capital of YGV Co, clearly stating any assumptions that you make. (5 marks)

(c) Calculate the effect of using the bond issue to finance the reduction in the overdraft on:

   (i) the interest coverage ratio;

   (ii) gearing. (4 marks)

(d) Evaluate the proposal to use the bond issue to finance the reduction in the overdraft and discuss alternative sources of finance that could be considered by YGV Co, given its current financial position. (12 marks)

(Total: 25 marks)

51 GM CO

GM Co is a listed company that plans to expand its business. One project, which will be funded via floating rate finance, will see GM Co venturing into a new, much riskier area of the market. The other project, funded via equity finance, will expand their current operations. Overall, there is expected to be little change in the company's market weighted capital gearing. Financial data for the company before the expansion are shown below:

Financial extracts for the year ending 31 March 20X8

	$ million	$ million
Ordinary shares, par value $0.50	225	
Retained earnings	801	
Total equity		1,026
14% loan notes	75	
9% bank loan	250	
Total non-current liabilities		325

The 14% loan notes are redeemable at par in five years' time. They have a current ex-interest market price of $110 per $100 loan note. GM Co pays tax on profits at an annual rate of 30%. The market price of the company's ordinary shares is currently $3.76.

GM Co's equity beta is estimated to be 1.2. The systematic risk of debt may be assumed to be zero. The risk free rate is 7% and the market return 13.5%.

The estimated equity beta of the main competitor in the same industry as the new venture is 1.8, and the competitor's capital gearing is 60% equity, 40% debt by market values.

Required:

(a) Calculate the current weighted average cost of capital of GM Co (10 marks)

(b) Estimate the risk adjusted cost of equity that GM Co should use when calculating the discount rate for its proposed investment in the new venture. State any assumptions that you make. (9 marks)

(c) Outline the main advantages and disadvantages of the CAPM when being used to calculate the required return on equity. (6 marks)

(Total 25 marks)

52   IRQ CO

IRQ Co has recently taken out a new variable rate bank loan to fund an expansion programme into the Middle East. The capital structure of the company is now as follows:

$400m par value of 50c shares trading at $2.30 – IRQ Co has an equity beta of 1.1.

$600m par value of 6% irredeemable loan notes trading at $107.

$100m variable rate bank loan – the current interest charge is 5%.

The directors of IRQ Co are keen to know what the weighted average cost of capital has now become in order to evaluate projects the company is considering.

Interest rates have risen in recent times and the company is paying more interest on the variable rate bank loan than was originally expected. The directors of IRQ Co are keen to understand how interest rates are determined and how they could hedge the interest rate risk on any future borrowings.

The expansion into the Middle East is progressing well and further expansion in the future is likely. During their trips to the Middle East a number of key clients and contacts have suggested that IRQ Co should consider the use of Islamic Finance for any future expansion.

The risk free rate is 4% and the market premium is 7%. Corporation tax is 28%.

Required:

(a) Calculate the WACC of IRQ Co. (8 marks)

(b) Explain the theoretical factors which determine the term structure of interest rates and hence the interest rates faced by a company such as IRQ Co. (5 marks)

(c) Explain briefly the over-the-counter and exchange traded methods that IRQ Co could use to hedge against future interest rate risk. Provide illustrative calculations of how a forward rate agreement could be used to protect the cost of future borrowings. (8 marks)

(d) Explain the key principles of Islamic Finance and describe how any future variable rate bank loan could be structured under the principles of Islamic Finance. (4 marks)

(Total: 25 marks)

53   DD CO (DEC 09)

DD Co has a dividend payout ratio of 40% and has maintained this payout ratio for several years. The current dividend per share of the company is 50c per share and it expects that its next dividend per share, payable in one year's time, will be 52c per share.

The capital structure of the company is as follows:

	$m	$m
Equity		
Ordinary shares (par value $1 per share)	25	
Reserves	35	
	───	
		60
Debt		
Bond A (par value $100)	20	
Bond B (par value $100)	10	
	───	
		30
		───
		90
		───

Bond A will be redeemed at par in ten years' time and pays annual interest of 9%. The current ex interest market price of the bond is $95.08.

Bond B will be redeemed at par in four years' time and pays annual interest of 8%. The cost of debt of this bond is 7.82% per year. The current ex interest market price of the bond is $102.01.

Bond A and Bond B were issued at the same time.

DD Co has an equity beta of 1.2. The risk-free rate of return is 4% per year and the average return on the market of 11% per year. Ignore taxation.

Required:

(a)   **Calculate the cost of debt of Bond A.**   **(3 marks)**

(b)   **Discuss the reasons why different bonds of the same company might have different costs of debt.**   **(6 marks)**

(c)   **Calculate the following values for DD Co:**

(i)   **cost of equity, using the capital asset pricing model;**   **(2 marks)**

(ii)   **ex dividend share price, using the dividend growth model;**   **(3 marks)**

(iii) **capital gearing (debt divided by debt plus equity) using market values; and**
                                                                           (2 marks)

(iv)   **market value weighted average cost of capital.**   **(2 marks)**

(d)   **Discuss whether a change in dividend policy will affect the share price of DD Co.**
                                                                           (7 marks)

                                                                     (Total: 25 marks)

BUSINESS VALUATIONS

54   QSX CO (JUNE 10)

A shareholder of QSX Co is concerned about the recent performance of the company and has collected the following financial information.

Year to 31 May	2009	2008	2007
Turnover	$6.8m	$6.8m	$6.6m
Earnings per share	58.9c	64.2c	61.7c
Dividend per share	40.0c	38.5c	37.0c
Closing ex dividend share price	$6.48	$8.35	$7.40
Return on equity predicted by CAPM	8%	12%	

One of the items discussed at a recent board meeting of QSX Co was the dividend payment for 2010. The finance director proposed that, in order to conserve cash within the company, no dividend would be paid in 2010, 2011 and 2012. It was expected that improved economic conditions at the end of this three-year period would make it possible to pay a dividend of 70c per share in 2013. The finance director expects that an annual dividend increase of 3% per year in subsequent years could be maintained.

The current cost of equity of QSX Co is 10% per year. Assume that dividends are paid at the end of each year.

Required:

(a)   **Calculate the dividend yield, capital gain and total shareholder return for 2008 and 2009, and briefly discuss your findings with respect to:**

   (i)   **the returns predicted by the capital asset pricing model (CAPM);**

   (ii)   **the other financial information provided.**   **(10 marks)**

(b)   **Calculate and comment on the share price of QSX Co using the dividend growth model in the following circumstances:**

   (i)   **based on the historical information provided;**

   (ii)   **if the proposed change in dividend policy is implemented.**   **(7 marks)**

(c)   **Discuss the relationship between investment decisions, dividend decisions and financing decisions in the context of financial management, illustrating your discussion with examples where appropriate.**   **(8 marks)**

(Total: 25 marks)

55   OCT

The directors of OCT Co, a listed hotel chain, are currently considering the possibility of a one for five rights issue, the net proceeds of which will be used to finance an expansion of the chain at an estimated cost of $12 million.

Issue costs for the rights issue will be 4% of the gross proceeds.

OCT currently has 25 million $1 ordinary shares in issue. In recent years it has maintained a dividend payout ratio of 50% and has paid dividends as follows:

Year	2007	2008	2009	2010
Dividend per share (cents)	17.77	18.52	19.30	20.00

If successful, the directors expect earnings per share to increase by 5 cents in the next year over and above the 2010 level. The dividend payout ratio and future dividend growth rates (after 2011) are expected to be consistent with historic patterns.

OCT Co has a cost of equity of 11%. The price/earnings ratio of OCT Co has remained fairly constant in recent years.

Required:

(a) Calculate the current ex-dividend share price of OCT Co using the dividend growth model. **(4 marks)**

(b) Calculate the ex-rights issue price per share that would provide sufficient net proceeds to allow the expansion to proceed. **(4 marks)**

(c) Assuming the rights issue takes place at the price you calculated in part (b) and ignoring the proposed use of the funds, calculate:

    (i)   the theoretical rights price per share; and

    (ii)   the market capitalisation of OCT Co at this point. **(4 marks)**

(d) Describe the efficient market hypothesis and distinguish between its three forms. Illustrate your answer by calculating the expected share price following the proposed business expansion using the price/earnings ratio method and comment on the implications of the hypothesis for the directors of OCT Co. **(13 marks)**

(Total: 25 marks)

56 HENDIL (PART II)

Hendil Inc, a manufacturer of electronic equipment, has prepared the following draft financial statements for the year that has just ended. These financial statements have not yet been made public.

Income statement

	$000
Sales revenue	9,600
Cost of sales	5,568
Gross profit	4,032
Operating expenses	3,408
Profit before interest and tax	624
Interest	156
Profit before tax	468
Taxation	140
Profit after tax	328
Dividends	300
Net change in equity (retained profits)	28

Statement of financial position

	$000	$000
Non-current assets		2,250
Current assets		
Inventories	1,660	
Receivables	2,110	
Cash	780	
	——	4,550
Total assets		6,800
Equity and liabilities		
Ordinary shares, par value 50¢		1,000
Retained profits		3,100
		——
Total equity		4,100
10% loan stock, repayable 2015		1,200
Current liabilities		
Trade payables	750	
Dividends	300	
Overdraft	450	
	——	1,500
		——
Total equity plus liabilities		6,800

Hendil Inc pays interest on its overdraft at an annual rate of 6%. The 10% loan stock is secured on the non-current assets of the company.

Average data on companies similar to Hendil Inc:

Interest cover	6 times
Long-term debt/ equity (book value basis)	50%
Long-term debt/ equity (market value basis)	25%

The ordinary shareholders of Hendil Inc require an annual return of 12%. Its ordinary shares are currently trading on the stock market at $1.80 per share. The dividend paid by the company has increased at a constant rate of 5% per year in recent years and, in the absence of further investment, the directors expect this dividend growth rate to continue for the foreseeable future.

Required:

(a) (i)   Calculate the ordinary share price of Hendil Inc, predicted by the dividend growth model. **(4 marks)**

(ii) Explain the concept of market efficiency and distinguish between strong form efficiency and semi-strong form efficiency. **(6 marks)**

(iii) Discuss why the share price predicted by the dividend growth model is different from the current market price. **(4 marks)**

(b) Hendil Inc plans to invest $1 million in a new product range and it has been suggested that the proposed investment could be financed by a new issue of loan stock with an interest rate of 8%, redeemable after 15 years and secured on existing assets of Hendil Inc. The existing loan stock of the company is trading at $113 per $100 nominal value. The directors of Hendil have estimated that the NPV of the proposed investment is +$832,000.

Required:

Evaluate and discuss the suggestion to finance the proposed investment with the new loan stock issue described above. Your answer should consider, but not be limited to, the effect of the new issue on:

(i) **interest cover;**

(ii) **gearing;**

(iii) **ordinary share price.** (11 marks)

(Total: 25 marks)

57 NN CO (DEC 10)

The following financial information refers to NN Co:

Current statement of financial position

	$m	$m	$m
Assets			
Non-current assets			101
Current assets			
Inventory		11	
Trade receivables		21	
Cash		10	
		——	42
Total assets			143
Equity and liabilities			
Ordinary share capital		50	
Preference share capital		25	
Retained earnings		19	
		——	
Total equity			94
Non-current liabilities			
Long-term borrowings		20	
Current liabilities			
Trade payables	22		
Other payables	7		
	——		
Total current liabilities		29	
		——	
Total liabilities			49
Total equity and liabilities			143

NN Co has just paid a dividend of 66 cents per share and has a cost of equity of 12%. The dividends of the company have grown in recent years by an average rate of 3% per year. The ordinary shares of the company have a par value of 50 cents per share and an ex div market value of $8.30 per share.

The long-term borrowings of NN Co consist of 7% bonds that are redeemable in six years' time at their par value of $100 per bond. The current ex interest market price of the bonds is $103.50.

The preference shares of NN Co have a nominal value of 50 cents per share and pay an annual dividend of 8%. The ex div market value of the preference shares is 67 cents per share.

NN Co pay profit tax at an annual rate of 25% per year.

Required:

(a)   Calculate the equity value of NN Co using the following business valuation methods:

(i)   the dividend growth model;

(ii)   net asset value.   **(5 marks)**

(b)   **Calculate the after-tax cost of debt of NN Co.**   **(4 marks)**

(c)   **Calculate the weighted average after-tax cost of capital of NN Co.**   **(6 marks)**

(d)   **Discuss the factors to be considered in formulating the dividend policy of a stock-exchange listed company.**   **(10 marks)**

                                                                                        (Total: 25 marks)

58   MAT CO

MAT Co operates a chain of stores selling furniture. It has a successful business model and is seeking to raise additional finance in order to grow further. MAT Co is currently listed on AIM (a secondary market) but the shares in the company are only traded infrequently. The following information refers to MAT Co:

Most recent statement of financial position

	$m	$m
Assets		
Non-current assets		71
Current assets		
Inventory	8	
Trade receivables	11	
Cash	15	
		34
Total assets		105
Equity and liabilities		
Ordinary share capital		40
Retained earnings	27	
Total equity		67
Non-current liabilities		
Long-term borrowings		18
Current liabilities		
Trade payables	20	
Total liabilities		38
Total equity and liabilities		105

MAT Co has paid the following dividends in recent years:

2008 – 4.1 cents

2009 – 4.3 cents

2010 – 4.7 cents

Since the most recent statement of financial position the company has declared a dividend of 5.0 cents and this will be paid shortly. The ordinary shares of the company have a par value of 25 cents and a market value of 66 cents per share. The equity beta of the company is estimated to be 1.15.

Prior to considering potential sources of finance the directors of MAT Co are keen to gain a better understanding of the value of the company. The directors are aware that the company has property with a current market value of $65m but a book value of only $52m. Additionally following a review of inventories the directors consider that a $2m write down is required.

The return on government bonds is currently 5% and the equity risk premium is 8%.

Required:

(a)   Calculate the total equity value of MAT Co using the following business valuation methods:

   (i)   the dividend growth model;

   (ii)   net asset value.   (9 marks)

(b)   Comment on the relevance of the total equity values calculated when compared to the total market value of the equity of the company.   (7 marks)

(c)   Explain the factors the directors of MAT Co should take into account when considering how to raise additional finance.   (9 marks)

(Total: 25 marks)

59   THP CO (JUNE 08) *Walk in the footsteps of a top tutor*

THP Co is planning to buy CRX Co, a company in the same business sector, and is considering paying cash for the shares of the company. The cash would be raised by THP Co through a 1 for 3 rights issue at a 20% discount to its current share price.

The purchase price of the 1 million issued shares of CRX Co would be equal to the rights issue funds raised, less issue costs of $320,000. Earnings per share of CRX Co at the time of acquisition would be 44.8c per share. As a result of acquiring CRX Co, THP Co expects to gain annual after-tax savings of $96,000.

THP Co maintains a payout ratio of 50% and earnings per share are currently 64c per share. Dividend growth of 5% per year is expected for the foreseeable future and the company has a cost of equity of 12% per year.

Information from THP Co's statement of financial position:

Equity and liabilities	$000
Shares ($1 par value)	3,000
Reserves	4,300
	7,300
Non-current liabilities	
8% loan notes	5,000
Current liabilities	2,200
Total equity and liabilities	14,500

Required:

(a)   Calculate the current ex dividend share price of THP Co and the current market capitalisation of THP Co using the dividend growth model.   (4 marks)

(b)   Assuming the rights issue takes place and ignoring the proposed use of the funds raised, calculate:

   (i)   the rights issue price per share;

(ii)   the cash raised;

(iii) the theoretical ex rights price per share; and

(iv)   the market capitalisation of THP Co.   **(5 marks)**

(c)   Using the price/earnings ratio method, calculate the share price and market capitalisation of CRX Co before the acquisition.   **(3 marks)**

(d)   Assuming a semi-strong form efficient capital market, calculate and comment on the post acquisition market capitalisation of THP Co in the following circumstances:

(i)   THP Co does not announce the expected annual after-tax savings; and

(ii)   the expected after-tax savings are made public.   **(5 marks)**

(e)   Discuss the factors that THP Co should consider, in its circumstances, in choosing between equity finance and debt finance as a source of finance from which to make a cash offer for CRX Co.   **(8 marks)**

                                                              (Total: 25 marks)

60   PHOBIS (DEC 07)

(a)   Phobis Co is considering a bid for Danoca Co. Both companies are stock-market listed and are in the same business sector. Financial information on Danoca Co, which is shortly to pay its annual dividend, is as follows:

Number of ordinary shares	5 million
Ordinary share price (ex div basis)	$3.30
Earnings per share	40.0c
Proposed payout ratio	60%
Dividend per share one year ago	23.3c
Dividend per share two years ago	22.0c
Equity beta	1.4

Other relevant financial information	
Average sector price/earnings ratio	10
Risk-free rate of return	4.6%
Return on the market	10.6%

Required:

Calculate the value of Danoca Co using the following methods:

(i)   **price/earnings ratio method;**

(ii)   **dividend growth model;**

and discuss the significance, to Phobis Co, of the values you have calculated, in comparison to the current market value of Danoca Co.   **(11 marks)**

(b)   Phobis Co has in issue 9% bonds which are redeemable at their par value of $100 in five years' time. Alternatively, each bond may be converted on that date into 20 ordinary shares of the company. The current ordinary share price of Phobis Co is $4.45 and this is expected to grow at a rate of 6.5% per year for the foreseeable future. Phobis Co has a cost of debt of 7% per year.

Required:

Calculate the following current values for each $100 convertible bond:

(i)   market value;

(ii)   floor value;

(iii)   conversion premium.   **(6 marks)**

(c)   Distinguish between weak form, semi-strong form and strong form stock market efficiency, and discuss the significance to a listed company if the stock market on which its shares are traded is shown to be semi-strong form efficient.   **(8 marks)**

(Total: 25 marks)

 Online question assistance

RISK MANAGEMENT

61   NG CO (DEC 09)

NG Co has exported products to Europe for several years and has an established market presence there. It now plans to increase its market share through investing in a storage, packing and distribution network. The investment will cost €13 million and is to be financed by equal amounts of equity and debt. The return in Euros before interest and taxation on the total amount invested is forecast to be 20% per year.

The debt finance will be provided by a €6.5 million bond issue on a large European stock market. The interest rate on the bond issue is 8% per year, with interest being payable in Euros on a six-monthly basis.

The equity finance will be raised in dollars by a rights issue in the home country of NG Co. Issue costs for the rights issue will be $312,000. The rights issue price will be at a 17% discount to the current share price. The current share price of NG Co is $4.00 per share and the market capitalisation of the company is $100 million.

NG Co pays taxation in its home country at a rate of 30% per year. The currency of its home country is the dollar. The current price/earnings ratio of the company, which is not expected to change as a result of the proposed investment, is 10 times.

The spot exchange rate is 1.3000 €/$. All European customers pay on a credit basis in Euros.

Required:

(a)   Calculate the theoretical ex rights price per share after the rights issue.   **(4 marks)**

(b)   Evaluate the effect of the European investment on:

(i)   the earnings per share of NG Co; and

(ii)   the wealth of the shareholders of NG Co.

Assume that the current spot rate and earnings from existing operations are both constant.   **(9 marks)**

(c) Explain the difference between transaction risk and translation risk, illustrating your answer using the information provided. **(4 marks)**

(d) The six-month forward rate is 1.2876 €/$ and the twelve-month forward rate is 1.2752 €/$. NG Co can earn 2.8% per year on short-term euro deposits and can borrow short-term in dollars at 5.3% per year.

Identify and briefly discuss exchange rate hedging methods that could be used by NG Co. Provide calculations that illustrate TWO of the hedging methods that you have identified. **(8 marks)**

(Total: 25 marks)

62   NEDWEN

Nedwen Co is a UK-based company which has the following expected transactions..

One month: Expected receipt of $240,000

One month: Expected payment of $140,000

Three months: Expected receipts of $300,000

The finance manager has collected the following information:

Spot rate ($ per £):   1.7820 ± 0.0002

One month forward rate ($ per £):   1.7829 ± 0.0003

Three months forward rate ($ per £): 1.7846 ± 0.0004

Money market rates for Nedwen Co:

	Borrowing	Deposit
One year sterling interest rate:	4.9%	4.6
One year dollar interest rate:	5.4%	5.1

Assume that it is now 1 April.

Required:

(a) Discuss the differences between transaction risk, translation risk and economic risk. **(6 marks)**

(b) Explain how inflation rates can be used to forecast exchange rates. **(6 marks)**

(c) Calculate the expected sterling receipts in one month and in three months using the forward market. **(3 marks)**

(d) Calculate the expected sterling receipts in three months using a money-market hedge and recommend whether a forward market hedge or a money market hedge should be used. **(5 marks)**

(e) Discuss how sterling currency futures contracts could be used to hedge the three-month dollar receipt. **(5 marks)**

(Total: 25 marks)

63   LAGRAG CO

The following data was published in the financial press on 1 January 20X7:

Redemption Yield (%)	As at 1/1/X7	As at 1/1/X6
Treasury 20X8	5.21	5.17
Treasury 20Y0-Y2	5.58	5.49
Exchequer 20Y6	6.46	6.33

Lagrag Co is a heavily indebted company which is keen to protect the interest payments on $10 million of borrowings which will be required in 3 months for a period of 4 months. The company has discovered that the following forward rate agreements are currently available to it:

3 v 4   7.45 – 7.34

3 v 7   7.53 – 7.43

4 v 7   7.58 – 7.45

Additionally Lagrag Co is keen to protect itself against interest rate movements on some of its other debt. However, the Finance Director cannot distinguish between futures and options on futures, and hence is unsure what to use.

Required:

(a)   **Explain what the redemption yield data indicate about interest rates and discuss possible reasons for the yields shown.**   **(8 marks)**

(b)   **Identify the appropriate forward rate agreement and show what the cash flows arising will be if the interest rate payable by Lagrag Co in 3 months is:**

   7.76%

   7.42%   **(6 marks)**

(c)   **Explain the difference between futures and options on futures and recommend which the Finance Director should choose.**   **(7 marks)**

(d)   **Explain the two major risks that are likely to arise if Lagrag Co sells to an overseas customer. For each risk identified explain a method by which the risk could be reduced.**   **(4 marks)**

(Total 25 marks)

64   BOLUJE CO (DEC 08)

Three years ago Boluje Co built a factory in its home country costing $3.2 million. To finance the construction of the factory, Boluje Co issued peso-denominated bonds in a foreign country whose currency is the peso. Interest rates at the time in the foreign country were historically low. The foreign bond issue raised 16 million pesos and the exchange rate at the time was 5.00 pesos/$.

Each foreign bond has a par value of 500 pesos and pays interest in pesos at the end of each year of 6.1%. The bonds will be redeemed in five years' time at par. The current cost of debt of peso-denominated bonds of similar risk is 7%.

In addition to domestic sales, Boluje Co exports goods to the foreign country and receives payment for export sales in pesos. Approximately 40% of production is exported to the foreign country.

The spot exchange rate is 6.00 pesos/$ and the 12-month forward exchange rate is 6.07 pesos/$. Boluje Co can borrow money on a short-term basis at 4% per year in its home currency and it can deposit money at 5% per year in the foreign country where the foreign bonds were issued. Taxation may be ignored in all calculation parts of this question.

Required:

(a) Briefly explain the reasons why a company may choose to finance a new investment by an issue of debt finance. **(7 marks)**

(b) Calculate the current total market value (in pesos) of the foreign bonds used to finance the building of the new factory. **(4 marks)**

(c) Assume that Boluje Co has no surplus cash at the present time:

(i) Explain and illustrate how a money market hedge could protect Boluje Co against exchange rate risk in relation to the dollar cost of the interest payment to be made in one year's time on its foreign bonds. **(4 marks)**

(ii) Compare the relative costs of a money market hedge and a forward market hedge. **(2 marks)**

(d) Describe other methods, including derivatives, that Boluje Co could use to hedge against exchange rate risk. **(8 marks)**

(Total: 25 marks)

 Online question assistance

65 **EXPORTERS PLC** *Walk in the footsteps of a top tutor*

(a) You are required to define a forward exchange contract and to explain the differences between fixed forward exchange contracts and option forward exchange contracts. **(2 marks)**

(b) Exporters plc, a UK company, is due to receive 500,000 Northland dollars in 6 months' time for goods supplied. The company decides to hedge its currency exposure by using the forward market. The short-term interest rate in the UK is 12% per annum and the equivalent rate in Northland is 15%. The spot rate of exchange is 2.5 Northland dollars to the pound.

Required:

(i) Calculate how much Exporters plc actually gains or losses as a result of the hedging transaction if, at the end of the six months, the pound, in relation to the Northland dollar, has:

(1) gained 4%,

(2) lost 2% or

(3) remained stable.

You may assume that the forward rate of exchange simply reflects the interest differential in the two countries (i.e. it reflects the Interest Rate Parity analysis of forward rates); **(7 marks)**

(ii)   **Explain the rationale behind the interest rate parity analysis of forward rates.**

(4 marks)

(iii)   **Compare a forward market currency hedge with:**

    (1)   a currency futures hedge,

    (2)   a currency options hedge.

    Indicate in each of the three cases how the hedging facility is actually provided, the nature of the costs and the potential outcomes of the hedge.

(12 marks)

(Total: 25 marks)

66   ELECT CO

Elect Co is a stock-market listed manufacturing company that is seeking additional finance of $5m to undertake a new project. The finance director of Elect Co is currently considering whether to raise the capital via debt or equity finance.

The capital structure of the company (before the new finance has been raised) is as follows:

	$m	$m
Equity		
Ordinary shares (par value 50c per share)	10	
Reserves	30	
	——	40
Debt		
Bond A (par value $100)	10	
Bank loan	5	
	——	15
		——
		55
		——

The ordinary shares are currently trading at $1.70 each. The company's cost of equity has been estimated at 15%.

Bond A will be redeemed at par in six years' time and pays a fixed annual interest of 8%. The pre-tax cost of this finance has been estimated at 10%.

The bank loan is repayable in two years' time. It is a floating rate loan at LIBOR + 1%. LIBOR is currently at 3%.

Some initial enquiries made by the finance director have indicated that further fixed rate debt finance could be raised at an annual post-tax cost of 7%. Floating rate debt finance could be obtained for LIBOR + 2%. Market experts are divided over the expectations of future interest rates with some expecting rates to remain steady for the foreseeable future and others predicting an increasing of up to 4%.

Elect Co pays corporation tax at a rate of 30%.

Required:

(a) Calculate the current market value of Bond A (2 marks)

(b) Calculate the current weighted average cost of capital of Elect Co (6 marks)

(c) Evaluate the impact on the weighted average cost of capital of raising the new finance via:

    (i) Equity

    (ii) Fixed rate debt

    State any assumptions that you make. (4 marks)

(d) Discuss the factors which should be considered when deciding between debt and equity finance. (7 marks)

(e) Discuss the factors affecting the choice between fixed and floating rate debt and describe two methods of hedging interest rate risk that may be appropriate for Elect Co. (6 marks)

(Total: 25 marks)

Section 2

ANSWERS TO PRACTICE QUESTIONS

FINANCIAL MANAGEMENT FUNCTION AND ENVIRONMENT

1   UUL CO

Key answer tips

This ratio combines a very examinable area (financial ratios) with the less frequently examined topic of stakeholder objectives and regulation.

Both parts (a) and (b) require some calculations to be performed. Critically though, you must also comment on these calculations.

To answer parts (c) and (d) you will need to think practically and considering the real world position of water companies should help you generate ideas.

The highlighted words are key phrases that markers are looking for.

(a)   Equivalent annual growth in dividends – $(7.1/4.2)^{0.25} - 1 = 14.0\%$

Equivalent annual growth in earnings – $(41.3/31.6)^{0.25} - 1 = 6.9\%$

Share price – 20X2 – 31.6c × 17 = $5.37

Share price – 20X6 – 41.3c × 22 = $9.09

Equivalent annual growth in share price – $(9.09/5.37)^{0.25} - 1 = 14.1\%$

The chairman states that the company has delivered above average performance. However, whilst dividend growth has exceeded the water industry average, the growth in earnings and the growth in share price is significantly behind the water industry average. Hence, it is hard to justify the statement made by the chairman.

Indeed, the shareholders should be concerned that given the growth in earnings, the current dividend growth rate does not seem sustainable.

On the positive side, given the inflation rate during this period, the company has delivered real growth in earnings, dividends and share price. Additionally, the P/E ratio has grown, which indicates the market is increasingly confident about the future of the company.

(b)   Total shareholder return = (7.1c + (909c – 912c))/912c = 0.45%

The total shareholder return is less than the inflation during this period and hence, in real terms, the shareholders have made an overall loss.

This conflicts with the statement by the chairman regarding performance. However, share prices are notoriously volatile and the decline in share price may have more to do with general market movements and may not necessarily accurately portray the performance of the company. To comment further it would be interesting to know the change in share price of similar competitors over the same period.

(c)   Three other key stakeholders in UUL Co are the local community in the area that the company operates, the customers of the company and the government.

The local community will be interested in the financial success of the company, as this will potentially generate jobs and wealth in their region. Equally, they will be keen to ensure that the company adheres to best practice in the treatment and disposal of sewage and that the risk of pollution is minimised.

Customers of the company will be keen that their cost for water is minimised. At the same time, they will be keen to make sure that they have a constant, reliable and safe water supply.

The government will be keen to extract tax receipts and will be keen to see the company succeed so that those tax receipts grow. The government will also want to make sure that all the operations of the company comply with the relevant environmental legislation and that all developments by the company, such as the development of a new reservoir, comply with planning laws.

Tutorial note:

Sensible references to other stakeholders would have also been acceptable.

(d)   The government will be keen to minimise the impact that the likely monopoly position of UUL Co will have on its customers. The monopoly position may itself be tolerated as the water industry is a natural monopoly where it would be hard to introduce competition and where the economies of scale necessary to justify the infrastructure investment make a monopoly acceptable. Hence, the government is very likely to control price increases and limit the return that the company is able to make in order to make sure that UUL Co does not take advantage of its monopoly position. Equally the government is likely to impose minimum service standards that UUL Co must provide to its customers, as the customers do not have a choice of provider.

The government will also intervene to make sure that UUL Co is carrying out its operations in a way that will not cause unnecessary environmental damage. For instance, Thames Water in the UK is having to invest considerable sums to make sure that the River Thames is no longer polluted by raw sewage during periods of heavy rain.

As a public company UUL Co will suffer all the costs associated with making sure that they have, and are seen to have, good corporate governance.

Additionally, UUL Co will suffer interference from government, as water is a strategic commodity and the government have an obligation to make sure that the country's anticipated needs are forecast and planned for.

2   CCC

Key answer tips

Part (a) is a tricky question on objective setting that requires a reasonable depth of knowledge of NFPs to score well. Part (b) is more straightforward but needs good application to the two companies concerned. The highlighted words are key phrases that markers are looking for.

(a)   The key criteria that need to be considered when objective setting are as follows:

Stakeholder expectations

All organisations need to identify key stakeholders, examine their expectations and try to set objectives to meet them.

For CCC stakeholders include:

- Local residents want to see the provision of quality health and education services and value for money in response to paying local taxes.

- Local businesses who will be interested in local infrastructure when deciding whether to invest in the area. In particular, CCC may be keen to ensure that DDD does not close its local offices, with resulting job losses, and move to the capital city.

- Central Government committees who make funding decisions based on local population and deprivation.

For DDD stakeholders include:

- Shareholders want to see their wealth increased through a mixture of growing dividends and an increasing share price. DDD has reflected this in the objective to increase shareholder wealth by 10% per annum.

- Customers will expect a certain level of quality and value for money, depending on the nature of products sold.

- The local communities affected by DDD will expect them to be good citizens and operate at high levels of corporate social responsibility.

Stakeholder power

All organisations will find conflicts between stakeholders so they need to consider how to prioritise them.

For a company like DDD the expectations of shareholders come first for the following reasons:

- This is usually reflected in companies' legislation where directors have a duty in law to put shareholder interests first. Many governance recommendations focus on protecting shareholder interests.

- Failure to deliver shareholder expectations will result in a falling share price and difficulties raising finance. Ultimately, shareholders have the power to remove directors should they feel dissatisfied.

However, this does not mean that other stakeholders' needs are ignored. Clearly if customers are unhappy then sales will be lost with a resulting fall in profitability and shareholder wealth.

For CCC the problem is more complex:

- It is much more difficult to prioritise stakeholder expectations. For example, given limited funds, should community health care needs come before educational ones?

- Even individual stakeholder groups have multiple conflicting objectives. For example, residents want to pay less tax and have better provision of services. Thus even if some groups are satisfied, other may still vote for changes in CCC.

- With companies, customers pay directly for the products they receive, ensuring that customer needs are addressed. With CCC the bulk of its funding comes from central government, not the local community who benefit from CCC's actions. Thus the needs of the funding body may take priority over locals needs, otherwise funding may be cut (note: this is less likely here as funding is mainly driven by population size).

Measurement issues

For an organisation like DDD, once shareholders have been prioritised, all decisions can be evaluated by reference to financial measures such as profitability. While non-financial targets will be incorporated as well, the 'bottom line' will be seen as key. Thus financial targets can be set for most objectives.

For CCC it is much more difficult to measure whether it is achieving its stated aims and hence to set targets.

- For example, how do you assess whether somewhere is an 'attractive place to live and work' or whether health and education provision is 'excellent'?

Other issues

All organisations need to ensure that objectives set relate to controllable factors to ensure staff is motivated to meet them.

All organisations need to differentiate between cause and effect and have objectives for both. For example, DDD may have an objective of customer satisfaction, which will need to be translated into objectives for quality, cost, etc.

(b) As described above, companies make decisions with the primary objective of maximising shareholder wealth.

Investment decisions

Potential investments should thus be assessed using NPV or SVA, rather than ROCE to ensure that shareholder wealth is increased.

This should be the case for both MS and DDD, though the former will have more difficulty determining a suitable discount rate, being unquoted.

Dividend decisions

Once shareholder value has been created, the firm needs to decide how to return those gains to shareholders – either as dividends or reinvested to enhance the share price further.

Modigliani and Miller argued that, given certain assumptions, dividend policy was irrelevant to shareholder wealth. If a dividend was cut, for example, shareholders could manufacture dividends by selling shares without any overall loss of wealth. Central to their theory was the idea that shareholders had perfect information and would understand why a dividend policy was changed.

In the case of MS, shareholders are also employees so will have full information regarding any change in dividend policy and will not thus perceive any information content in the dividends themselves. However, should the dividend be cut, shareholders who require income will not be able to sell shares to generate cash as the company is unquoted. MS should thus try to continue the stable dividend policy it has adopted to date, even though historical dividend cover is lower than the 'rule of thumb' of two.

In the case of DDD, major institutional shareholders will have good information from the company but may have tax preferences regarding income and capital gains so DDD should adopt a consistent dividend policy to meet their requirements. DDD will probably have attracted a certain clientele of shareholder based on previous policies.

Financing decisions

Both firms need to raise finance in order to undertake new investments to increase shareholder wealth. The issue here is whether the finance used ultimately affects shareholder wealth as well.

From a theoretical point of view, Modigliani and Miller argued that in the absence of taxation, and certain other assumptions, the choice between debt or equity finance was irrelevant. With corporation tax they concluded that debt finance was preferable, due to the benefits of the tax shield. With personal taxes the conclusions depend on the specific circumstances of the company and its shareholders. Incorporating real world factors, many analysts argue that there is an optimal gearing level for each company.

DDD is already at the typical gearing ratio for its industry so it would reasonable to assume that this is their optimal gearing level. Future financing should involve a mixture of debt and equity to maintain this ratio.

MS is all-equity financed at present so it should seek to raise at least some of the $15 million required using debt finance to take advantage of the tax relief and low costs involved.

Interrelationships

All three types of decisions are inter-related, thus the financing decision will affect the cost of capital, and as a consequence, the net benefits obtainable from a particular project, thereby influencing the investment decision, while the financing decision concerning gearing will affect both the other decisions.

The dividend decision, in determining the level of retentions, will affect the cash available for investment, and the extent to which external sources of funds need to be sought in financing to optimise operations.

3   NEIGHBOURING COUNTRIES

Key answer tips

A careful read of the specifics of all parts of the question was needed to ensure you answered the requirement in full and didn't end up discussing areas that wouldn't earn marks. The highlighted words are key phrases that markers are looking for.

(a)   The objectives of the nationalised industry in Country A are likely to be influenced by the government, rather than by financial matters. The major objectives are likely to be the provision of a service to the public, and the provision of electricity for the economic development of the country. This may mean providing electricity at considerable cost to outlying areas, or to areas which the government wishes to develop. The financial objectives will be secondary, and will probably attempt to achieve a target rate of return, although the government may be prepared to accept a negative return in order to achieve its political objectives.

The primary objectives of the private sector companies in Country B will probably be the maximisation of shareholder wealth. The companies' managements will decide the objectives, which may be merely 'satisficing', with other non-financial objectives such as good working conditions for employees, market share and provision of a good service to customers. An important industry such as the provision of electricity will, however, be subject to strong government influences and constraints.

Investment planning and appraisal techniques will differ largely as a result of the differing objectives.

In the nationalised industry, strategic investment planning will be instigated by the government, with the tactical decisions left to the management of the industry. The amount of capital investment involved will be determined by the government, which is responsible for the supply of funds.

Appraisal techniques will be designed to ensure that the government targets are met, e.g. ROCE and budgetary control.

In the private sector, investment will be influenced by market forces, with managements attempting to maximise shareholder wealth, or at least satisfy their shareholders while meeting other objectives. Managements will be responsible for both strategic and tactical decisions.

Appraisal techniques will be introduced to ensure that the objectives are met, and will almost certainly include DCF and budgetary control. Failure to meet the objectives may have serious consequences on the share price, with the risk of take-over and possible job losses.

In conclusion, it may be that both the nationalised industry and the privately-controlled industry use the same evaluation techniques. It will be the objectives that are likely to be different, with the consequences of failure being more serious in the private sector.

(b)   (i)   Responding to various stakeholder groups

If a company has a single objective in terms of maximising profitability then it is only responding to one stakeholder group, namely shareholders. However, companies can no longer fail to respond to the interests and concerns of a wider range of groups, particularly with respect to those who may have a non-financial interest in the organisation. Stakeholder groups with a non-financial interest can therefore generate for companies non-financial objectives and place constraints on their operations to the extent that the company is prepared to respond to such groups.

Various stakeholder groupings can emerge. The following represents examples of likely groups, their non-financial objectives and/or the constraints they may place on a business:

Stakeholder	Objective	Constraints
Employees	Employee welfare	Maximum hours worked
Community	Responding to community concerns	Limits on activities
Customers	Product or service levels	Minimum quality standards
Suppliers	Good trading relationships	
Government	Protecting the consumer	Minimum standards on products or services
Trade bodies	Protecting professional reputation	Minimum standards on products or services

(ii) The difficulties associated with managing organisations with multiple objectives

To the extent that an organisation faces a range of stakeholders, then they also face multiple objectives. This would not particularly be a problem if the multiple objectives were congruent, but they normally are not. There are a number of difficulties:

- Multiple stakeholders imply multiple objectives. To the extent that they conflict then compromises must be made. This will lead potentially to opportunity costs in that maximisation of profitability will potentially be reduced.

- Responding to stakeholders other than shareholders involves costs, either in management time or in directly responding to their needs.

- Some objectives are not clearly defined, for example what is actually meant by 'protecting the consumer'? It will therefore not always be clear to the organisation that they have met the needs of all of their stakeholders.

- Some of the objectives may actually be conflicting where compromise is not possible. Prioritisation and ranking will then have to take place. Questions then arise as to who is the most important stakeholder or what ranking should be assigned?

- New stakeholder groups often emerge. This can create a problem of longer-term strategic management in that plans can be diverted if new pressures arise. For example, environmental issues were not so important 20 years ago.

- Management of the organisation becomes complex when multiple objectives have to be satisfied. Each managerial decision is likely to face many constraints.

(c) The role of financial intermediaries include:

1 **Risk diversification** – Allowing one investor to invest in many companies.

2 **Aggregation** – Allowing one company (borrower) to borrow from many investors.

3 **Maturity transformation** – By 'borrowing short and lending long' the intermediaries allow investors the opportunity to withdraw in the short term but give companies the funds for the long term.

4 **Hedging** – The intermediary may offer an opportunity for an organisation to reduce risk and uncertainty in relation to things such as interest rates and exchange rates.

5 **Making a market** – They provide a market for the funds.

6 **Advice** – A key role of intermediaries is to advise lenders and borrowers of their options.

4 RZP CO

Key answer tips

Part (a) required a large volume of albeit, relatively straightforward calculations. You must be careful not to spend too much time on the numbers at the expense of the commentary. Parts (b) and (c) were more straightforward. The highlighted words are key phrases that markers are looking for.

(a) **Analysis of data provided**

Year	20X4	20X3	20X2	20X1	20X0
Dividend per share	2.8¢	2.3¢	2.2¢	2.2¢	1.7¢
Annual dividend growth	21.7%	4.5%	Nil	29.4%	
Earnings per share	19.04¢	14.95¢	11.22¢	15.84¢	13.43¢
Annual earnings growth	27.3%	33.2%	−29.2%	17.9%	
Price/earnings ratio	22.0	33.5	25.5	17.2	15.2
Share price P/E×EPS	418.9¢	500.8¢	286.1¢	272.4¢	204.1¢
Annual share price growth	−16.3%	75.0%	5.0%	33.5%	
Dividend per share	2.8¢	2.3¢	2.2¢	2.2¢	1.7¢
General price index	117	113	110	105	100
Real dividend per share	2.4¢	2.0¢	2.0¢	2.1¢	1.7¢
Annual dividend growth	20.0%	Nil	−4.8%	23.5%	

Average dividend growth:

Arithmetic mean $= (21.7 + 4.5 + 0 + 29.4)/4 = 55.6/4 = 13.9\%$
Equivalent annual growth rate $= [(2.8/1.7)^{0.25} - 1] \times 100 = 13.3\%$

Average earnings per share growth:

Arithmetic mean $= (27.3 + 33.2 - 29.2 + 17.9)/4 = 49.2/4 = 12.3\%$
Equivalent annual growth rate $= [(19.04/13.43)^{0.25} - 1] \times 100 = 9.1\%$

Average share price growth:

Arithmetic mean	= (−16.3 + 75.0 + 5.0 + 33.5)/4 = 97.2/4 = 24.3%
Equivalent annual growth rate	= [(418.9/204.1)$^{0.25}$ − 1] × 100 = 19.7%

Average real dividend growth:

Arithmetic mean	= (20.0 + 0 − 4.8 + 23.5)/4 = 38.7/4 = 9.7%
Equivalent annual growth rate	= [(2.4/1.7)$^{0.25}$ − 1] × 100 = 9.0%

Discussion of analysis and views expressed by chairman

The chairman's statement claims that RZP Co has delivered growth in every year in dividends, earnings and ordinary share price, apart from 20X2. Analysis shows that the chairman is correct in excluding 20X2, when no growth occurred in dividends, earnings fell by 29.2%, and real dividends fell by 4.8%. Analysis also shows that no growth in real dividends occurred in 20X3 and that the company's share price fell by 16.3% in 20X4. It is possible the chairman may not have been referring to real dividend growth, in which case his statement could be amended. However, shareholders will be aware of the decline in share price in 20X4 or could calculate the decline from the information provided, so the chairman cannot claim that RZP Co has delivered share price growth in 20X4. In fact, the statement could explain the reasons for the decline in share price in order to reassure shareholders. It also possible for the five-year summary to be extended to include annual share price data, such as maximum, minimum and average share price, so that shareholders have this information readily available.

The chairman's statement claims that RZP Co has consistently delivered above-average performance. The company may have delivered above- or below-average performance in individual years but without further information in the form of sector averages for individual years, it is not possible to reach a conclusion on this point. The average growth rates for the sector cannot therefore be used to comment on the performance of RZP Co in individual years. If the company has consistently delivered above-average performance, however, the company's average annual growth rates should be greater than the sector averages.

The growth rates can be compared as follows:

	Arithmetic mean	*Equivalent annual rate*	*Sector*
Nominal dividends	13.9%	13.3%	10%
Real dividends	9.7%	9.0%	9%
Earnings per share	12.3%	9.1%	10%
Share price	24.3%	19.7%	20%

It can be seen that if the sector average growth rates are arithmetic mean growth rates, the chairman's statement is correct. If the sector average growth rates are equivalent annual growth rates, however, only the nominal dividend growth rate is greater than the sector average. The basis on which the sector average growth rates have been prepared should therefore be clarified in order to determine whether the chairman's statement is correct.

(b) The dividend yield and capital growth for 20X4 must be calculated with reference to the 20X3 end-of-year share price. The dividend yield is 0.56% (100 × 2.8/500.8) and the capital growth is −16.35% (100 × (418.9 − 500.8)/500.8), so the total shareholder return is −15.79% or −15.8% (0.56 − 16.35). A negative return of 15.8% looks even worse when it is noted that annual inflation for 20X4 was 3.5% (117/113).

While the negative total shareholder return is at odds with the chairman's claim to have delivered growth in dividends and share price in 20X4, a different view might have emerged if average share prices had been used, since the return calculation ignores share price volatility. The chairman should also be aware that share prices may be affected by other factors than corporate activity, so a good performance in share price terms may not be due to managerial excellence. It also possible that the negative return may represent a good performance when compared to the sector as a whole in 20X4: further information is needed to assess this.

Note that total shareholder return can also be found as (100 × (2.8 + 418.9 − 500.8)/500.8).

(c)   The objectives of managers may conflict with the objectives of shareholders, particularly with the objective of maximisation of shareholder wealth. Management remuneration package are one way in which goal congruence between managers and shareholders may be increased. Such packages should motivate managers while supporting the achievement of shareholder wealth maximisation. The following factors should be considered when deciding on a remuneration package intended to encourage directors to act in ways that maximise shareholder wealth.

Clarity and transparency

The terms of the remuneration package should be clear and transparent so that directors and shareholders are in no doubt as to when rewards have been earned or the basis on which rewards have been calculated.

Appropriate performance measure

The managerial performance measure selected for use in the remuneration package should support the achievement of shareholder wealth maximisation. It is therefore likely that the performance measure could be linked to share price changes.

Quantitative performance measure

The managerial performance measure should be quantitative and the manner in which it is to be calculated should be specified. The managerial performance measure should ideally be linked to a benchmark comparing the company's performance with that of its peers. The managerial performance measure should not be open to manipulation by management.

Time horizon

The remuneration package should have a time horizon that is linked to that of shareholders. If shareholders desire long-term capital growth, for example, the remuneration package should discourage decisions whose objective is to maximise short-term profits at the expense of long-term growth.

Impartiality

In recent years there has been an increased emphasis on decisions about managerial remuneration packages being removed from the control of managers who benefit from them. The use of remuneration committees in listed companies is an example of this. The impartial decisions of non-executive directors, it is believed, will eliminate or reduce managerial self-interest and encourage remuneration packages that support the achievement of shareholder rather than managerial goals.

Appropriate management remuneration packages for RZP Co

Remuneration packages may be based on a performance measure linked to values in the income statement. A bonus could be awarded, for example, based on growth in sales revenue, profit before tax, or earnings (earnings per share). Such performance measures could lead to maximisation of profit in the short-term rather than in the long-term, for example by deferring capital expenditure required to reduce environmental pollution, and may encourage managers to manipulate reported financial information in order to achieve bonus targets. They could also lead to sub-optimal managerial performance if managers do enough to earn their bonus, but then reduce their efforts once their target has been achieved.

RZP Co has achieved earnings growth of more than 20% in both 20X3 and 20X4, but this is likely to reflect in part a recovery from the negative earnings growth in 20X1, since over the five-year period its earnings growth is not very different from its sector's (it may be worse). If annual earnings growth were to be part of a remuneration package for RZP Co, earnings growth could perhaps be compared to the sector and any bonus made conditional upon ongoing performance in order to discourage a short-term focus.

Remuneration packages may be based on a performance measure linked to relative stock market performance, e.g. share price growth over the year compared to average share price growth for the company's sector, or compared to growth in a stock market index, such as the FTSE 100. This would have the advantage that managers would be encouraged to make decisions that had a positive effect on the company's share price and hence are likely to be consistent with shareholder wealth maximisation. However, as noted earlier, other factors than managerial decisions can have a continuing effect on share prices and so managers may fail to be rewarded for good performance due to general economic changes or market conditions.

RZP Co recorded negative share price growth in 20X4 and the reasons for this should be investigated. In the circumstances, a remuneration package linked to benchmarked share price growth could focus the attention of RZP managers on decisions likely to increase shareholder wealth. The effect of such a remuneration package could be enhanced if the reward received by managers were partly or wholly in the form of shares or share options. Apart from emphasising the focus on share price growth, such a reward scheme would encourage goal congruence between shareholders and managers by turning managers into shareholders.

5   JJG CO

Key answer tips

This question may cause problems for some students, especially regarding the level of depth to go into on part (a).

Part (a) requires an evaluation of the performance of JJG. The provision of information on industry averages gives some clear indications of the ratios which any analysis should focus on.

Part (b) is a relatively straightforward calculation of the impact of a rights issue.

Part (c) gives plenty of opportunity to gain easy marks although the final words "for the expansion" means comments must be specific to the scenario presented.

The highlighted words are key phrases that markers are looking for.

(a) **Financial Analysis**

	2008	2007	2006	2005
Turnover ($m)	28.0	24.0	19.1	16.8
Turnover growth	17%	26%	14%	
Geometric average growth: 18.6%				
Profit before interest and tax ($m)	9.8	8.5	7.5	6.8
PBIT growth	15%	13%	10%	
Geometric average growth: 13.0%				
Earnings ($m)	5.5	4.7	4.1	3.6
Earnings per share (cents)	100	85	75	66
EPS growth	18%	13%	14%	
Geometric average growth: 14.9%				
Dividends ($m)	2.2	1.9	1.6	1.6
Dividends per share (cents)	40	35	29	29
DPS growth	14%	21%	nil	
Geometric average growth: 11.3%				
Ordinary shares ($m)	5.5	5.5	5.5	5.5
Reserves ($m)	13.7	10.4	7.6	5.1
Shareholders' funds ($)	19.2	15.9	13.1	10.6
8% Bonds, redeemable 2015 ($m)	20	20	20	20
Capital employed ($m)	39.2	35.9	33.1	30.6
Profit before interest and tax ($m)	9.8	8.5	7.5	6.8
Return on capital employed	25%	24%	23%	22%
Earnings ($m)	5.5	4.7	4.1	3.6
Return on shareholders' funds	29%	30%	31%	34%
8% Bonds, redeemable 2015 ($m)	20	20	20	20
Market value of equity ($m)	47.5	31.6	18.4	14.7
Debt/equity ratio (market value)	42%	63%	109%	136%
Share price (cents)	864	574	335	267
Dividends per share (cents)	40	35	29	29
Total shareholder return	58%	82%	36%	

Achievement of corporate objectives

JJG Co has shareholder wealth maximisation as an objective. The wealth of shareholders is increased by dividends received and capital gains on shares owned. Total shareholder return compares the sum of the dividend received and the capital gain with the opening share price. The shareholders of JJG Co had a return of 58% in 2008, compared with a return predicted by the capital asset pricing model of 14%. The lowest return shareholders have received was 21% and the highest return was 82%. On this basis, the shareholders of the company have experienced a significant increase in wealth. It is debatable whether this has been as a result of the actions of the company, however. Share prices may increase irrespective of the actions and decisions of managers, or even despite them. In fact, looking at the dividend per share history of the company, there was one year (2006) where dividends were constant, even though earnings per share increased. It is also difficult to know when wealth has been maximised.

Another objective of the company was to achieve a continuous increase in earnings per share. Analysis shows that earnings per share increased every year, with an average increase of 14.9%. This objective appears to have been achieved.

Comment on financial performance

Return on capital employed (ROCE) has been growing towards the sector average of 25% on a year-by-year basis from 22% in 2005. This steady growth in the primary accounting ratio can be contrasted with irregular growth in turnover, the reasons for which are unknown.

Return on shareholders' funds has been consistently higher than the average for the sector. This may be due more to the capital structure of JJG Co than to good performance by the company, however, in the sense that shareholders' funds are smaller on a book value basis than the long-term debt capital. In every previous year but 2008 the gearing of the company was higher than the sector average.

(b) **Calculation of theoretical ex rights per share**

Current share price = $8.64 per share

Current number of shares = 5.5 million shares

Finance to be raised = $15m

Rights issue price = $7.50 per share

Number of shares issued = 15m/7.50 = 2 million shares

Theoretical ex rights price per share = ((5.5m × 8.64) + (2m × 7.50))/7.5m = $8.34 per share

The share price would fall from $8.64 to $8.34 per share However, there would be no effect on shareholder wealth

Effect of rights issue on earnings per share

Current EPS = 100 cents per share

Revised EPS = 100 × 5.5m/7.5m = 73 cents per share

The EPS would fall from 100 cents per share to 73 cents per share However, as mentioned earlier, there would be no effect on shareholder wealth

Effect of rights issue on the debt/equity ratio

Current debt/equity ratio = 100 × 20/47.5 = 42%

Revised market value of equity = 7.5m × 8.34 = $62.55 million

Revised debt/equity ratio = 100 × 20/62.55 = 32%

The debt/equity ratio would fall from 42% to 32%, which is well below the sector average value and would signal a reduction in financial risk

(c) The current debt/equity ratio of JJG Co is 42% (20/47.5). Although this is less than the sector average value of 50%, it is more useful from a financial risk perspective to look at the extent to which interest payments are covered by profits.

	2008	*2007*	*2006*	*2005*
Profit before interest and tax ($m)	9.8	8.5	7.5	6.8
Bond interest ($m)	1.6	1.6	1.6	1.6
Interest coverage ratio (times)	6.1	5.3	4.7	4.3

The interest on the bond issue is $1.6 million (8% of $20m), giving an interest coverage ratio of 6.1 times. If JJG Co has overdraft finance, the interest coverage ratio will be lower than this, but there is insufficient information to determine if an overdraft exists. The interest coverage ratio is not only below the sector average, it is also low enough to be a cause for concern. While the ratio shows an upward trend over the period under consideration, it still indicates that an issue of further debt would be unwise.

A placing, or any issue of new shares such as a rights issue or a public offer, would decrease gearing. If the expansion of business results in an increase in profit before interest and tax, the interest coverage ratio will increase and financial risk will fall. Given the current financial position of JJG Co, a decrease in financial risk is certainly preferable to an increase.

A placing will dilute ownership and control, providing the new equity issue is taken up by new institutional shareholders, while a rights issue will not dilute ownership and control, providing existing shareholders take up their rights. A bond issue does not have ownership and control implications, although restrictive or negative covenants in bond issue documents can limit the actions of a company and its managers.

All three financing choices are long-term sources of finance and so are appropriate for a long-term investment such as the proposed expansion of existing business.

Equity issues such as a placing and a rights issue do not require security. No information is provided on the non-current assets of JJG Co, but it is likely that the existing bond issue is secured. If a new bond issue was being considered, JJG Co would need to consider whether it had sufficient non-current assets to offer as security, although it is likely that new non-current assets would be bought as part of the business expansion.

ACCA marking scheme		
		Marks
(a)	Relevant financial analysis	6 – 7
	Shareholder wealth discussion	2 – 3
	Earnings per share discussion	2 – 3
	Comment on financial performance	1 – 2
		———
	Maximum	12
		———
(b)	Share price calculation and comment	2 – 3
	Earnings per share calculation and comment	2 – 3
	Debt / equity ratio calculation and comment	1 – 2
		———
	Maximum	6
		———
(c)	Financial analysis	1 – 2
	Discussion of rights issue and placing	2 – 3
	Discussion of bond issue	2 – 3
		———
	Maximum	7
		———
Total		25

Examiner's comments

This question provided historical information relating to a company and average values for its business sector.

In part (a), candidates were required to evaluate the financial performance of the company and to discuss the extent to which it had achieved its objectives of maximising shareholder wealth and continuous growth in earnings per share (EPS).

Many candidates had difficulty in calculating accounting ratios to compare with the sector averages provided. Accounting ratios have standard names and standard definitions and candidates should know these. Some candidates calculated profit after tax, even though the question gave annual earnings for each of four years. Some candidates averaged the four years of data provided, simply because the question provided average sector data. Some candidates calculated ratios for one year only and ignored the three other years.

Many candidates did not understand the significance of the inclusion in the question of an average sector value for the return predicted by the capital asset pricing model (CAPM). This value (14%) provided a way to assess whether the company had achieved its objective of maximising the wealth of shareholders. If the return that shareholders had received each year, in the form of capital gains and dividend, exceeded the return predicted by the CAPM, it could be argued that the objective had been achieved, since the company had outperformed the business sector as a whole. Since total shareholder return was 36%, 82% and 58%, this certainly seemed to be the case here. Some candidates argued that this objective had been achieved on the basis of inappropriate analysis, such as that the amount of reserves or the return on capital employed had increased each year.

It could be demonstrated that the objective of achieving continuous growth in EPS had been achieved by calculating the EPS figure for each year.

Part (b) asked candidates to calculate and comment on the effect of the rights issue on the company's share price, earnings per share (EPS) and debt/equity ratio. To do this, candidates had to calculate the number of shares issued by dividing the amount of cash to be raised ($15 million) by the rights issue price ($7.50 per share). Weaker answers were unable to do this and, instead, assumed a form for the rights issue (such as 1 for 2 or 1 for 4). Better answers calculated all three values and commented on the changes with respect to their historical values, noting that a rights issue has no effect on shareholder wealth and that a fall in the EPS does mean that shareholder wealth has decreased.

Part (c) asked for an analysis and discussion of the relative merits of a rights issue, a placing and an issue of bonds as ways of raising the $15 million of finance needed. Better answers started with analysis and used this as the basis for discussion. The effect of raising the $15 million of finance on gearing and interest cover, for example, had to be assessed before an informed answer could be offered.

Many answers had little or no analysis and compared the three financing methods in general terms, for example looking at ownership and control, increase or decrease in gearing and financial risk, issue costs, servicing costs and maturity.

6   DARTIG CO *Walk in the footsteps of a top tutor*

Key answer tips

This question has a few trickier elements that may unnerve some students.

Part (e) gives the easiest opportunity to grab marks. A straightforward explanation of the agency problem as well as how share options could be used to reduce the issue should allow most students to score highly. Being unrelated to the other parts, it should be tackled first.

The other four parts to the question all require some degree of calculations. Part (a) is also straightforward, and should result in full marks for most candidates.

Part (d) should be reasonable for most candidates. The highlighted words are key phrases that markers are looking for.

(a)   Rights issue price = 2.5 × 0.8 = $2.00 per share

Theoretical ex rights price = ((2.50 × 4) + (1 × 2.00)/5=$2.40 per share

(Alternatively, number of rights shares issued = $5m/$2.00 = 2.5m shares

Existing number of shares = 4 × 2.5m = 10m shares

Theoretical ex rights price per share = ((10m × 2.50) + (2.5m × 2.00))/12.5m = $2.40)

Tutor's top tips:

In parts (b) and (c), students may be thrown by the assertion that "the expansion of existing business will allow the average growth rate of earnings per share over the last four years to be maintained". A rights issue would normally result in a fall in EPS due to the higher number of shares in issue. In this case though, the new finance from the rights issue will be invested and will earn a sufficiently high return to avoid the usual reduction. Indeed, growth of 4% is being predicted.

Some background calculations may help to illustrate this further:

$$\frac{\$5m}{\$2.50 \times 80\%} = 2.5 \text{ million new shares to be issued.}$$

A 1 for 4 rights issue therefore implies the company must have 10 million shares in issue at present and will have 12.5 million after the rights issue.

Current EPS = 32.4 cents. Total earnings is therefore 0.324 × 10 million = $3.24 million

New total earnings will be 12.5 million × $0.324 × 1.04 = $4.21 million.

In the cold light of day it is not unreasonable to expect the finance raised to increase earnings by this amount (an annual return of just under 20%). However, such rational thought often escapes candidates within the pressure of the exam hall.

(b)   Current price/earnings ratio = 250/32.4 = 7.7 times

Average growth rate of earnings per share = $100 \times ((32.4/27.7)^{0.25} - 1) = 4.0\%$

Earnings per share following expansion = 32.4 × 1.04 = 33.7 cents per share

Share price predicted by price/earnings ratio method = 33.7 × 7.7 = $2.60

Since the price/earnings ratio of Dartig Co has remained constant in recent years and the expansion is of existing business, it seems reasonable to apply the existing price/earnings ratio to the revised earnings per share value.

(c)   The proposed business expansion will be an acceptable use of the rights issue funds if it increases the wealth of the shareholders. The share price predicted by the price/earnings ratio method is $2.60. This is greater than the current share price of $2.50, but this is not a valid comparison, since it ignores the effect of the rights issue on the share price. The rights issue has a neutral effect on shareholder wealth, but the cum rights price is changed by the increase in the number of shares and by the transformation of cash wealth into security wealth from a shareholder point of view. The correct comparison is with the theoretical ex rights price, which was found earlier to be $2.40. Dartig Co shareholders will experience a capital gain due to the business expansion of $2.60 – 2.40 = 20 cents per share. However, these share prices are one year apart and hence not directly comparable.

If the dividend yield remains at 6% per year (100 × 15.0/250), the dividend per share for 2008 will be 15.6 cents (other estimates of the 2008 dividend per share are possible). Adding this to the capital gain of 20 cents gives a total shareholder return of 35.6 cents or 14.24% (100 × 35.6/240). This is greater than the cost of equity of 10% and so shareholder wealth has increased.

Tutor's top tips:

The model answer for both parts (b) and (c) both illustrate an approach to the question set but it is doubtful that many students actually produced the results presented, especially regarding the total shareholder return. However, even if you have difficulties getting your head around the situation, it is still possible to gather many of the marks. Method marks are available for any students who demonstrate a logical approach and utilise the basic price/earnings ratio method.

(d)   In order to use the dividend growth model, the expected future dividend growth rate is needed. Here, it may be assumed that the historical trend of dividend per share payments will continue into the future. The geometric average historical dividend growth rate = $100 \times ((15.0/12.8)^{0.25} - 1) = 4\%$ per year.

(Alternatively, the arithmetical average of annual dividend growth rates could be used. This will be (5.5 + 0.0 + 7.4 + 3.5)/4 = 4.1%. Another possibility is to use the Gordon growth model. The average payout ratio over the last 4 years has been 47%, so the average retention ratio has been 53%. Assuming that the cost of equity represents an acceptable return on shareholders' funds, the dividend growth rate is approximately 53% × 10% = 5.3% per year.)

Using the formula for the dividend growth model from the formula sheet, the ex dividend share price = (15.0 × 1.04)/(0.1 – 0.04) = $2.60

This is 10 cents per share more than the current share price of Dartig Co. There are several reasons why there may be a difference between the two share prices. The future dividend growth rate for example, may differ from the average historical dividend growth rate, and the current share price may factor in a more reasonable estimate of the future dividend growth rate than the 4% used here. The cost of equity of Dartig Co may not be exactly equal to 10%. More generally, there may be a degree of inefficiency in the capital market on which the shares of Dartig Co are traded.

(e)   The primary financial management objective of a company is usually taken to be the maximisation of shareholder wealth. In practice, the managers of a company acting as agents for the principals (the shareholders) may act in ways which do not lead to shareholder wealth maximisation. The failure of managers to maximise shareholder wealth is referred to as the agency problem.

Shareholder wealth increases through payment of dividends and through appreciation of share prices. Since share prices reflect the value placed by buyers on the right to receive future dividends, analysis of changes in shareholder wealth focuses on changes in share prices. The objective of maximising share prices is commonly used as a substitute objective for that of maximising shareholder wealth.

The agency problem arises because the objectives of managers differ from those of shareholders: because there is a divorce or separation of ownership from control in modern companies; and because there is an asymmetry of information between shareholders and managers which prevents shareholders being aware of most managerial decisions.

One way to encourage managers to act in ways that increase shareholder wealth is to offer them share options. These are rights to buy shares on a future date at a price which is fixed when the share options are issued. Share options will encourage managers to make decisions that are likely to lead to share price increases (such as investing in projects with positive net present values), since this will increase the rewards they receive from share options. The higher the share price in the market when the share options are exercised, the greater will be the capital gain that could be made by managers owning the options.

Share options therefore go some way towards reducing the differences between the objectives of shareholders and managers. However, it is possible that managers may be rewarded for poor performance if share prices in general are increasing. It is also possible that managers may not be rewarded for good performance if share prices in general are falling. It is difficult to decide on a share option exercise price and a share option exercise date that will encourage managers to focus on increasing shareholder wealth while still remaining challenging, rather than being easily achievable.

	ACCA marking scheme		
			Marks
(a)	Rights issue price	1	
	Theoretical ex rights price per share	2	
		———	
			3
(b)	Existing price/earnings ratio	1	
	Revised earnings per share	1	
	Share price using price/earnings method	1	
		———	
			3
(c)	Discussion of share price comparisons	3 – 4	
	Calculation of capital gain and comment	1 – 2	
		———	
			Max 5
(d)	Average dividend growth rate	2	
	Ex div market price per share	2	
	Discussion	2	
		———	
			6
(e)	Discussion of agency problem	4 – 5	
	Discussion of share option schemes	4 – 5	
		———	
			Max 8
			———
Total			25
			———

Examiner's comments

In part (a), candidates were asked to calculate a theoretical ex rights price per share. Many candidates gained full marks for their calculations. Weaker answers made errors as regards the form of the issue (it was 1 for 4, not 4 for 1), or thought the theoretical ex rights price was the rights issue price, or calculated the value of the rights.

Part (b) required the calculation of the share price after the business expansion, using the price/earnings ratio method. The first step was to calculate the current price/earnings ratio. The second step was to calculate the earnings per share (EPS) after the proposed business expansion. The final step was to calculate the future share price by multiplying the two together.

A number of candidates were not able to calculate the price/earnings ratio by dividing the current share price by the current EPS. Calculating the EPS after the expansion by multiplying the current EPS by the average historic EPS growth rate was also a problem for some candidates, who were unable to calculate average historic growth rate, or who applied the growth rate to the average EPS rather than the current EPS.

Some students were also unfamiliar with the PER valuation method, even though this is discussed in the study texts.

Part (c) asked for a discussion of whether the business expansion was an acceptable use of the rights issue funds, and an evaluation of the effect of the expansion on the wealth of shareholders. The two parts of the question are linked, since the question of whether the use made of the finance is acceptable depends on the effect on the wealth of shareholders.

If shareholder wealth increases, the proposed use of the finance is acceptable. Better answers therefore looked to compare the theoretical rights price per share (the share price before the rights issue funds were invested) with the share price after the investment had taken place (for example the share price calculated in part (b)), or to compare the return from the investment (for example, total shareholder return, which is the sum of capital gain and divided yield) with the cost of equity.

Part (d) required candidates to calculate the share price predicted by the dividend growth model and compare it with the current share price, explaining any difference that might be found. Many candidates gained full marks for their answer to this question. Marks were lost where candidates used EPS rather than dividend per share in the dividend growth model, or were not able to calculate the dividend growth rate, or used incorrect values in the dividend growth model. A surprising number of candidates did not use the dividend growth model given in the formula sheet, but used the rearranged version of the formula that is used to calculate the cost of equity. Some candidates mistakenly thought that the cost of equity calculated by this formula was the same as the share price.

Part (e) required candidates to explain the nature of the agency problem and to discuss using share option schemes to reduce it in a stock-market listed company. The agency problem is that managers may act in ways that do not lead to the maximisation of shareholder wealth. Shareholder wealth increases through receiving dividends and through capital gains in share prices, and is usually assessed through changes in share prices. Better answers referred to these key financial management concepts.

Share option schemes, in making managers into shareholders, lead to convergence of objectives, if only on a shared focus on increased wealth through increasing share prices. Unfortunately, while share prices increases can arise from good managerial decisions, share price changes can arise for other reasons as well. There was scope here for candidates to discuss a range of issues relating to the difficulty of designing a share option scheme that rewarded managers for good performance, but not for poor performance.

7   NEWS FOR YOU

Key answer tips

To score well on part (a), you must ensure you apply your basic knowledge of economics to the specifics of News For You's situation. In part (b) the majority of marks are available for the justifications you provide as opposed to the conclusion you reach. The highlighted words are key phrases that markers are looking for.

(a)   Economic opinion on the effect of an **interest rate change** on News For You might vary. Keynesian economists argue that if base rate (and other interest rates) fall, this will lead to an increase in consumer demand (i.e. consumer spending). Unfortunately, however, even if the recent drop in the base rate increases consumer demand, it is unlikely to have any significant impact on the particular business of News For You. Sales are likely to remain unchanged, because newspapers and small confectionery items are low cost purchases, often bought on impulse. Interest rate movements will not make such items suddenly affordable where before they were not.

News For You needs to think about other ways in which the interest rate change might affect its business, and particularly its impact on business costs. If the company has an overdraft facility, its cost of borrowing will have been reduced. At the same time, the expansion plans require the business to raise $2 million, and changes in interest rates affect the cost of all types of capital, both loans and equity. Corporate borrowing rates are generally linked to the prevailing base rate or inter-bank lending rate, with companies paying a premium above base or interbank rate for their loans.

The drop in interest rates will therefore affect the required return on the finance needed to fund the proposed expansion. If News For You uses Discounted Cash Flow analysis for investment appraisals, the fall in the cost of capital resulting from the drop in the base rate will mean that a lower discount rate can be applied to the investment evaluation. A lower rate of discount will result in a higher Net Present Value for any given proposal.

Keynesian economists, however, do not agree that changes in interest rates affect corporate investment decisions. They argue that investments are more dependent on the level of business confidence. It might be possible to suggest that News For You will see the fall in the base rate as stimulating general economic confidence. If so, it will be more confident about the future of its business, and so regardless of any changes in the cost of capital, it might be more willing to undertake the expansionary investment. (On the other hand, a fall in interest rates could be a response to a deterioration in the economy, and a loss of business confidence.)

The **inflation figures** are useful to News For You because they can directly affect profit and cash flow forecasts. The impact of inflation on cash flows and profit will be dependent to a large degree on the relative rates of increase in wages, the cost of wholesale supplies for the shop, and the prices that News For You can charge its customers. The quoted rate of inflation is very low at just over 1% per year and, although the rate is not expected to fall any further, its current level is unlikely to have a dramatic effect on the ability of the business to trade profitably. The greater risk for the business might come from the problem that, because inflation is so low, customers are not prepared to tolerate any price rises at all. If so, News For You might become more vulnerable to loss of business to the large food stores which can draw away customers via price cutting campaigns.

Personal and corporation tax rates are relevant to the owners of News For You because they will affect the net gain to the business that may be generated by expansion. As with interest rates, tax rates can affect personal spending patterns and therefore affect the sales revenue of a particular business. News For You, however, is unlikely to have a business that is sensitive to tax rates, because its products are basic essentials and low cost items. Nonetheless, the information that tax rates will remain unchanged is useful because it allows the business to be certain of the amount of tax relief that may be available on loan finance, and the relief that equity investors may claim for investing in a small unquoted company. This information might be useful in deciding whether or not to go ahead with the expansion, because it may affect the relative cost and availability of capital.

The **changes in taxes on tobacco** might be expected to have had a significant effect on News For You because it is one of the relatively high value products sold by the stores. The question indicates that tobacco sales have been falling, but it is unclear whether this drop is linked to the 10% rise in tax over the last twelve months, or simply a result of the population becoming more health conscious and so buying fewer cigarettes. If customers are price-sensitive in their purchasing of tobacco, News For You might once again find itself vulnerable to competition from the food retailers that can exercise greater buying power and sell similar products at lower prices. The high cost of these items also means that inventory holding costs are high, and if inventory turnover is reduced because of tax increase, then the amount of working capital required by News For You will rise.

The **investigation into the food sector** might prove detrimental to News For You if it serves to initiate a price war amongst the retailers, all of whom will be anxious to prove that they look after their customers. The business grew very quickly between

20X2 and 20X6, but since then sales revenue has increased by just 2% per year, and the owners must be concerned that further growth potential is limited, at least within the existing outlets. Moving into the sale of basic foodstuffs has been used as a strategy to compensate for loss of sales in other products such as tobacco, but in many countries a large proportion of people do their food shopping in large retail outlets. By expanding their product range, News For You has also created for itself another set of competitors in the form of food retailers. The only way in which the business might gain from this investigation is if it also covers food wholesaling, and the result is a drop in the prices that News For You have to pay for their inventory.

(b) **Arguments in favour of the expansion include the following:**

- The sales revenue figures suggest that there is only limited opportunity for the business to continue to grow organically. The business is seeking to replace sales of tobacco and newspapers with sales of foods, but as suggested in answer to (a), the potential of this side of the business may be limited. News For You may be advised to try to grow sales revenue by means of acquiring new outlets instead.

- If News For You is being forced into paying relatively high prices for supplies from a local wholesaler, then expansion may allow it to gain more bargaining power, and purchase at reduced rates from a national wholesale chain. Increased size will offer the opportunity to take advantage of possible economies of scale via bulk ordering. In this way, margins could be widened and the overall business made more profitable.

- With a larger number of stores covering a wider geographic area, News For You will be able to broaden the nature of their business base, so that it will be less vulnerable to regional economic trends.

Arguments against any expansion include the following:

- The potential to increase sales substantially via food sales is very limited. The majority of people purchase most of their food from larger stores, and will only use a local shop for small low cost items, for which it is not worthwhile making a special car journey to the supermarket. It is unlikely a profitable business can be created based on this type of sale.

- The widespread ownership of televisions and access to differing forms of mass media communications is likely to mean that fewer people will purchase newspapers on a daily basis. This is particularly true of those papers that are also published in electronic form. Many newsagents are dependent for the bulk of their sales on customers who come into the shop to buy a newspaper and then purchase additional items at the same time. If customers do not come in for a newspaper, then the associated sales income will also be lost. Expanding a business where there is such a risk of demand falling away may be regarded as very risky.

- The information in the question suggests that the competitive environment for News For You is becoming much tougher on a number of different fronts simultaneously, with rising excise duties, powerful food retailers and a reduction in tobacco and newspaper purchases. Expansion usually occurs because a business is very confident of the future, but in this case it is questionable whether News For You has much about which to be confident.

It would therefore seem advisable for News For You to postpone its expansion plans, and perhaps look at ways of using its existing outlets to sell very different products, thereby 're-inventing' their business, perhaps by moving completely away from confectionery and into, for example, video rental.

8   CC CO

Key answer tips

Part (c) can easily be attempted in isolation and could be tackled first to capture the knowledge level marks early within your allotted time.

Part (b) is dependent on your answer to part (a) although the own figure rule will apply when part (b) is marked. A methodical approach should yield some easy marks

The highlighted words in the written sections are key phrases that markers are looking for.

(a)   **Using a forward market hedge**

Dollar value of payment = €1.5m/0.698 = $2.149m

Using a money market hedge

Expected payment after 3 months = €1.5m

Euro interest rate over three months = 2.9/4 = 0.725%

Euros to invest now to have €1.5m asset after 3 months = €1.5m/1.00725 = €1.4892m

Spot rate for buying Euros = 0.70 €/$

Dollar loan needed for Euros deposited = €1.4892 / 0.7 = $2.127m

Dollar interest rate over three months = 5.5/ 4 = 1.375%

Value in 3 months of dollar loan = €2.127 × 1.01375 = $2.1567

The forward market is marginally preferable to the money market hedge for the Euro payment expected after 3 months.

(b)

Year	0	1	2	3	4	5
		$000	$000	$000	$000	$000
Contribution (W1)		1,330	2,830	2,408	1,280	
Fixed costs (W2)		(265)	(281)	(298)	(316)	
Taxable cash flow		1,065	2,549	2,110	964	
Taxation			(320)	(765)	(633)	(289)
Initial investment	(2,149)					
CA tax benefits (W3)			161	161	161	161
After-tax cash flow	(2,149)	1,065	2,390	1,506	492	(128)
Discount at 10% (W4)	1	0.909	0.826	0.751	0.683	0.621
Present values	(2,149)	968	1,974	1,131	336	(79)

Net present value = $2,181,000. The net present value is positive and so the investment is financially acceptable.

Workings

(W1) Annual contribution

Year	0	1	2	3	4
Sales volume (units/yr)		250,000	500,000	400,000	200,000
Selling price ($/unit)		12.60	13.23	13.89	14.59
Variable cost ($/unit)		7.28	7.57	7.87	8.19
Contribution ($/unit)		5.32	5.66	6.02	6.40
Contribution ($/yr)		1,330,000	2,830,000	2,408,000	1,280,000

(W2) Fixed costs

$250,000 inflating at 6% p.a. = $265,000 in T1 etc

(W3) Capital allowance (CA) tax benefits

Capital allowance is on a straight-line basis over the four-year life of the asset.

$2.149m ÷ 4 years = $537,250 per annum

Tax benefit = $537,250 × 30% = $161,175

(W4) Discount factor

$(1 + i) = (1 + r) \times (1 + h)$

$(1 + i) = (1 + 0.051) \times (1 + 0.047)$

$(1 + i) = 1.1004$

$i = 10\%$

(c)

Tutorial note:

More has been noted in this answer than would be needed to score highly.

Inflation is an increase in the general level of prices in an economy that is sustained over a period of time. Rising price levels and uncertainty as to future rates of inflation make financial decisions more difficult and more important. As prices of different commodities change at different rates, the timing of purchase, sale, borrowing and repayment of debt becomes critical to the success of organisations and their projects.

The real effects on the level of profits and the cash flow position of a business of a sustained rate of inflation depend on the form that inflation is taking and the nature of the markets in which the company is operating. One way of analysing inflation is to distinguish between demand-pull inflation and cost-push inflation.

Demand-pull inflation might occur when excess aggregate monetary demand in the economy and hence demand for particular goods and services enable companies to raise prices and expand profit margins.

Cost-push inflation will occur when there are increases in production costs independent of the state of demand, e.g. rising raw material costs or rising labour costs. The initial effect is to reduce profit margins and the extent to which these can be restored depends on the ability of companies to pass on cost increases as price increases for customers.

One would expect that the effect of cost-push inflation on company profits and cash flow would always be negative, but that with demand-pull inflation, profits and cash flow might be increased, at least in nominal terms and in the short run. In practice, however, even demand-pull inflation may have negative effects on profits and cash flow in the longer-term as it works through cost. This is especially true if companies use pricing strategies in which prices are determined by cost plus some mark-up.

- Excess demand for goods leads companies to expand output.
- This leads to excess demand for factors of production, especially labour, so costs (e.g. wages) rise.
- Companies pass on the increased cost as higher prices.
- In most cases inflation will reduce profits and cash flow, especially in the long run.

Another effect of inflation on companies is the role it plays in determining exchange rates. Purchasing power parity theory (PPPT) claims that the rate of exchange between two currencies depends on the relative inflation rates within the respective countries. PPPT is based on 'the law of one price'. In equilibrium, identical goods must cost the same, regardless of the currency in which they are sold.

The main function of an exchange rate is to provide a means of translating prices expressed in one currency into another currency. The implication is that the exchange rate will be determined in some way by the relationship between these prices. This arises from the law of one price.

The law of one price states that in a free market with no barriers to trade and no transport or transactions costs, the competitive process will ensure that there will only be one price for any given good. If price differences occurred they would be removed by arbitrage; entrepreneurs would buy in the low market and resell in the high market. This would eradicate the price difference.

If this law is applied to international transactions, it suggests that exchange rates will always adjust to ensure that only one price exists between countries where there is relatively free trade.

An estimate of expected future spot rates can be made using the formula:

$$S_1 = S_0 \times \frac{(1+h_c)}{(1+h_b)}$$

Where:

S_0 = current spot rate

S_1 = expected future spot rate

h_b = inflation rate in country for which the spot is quoted (base currency)

h_c = inflation rate in the other country (counter currency)

Thus, a high level of inflation in an economy, relative to the inflation rates overseas will result in a depreciation of the currency. As a result of the currency fluctuation imports will cost more but it may be easier to export since goods will appear cheaper to overseas purchasers.

9   RWF

Key answer tips

The is a very common style question and the open-ended nature of part (a) of the requirement will require a logical and methodical approach to ensure you capture all of the marks. Make sure you balance the calculation of ratios with a discussion of their meaning.

The highlighted words in the written sections are key phrases that markers are looking for.

(a)   **Impact on corporate objectives**

Financial gearing:

Current	50,000/90,000 = 55.5%
Proposed – Debt issue	(50,000 + 9,000)/(90,000 + 6,670) = 61.0%
Proposed – Rights issue	(50,000/(90,000 + 9,000 + 6,800) = 47.3%

Earnings per share:

Current	$6.3m/12m = 52.5c
Proposed – debt issue	$9.17m/12m = 76.4c

New shares to be issued if rights issue used – $9m/$6 = 1.5m

Proposed – rights issue	$9.8/(12 + 1.5) = 72.6c

Impact on other key ratios

Required:

Operating gearing:

Using fixed costs/total costs:

Current	(9,000 + 16,000)/(32,000 + 9,000 + 16,000) = 43.9%
Proposed	(16,000 + 17,000)/(34,000 + 16,000 + 17,000) = 49.3%

This will be the same for either financing option.

The administration costs are assumed to be fixed in nature.

Tutorial note:

Credit will be given for a further 2 relevant ratios only. It is possible that students may have attempted other ratios than those shown below.

ROCE (based on opening capital employed):

Current	13,000/(90,000+50,000-4,300) = 9.58%
Proposed – Debt issue or rights issue	18,000/(90,000+50,000+9,000) = 12.08%

Interest cover:

Current	13,000/4,000 = 3.25 times
Proposed – Debt issue	18,000/4,900 = 3.67 times
Proposed – Rights issue	18,000/4,000 = 4.5 times

Comment

The financial gearing is currently within the target of 60% and will fall if a rights issue is made. However it will increase marginally above the 60% target if debt is raised. Furthermore at the start of the forecast period when the debt has been raised but no profits have yet been earned the gearing will be as high as (59,000/90,000) 65.6%.

The EPS will rise irrespective of the type of finance used. The greatest rise is if a debt issue is made. Whilst this is good for the shareholders they will of course be taking more financial risk than if a rights issue is used. The percentage rise in EPS is 46% if debt is raised and 38% if a rights issue is used. As both of these exceed the 5% inflation rate the company will achieve its target of providing real growth in EPS.

The operational gearing will rise as a result of undertaking the project. Hence the operational or business risk of the company will increase due to the company having a higher proportion of fixed costs. As a result of this the company may be wary of taking on more financial risk.

ROCE is an important performance measure which is often used by investors. The expansion project will significantly increase ROCE albeit from a rather low level.

If financial risk is measured by interest cover the situation improves if either a rights issue or the debt is used. This may suggest that the company could afford to take on more debt/financial risk.

In order to comment further it would be useful to know industry average data as considering RWF Co in isolation is of limited use.

Recommendation

In order to keep the financial gearing within the target set by the company and as a result of the expected increase in operating gearing I suggest that the new finance required is raised by means of a rights issue.

(b)   **Criticisms of the corporate objectives stated include:**

Although the objectives focus on two separate and critical areas of performance (profitability and gearing), they are both financial in nature. A company should set both financial and non-financial objectives.

Depending upon the industry average gearing or the optimal gearing for RWF Co the gearing objective may be inappropriate.

Only having two objectives could promote manipulation especially if the achievement of these objectives results in the payment of bonuses.

Neither objective will necessarily result in the company maximising the wealth of shareholders which should be the primary objective of a company.

Recommendations

It is recommended that RWF Co adopts the corporate objective of maximising shareholder wealth subject to satisficing other key stakeholders. In order to ensure this objective is met the company should adopt a broad range of performance measures and these should be both financial and non-financial.

(c)   The key factors a company should consider when taking the three key financial management decisions are the objectives of the company and the economic environment within which the company is operating.

For instance if a company were to have as one its objectives the desire to develop a leading reputation for quality then when taking its investment decisions the company would need to consider investing in a suitable quality assurance system.

Equally if the economic environment was such that increases in interest rates were expected the company would consider this when taking its financing decisions. Hence the company may choose to hedge against interest rate risk or move into fixed rate borrowings.

WORKING CAPITAL MANAGEMENT

10   GORWA CO

Key answer tips

In part (a) students may go into more depth about how to hedge interest rate risk and miss marks for analysing the effects of an increase in interest rates on the company concerned. Although the model answer presents a number of calculations that could be performed, there are only 1 – 2 marks available for the financial analysis. This is another reminder that the F9 paper is far from wholly numerical.

In part (b), again a huge range of calculations are possible. If students only manage a selection of those presented in the model answer, they should still be able to score highly. The weighting between calculations and discussion is 50:50 and the discussion provided in the model answer demonstrates the style the examiner is hoping for.

Part (c) is a fairly straightforward appraisal of the costs and benefits involved in a factoring agreement. With a requirement of "evaluate", it is clear that this section will require a good number of calculations.

(a)   **Financial analysis**

Fixed interest debt proportion (2006) = 100 × 2,425/(2,425 + 1,600) = 60%

Fixed interest debt proportion (2007) = 100 × 2,425/(2,425 + 3,225) = 43%

Fixed interest payments = 2,425 × 0.08 = $194,000

Variable interest payments (2006) = 274 – 194 = $80,000 or 29%

Variable interest payments (2007) = 355 – 194 = $161,000 or 45%

(Alternatively, considering the overdraft amounts and the average variable overdraft interest rate of 5% per year:

Variable interest payments (2006) = 1.6m × 0.05 = $80,000 or 29%

Variable interest payments (2007) = 3.225m × 0.05 = $161,250 or 45%)

Interest coverage ratio (2006) = 2,939/ 274 = 10.7 times

Interest coverage ratio (2007) = 2,992/ 355 = 8.4 times

Debt/equity ratio (2006) = 100 × 2,425/ 11,325 = 21%

Debt/equity ratio (2007) = 100 × 2,425/ 12,432 = 20%

Total debt/equity ratio (2006) = 100 × (2,425 + 1,600)/ 11,325 = 35%

Total debt/equity ratio (2007) = 100 × (2,425 + 3,225)/ 12,432 = 45%

Discussion

Gorwa Co has both fixed interest debt and variable interest rate debt amongst its sources of finance. The fixed interest bonds have ten years to go before they need to be redeemed and they therefore offer Gorwa Co long term protection against an increase in interest rates.

In 2006, 60% of the company's debt was fixed interest in nature, but in 2007 this had fallen to 43%. The floating-rate proportion of the company's debt therefore increased from 40% in 2006 to 57% in 2007. The interest coverage ratio fell from 10.7 times in 2006 to 8.4 times in 2007, a decrease which will be a cause for concern to the company if it were to continue. The debt/equity ratio (including the overdraft due to its size) increased over the same period from 35% to 45% (if the overdraft is excluded, the debt/equity ratio declines slightly from 21% to 20%). From the perspective of an increase in interest rates, the financial risk of Gorwa Co has increased and may continue to increase if the company does not take action to halt the growth of its variable interest rate overdraft. The proportion of interest payments linked to floating rate debt has increased from 29% in 2006 to 45% in 2007. An increase in interest rates will further reduce profit before taxation, which is lower in 2007 than in 2006, despite a 40% increase in turnover.

One way to hedge against an increase in interest rates is to exchange some or all of the variable-rate overdraft into long-term fixed-rate debt. There is likely to be an increase in interest payments because long-term debt is usually more expensive than short-term debt. Gorwa would also be unable to benefit from falling interest rates if most of its debt paid fixed rather than floating rate interest.

Interest rate options and interest rate futures may be of use in the short term, depending on the company's plans to deal with its increasing overdraft.

For the longer term, Gorwa Co could consider raising a variable-rate bank loan, linked to a variable rate-fixed interest rate swap.

(b) **Financial analysis**

		2007	2006
Inventory days	(365 × 2,400)/23,781		37 days
	(365 × 4,600)/34,408	49 days	
Receivables days	(365 × 2,200)/26,720		30 days
	(365 × 4,600)/37,400	45 days	
Payables days	(365 × 2,000)/23,781		31 days
	(365 × 4,750)/34,408	51 days	
Current ratio	4,600/3,600		1.3 times
	9,200/7,975	1.15 times	
Quick ratio	2,200/3,600		0.61 times
	4,600/7,975	0.58 times	
Sales/net working capital	26,720/1,000		26.7 times
	37,400/1,225	30.5 times	
Turnover increase	37,400/26,720	40%	
Non-current assets increase	13,632/12,750	7%	
Inventory increase	4,600/2,400	92%	
Receivables increase	4,600/2,200	109%	
Payables increase	4,750/2,000	138%	
Overdraft increase	3,225/1,600	102%	

Discussion

Overtrading or undercapitalisation arises when a company has too small a capital base to support its level of business activity. Difficulties with liquidity may arise as an overtrading company may have insufficient capital to meet its liabilities as they fall due. Overtrading is often associated with a rapid increase in turnover and Gorwa Co has experienced a 40% increase in turnover over the last year. Investment in working capital has not matched the increase in sales, however, since the sales/net working capital ratio has increased from 26.7 times to 30.5 times.

Overtrading could be indicated by a deterioration in inventory days. Here, inventory days have increased from 37 days to 49 days, while inventory has increased by 92% compared to the 40% increase in turnover. It is possible that inventory has been stockpiled in anticipation of a further increase in turnover, leading to an increase in operating costs.

Overtrading could also be indicated by deterioration in receivables days. In this case, receivables have increased by 109% compared to the 40% increase in turnover. The increase in turnover may have been fuelled in part by a relaxation of credit terms.

As the liquidity problem associated with overtrading deepens, the overtrading company increases its reliance on short-term sources of finance, including overdraft, trade payables and leasing. The overdraft of Gorwa Co has more than doubled in size to $3.225 million, while trade payables have increased by $2.74 million or 137%. Both increases are much greater than the 40% increase in turnover. There is evidence here of an increased reliance on short-term finance sources.

Overtrading can also be indicated by decreases in the current ratio and the quick ratio. The current ratio of Gorwa Co has fallen from 1.3 times to 1.15 times, while its quick ratio has fallen from 0.61 times to 0.58 times.

There are clear indications that Gorwa Co is experiencing the kinds of symptoms usually associated with overtrading. A more complete and meaningful analysis could be undertaken if appropriate benchmarks were available, such as key ratios from comparable companies in the same industry sector, or additional financial information from prior years so as to establish trends in key ratios.

(c)   Current receivables = $4,600,000

Receivables under factor = 37,400,000 × 30/365 = $3,074,000

Reduction in receivables = 4,600 – 3,074 = $1,526,000

Reduction in finance cost = 1,526,000 × 0.05 = $76,300 per year

Administration cost savings = $100,000 per year

Bad debt savings = $350,000 per year

Factor's annual fee = 37,400,000 × 0.03 = $1,122,000 per year

Extra interest cost on advance = 3,074,000 × 80% × (7% – 5%) = $49,184 per year

Net cost of factoring = 76,300 + 100,000 + 350,000 – 1,122,000 – 49,184 = $644,884

The factor's offer cannot be recommended, since the evaluation shows no financial benefit arising.

ACCA marking scheme			
			Marks
(a)	Discussion of effects of interest rate increase	3 – 4	
	Relevant financial analysis	1 – 2	
	Interest rate hedging	2 – 3	
		———	
			Max 7
(b)	Financial analysis	5 – 6	
	Discussion of overtrading	4 – 5	
	Conclusion as to overtrading	1	
		———	
			Max 10
(c)	Reduction in financing cost	3	
	Factor's fee	1	
	Interest on advance	2	
	Net cost of factoring	1	
	Conclusion	1	
		———	
		8	
Total		———	
		25	
		———	

Examiner's comments

Part (a) asked for a discussion, with supporting calculations, of the possible effects on a company of an increase in interest rates, and advice on how to protect against interest rate risk.

Some candidates were not aware of the difference between interest rate and interest payment, and consequently discussed how the company's finance costs (interest payments) had increased from one year to the next. Analysis would have shown that the increase in the finance cost was due to the increase in the overdraft and that the interest rate applied to the overdraft was 5% in each year, i.e. the interest rate had not changed. The bonds were fixed-rate in nature, as they were given in the balance sheet as 8% bonds. As the question asked about hedging interest rate risk, looking at the balance between fixed rate debt (bonds) and floating rate debt (overdraft) was also relevant here, as was a consideration of gearing and interest cover.

The question was, in fact, very open in nature, and a discussion of the effects of an increase in interest rates could look at an increase in financial risk, a decrease in sales due to a fall in demand, an increase in operating costs and a cutting back of investment plans.

Many answers offered a number of ways of protecting (hedging) against interest rate risk, including matching and smoothing: using forward rate agreements, interest rate futures, interest rate options and interest rates swaps; and taking steps to decrease the dependency on variable-rate overdraft finance and hence the exposure to interest rate increases, for example by improving working capital management.

In part (b), the requirement was to discuss, with supporting calculations, whether a company was overtrading (undercapitalised). Relevant financial analysis, including ratio analysis, therefore needed to look at the level of business activity and the area of working capital management.

Better answers calculated a series of accounting ratios, perhaps adding some growth rates and changes in financial statement entries, and used this analysis to look at the increasing dependence of the company on short-term sources of finance while sales were expanding at a high rate. Some answers noted that short-term finance had been used to acquire additional non-current assets, that inventory growth exceeded sales growth, and so on. Weaker answers often did little more than repeat in words the financial ratios that had been already calculated, without explaining how or why the identified changes supported the idea that the company was overtrading.

Part (c) required the evaluation of an offer from a factor using cost-benefit analysis.

Many candidates seemed to be unfamiliar with the relationship between credit sales, the level of trade receivables in the balance sheet, trade receivables days (the trade receivables collection period), and the cost of financing trade receivables. This unfamiliarity led to applying the revised trade receivables days to the current level of receivables instead of to credit sales: calculating the factor's advance on the current level of receivables rather than on the revised level of receivables: and calculating the factor's fee on the level of receivables rather than on credit sales.

Since marks were available for each element of the cost-benefit analysis, most candidates were able to obtain reasonable marks on this part of question 3, even where answers were incomplete or contained some of the errors identified above.

11 FLG CO

Key answer tips

Parts (a) and (b) are both standard textbook material. In part (a), for six marks you should discuss at least three factors. Don't forget the requirement is to "discuss" not "state" so you must give some commentary: 'the length of the working capital cycle' will not get the full marks available.

In part (b) the requirement is again to "discuss". Given the emphasis is on how both factoring and invoice discounting can assist in the **management** of accounts receivable, there should be more discussion on factoring than invoice discounting (the latter being a tool for managing cash flow rather than managing accounts receivable). Don't forget to define each of the terms to collect some easy marks.

The calculation in part (c) requires some "out of the box" thinking in order to see how the brief information provided can be used to work out the size of the overdraft. Not only does it involve re-arranging the usual working capital ratios we're used to seeing, it also requires a disaggregation of the operating cycle to reveal the inventory holding period.

In contrast, part (d) is a fairly straightforward application of the EOQ model which shouldn't pose many difficulties. The highlighted words are key phrases that markers are looking for.

(a) There are a number of factors that determine the level of investment in current assets and their relative importance varies from company to company.

Length of working capital cycle

The working capital cycle or operating cycle is the period of time between when a company settles its accounts payable and when it receives cash from its accounts receivable. Operating activities during this period need to be financed and as the operating period lengthens, the amount of finance needed increases. Companies with comparatively longer operating cycles than others in the same industry sector, will therefore require comparatively higher levels of investment in current assets.

Terms of trade

These determine the period of credit extended to customers, any discounts offered for early settlement or bulk purchases, and any penalties for late payment. A company whose terms of trade are more generous than another company in the same industry sector will therefore need a comparatively higher investment in current assets.

Policy on level of investment in current assets

Even within the same industry sector, companies will have different policies regarding the level of investment in current assets, depending on their attitude to risk. A company with a comparatively conservative approach to the level of investment in current assets would maintain higher levels of inventory, offer more generous credit terms and have higher levels of cash in reserve than a company with a comparatively aggressive approach. While the more aggressive approach would be more profitable because of the lower level of investment in current assets, it would also be more risky, for example in terms of running out of inventory in periods of fluctuating demand, of failing to have the particular goods required by a customer, of failing to retain customers who migrate to more generous credit terms elsewhere, and of being less able to meet unexpected demands for payment.

Industry in which organisation operates

Another factor that influences the level of investment in current assets is the industry within which an organisation operates. Some industries, such as aircraft construction, will have long operating cycles due to the length of time needed to manufacture finished goods and so will have comparatively higher levels of investment in current assets than industries such as supermarket chains, where goods are bought in for resale with minimal additional processing and where many goods have short shelf-lives.

(b)   Factoring involves a company turning over administration of its sales ledger to a factor, which is a financial institution with expertise in this area. The factor will assess the creditworthiness of new customers, record sales, send out statements and reminders, collect payment, identify late payers and chase them for settlement, and take appropriate legal action to recover debts where necessary.

The factor will also offer finance to a company based on invoices raised for goods sold or services provided. This is usually up to 80% of the face value of invoices raised. The finance is repaid from the settled invoices, with the balance being passed to the issuing company after deduction of a fee equivalent to an interest charge on cash advanced.

If factoring is without recourse, the factor rather than the company will carry the cost of any bad debts that arise on overdue accounts. Factoring without recourse therefore offers credit protection to the selling company, although the factor's fee (a percentage of credit sales) will be comparatively higher than with non-recourse factoring to reflect the cost of the insurance offered.

Invoice discounting is a way of raising finance against the security of invoices raised, rather than employing the credit management and administration services of a factor. A number of good quality invoices may be discounted, rather than all invoices, and the service is usually only offered to companies meeting a minimum turnover criterion.

(c)   **Calculation of size of overdraft**

Inventory period = operating cycle + payables period − receivables period = 3 + 1 − 2 = 2 months

Inventory = 1.89m × 2/12 = $315,000

Accounts receivable = 4.2m × 2/12 = $700,000

Current assets = 315,000 + 700,000 = $1,015,000

Current liabilities = current assets/current ratio = 1,015,000/1.4 = $725,000

Accounts payable = 1.89m × 1/12 = $157,500

Overdraft = 725,000 − 157,500 = $567,500

Net working capital = current assets − current liabilities = 1,015,000 − 725,000 = $290,000

Short-term financing cost = 567,500 × 0.07 = $39,725

Long-term financing cost = 290,000 × 0.11 = $31,900

Total cost of financing current assets = 39,725 + 31,900 = $71,625

(d)   (i)   Economic order quantity = (2 × 6 × 60,000/0.5)0.5 = 1,200 units

Number of orders = 60,000/1,200 = 50 order per year

Annual ordering cost = 50 × 6 = $300 per year

Average inventory = 1,200/2 = 600 units

Annual holding cost = 600 × 0.5 = $300 per year

Inventory cost = 60,000 × 12 = $720,000

Total cost of inventory with EOQ policy = 720,000 + 300 + 300 = $720,600 per year

(ii)   Order size for bulk discounts = 10,000 units

Number of orders = 60,000/10,000 = 6 orders per year

Annual ordering cost = 6 × 6 = $36 per year

Average inventory = 10,000/2 =5,000 units

Annual holding cost = 5,000 × 2 = $10,000 per year

Discounted material cost =12 × 0.99 = $11.88 per unit

Inventory cost = 60,000 × 11.88 = $712,800

Total cost of inventory with discount = 712,800 + 36 + 10,000 = $722,836 per year

The EOQ approach results in a slightly lower total inventory cost

ACCA marking scheme			
			Marks
(a)	Discussion of key factors	Maximum	6
(b)	Discussion of factoring		4–5
	Discussion of Invoice discounting		1–2
			—
	Maximum		6
(c)	Value of inventory		1
	Accounts receivable and accounts payable		1
	Current liabilities		1
	Size of overdraft		1
	Net working capital		1
	Total cost of financing working capital		1
			—
			6
(d)	(i) Economic order quantity		1
	Ordering cost and holding cost under EOQ		1
	Inventory cost under EOQ		1
	Total cost of inventory with EOQ policy		1
			—
			4
	(ii) Ordering cost and holding cost with discount		1
	Inventory cost with discount		1
	Total cost of inventory with bulk purchase discount		1
	Conclusion		1
			—
	Maximum		3
			—
Total			25
			—

Examiner's comments

Part (a) asked for a discussion of the factors which determine the level of investment in current assets. Although this topic is clearly identified in the F9 Study Guide (C3a), answers often referred incorrectly to working capital funding strategies (C3b). The suggested answer to this question refers to factors mentioned in the F9 Study Guide, such as length of working capital cycle, terms of trade, working capital policy and so on. Answers that discussed these or similar factors gained high marks.

Part (b) asked for a discussion of the ways in which factoring and invoice discounting could help in managing accounts receivable. Many candidates discussed relevant points in relation to factoring and received credit accordingly. Discussions of invoice discounting tended to be variable in quality, with a significant number of students believing incorrectly that invoice discounting meant early settlement discounts.

In part (c), candidates were asked to calculate the size of an overdraft, the net working capital, and the total cost of financing current assets.

The variable quality of the answers indicates a need for candidates to ensure, not only that they are familiar with accounting ratios, but also that they are familiar with the accounting items to which the ratios relate, in this case sales, cost of sales, inventory, trade receivables, trade payables and so on. Many candidates were unable to calculate the inventory turnover period, given the operating cycle, the average collection period and the average payable period. Many candidates were also unable to work backwards from the provided ratios, for example to calculate the level of receivables given the average collection period and the amount of credit sales. Some candidates omitted the overdraft when calculating net working capital, indicating unfamiliarity with the structure of the balance sheet.

Part (d) asked candidates to calculate the total cost of inventory using the economic order quantity model (EOQ) and to evaluate a discount offered by a supplier. Many candidates gained high marks here by offering a comprehensive answer. Candidates who did not gain high marks appeared to be unsure of the meaning of the variables in the EOQ, even though the units of each were clearly specified in the question.

---

12   PKA CO   *Walk in the footsteps of a top tutor*

Key answer tips

This question combines elements from throughout the working capital management area of the syllabus with the foreign currency risk section. It is a good reflection of the examiner's style. The highlighted words are key phrases that markers are looking for.

Tutor's top tips:

Within the 15 minutes reading time, you should have managed a detailed read of the requirement and perhaps a quick skim read of the scenario. This will have highlighted that the question is a good balance of words and calculations and that parts (a) & (c) give an opportunity to capture some easy marks. You should consider doing these sections first.

Tutor's top tips:

Part (a) covers two aspects; the objectives of working capital management and the conflicts between them. Use the requirement to help structure your answer by picking out words that can be used as sub-headings. Any discussion on working capital can be reduced to a balance between profitability and liquidity, these being the overriding objectives. You will need to give definitions for both before moving on to talk about how they might conflict. Giving examples can be an easy way to explain things and will make the topic come to life.

(a)   The objectives of working capital management are profitability and liquidity. The objective of profitability supports the primary financial management objective, which is shareholder wealth maximisation. The objective of liquidity ensures that companies are able to meet their liabilities as they fall due, and thus remain in business.

However, funds held in the form of cash do not earn a return, while near-liquid assets such as short-term investments earn only a small return. Meeting the objective of liquidity will therefore conflict with the objective of profitability, which is met by investing over the longer term in order to achieve higher returns.

Good working capital management therefore needs to achieve a balance between the objectives of profitability and liquidity if shareholder wealth is to be maximised.

Tutor's top tips:

Part (b) will require a bit more thought. This is a fairly common exam question but the complexity of it can change depending on the information given. Your starting point should be to work out the economic order quantity (EOQ). We're given the formula in the exam so it's really just a case of finding the three pieces of information required, all of which are clearly stated in the scenario. Having calculated the EOQ, you are now equipped to work out the relative costs of the current policy compared to a potential new policy based on the EOQ. You will need to calculate:

—   *Total order costs (using annual demand, order size and cost per order)*

—   *Total holding costs (using the cost of holding one unit and the average level of inventory)*

Four of these five things are given to us in the scenario or have already been calculated. The tricky one is the average level of inventory as we need to consider not only the size of the order but also the level of buffer stocks held. You would be forgiven for thinking the buffer stock is 35,000 units, however you would be wrong. Some of these units would in fact be used in the two weeks it takes for the order to arrive. The information provided on annual demand will enable us to calculated how many units would be used in those two weeks, from which we can work out the level of inventory just prior to the order being delivered. This is by far the trickiest part of this question and it's important to keep it in context. Had you not spotted this, you would only have lost 2 marks. Don't forget, the requirement asks for the saving – be sure that you specifically calculate this to get all the marks.

(b) **Cost of current ordering policy of PKA Co**

Ordering cost = €250 × (625,000/100,000) = €1,563 per year

Weekly demand = 625,000/50 = 12,500 units per week

Consumption during 2 weeks lead time = 12,500 × 2 = 25,000 units

Buffer stock = re-order level less usage during lead time = 35,000 − 25,000 = 10,000 units

Average stock held during the year = 10,000 + (100,000/2) = 60,000 units

Holding cost = 60,000 × €0.50 = €30,000 per year

Total cost = ordering cost plus holding cost = €1,563 + €30,000 = €31,563 per year

Economic order quantity = $((2 \times 250 \times 625{,}000)/0.5)_{1/2}$ = 25,000 units

Number of orders per year = 625,000/25,000 = 25 per year

Ordering cost = €250 × 25 = €6,250 per year

Holding cost (ignoring buffer stock) = €0.50 × (25,000/2) = €0.50 × 12,500 = €6,250 per year

Holding cost (including buffer stock) = €0.50 × (10,000 + 12,500) = €11,250 per year

Total cost of EOQ-based ordering policy = €6,250 + €11,250 = €17,500 per year

Saving for PKA Co by using EOQ-based ordering policy = €31,563 − €17,500 = €14,063 per year

---

Tutor's top tips:

A quick read of the scenario for accounts receivable management gives us some ideas for sub-headings to use to answer part (c); accounts receivable period and bad debts. For 7 marks you should be aiming for a couple of points under each heading.

(c) The information gathered by the Financial Manager of PKA Co indicates that two areas of concern in the management of domestic accounts receivable are the increasing level of bad debts as a percentage of credit sales and the excessive credit period being taken by credit customers.

Reducing bad debts

The incidence of bad debts, which has increased from 5% to 8% of credit sales in the last year, can be reduced by assessing the creditworthiness of new customers before offering them credit and PKA Co needs to introduce a policy detailing how this should be done, or review its existing policy, if it has one, since it is clearly not working very well. In order to do this, information about the solvency, character and credit history of new clients is needed. This information can come from a variety of sources, such as bank references, trade references and credit reports from credit reference agencies. Whether credit is offered to the new customer and the terms of the credit offered can then be based on an explicit and informed assessment of default risk.

Reduction of average accounts receivable period

Customers have taken an average of 75 days credit over the last year rather than the 30 days offered by PKA Co, i.e. more than twice the agreed credit period. As a result, PKA Co will be incurring a substantial opportunity cost, either from the additional interest cost on the short-term financing of accounts receivable or from the incremental profit lost by not investing the additional finance tied up by the longer average accounts receivable period. PKA Co needs to find ways to encourage accounts receivable to be settled closer to the agreed date.

Assuming that the credit period offered by PKA Co is in line with that of its competitors, the company should determine whether they too are suffering from similar difficulties with late payers. If they are not, PKA Co should determine in what way its own terms differ from those of its competitors and consider whether offering the same trade terms would have an impact on its accounts receivable. For example, its competitors may offer a discount for early settlement while PKA Co does not and introducing a discount may achieve the desired reduction in the average accounts receivable period. If its competitors are experiencing a similar accounts receivable problem, PKA Co could take the initiative by introducing more favourable early settlement terms and perhaps generate increased business as well as reducing the average accounts receivable period.

PKA Co should also investigate the efficiency with which accounts receivable are managed. Are statements sent regularly to customers? Is an aged accounts receivable analysis produced at the end of each month? Are outstanding accounts receivable contacted regularly to encourage payment? Is credit denied to any overdue accounts seeking further business? Is interest charged on overdue accounts? These are all matters that could be included by PKA Co in a revised policy on accounts receivable management.

Tutor's top tips:

Finally, in part (d), you must be very clear on the scenario before your start. PKA has a foreign supplier so to settle their debts, PKA will need to buy Dollars. If PKA is buying, the bank will be selling (remember the rhyme – the bank will always sell low (sounds like hello) and buy high (sounds like bye bye)!) We therefore know the appropriate spot rate is 1.998 – 0.002 = \$1.996:€ and the appropriate forward rate is 1.979 – 0.004 = \$1.975:€.

Once you're happy on which rates are to be used, you can calculate the Euros payable under the forward market hedge (don't let this term confuse you – it simply means a forward exchange contract) using the forward rate. You can also start the calculation for the lead payment using the spot rate. Finish this by thinking about the interest payable on the required loan. Since this is a Euro loan, you need half of the one year Euro borrowing rate.

Lastly, you can work on the money market hedge. Start by drawing out a diagram of the process, remembering the purpose is to eliminate the exchange risk by doing the translation now but then making sure that money continues to work for us by investing it in a Dollar bank account to earn interest.

(d)   **Money market hedge**

PKA Co should place sufficient dollars on deposit now so that, with accumulated interest, the six-month liability of $250,000 can be met. Since the company has no surplus cash at the present time, the cost of these dollars must be met by a short-term euro loan.

Six-month dollar deposit rate = 3.5/2 = 1.75%

Current spot selling rate = 1.998 – 0.002 = $1.996 per euro

Six-month euro borrowing rate = 6.1/2 = 3.05%

Dollars deposited now = 250,000/1.0175 = $245,700

Cost of these dollars at spot = 245,700/1.996 = 123,096 euros

Euro value of loan in six months' time = 123,096 × 1.0305 = 126,850 euros

Forward market hedge

Six months forward selling rate = 1.979 – 0.004 = $1.975 per euro

Euro cost using forward market hedge = 250,000/1.975 = 126,582 euros

Lead payment

Since the dollar is appreciating against the euro, a lead payment may be worthwhile.

Euro cost now = 250,000/1.996 = 125,251 euros

This cost must be met by a short-term loan at a six-month interest rate of 3.05%

Euro value of loan in six months' time = 125,251 × 1.0305 = 129,071 euros

Evaluation of hedges

The relative costs of the three hedges can be compared since they have been referenced to the same point in time, i.e. six months in the future. The most expensive hedge is the lead payment, while the cheapest is the forward market hedge. Using the forward market to hedge the account payable currency risk can therefore be recommended.

Tutor's top tips:

The key learning points from this question are the importance of doing the easy parts of the question first and making sure you maintain good time discipline to ensure you don't get bogged down in one part of the question at the expense of another part.

ACCA marking scheme

		Marks
(a)	Profitability and liquidity	1
	Discussion of conflict between objectives	2
		——
		3
		——
(b)	Cost of current ordering policy	3
	Cost of EOQ-based ordering policy	3
	Saving by using EOQ model	1
		——
		7
		——
(c)	Reduction of bad debts	3–4
	Reduction of average accounts receivable period	3–4
	Discussion of other improvements	1–2
		——
		7
		——
d)	Money market hedge	3
	Forward market hedge	2
	Lead payment	2
	Evaluation	1
		——
		8
Total		——
		25
		——

Examiner's comments

Part (a) of this question asked candidates to identify the objectives of working capital management and to discuss the conflict that might arise between them. There were many good answers here and most candidates gained high marks. However, some answers tended to be somewhat general rather than focussing on the objectives of working capital management and some answers were much too long for the three marks on offer.

In part (b) candidates were asked to calculate the cost of a company's current ordering policy and to determine the saving that could be made by using the economic order quantity (EOQ) model. Many candidates gained high marks for their answers to this part of

question 4, calculating correctly the ordering costs of both the current and the EOQ policies, and comparing the total costs of each policy to show the saving arising from adoption of the EOQ policy. Many of these comparisons, however, were based on incorrect calculations of the holding costs of each policy.

Some candidates failed to consider the buffer inventory in calculating holding costs. Others used the re-order inventory level as the buffer level, failing to reduce inventory by consumption during the lead time it took for orders to arrive after being placed. Others added the re-order level to order quantity before dividing by two to calculate average inventory level, when only the order quantity is averaged.

Part (c) required candidates to discuss the ways in which a company could improve the management of domestic accounts receivable and many gained full marks here. Candidates failing to gain high marks tended to offer a limited number of possible methods, for example by focussing at length on factoring to the exclusion of internal accounts receivables management methods. Despite the requirement to discuss domestic accounts receivable, some candidates discussed export factoring and exchange rate hedging.

In part (d) candidates were required to evaluate whether a money market hedge, a forward market hedge or a lead payment should be used to hedge a foreign account payable. Some candidates offered discursive answers, for which they gained little credit since the question asked for an evaluation of hedging methods.

Many candidates were unable to calculate correctly the spot and forward exchange rates from the information provided. Many candidates failed to compare all three hedges from a common time horizon perspective, i.e. either from the current time or from three months hence.

Since it was a foreign currency account payable that was being hedged (a liability), the money market hedge involved creating a foreign currency asset (a deposit). The hedging company therefore needed to borrow euros, exchange them into dollars and place these dollars on deposit. Some candidates offered the opposite hedge, i.e. borrowing dollars and exchanging them into euros.

13 ULNAD

Key answer tips

This question covers two of the key elements within the working capital management section of the syllabus. Part (a) requires a methodical approach, working though the impact of the proposed change. Part (b) is more straightforward given that the Miller Orr formula is provided in the exam; .don't neglect to explain the relevance of the values though. Parts (c) and (d) cover common discursive areas and should give an opportunity to just learn and churn. The highlighted words are key phrases that markers are looking for.

(a) **Evaluation of change in credit policy**

Current average collection period = 30 + 10 = 40 days

Current accounts receivable = 6m × 40/365 = $657,534

Average collection period under new policy = (0.3 × 15) + (0.7 × 60) = 46.5 days

New level of credit sales = $6.3 million

Accounts receivable after policy change = 6.3 × 46.5/ 365 = $802,603

Increase in financing cost = (802,603 − 657,534) × 0.07 = $10,155

	$
Increase in financing cost	10,155
Incremental costs = 6.3m × 0.005 =	31,500
Cost of discount = 6.3m × 0.015 × 0.3 =	28,350
Increase in costs	70,005
Contribution from increased sales = 6m × 0.05 × 0.6 =	180,000
Net benefit of policy change	109,995

The proposed policy change will increase the profitability of Ulnad Co

(b)   Determination of spread:

Daily interest rate = 5.11/ 365 = 0.014% per day

Variance of cash flows = 1,000 × 1,000 = $1,000,000 per day

Transaction cost = $18 per transaction

Spread   = 3 × ((0.75 × transaction cost × variance)/interest rate)$^{1/3}$
          = 3 × ((0.75 × 18 × 1,000,000)/0.00014)$^{1/3}$ = 3 × 4,585.7 = $13,757

Lower limit (set by Renpec Co) = $7,500

Upper limit = 7,500 + 13,757 =$21,257

Return point = 7,500 + (13,757/3) = $12,086

The Miller-Orr model takes account of uncertainty in relation to receipts and payment. The cash balance of Renpec Co is allowed to vary between the lower and upper limits calculated by the model. If the lower limit is reached, an amount of cash equal to the difference between the return point and the lower limit is raised by selling short-term investments. If the upper limit is reached an amount of cash equal to the difference between the upper limit and the return point is used to buy short-term investments. The model therefore helps Renpec Co to decrease the risk of running out of cash, while avoiding the loss of profit caused by having unnecessarily high cash balances.

(c)   There are four key areas of accounts receivable management: policy formulation, credit analysis, credit control and collection of amounts due.

Policy formulation

This is concerned with establishing the framework within which management of accounts receivable in an individual company takes place. The elements to be considered include establishing terms of trade, such as period of credit offered and early settlement discounts: deciding whether to charge interest on overdue accounts; determining procedures to be followed when granting credit to new customers; establishing procedures to be followed when accounts become overdue, and so on.

Credit analysis

Assessment of creditworthiness depends on the analysis of information relating to the new customer. This information is often generated by a third party and includes bank references, trade references and credit reference agency reports. The depth of credit analysis depends on the amount of credit being granted, as well as the possibility of repeat business.

Credit control

Once credit has been granted, it is important to review outstanding accounts on a regular basis so overdue accounts can be identified. This can be done, for example, by an aged receivables analysis. It is also important to ensure that administrative procedures are timely and robust, for example sending out invoices and statements of account, communicating with customers by telephone or e-mail, and maintaining account records.

Collection of amounts due

Ideally, all customers will settle within the agreed terms of trade. If this does not happen, a company needs to have in place agreed procedures for dealing with overdue accounts. These could cover logged telephone calls, personal visits, charging interest on outstanding amounts, refusing to grant further credit and, as a last resort, legal action. With any action, potential benefit should always exceed expected cost.

(d) When considering how working capital is financed, it is useful to divide assets into non-current assets, permanent current assets and fluctuating current assets. Permanent current assets represent the core level of working capital investment needed to support a given level of sales. As sales increase, this core level of working capital also increases. Fluctuating current assets represent the changes in working capital that arise in the normal course of business operations, for example when some accounts receivable are settled later than expected, or when inventory moves more slowly than planned.

The matching principle suggests that long-term finance should be used for long-term assets. Under a matching working capital funding policy, therefore, long-term finance is used for both permanent current assets and non-current assets. Short-term finance is used to cover the short-term changes in current assets represented by fluctuating current assets.

Long-term debt has a higher cost than short-term debt in normal circumstances, for example because lenders require higher compensation for lending for longer periods, or because the risk of default increases with longer lending periods. However, long-term debt is more secure from a company point of view than short-term debt since, provided interest payments are made when due and the requirements of restrictive covenants are met, terms are fixed to maturity. Short-term debt is riskier than long-term debt because, for example, an overdraft is repayable on demand and short-term debt may be renewed on less favourable terms.

A conservative working capital funding policy will use a higher proportion of long-term finance than a matching policy, thereby financing some of the fluctuating current assets from a long-term source. This will be less risky and less profitable than a matching policy, and will give rise to occasional short-term cash surpluses.

An aggressive working capital funding policy will use a lower proportion of long-term finance than a matching policy, financing some of the permanent current assets from a short-term source such as an overdraft. This will be more risky and more profitable than a matching policy.

Other factors that influence a working capital funding policy include management attitudes to risk, previous funding decisions, and organisation size. Management attitudes to risk will determine whether there is a preference for a conservative, an aggressive or a matching approach. Previous funding decisions will determine the current position being considered in policy formulation. The size of the organisation will influence its ability to access different sources of finance. A small company, for example, may be forced to adopt an aggressive working capital funding policy because it is unable to raise additional long-term finance, whether equity of debt.

ACCA marking scheme			
			Marks
(a)	Increase in financing cost	2 marks	
	Incremental costs	1 mark	
	Cost of discount	1 mark	
	Contribution from increased sales	1 mark	
	Conclusion	1 mark	
			6
(b)	Calculation of spread	2 marks	
	Calculation of upper limit	1 mark	
	Calculation of return point	1 mark	
	Explanation of findings	2 marks	
			6
(c)	Policy formulation	1–2 marks	
	Credit analysis	1–2 marks	
	Credit control	1–2 marks	
	Collection of amounts due	1–2 marks	
	Maximum		6
(d)	Analysis of assets	1–2 marks	
	Short-term and long-term debt	2–3 marks	
	Discussion of policies	2–3 marks	
	Other factors	1–2 marks	
	Maximum		7
			——
Total			25
			——

14 APX CO

Key answer tips

This question approaches the topic of working capital management from a less frequently examined angle; providing a series of accounting ratios and asking students to work back to a forecast income statement and statement of financial position. What makes this question tough is that parts (c) and (d) cannot be attempted without some stab at an answer to part (b). This means there are very few obvious "easy" marks on this question. The highlighted words are key phrases that markers are looking for.

(a) The role of financial intermediaries in providing short-term finance for use by business organisations is to provide a link between investors who have surplus cash and borrowers who have financing needs. The amounts of cash provided by individual investors may be small, whereas borrowers need large amounts of cash: one of the functions of financial intermediaries is therefore to aggregate invested funds in order to meet the needs of borrowers. In so doing, they provide a convenient and readily accessible route for business organisations to obtain necessary funds.

Small investors are likely to be averse to losing any capital value, so financial intermediaries will assume the risk of loss on short-term funds borrowed by business organisations, either individually or by pooling risks between financial intermediaries. This aspect of the role of financial intermediaries is referred to as risk transformation. Financial intermediaries also offer maturity transformation, in that investors can deposit funds for a long period of time while borrowers may require funds on a short-term basis only, and vice versa. In this way the needs of both borrowers and lenders can be satisfied.

(b)   **Forecast income statement**

	$m
Turnover = 16.00m × 1.084 =	17.344
Cost of sales = 17.344m – 5.203m =	12.141
Gross profit = 17.344m × 30% =	5.203
Other expenses = 5.203m – 3.469m =	1.734
Net profit = 17.344m × 20% =	3.469
Interest = (10m × 0.08) + 0.140m =	0.940
Profit before tax	2.529
Tax = 2.529m × 0.3 =	0.759
Profit after tax	1.770
Dividends = 1.770m × 50% =	0.885
Retained profit	0.885

Tutor's top tips:

The best way to approach this part of the requirement is to work through the income statement and statement of financial position line by line, recognising that the overdraft will be your balancing figure.

Forecast statement of financial position

	$m	$m
Non-current assets		22.00
Current assets		
Inventory	3.66	
Trade receivables	3.09	
		6.75
Total assets		28.75
Equity finance:		
Ordinary shares	5.00	
Reserves	8.39	
		13.39
Bank loan		10.00
		23.39
Current liabilities		
Trade payables	2.49	
Overdraft	2.87	
		5.36
Total liabilities		28.75

Workings

Inventory = 12.141m × (110/365) = $3.66m

Trade receivables = 17.344m × (65/365) = $3.09m

Trade payables = 12.141m × (75/365) = $2.49m

Reserves = 7.5m + 0.885m = $8.39m

Overdraft = 28.75m − 23.39m − 2.49 = $2.87m (balancing figure)

(c) Working capital financing policies can be classified into conservative, moderate (or matching) and aggressive, depending on the extent to which fluctuating current assets and permanent current assets are financed by short-term sources of finance. Permanent current assets are the core level of investment in current assets needed to support a given level of business activity or turnover, while fluctuating current assets are the changes in the levels of current assets arising from the unpredictable nature of some aspects of business activity.

A conservative working capital financing policy uses long-term funds to finance non-current assets and permanent current assets, as well as a proportion of fluctuating current assets. This policy is less risky and less profitable than an aggressive working capital financing policy, which uses short-term funds to finance fluctuating current assets and a proportion of permanent current assets as well. Between these two extremes lies the moderate (or matching) policy, which uses long-term funds to finance long-term assets (non-current assets and permanent current assets) and short-term funds to finance short-term assets (fluctuating current assets).

The current statement of financial position shows that APX Co uses trade payables and an overdraft as sources of short-term finance. In terms of the balance between short- and long-term finance, 89% of current assets (100 × 4.1/4.6) are financed from short-term sources and only 11% are financed from long-term sources. Since a high proportion of current assets are permanent in nature, this appears to be a very aggressive working capital financing policy which carries significant risk. If the overdraft were called in, for example, APX Co might have to turn to more expensive short-term financing.

The forecast statement of financial position shows a lower reliance on short-term finance, since 79% of current assets (100 × 5.36/6.75) are financed from short-term sources and 21% are financed from long-term sources. This decreased reliance on an aggressive financing policy is sensible, although with a forecast interest coverage ratio of only 3.7 times (3.469/0.94), APX Co has little scope for taking on more long-term debt. An increase in equity funding to decrease reliance on short-term finance could be considered.

(d) **Working capital management**

Financial analysis shows deterioration in key working capital ratios. The inventory turnover period is expected to increase from 81 days to 110 days, the trade receivables period is expected to increase from 50 days to 65 days and the trade payables period is expected to increase from 64 days to 75 days. It is also a cause for concern here that the values of these working capital ratios for the next year are forecast, i.e. APX Co appears to be anticipating a worsening in its working capital position. The current and forecast values could be compared to average or sector values in order to confirm whether this is in fact the case.

Because current assets are expected to increase by more than current liabilities, the current ratio and the quick ratio are both expected to increase in the next year, the current ratio from 1.12 times to 1.26 times and the quick ratio from 0.54 times to 0.58 times. Again, comparison with sector average values for these ratios would be useful in making an assessment of the working capital management of APX Co. The balance between trade payables and overdraft finance is approximately the same in both years (trade payables are 46% of current liabilities in the current statement of financial position and 47% of current liabilities in the forecast statement of financial position), although reliance on short-term finance is expected to fall slightly in the next year.

The deteriorating working capital position may be linked to an expected deterioration in the overall financial performance of APX Co. For example, the forecast gross profit margin (30%) and net profit margin (20%) are both less than the current values of these ratios (32% and 23% respectively), and despite the increase in turnover, return on capital employed (ROCE) is expected to fall from 16.35% to 14.83%.

Analysis

Extracts from current income statement:

	$m
Turnover	16.00
Cost of sales	10.88
Gross profit	5.12
Other expenses	1.44
Net profit	3.68

	Current	Forecast
Gross profit margin (100 × 5.12/16.00)	32%	
		30%
Net profit margin (100 × 3.68/16.00)	23%	
		20%
ROCE (100 × 3.68/22.5)	16.35%	
(100 × 3.469/23.39)		14.83%
Inventory period (365 × 2.4/10.88)	81 days	
		110 days
Receivables period (365 × 2.2/16.00)	50 days	
		65 days
Payables period (365 × 1.9/10.88)	64 days	
		75 days
Current ratio (4.6/4.1)	1.12 times	
(6.75/5.36)		1.26 times
Quick ratio (2.2/4.1)	0.54 times	
(3.09/5.36)		0.58 times

	ACCA marking scheme		
			Marks
(a)	Relevant discussion on financial intermediaries		4.0
			───
		Maximum	4.0
			───
(b)	Gross profit		1.0
	Net profit		1.0
	Profit before tax		1.0
	Retained profit		1.0
	Inventory		1.0
	Trade receivables		1.0
	Trade payables		1.0
	Reserves		1.0
	Overdraft		1.0
	Layout and format		1.0
			───
		Maximum	9.0
			───
(c)	Working capital financing policies		2–3
	Financial analysis		1–2
	Working capital financing policy of company		2–3
			───
		Maximum	6.0
			───
(d)	Discussion of working capital management		3–4
	Financial analysis		2–4
			───
		Maximum	6.0
			───
Total			25
			───

Examiner's comments

Candidates often gained high marks in part (b) of this question, but answers to part (a) were usually of a poor standard, while answers to parts (c) and (d) lacked focus.

Part (a) asked candidates to discuss the role of financial intermediaries in providing short-term finance for business organisations. Better answers discussed providing a link between investors and borrowers, aggregation of invested funds, maturity transformation and risk transformation.

Rather than discussing the role of financial intermediaries, weaker answers tended to discuss short-term sources of finance (products) and the range and type of financial intermediaries (providers).

Part (b) required candidates to prepare a forecast income statement and a forecast statement of financial position. Many answers were of a very good standard and gained full marks.

Some candidates ignored the forecast financial ratios and applied the expected turnover growth rate to cost of sales and other expenses. Other candidates showed a lack of knowledge of the structure of the income statement by calculating the tax liability before subtracting the interest payments. Candidates should recognise that a good understanding of accounting ratios is needed if they expect to achieve a pass standard and they are advised to study the suggested answer carefully in comparison to the question set in the question paper.

Part (c) asked for an analysis and discussion of the working capital financing policy of the company in the question. Many students were not aware of the conservative, aggressive and matching approaches to working capital financing policy, and so were ill-prepared for this question.

Analysis of the statement of financial position shows that 89% of the current assets of the company are financed from a short-term source, while only 11% are financed from a long-term source. Noting this, good answers discussed the aggressive nature of the company's working capital financing policy and the risks to which it gave rise.

Weaker answers discussed conservative and aggressive approaches to the level of investment in working capital, or focused on the cash conversion cycle (operating cycle) of the company, or combined part (c) with part (d).

Part (d) asked for a discussion of the forecast financial performance of the company in terms of working capital management. Comparing the current position with the forecast position showed that a deterioration in financial performance was expected. Better answers recognised this and made appropriate comments. Weaker answers failed to focus on working capital ratios (for example by calculating and discussing ratios such as interest coverage, debt/equity ratio and dividend per share), or offered only general discussions of areas of working capital management (such as explaining ways in which inventory control or credit management could be improved).

15 HGR CO

Key answer tips

The generic requirement of part (a), to "discuss the working capital financing strategy of HGR" can result in a lack of direction and focus in your answer. This sort of question highlights the importance of good exam preparation that includes sitting as many past exam questions as possible as requirements such as this are not unusual.

Part (b) may overwhelm some students as the initial perception is that many calculations need to be made. However, this is not the case. Part (i) (for 2 marks) involves simply plugging in the numbers provided before doing a quick calculation of overdraft interest. In part (ii), (for 5 marks) you need to evaluate the impact of the finance director's proposals surrounding both accounts receivable and inventory management. Both calculations involve a manipulation of the standard working capital cycle formulae that students should be familiar, although this might not be obvious to some students. The model answer shows the most efficient way of laying out the answer. Of the 10 marks available for part (b), up to 4 are available for commenting on the forecast position and making suitable recommendations. This could easily be overlooked if you're not careful.

Finally, part (c) gives a good opportunity to pick up some easier marks. This part of the question should be attempted first. The highlighted words are key phrases that markers are looking for.

(a) When considering the financing of working capital, it is useful to divide current assets into fluctuating current assets and permanent current assets. Fluctuating current assets represent changes in the level of current assets due to the unpredictability of business activity. Permanent current assets represent the core level of investment in current assets needed to support a given level of turnover or business activity. As turnover or level of business activity increases, the level of permanent current assets will also increase. This relationship can be measured by the ratio of turnover to net current assets.

The financing choice as far as working capital is concerned is between short-term and long-term finance. Short-term finance is more flexible than long-term finance: an overdraft, for example, is used by a business organisation as the need arises and variable interest is charged on the outstanding balance. Short-term finance is also more risky than long-term finance: an overdraft facility may be withdrawn, or a short-term loan may be renewed on less favourable terms. In terms of cost, the term structure of interest rates suggests that short-term debt finance has a lower cost than long-term debt finance.

The matching principle suggests that long-term finance should be used for long-term investment. Applying this principle to working capital financing, long-term finance should be matched with permanent current assets and non-current assets. A financing policy with this objective is called a 'matching policy'. HGR Co is not using this financing policy, since of the $16,935,000 of current assets, $14,000,000 or 83% is financed from short-term sources (overdraft and trade payables) and only $2,935,000 or 17% is financed from a long-term source, in this case equity finance (shareholders' funds) or traded bonds.

The financing policy or approach taken by HGR Co towards the financing of working capital, where short-term finance is preferred, is called an aggressive policy. Reliance on short-term finance makes this riskier than a matching approach, but also more profitable due to the lower cost of short-term finance. Following an aggressive approach to financing can lead to overtrading (undercapitalisation) and the possibility of liquidity problems.

(b) Bank balance in three months' time if no action is taken:

Month	1	2	3
	$000	$000	$000
Receipts	4,220	4,350	3,808
Payments	(3,950)	(4,100)	(3,750)
Interest on bonds		(200)	
Overdraft interest	(19)	(18)	(18)
Capital investment			(2,000)
	___	___	___
Net cash flow	251	32	(1,960)
Opening balance	(3,800)	(3,549)	(3,517)
	___	___	___
Closing balance	(3,549)	(3,517)	(5,477)

Bank balance in three months' time if the finance director's proposals are implemented:

Month	1	2	3
	$000	$000	$000
Receipts	4,220	4,350	3,808
Payments	(3,950)	(4,100)	(3,750)
Interest on bonds		(200)	
Overdraft interest	(19)	(15)	(13)
Capital investment			(2,000)
Accounts receivable	270	270	270
Inventory	204	204	204
	———	———	———
Net cash flow	725	509	(1,481)
Opening balance	(3,800)	(3,075)	(2,566)
	———	———	———
Closing balance	(3,075)	(2,566)	(4,047)
	———	———	———

Workings:

Reduction in accounts receivable days

Current accounts receivable days = (8,775/49,275) × 365 = 65 days

Reduction in days over six months = 65 – 53 = 12 days

Monthly reduction = 12/6 = 2 days

Each receivables day is equivalent to 8,775,000/65 =$135,000 (Alternatively, each receivables day is equivalent to 49,275,000/365 =$135,000)

Monthly reduction in accounts receivable = 2 × 135,000 = $270,000

Reduction in inventory days

Current inventory days = (8,160/37,230) × 365 = 80 days

Each inventory day is equivalent to 8,160,000/80 = $102,000 (Alternatively, each inventory day = 37,230,000/365 = $102,000)

Monthly reduction in inventory = 102,000 × 2 = $204,000

Overdraft interest calculations

Monthly overdraft interest rate = 1.06171/12 = 1.005 or 0.5%

If no action is taken:

Period 1 interest = 3,800,000 × 0.005 = $19,000

Period 2 interest = 3,549,000 × 0.005 = $17,745 or $18,000

Period 3 interest = 3,517,000 × 0.005 = $17,585 or $18,000

If action is taken:

Period 1 interest = 3,800,000 × 0.005 = $19,000

Period 2 interest = 3,075,000 × 0.005 = $15,375 or $15,000

Period 3 interest = 2,566,000 × 0.005 = $12,830 or $13,000

Discussion

If no action is taken, the cash flow forecast shows that HGR Co will exceed its overdraft limit of $4 million by $1.48 million in three months' time. If the finance director's proposals are implemented, there is a positive effect on the bank balance, but the overdraft limit is still exceeded in three months' time, although only by $47,000 rather than by $1.47 million.

In each of the three months following that, the continuing reduction in accounts receivable days will improve the bank balance by $270,000 per month. Without further information on operating receipts and payments, it cannot be forecast whether the bank balance will return to less than the limit, or even continue to improve.

The main reason for the problem with the bank balance is the $2 million capital expenditure. Purchase of non-current assets should not be financed by an overdraft, but a long-term source of finance such as equity or bonds. If the capital expenditure were removed from the area of working capital management, the overdraft balance at the end of three months would be $3.48 million if no action were taken and $2.05 million if the finance director's proposals were implemented. Given that HGR Co has almost $50 million of non-current assets that could possibly be used as security, raising long-term debt through either a bank loan or a bond issue appears to be sensible. Assuming a bond interest rate of 10% per year, current long-term debt in the form of traded bonds is approximately ($200m × 2)/0.1 = $4m, which is much less than the amount of noncurrent assets.

A suitable course of action for HGR Co to follow would therefore be, firstly, to implement the finance director's proposals and, secondly, to finance the capital expenditure from a long-term source. Consideration could also be given to using some long-term debt finance to reduce the overdraft and to reduce the level of accounts payable, currently standing at 100 days.

(c) When credit is granted to foreign customers, two problems may become especially significant. First, the longer distances over which trade takes place and the more complex nature of trade transactions and their elements means foreign accounts receivable need more investment than their domestic counterparts. Longer transaction times increase accounts receivable balances and hence the level of financing and financing costs. Second, the risk of bad debts is higher with foreign accounts receivable than with their domestic counterparts. In order to manage and reduce credit risks, therefore, exporters seek to reduce the risk of bad debt and to reduce the level of investment in foreign accounts receivable.

Many foreign transactions are on 'open account', which is an agreement to settle the amount outstanding on a predetermined date. Open account reflects a good business relationship between importer and exporter. It also carries the highest risk of non-payment.

One way to reduce investment in foreign accounts receivable is to agree early payment with an importer, for example by payment in advance, payment on shipment, or cash on delivery. These terms of trade are unlikely to be competitive, however, and it is more likely that an exporter will seek to receive cash in advance of payment being made by the customer.

One way to accelerate cash receipts is to use bill finance. Bills of exchange with a signed agreement to pay the exporter on an agreed future date, supported by a documentary letter of credit, can be discounted by a bank to give immediate funds.

This discounting is without recourse if bills of exchange have been countersigned by the importer's bank.

Documentary letters of credit are a payment guarantee backed by one or more banks. They carry almost no risk, provided the exporter complies with the terms and conditions contained in the letter of credit. The exporter must present the documents stated in the letter, such as bills of lading, shipping documents, bills of exchange, and so on, when seeking payment. As each supporting document relates to a key aspect of the overall transaction, letters of credit give security to the importer as well as the exporter.

Companies can also manage and reduce risk by gathering appropriate information with which to assess the creditworthiness of new customers, such as bank references and credit reports.

Insurance can also be used to cover some of the risks associated with giving credit to foreign customers. This would avoid the cost of seeking to recover cash due from foreign accounts receivable through a foreign legal system, where the exporter could be at a disadvantage due to a lack of local or specialist knowledge.

Export factoring can also be considered, where the exporter pays for the specialist expertise of the factor as a way of reducing investment in foreign accounts receivable and reducing the incidence of bad debts.

ACCA marking scheme			
			Marks
(a)	Analysis of current assets	1 – 2	
	Short-term and long-term finance	2 – 3	
	Matching principle	1 – 2	
	Financing approach used by company	1 – 2	
		Maximum	7
(b)	Bank balance if no action is taken	2	
	Bank balance if action is taken	5	
	Working capital management implications	1 – 2	
	Advice on course of action	1 – 2	
		Maximum	10
(c)	Relevant discussion		8
Total			25

Examiner's comments

Part (a) required candidates to discuss the working capital financing strategy of a company. Some candidates ignored the word 'financing' and discussed working capital strategy in general. Other candidates took 'working capital financing strategy' to mean the proposals in the question to reduce the level of account receivables and inventory by operational improvements.

The question gave extracts from a statement of financial position which showed that the company was financing 83% of its current assets from short-term sources, namely a bank overdraft and trade receivables. This is an aggressive rather than a conservative financing strategy and better answers recognised this, discussing how current assets could be divided into fluctuating and permanent current assets, and linking this analysis of current assets via the matching principle to the use of short-term and long-term finance.

Part (b) asked candidates to calculate the bank balance in three months' time if no action were taken, and if the proposals were implemented. Many candidates had great difficulty in rolling forward the current cash balance (the overdraft of $3.8 million) using the receipts and payments given in the question, while allowing for one month's interest on the balance of the account at the start of each month. Common errors included failing to recognise that the opening balance was the overdraft and therefore having no opening balance: calculating annual interest rather than monthly interest; and including cash flows other

than those given in the question (for example from the credit sales and cost of sales figures given in the question). All candidates are expected to be able to prepare cash flow forecasts and the general standard of answers to this question showed that many candidates need further preparation in this important area.

Part (c) required candidates to discuss how risks arising from granting credit to foreign customers could be managed and reduced. Many candidates gave answers of a good standard, although some answers were one-sided, concentrating on exchange rate risk rather than on credit risk. Since the question referred to foreign customers, it was inappropriate to limit answers to a discussion of domestic receivables management.

16   ANJO

Key answer tips

This is a fairly straightforward question with some easier written marks within part (c). Tackle these first to ensure you give yourself the most amount of time for the calculations. The highlighted words are key phrases that markers are looking for.

(a)   **Calculation of ratios**

Inventory days	20X6:	(3,000/9,300) × 365	= 118 days
	20X5:	(1,300/6,600) × 365	= 72 days
		Sector average: 90 days	
Receivables days	20X6:	(3,800/15,600) × 365	= 89 days
	20X5:	(1,850/11,100) × 365	= 61 days
		Sector average: 60 days	
Payables days	20X6:	(2,870/9,300 × 0.95) × 365	= 119 days
	20X5:	(1,600/6,600 × 0.95) × 365	= 93 days
		Sector average: 80 days	

In each case, the ratio in 20X6 is higher than the ratio in 20X5, indicating that deterioration has occurred in the management of inventories, receivables and payables in 20X6.

Inventory days have increased by 46 days or 64%, moving from below the sector average to 28 days – one month – more than it. Given the rapid increase in sales revenue (40%) in 20X6, Anjo Inc may be expecting a continuing increase in the future and may have built up inventories in preparation for this, i.e. inventory levels reflect future sales rather than past sales. Accounting statements from several previous years and sales forecasts for the next period would help to clarify this point.

Receivables days have increased by 28 days or 46% in 20X6 and are now 29 days above the sector average. It is possible that more generous credit terms have been offered in order to stimulate sales. The increased sales revenue does not appear to be due to offering lower prices, since both gross profit margin (40%) and net profit margin (34%) are unchanged.

In 20X5, only management of payables was a cause for concern, with Anjo Inc taking 13 more days on average to settle liabilities with trade payables than the sector. This has increased to 39 days more than the sector in 20X6. This could lead to difficulties between the company and its suppliers if it is exceeding the credit periods they have specified. Anjo Inc has no long-term debt and the balance sheet (statement of financial position) indicates an increased reliance on short-term finance, since cash has reduced by $780,000 or 87% and the overdraft has increased by $850,000 to $1 million.

Perhaps the company should investigate whether it is undercapitalised (overtrading). It is unusual for a company of this size to have no long-term debt.

(b) Cash operating cycle (20X5) = 72 + 61 − 93 = 40 days

Cash operating cycle (20X6) = 118 + 89 − 119 = 88 days

The cash operating cycle or working capital cycle gives the average time it takes for the company to receive payment from receivables after it has paid its trade payables. This represents the period of time for which payables require financing. The cash operating cycle of Anjo Inc has lengthened by 48 days in 20X6 compared with 20X5. This represents an increase in working capital requirement of approximately $15,600,000 × 48/365 = $2.05 million.

(c) Just-in-time (JIT) inventory management methods seek to eliminate any waste that arises in the manufacturing process as a result of using inventory. JIT purchasing methods apply the JIT principle to deliveries of material from suppliers. With JIT production methods, inventory levels of raw materials, work-in-progress and finished goods are reduced to a minimum or eliminated altogether by improved work-flow planning and closer relationships with suppliers.

Advantages

- JIT inventory management methods seek to eliminate waste at all stages of the manufacturing process by minimising or eliminating stock, defects, breakdowns and production delays. This is achieved by improved workflow planning, an emphasis on quality control and firm contracts between buyer and supplier.

- One advantage of JIT inventory management methods is a stronger relationship between buyer and supplier. This offers security to the supplier, who benefits from regular orders, continuing future business and more certain production planning. The buyer benefits from lower inventory holding costs, lower investment in inventory and work in progress, and the transfer of inventory management problems to the supplier. The buyer may also benefit from bulk purchase discounts or lower purchase costs.

- The emphasis on quality control in the production process reduces scrap, reworking and set-up costs, while improved production design can reduce or even eliminate unnecessary material movements. The result is a smooth flow of material and work through the production system, with no queues or idle time.

Disadvantages

- A JIT system may not run as smoothly in practice as theory may predict, since there may be little room for manoeuvre in the event of unforeseen delays. There is little room for error, for example, on delivery times.

- The buyer is also dependent on the supplier for maintaining the quality of delivered materials and components. If delivered quality is not up to the required standard, expensive downtime or a production standstill may arise, although the buyer can protect against this eventuality by including guarantees and penalties in to the supplier's contract. If the supplier increases prices, the buyer may find that it is not easy to find an alternative supplier who is able, at short notice, to meet his needs.

(d)

	$000
Current receivables =	3,800
Receivables under factor = 3,800 × 0.7 =	2,660
	———
Reduction in receivables =	1,140
	———

	$000
Finance cost saving = 1,140 × 0.08 =	91.2
Administration cost saving = 1,000 × 0.02 =	20.0
Interest on advance = 2,660 × 0.8 × 0.01 =	(21.3)
Factor's annual fee = 15,600 × 0.005 =	(78.0)
	———
Net benefit of accepting factor's offer	11.9
	———

Although the terms of the factor's offer are financially acceptable, suggesting a net financial benefit of $11,900, this benefit is small compared with annual sales revenue of $15.6 million. Other benefits, such as the application of the factor's expertise to the receivables management of Anjo Inc, might also be influential in the decision on whether to accept the offer.

17 ZSE CO

Key answer tips

This question combines the key area of working capital management with the slightly less examined area of probability analysis and expected values. The calculations required in part (a) are fairly straightforward. However, the unusual combination of these two syllabus areas may confuse some students. Parts (b) and (c) require a 'learn and churn' type discussion so students should feel more comfortable with this. The highlighted words are key phrases that markers are looking for.

(a) (i) **Period 1 closing balance**

Opening balance	Cash flow	Closing balance	Probability	Expected value
$000	$000	$000	$000	$000
(500)	8,000	7,500	0.1	750
(500)	4,000	3,500	0.6	2,100
(500)	(2,000)	(2,500)	0.3	(750)
				————
				2,100
				————

The expected value of the period 1 closing balance is $2,100,000

Tutorial note:

An alternative approach to this part of the question is to calculate the expected value of the cash flow in period 1, and then add this to the opening balance. This could be achieved as follows:

(8,000 × 0.1) + (4,000 × 0.6) – (2,000 × 0.3) = 2,600

(500) + 2,600 = $2,100k

(ii) **Period 2 closing balance**

Period 1 closing balance	Probability	Period 2 cash flow	Probability	Period 2 closing balance	Joint probability	Expected value
$000		$000		$000		$000
7,500	0.1	7,000	0.3	14,500	0.03	435
		3,000	0.5	10,500	0.05	525
		(9,000)	0.2	(1,500)	0.02	(30)
3,500	0·6	7,000	0.3	10,500	0.18	1,890
		3,000	0.5	6,500	0.30	1,950
		(9,000)	0.2	(5,500)	0.12	(660)
(2,500)	0·3	7,000	0.3	4,500	0.09	405
		3,000	0.5	500	0.15	75
		(9,000)	0.2	(11,500)	0.06	(690)
						————
						3,900
						————

The expected value of the period 2 closing balance is $3,900,000

(iii)

Tutorial note:

The key to answering parts (iii) and (iv) is to consider the net effect of the flows. For part (iii), if the period 2 cash flow was ($9,000,000) then it wouldn't matter what the period 1 cash flow was, the balance would be negative at the end of period 2. With any of the other two possibilities, the balance would be positive, regardless of what cash flow arose in period 1. The answer is therefore the probability of the $9,000,000 cash outflow in period 2 which is 20%.

For part (iv), the same thought process can be used, except this time you're not looking at whether the balance is above or below zero; your benchmark changes to the overdraft limit of $2m.

The probability of a negative cash balance at the end of period 2 = 0.02 + 0.12 + 0.06 = 20%

(iv)   The probability of exceeding the overdraft limit in period 2 is 0.12 + 0.06 = 18%

Tutor's top tips:

Ensure you cover off all parts of the requirement. In part (a) it is easy to drop marks by failing to discuss whether your analysis can assist the company in managing its cash flows.

Discussion

The expected value analysis has shown that, on an average basis, ZSE Co will have a positive cash balance at the end of period 1 of $2.1 million and a positive cash balance at the end of period 2 of $3.9 million. However, the cash balances that are expected to occur are the specific balances that have been averaged, rather than the average values themselves.

There could be serious consequences for ZSE Co if it exceeds its overdraft limit. For example, the overdraft facility could be withdrawn. There is a 30% chance that the overdraft limit will be exceeded in period 1 and a lower probability, 18%, that the overdraft limit will be exceeded in period 2. To guard against exceeding its overdraft limit in period 1, ZSE Co must find additional finance of $0.5 million ($2.5m − $2.0m). However, to guard against exceeding its overdraft limit in period 2, the company could need up to $9.5 million ($11.5m − $2.0m). Renegotiating the overdraft limit in period 1 would therefore be only a short-term solution.

One strategy is to find now additional finance of $0.5 million and then to re-evaluate the cash flow forecasts at the end of period 1. If the most likely outcome occurs in period 1, the need for additional finance in period 2 to guard against exceeding the overdraft limit is much lower.

The expected value analysis has been useful in illustrating the cash flow risks faced by ZSE Co. Although the cash flow forecasting model has been built with the aid of a firm of financial consultants, the assumptions used in the model must be reviewed before decisions are made based on the forecast cash flows and their associated probabilities.

Expected values are more useful for repeat decisions rather than one-off activities, as they are based on averages. They illustrate what the average outcome would be if an activity was repeated a large number of times. In fact, each period and its cash flows will occur only once and the expected values of the closing balances are not closing balances that are forecast to arise in practice. In period 1, for example, the expected value closing balance of $2.1 million is not forecast to occur, while a closing balance of $3.5 million is likely to occur.

(b)   The factors to be considered in formulating a policy to manage the trade receivables of ZSE Co will relate to the key areas of credit assessment or analysis, credit control and collection procedures. A key factor is the turbulence in the company's business environment and the way it affects the company's customers.

Credit analysis

The main objective of credit analysis is to ensure that credit is granted to customers who will settle their account at regular intervals in accordance with the agreed terms of sale. The risk of bad debts must be minimised as much as possible.

Key factors to consider here are the source and quality of the information used by ZSE Co to assess customer creditworthiness. The information sources could include bank references, trade references, public information such as published accounts, credit reference agencies and personal experience. The quality of the information needs to be confirmed as part of the credit analysis process. Some organisations have developed credit scoring systems to assist in the assessment of creditworthiness.

Credit control

Once credit has been granted, it is essential to ensure that agreed terms and conditions are adhered to while the credit is outstanding. This can be achieved by careful monitoring of customer accounts and the periodic preparation of aged debtor analyses. A key factor here is the quality of the staff involved with credit control and the systems and procedures they use to maintain regular contact with customers, for example invoices, statements, reminders, letters and telephone contacts.

ZSE Co has been experiencing difficulties in collecting amounts due because its customers have been experiencing difficult trading conditions. Close contact with customers is essential here in order to determine where revised terms can be negotiated when payment is proving hard, and perhaps to provide advance warning of serious customer liquidity or going concern problems.

Collection procedures

The objective here is to ensure timely and secure transfer of funds when they are due, whether by physical means or by electronic means. A key factor here is the need to ensure that the terms of trade are clearly understood by the customer from the point at which credit is granted. Offering credit represents a cost to the seller and ensuring that payment occurs as agreed prevents this cost from exceeding budgeted expectations.

Procedures for chasing late payers should be clearly formulated and trained personnel must be made responsible for ensuring that these procedures are followed. Legal action should only be considered as a last resort, since it often represents the termination of the business relationship with a customer.

(c) Profitability and liquidity are usually cited as the twin objectives of working capital management. The profitability objective reflects the primary financial management objective of maximising shareholder wealth, while liquidity is needed in order to ensure that financial claims on an organisation can be settled as they become liable for payment.

The two objectives are in conflict because liquid assets such as bank accounts earn very little return or no return, so liquid assets decrease profitability. Liquid assets in fact incur an opportunity cost equivalent either to the cost of short-term finance or to the profit lost by not investing in profitable projects.

Whether profitability is a more important objective than liquidity depends in part on the particular circumstances of an organisation. Liquidity may be the more important objective when short-term finance is hard to find, while profitability may become a more important objective when cash management has become too conservative. In short, both objectives are important and neither can be neglected.

ACCA marking scheme		
		Marks
(a)	Expected value of period 1 closing balance	2
	Expected value of period 2 closing balance	5
	Probability of negative cash balance	1
	Probability of exceeding overdraft limit	2
	Discussion of expected value analysis	3
	Maximum	13
(b)	Credit analysis	2–3
	Credit control	2–3
	Collection procedures	2–3
	Maximum	8
(c)	Relevant discussion	4
Total		25

Examiner's comments

This part (a) required candidates to calculate expected values and probabilities from data given in the question, and to discuss the usefulness of expected value analysis.

A number of candidates lost marks by calculating the expected values of the cash flows for period 1 and period 2, but not calculating the closing balances for period 1 and period 2, which is what the question had asked for. There is clearly a difference between cash flow and closing balance.

Candidates were expected to calculate the closing balances using a probability table approach, but many candidates calculated the closing balances using an average cash flow approach. While this provided correct values for the closing balances and hence was given full credit, it did not help with calculating the probability of a negative closing balance in period 2, and it did not help with calculating the probability of exceeding the overdraft limit at the end of period 2. Many candidates were unable to calculate these probabilities because they did appreciate the importance of the joint probabilities used in a probability table.

Candidates were then asked to discuss whether the expected value analysis could assist the company to manage its cash flows. Many candidates tended to discuss ways in which the company could manage cash flows in general, even in some cases discussing cash management models, rather than discussing the usefulness of an expected value analysis. Better answers discussed the benefits and limitations of the analysis that had been undertaken.

In part (b), candidates were asked to identify and discuss factors relevant to formulating a trade receivables management policy. While many candidates gained good marks here, there was a very strong tendency for answers to be framed around lists of ways of improving trade receivables management (a question that has been asked in the past), rather than around factors influencing trade receivables policy. Fortunately, a strong relationship exists between the two areas, and it was possible to give credit for knowledge about the management of trade receivables.

Part (c) asked candidates to discuss whether profitability or liquidity was the primary objective of working capital management. Many candidates answered appropriately that both profitability and liquidity were important: profitability because it related to the overall objective of wealth maximisation and liquidity because of the need to meet liabilities as they became due for settlement.

18   PNP PLC

Key answer tips

Part (a) requires the usual comparison of the costs and benefits of implementing a discount. The complexity of the question means there are a large number of elements to consider and key to tackling the calculations is to recognise that the average payment period per class of receivable will equal the receivables days. Remember, each individual calculation will earn marks so you don't need to have identified all of them to score well. Both parts (a) and (b) of this question require a significant amount of workings. Laying your workings out neatly and clearly cross referencing them to your answer will ensure you have the best chance of scoring well. When laying out your answer to part (d), use plenty of sub-headings to clearly indicate to your marker the points you are making. The highlighted words are key phrases that markers are looking for.

(a) **Effect on profitability of implementing the proposal**

	£	£
Benefits:		
Increased contribution (W1)	200,000	
Decrease in irrecoverable debts (W2)	6,300	
		206,300
Costs		
Increase in current Class 1 discount (W3)	12,167	
Discount from transferring Class 2 receivables (W4)	11,498	
Discount from new Class 1 receivables (W5)	3,750	
Increase in irrecoverable debts, new Class 2 receivables (W6)	2,055	
Increase in financing cost from new receivables (W7)	4,932	34,402
Net benefit of implementing the proposal		171,898

The proposed change appears to be financially acceptable and so may be recommended. Uncertainty with respect to some of the assumptions underlying the financial evaluation would be unlikely to change the favourable recommendation.

Workings

Contribution/sales ratio = $100 \times (5,242 - 3,145)/5,242 = 40\%$

Irrecoverable debts ratio for Class 2 receivables = $100 \times (12,600/252,000) = 5\%$

Increase in Class 1 receivables from new business = $250,000 \times 30/365 = £20,548$

Increase in Class 2 receivables from new business = $250,000 \times 60/365 = £41,096$

(W1) Contribution from increased business = $500,000 \times 40\% = £200,000$

(W2) Decrease in irrecoverable debts for transferring current Class 2 receivables = $12,600 \times 0.5 = £6,300$

(Note that other assumptions regarding irrecoverable debts are possible here)

(W3) Current sales of Class 1 receivables = $200,000 \times (365/30) = £2,433,333$

Rise in discount cost for current Class 1 receivables = $2,433,333 \times 0.005 = £12,167$

(W4) Current sales of Class 2 receivables = $252,000 \times (365/60) = £1,533,000$

Discount cost of transferring Class 2 receivables = $1,533,000 \times 0.5 \times 0.015 = £11,498$

(W5) Discount cost for new Class 1 receivables = $250,000 \times 0.015 = £3,750$

(W6) Irrecoverable debts arising from new Class 2 receivables = $41,096 \times 0.05 = £2,055$

(Note that other assumptions regarding irrecoverable debts are possible here)

(W7) Increase in financing cost from new receivables = $(20,548 + 41,096) \times 0.08 = £4,932$

(**Note** that it could be assumed that transferring receivables pay after 30 days rather than 60 days)

Examiner's Note: because of the various assumptions that could be made regarding irrecoverable debts and payment period, other approaches to a solution are also acceptable.

Tutorial note:

An alternative approach to this part of the question is to lay out all of the calculations regarding the current and revised position before getting into the detail. This can often allow a clearer thought process and a more time efficient approach to the question.

You know from your studies that the main costs and benefits to consider when deciding on a level of discount to offer are:

— *The cost of the discount itself (for this you will need to know the value of sales for each class)*

— *The benefit of reduced financing costs (for this you will need to know the level of receivables under the current strategy and the proposed strategy*

— *The benefit of reduced irrecoverable debts (for this you will need to know the new level of receivables by class together with the typical ratio of bad debts)*

In this particular case, we will also need to consider the contribution that will be earned on the additional sales resulting from the revised policy.

Now we know the information we will require, we can set about obtaining it

	Current level of discount		Revised level of discount	
		£000		*£000*
Class 1 sales	*£200k × 365/30*	*2,433.3*	*£2,433.3k + £250k (being half of the new sales) + £766.5k (being half of the previous class 2 receivables)*	*3,449.8*
Class 1 receivables	*Per question*	*200*	*£3,449.8k × 30/365*	*283.5*
Cost of financing class 1 receivables	*£200k × 8%*	*16*	*£283.5k × 8%*	*22.7*
Class 2 sales	*£252k × 365/60*	*1,533*	*£1,533k / 2 + £250k*	*1,016.5*
Class 2 receivables	*Per question*	*252*	*£1,016.5k × 60/365*	*167*
Cost of financing class 2 receivables	*£252k × 8%*	*20.2*	*£167k × 8%*	*13.4*

The other pieces of information required were shown at the beginning of this answer; the contribution/sales ratio of 40% and the irrecoverable debts ratio for class 2 receivables of 5%.

Having gathered all of the information, it is quite a simple job to detail out the costs and benefits.

> *Costs*
>
> *Additional discount*
>
> *Remember this will need to reflect both the additional 0.5% payable on existing class 1 sales as well as the full 1.5% payable on all new sales and the previous class 2 sales that will now pay promptly.*
>
> | | |
> |---|---|
> | *£2,433.3k × 0.5%* | *= £12.2k* |
> | *(£3,449.8k – £2,433.3k) × 1.5%* | *= £15.2k* |
> | ***Total cost*** | ***= £27.4k*** |
> | ***Benefits*** | |
> | *Additional contribution* | |
> | *£500k × 40%* | *= £200k* |
> | *Reduction in irrecoverable debts* | |
> | *(£167k – £252k) × 5%* | *= £4.2k* |
> | *Reduction in financing costs* | |
> | *(£16k + £20.2k) – (£22.7k + £13.4k)* | *= £0.1k* |
> | ***Total benefit*** | ***= £204.3k*** |
> | ***Net benefit*** | ***= £176.9k*** |
>
> *Note: this answer differs from that presented above due to the approach taken. It would however, score in full.*

(b)   Current cash operating cycle:

Inventory days = (603/3,145) × 365 = 70 days

Payables days = (574.5/3,145) × 365 = 67 days

Average receivables days = (744.5/5,242) × 365 = 52 days

Cash operating cycle = 70 + 52 – 67 = 55 days

After implementation of the proposal, it is reasonable to assume that inventory days and payables days remain unchanged. Total receivables have increased by £61,644 to £806,144 and sales revenue has increased to £5.742m. Average receivables days are now 365 × (806/5,742) = 51 days. The cash operating cycle has marginally decreased by one day to 54 days (70 + 51 – 67).

(c)   Current sterling value of overseas receivables = £182,500

Current dollar value of overseas receivables = 182,500 × 1.7348 = $316,601

A forward market hedge (i.e. a forward exchange contract) will lock the sterling value of the receivables at the three-month forward rate.

Hedged sterling value of overseas receivables in three months = 316,601/1.7367 = £182,300

This is less than the current sterling value of the overseas receivables because sterling is expected to appreciate against the dollar.

(d)   The key elements of a receivables management system may be described as establishing a credit policy, credit assessment, credit control and collection of amounts due.

Establishing credit policy

The credit policy provides the overall framework within which the receivables management system of PNP plc operates and will cover key issues such as the procedures to be followed when granting credit, the usual credit period offered, the maximum credit period that may be granted, any discounts for early settlement, whether interest is charged on overdue balances, and actions to be taken with accounts that have not been settled in the agreed credit period. These terms of trade will depend to a considerable extent on the terms offered by competitors to PNP plc, but they will also depend on the ability of the company to finance its receivables (financing costs), the need to meet the costs of administering the system (administrative costs) and the risk of irrecoverable debts.

Credit assessment

In order to minimise the risk of irrecoverable debts, PNP plc should assess potential customers as to their creditworthiness before offering them credit. The depth of the credit check depends on the amount of business being considered, the size of the client and the potential for repeat business. The credit assessment requires information about the customer, whether from a third party as in a trade reference, a bank reference or a credit report, or from PNP itself through, for example, its analysis of a client's published accounts. The benefits of granting credit must always be greater than the cost involved. There is no point, therefore, in PNP plc paying for a detailed credit report from a credit reference agency for a small credit sale.

Credit control

Once PNP plc has granted credit to a customer, it should monitor the account at regular intervals to make sure that the agreed terms are being followed. An aged receivables analysis is useful in this respect since it helps the company focus on those clients who are the most cause for concern. Customers should be reminded of their debts by prompt despatch of invoices and regular statements of account. Customers in arrears should not be allowed to take further goods on credit.

Collection of amounts due

The customers of PNP plc should ideally settle their accounts within the agreed credit period. There is no indication as to what this might be, but the company clearly feels that a segmental analysis of its clients is possible given their payment histories, their potential for irrecoverable debts and their geographical origin. Clear guidelines are needed over the action to take when customers are late in settling their accounts or become irrecoverable debts, for example indicating at what stage legal action should be initiated.

Overseas receivables

PNP plc will need to consider the ways in which overseas receivables differ from domestic receivables. For example, overseas receivables tend to take longer to pay and so will need financing for longer. Overseas receivables will also give rise to exchange rate risk, which will probably need to be managed. The credit risk associated with overseas customers can be reduced in several ways, however, for example by using advances against collection, requiring payment through bills of exchange, arranging documentary letters of credit or using export factoring.

19   WQZ

Key answer tips

This question covers two popular areas of working capital management: inventory and accounts receivable management. The calculations in part (a) give some early chances to pick up some relatively easy marks. Part (b) and (d) are both discursive requirements that should also prove relatively straightforward. The trickiest element is part (c) although the requirement to calculate the maximum early settlement discount that could be offered is only worth one mark: don't let this put you off gathering the marks for the earlier parts of the process. The highlighted words are key phrases that markers are looking for.

(a)   **Cost of the current ordering policy**

Order size = 10% of 160,000 = 16,000 units per order

Number of orders per year = 160,000/16,000 = 10 orders per year

Annual ordering cost = 10 × 400 = $4,000 per year

Holding cost ignoring buffer stock = 5.12 × (16,000/2) = $40,960 per year

Holding cost of buffer inventory = 5.12 × 5,000 = $25,600 per year

Total cost of current policy = 4,000 + 40,960 + 25,600 = $70,560 per year

Cost of the ordering policy using the EOQ model

Order size = $(2 \times 400 \times 160,000/5.12)^{0.5}$ = 5,000 units per order

Number of orders per year = 160,000/5,000 = 32 orders per year

Annual ordering cost = 32 × 400 = $12,800 per year

Holding cost ignoring buffer stock = 5.12 × (5,000/2) = $12,800 per year

Holding cost of buffer inventory = 5.12 × 5,000 = $25,600 per year

Total cost of current policy = 12,800 + 12,800 + 25,600 = $51,200 per year

Change in costs of inventory management by using EOQ model

Decrease in costs = 70,560 − 51,200 = $19,360

Tutorial note:

Since the buffer inventory is the same in both scenarios, its holding costs do not need to be included in calculating the change in inventory management costs.

(b)   Holding costs can be reduced by reducing the level of inventory held by a company. Holding costs can be reduced to a minimum if a company orders supplies only when it needs them, avoiding the need to have any inventory at all of inputs to the production process. This approach to inventory management is called just-in-time (JIT) procurement.

The benefits of a JIT procurement policy include a lower level of investment in working capital, since inventory levels have been minimised: a reduction in inventory holding costs; a reduction in materials handling costs, due to improved materials flow through the production process; an improved relationship with suppliers, since supplier and customer need to work closely together in order to make JIT procurement a success; improved operating efficiency, due to the need to streamline production methods in order to eliminate inventory between different stages of the production process; and lower reworking costs due to the increased emphasis on the quality of supplies, since hold-ups in production must be avoided when inventory between production stages has been eliminated.

(c) **Evaluation of changes in receivables management**

Tutor's top tips:

When asked to evaluate a proposed change in policy you should always focus on quantifying the additional costs and benefits. Start by listing them out, and then begin with the easier calculations first. You don't need to complete the evaluation in order to score reasonable marks.

The current level of receivables days = (18/87.6) × 365 = 75 days

Since 25% of credit customers will take the discount, 75% will not be doing so.

The revised level of receivables days = (0.25 × 30) + (0.75 × 60) = 52.5 days

Current level of trade receivables = $18m

Revised level of trade receivables = 87.6 × (52.5/365) = $12.6m

Reduction level of trade receivables = 18 – 12.6 = $5.4m

Cost of short-term finance = 5.5%

Reduction in financing cost = 5.4m × 0.055 = $297,000

Administration and operating cost savings = $753,000

Total benefits = 297,000 + 753,000 = $1,050,000

Cost of early settlement discount = 87.6m × 0.25 × 0.01 = $219,000

Net benefit of early settlement discount = 1,050,000 – 219,000 = $831,000

The proposed changes in receivables management are therefore financially acceptable, although they depend heavily on the forecast savings in administration and operating costs.

Maximum early settlement discount

Tutor's top tips:

To calculate this you must start with the awareness that the maximum discount that could be offered is one where the cost equals the benefit. Anything above this, and it wouldn't be worth offering the discount.

You've already calculated the value of the benefit, so all that remains is to convert this figure into a percentage of sales revenue, remembering that only 25% of customers are expected to take up the offer.

Comparing the total benefits of $1,050,000 with 25% of annual credit sales of $87,600,000, which is $21,900,000, the maximum early settlement discount that could be offered is 4.8% (100 × (1.050k/21.9m)).

(d) Factors that should be considered when formulating working capital policy on the management of trade receivables include the following:

The level of investment in trade receivables

If the amount of finance tied up in trade receivables is substantial, receivables management policy may be formulated with the intention of reducing the level of investment by tighter control over the way in which credit is granted and improved methods of assessing client creditworthiness.

The cost of financing trade credit

If the cost of financing trade credit is high, there will be pressure to reduce the amount of credit offered and to reduce the period for which credit is offered.

The terms of trade offered by competitors

In order to compete effectively, a company will need to match the terms offered by its competitors, otherwise customers will migrate to competitors, unless there are other factors that will encourage them to be loyal, such as better quality products or a more valuable after-sales service.

The level of risk acceptable to the company

Some companies may feel that more relaxed trade credit terms will increase the volume of business to an extent that compensates for a higher risk of bad debts. The level of risk of bad debts that is acceptable will vary from company to company. Some companies may seek to reduce this risk through a policy of insuring against non-payment by clients.

The need for liquidity

Where the need for liquidity is relatively high, a company may choose to accelerate cash inflow from credit customers by using invoice discounting or by factoring.

The expertise available within the company

Where expertise in the assessment of creditworthiness and the monitoring of customer accounts is not to a sufficiently high standard, a company may choose to outsource its receivables management to a third party, i.e. a factor.

ACCA marking scheme		
		Marks
(a) Current policy:		
Annual ordering cost		1
Annual holding cost		1
Total annual cost		1
EOQ policy:		
Annual order size		1
Annual ordering cost and holding cost		1
Change in inventory management cost		1
		___
	Maximum	6
(b) Benefits of JIT procurement policy		5
(c) Reduction in trade receivables		2
Financing cost saving		1
Cost of early settlement discount		1
Comment on net benefit		1
Maximum early settlement discount		1
		___
	Maximum	6
(d) Relevant discussion		8
		___
Total		25
		___

Examiner's comments

Many candidates gained full marks in answering part (a), picked up reasonable marks on parts (b) and (d), but in many cases gave poor answers to part (c).

Part (a) required candidates to calculate the cost of a current inventory ordering policy, and the change in inventory management costs when the economic ordering quantity (EOQ) model was used to find the optimum order size.

A number of answers failed to gain full marks because they did not calculate the change in inventory management costs, even after correctly calculating these costs under the current ordering policy and after applying the EOQ model.

Poorer answers showed a lack of understanding of the relationship between ordering costs and holding costs, and an inability to calculate these costs.

In part (b), candidates were required to describe briefly the benefits of a just-in-time (JIT) procurement policy. No credit was given for discussing the disadvantages of such a policy, as these were not required. Many answers gave a short list of benefits, rather than a description of the benefits, and so were not able to gain full marks.

Part (c) asked candidates to calculate and comment on whether a proposed change in receivables management (offering an early settlement discount) was acceptable, and to calculate the maximum discount that could be offered.

Some candidates gained full marks for calculating correctly the reduction in financing cost, the cost of the discount and the net benefit of offering the discount. The reduction in financing cost and the cost of the discount were both based on credit sales for the year of $87.6 million.

Poorer answers based their calculations on current trade receivables of $18 million, even though the question stated that the early settlement discount would be offered to 25% of credit customers. Comparing current trade receivables and current credit sales showed that current receivables paid on average after 75 days, a credit period that would be reduced to 60 days through improved operational procedures. Some candidates assumed incorrectly that the current trade receivables period was 60 days and made incorrect calculations as a result.

The maximum discount that could be offered would be equal to the benefit gained from the discount, i.e. the saving in administration and operating costs added to the reduction in financing cost

Feedback from markers indicated that some answers to this part of question 3 were disorganised, with unlabelled calculations and a lack of explanation. It is important to help the marking process by labelling calculations, explaining workings and using correct notation, e.g. '$ per year', '$m', 'days' and so on.

Part (d) required candidates to discuss the factors that should be considered in formulating working capital policy on the management of trade receivables.

Poorer answers offered a list of actions that could be met in trade receivables management, such as "send out letters to trade receivables", "call customers on the telephone", "produce an aged receivables analysis regularly". Working capital policy on trade receivables management should consider what period of credit to offer, how to determine the amount of credit offered, when creditworthiness needs to be assessed and to what extent, and so on, and it is often informed by the trade receivables management policies of competitors. The policy should provide the framework within which the actions referred to above would be undertaken.

INVESTMENT APPRAISAL

20 ARMCLIFF CO

Key answer tips

In part (a) the first part of the data in the question relates to current operations – try to think why the examiner has given you this. The requirement is to determine whether the proposed project is attractive to *Armcliff* – not the parent company. Presumably what will make a project attractive to a division's management is one that will improve their current performance measure. Thus it is useful to know what the current level of ARR being achieved. This can then be compared with the project ARR.

Remember that the ARR is a financial accounting based measure – returns are in terms of accounting profits, and investments valued at balance sheet amounts – you must try to put all 'relevant cost' principles to the back of your mind. Whilst there are various possible definitions of the ARR (a point that can be raised in (b)) here you are given precise directions, so make sure you follow them. Both average profits and average investment need to be ascertained.

Don't forget to conclude by comparison with both current and required rates of return.

In part (b) the question requires you to show both theoretical and practical knowledge about investment appraisal methods.

In part (c), even though this is a examining a general area of credit management, try wherever you can to relate your points to the business in the question – it is stated that Armcliff intends to extend its credit to improve sales. Again make sure that you explain points enough to get the marks available, whilst still offering sufficient variety. Note that it is not enough simply to say that the advantage of ARR is its simplicity. With spreadsheets, this is hardly going to be a consideration. Show instead that you appreciate that mangers are influenced by the methods used for their performance measurement – both internally and externally. The highlighted words are key phrases that markers are looking for.

(a) **Current return on capital employed**

= Operating profit/capital employed

= $20m/($75m + $25m) = $20m/$100m = 20%.

Analysis of the project

Project capital requirements are $14 million fixed capital plus $0.5 million inventory. The annual depreciation charge (straight line) is:

($14m – expected residual value of $2m)/4 = $3 million per annum.

Profit profile ($m)

Year	1	2	3	4
Sales revenue	(5.00 × 2m) = 10.00	(4.50 × 1.8m) = 8.10	(4.00 × 1.6m) = 6.40	(3.50 × 1.6m) = 5.60
Operating costs	(2.00)	(1.80)	(1.60)	(1.60)
Fixed costs	(1.50)	(1.35)	(1.20)	(1.20)
Depreciation	(3.00)	(3.00)	(3.00)	(3.00)
Profit	3.50	1.95	0.60	(0.20)

Total profit over four years = $5.85 million.

Capital employed (start-of-year):

Non-current assets	14.00	11.00	8.00	5.00
Inventories	0.50	0.50	0.50	0.50
Profit	14.50	11.50	8.50	5.50

Average capital employed = (14.50 + 11.50 + 8.50 + 5.50)/4 = $10 million.

$$\text{Average rate of return} = \frac{\text{Average profit}}{\text{Average capital employed}} = \frac{\$5.85m\,/\,4}{\$10.0m} = \frac{\$1.46m}{\$10.0m}$$

= 14.6%

Note: If receivables were to be included in the definition of capital employed, this would reduce the calculated rate of return, while the inclusion of payables would have an offsetting effect. However, using the ARR criterion as defined, the proposal has an expected return above the minimum stipulated by Shevin Inc. It is unlikely that the managers of Armcliff will propose projects which offer a rate of return below the present 20% even where the expected return exceeds the minimum of 10%. To undertake projects with returns in this range will depress the overall divisional return and cast managerial performance in a weaker light.

However, it is unlikely that the senior managers of the Armcliff subsidiary would want to undertake the project.

(b)   (i)   The **ARR can be expressed in a variety of ways**, and is therefore susceptible to manipulation. Although the question specifies average profit to average capital employed, many other variants are possible, such as average profit to initial capital, which would raise the computed rate of return.

It is also **susceptible to variation in accounting policy** by the same firm over time, or as between different firms at a point in time. For example, different methods of depreciation produce different profit figures and hence different rates of return.

Perhaps, most fundamentally, it is **based on accounting profits expressed net of deduction for depreciation provisions, rather than cash flows**. This effectively results in double-counting for the initial outlay i.e. the capital cost is allowed for twice over, both in the numerator of the ARR calculation and also in the denominator. This is likely to depress the measured profitability of a project and result in rejection of some worthwhile investment.

Finally, because it simply averages the profits, it **makes no allowance for the timing of the returns** from the project.

(ii)   The continuing use of the ARR method can by explained largely by its utilisation of balance sheet (statement of financial position) and income statement magnitudes familiar to managers, namely 'profit' and 'capital employed'. In addition, the impact of the project on a company's financial statements can also be specified. Return on capital employed is still the commonest way in which business unit performance is measured and evaluated, and is certainly the most visible to shareholders. It is thus not surprising that some managers may be happiest in expressing project attractiveness in the same terms in which their performance will be reported to shareholders, and according to which they will be evaluated and rewarded.

(c)   Armcliff intends to achieve a sales increase by extending its receivables collection period. This policy carries several dangers. It implies that credit will be extended to customers for whom credit is an important determinant of supplier selection, hinting at financial instability on their part. Consequently, the risk of later than expected, or even no payment, is likely to increase. Although losses due to default are limited to the incremental costs of making these sales rather than the invoiced value, Armcliff should recognise that there is an opportunity cost involved in tying up capital for lengthy periods. In addition, companies which are slow payers often attempt to claim discounts to which they are not entitled. Armcliff may then face the difficult choice between acquiescence to such demands versus rejection, in which case, it may lose repeat sales.

The creditworthiness of customers can be assessed in several ways as follows.

Analysis of accounting statements

In the case of companies that have to publish their annual accounts, key financial ratios can be examined to assess their financial stability. However, these almost certainly will be provided in arrears and may not give a true indication of the companies' current situation. Some customers may be prepared to supply more up-to-date accounts directly to the seller, although these are unlikely to have been audited.

Analysis of credit reports

It may be possible to obtain detailed assessment of the creditworthiness of customers from other sources, such as their bankers, specialist credit assessment agencies such as Dun & Bradstreet, and from trade sources such as other companies who supply them. These assessments are likely to be more up-to-date than company accounts, but will inevitably be more subjective.

Previous experience

If the firm has supplied the customer in the past, its previous payment record will be available.

Cash-only trial period

If accounting and other data is sparse, and there is no previous trading record with the customer, the seller may offer a trial period over which cash is required, but if the payment record is acceptable (e.g. if the customer's cheques always clear quickly), further transactions may be conducted on credit.

Background information

General background information on the industry in which the customer operates will generate insights into the financial health of companies in that sector, and by implication, that of the customer. Many agencies supply such information, although it should only be used as a back-up to other assessments.

21 DAIRY CO

Key answer tips

Tackling this question requires a methodical and logical approach. The requirements must be attempted in the order given. It is an excellent test of your understanding on the key investment appraisal topic. The highlighted words are key phrases that markers are looking for.

(a)

Tutor's top tips:

A careful read of the question is essential. For example, the increases in maintenance payments only occur after the first payment (which will be made at the end of the first year of the project i.e. T_1). This could easily have been mis-interpreted. Writing down the timescales is a good way of ensuring you have everything clear in your mind.

With so many calculations, be careful to layout your workings neatly and cross reference fully where applicable.

Option 1 – Replace the machine:

Year	Capital cost and maintenance			Contribution $	Net cash flow $	Discount factors	Present value $
0	450,000				(450,000)	1.000	(450,000)
1	25,000			150,000	125,000	0.893	111,625
2	25,000 × 1.075	= 26,875		170,000	143,125	0.797	114,071
3	25,000 × 1.075^2	= 28,891		190,000	161,109	0.712	114,710
4	25,000 × 1.075^3	= 31,057		210,000	178,943	0.636	113,808
5	25,000 × 1.075^4	= 33,387		220,000	186,613	0.567	105,810

Net present value 110,024

Option 2 – Overhaul the machine:

Year	Capital cost and maintenance			Contribution $	Net cash flow $	Discount factors	Present value $
0	275,000				(275,000)	1.000	(275,000)
1	40,000			130,000	90,000	0.893	80,370
2	40,000 × 1.105	= 44,200		145,000	100,800	0.797	80,338
3	40,000 × 1.105^2	= 48,841		155,000	106,159	0.712	75,585
4	40,000 × 1.105^3	= 53,969		160,000	106,031	0.636	67,436
5	40,000 × 1.105^4	= 59,636		160,000	100,364	0.567	56,906

Net present value 85,635

(b)   **Discounted payback**

	Replace the machine		Overhaul the machine	
Year	Net discounted cash flow	Cumulative present value	Net discounted cash flow	Cumulative present value
	$	$	$	$
0	(450,000)	(450,000)	(275,000)	(275,000)
1	111,625	(338,375)	80,370	(194,630)
2	114,071	(224,304)	80,338	(114,292)
3	114,710	(109,594)	75,585	(38,707)
4	113,808	4,214	67,436	28,729
5	105,810	110,024	56,906	85,635

Tutor's top tips:

The above shows a really efficient layout for your workings since it minimises the number of times you need to copy down information.

Option 1 – Replace the machine:

Discounted payback period = 3 years + $\dfrac{109,594}{113,808}$ × 12 months = 3 years 11.6 month

Option 2 – Overhaul existing machine:

Discounted payback period = 3 years + $\dfrac{38,707}{67,436}$ × 12 months = 3 years 6.9 months

(c)

		Replace the machine		Overhaul the machine	
Year	Discount factor (20%)	Net cash flow	Present value	Net cash flow	Present value
		$	$	$	$
0	1.000	(450,000)	(450,000)	(275,000)	(275,000)
1	0.833	125,000	104,125	90,000	74,970
2	0.694	143,125	99,329	100,800	69,955
3	0.579	161,109	93,282	106,159	61,466
4	0.482	178,943	86,251	106,031	51,107
5	0.402	186,613	75,018	100,364	40,346
			8,005		**22,844**

IRR of replacement = 12% + $\dfrac{110,024}{110,024 \quad 8,005}$ × (20% – 12%) = 12 + 8.6 = 20.6%

IRR of overhaul = 12% + $\dfrac{85,635}{85,635 \quad 22,844}$ × (20% – 12%) = 12 + 10.9 = 22.9%

Tutor's top tips:

Don't forget, the IRR formula is not supplied in the exam so you will need to memorise it.

Tutorial note:

20% is not the only possible discount factor to use here; any value over 12% is acceptable. The IRR may differ slightly, but should not be significantly different if alternative values are used.

(d)

Tutor's top tips:

This part of the question is just about clearly stating what all of your calculations mean and why.

All three methods of investment appraisal use relevant cash flows to appraise the alternative investments and take account of the time value of money.

The discounted payback period calculates the time taken to pay back the initial investment. Using this criterion, overhauling the machine is the better option, with the slightly shorter payback period.

The net present value is the profit in present value terms. If the cost of capital is 12%, the machine should be replaced, since this option has the higher NPV.

The internal rate of return is the percentage return on the investment, taking into account the time value of money. The higher the return, the better. Overhauling the current machine has a higher IRR and so should be chosen using this appraisal technique.

Overall, to maximise shareholder wealth, the project with the highest NPV should be chosen which means that, provided the outcomes are not risky and 12% is the appropriate cost of capital, the machine should be replaced.

(e)   **Finance department**

When considering a new investment, the finance department will perform the investment appraisal calculations. This will involve identifying and forecasting costs and revenues, and deciding which method(s) of investment appraisal should be used (e.g. NPV, payback period, or other alternative methods).

If the directors decide to go ahead with a project, the finance department will then negotiate the terms of contracts, and will oversee the implementation of the project, investigating any variances as they arise.

Treasury department

The treasury department will calculate the necessary cost of capital for the project appraisal. If new finance is required, the treasury department will decide whether equity or debt finance should be used, and will liaise with finance providers to ensure that financing costs are kept to a minimum.

The treasury department will also identify any risks which might arise on the project (e.g. currency risks, credit risks) and will manage these risks by setting up hedging strategies.

Need for liaison

Before the finance department can perform an investment appraisal calculation, the treasury department will need to calculate a suitable cost of capital. There will need to be close liaison here, to ensure that the calculated cost of capital reflects the business risk of the new project and also the likely financing position of the business.

The finance department will need to keep the treasury department fully informed about the financing requirement for the new project, so that the treasury department can arrange any extra financing as required.

22 INVESTMENT APPRAISAL

Key answer tips

Parts (a) & (b)(i) should present an opportunity to gain some easy marks by outlining some basic areas of the syllabus. The calculations in part (b) (ii) were relatively straightforward. Make sure you don't neglect the final part of the requirement – to identify other factors that the company should take into account when deciding of the optimal cycle. The highlighted words are key phrases that markers are looking for.

(a) Accounting rate of return (ARR) is a measure of the return on an investment where the annual profit before interest and tax is expressed as a percentage of the capital sum invested. There are a number of alternative formulae which can be used to calculate ARR, which differ in the way in which they define capital cost. The more common alternative measures available are:

- average annual profit to initial capital invested, and

- average annual profit to average capital invested.

The method selected will affect the resulting ARR figure, and for this reason it is important to recognise that the measure might be subject to manipulation by managers seeking approval for their investment proposals. The value for average annual profit is calculated after allowances for depreciation, as shown in the example below:

Suppose ARR is defined as: $\dfrac{\text{Average profit (after depreciation)}}{\text{Initial capital invested}} \times 100\%$

A project costing \$5 million, and yielding average profits of \$1,250,000 per year after depreciation charges of \$500,000 per year, would give an ARR of:

1,250,000/5,000,000 × 100% = 25%

If the depreciation charged were to be increased to $750,000 per year, for example as a result of technological changes reducing the expected life of an asset, the ARR becomes:

1,000,000/5,000,000 × 100% = 20%

The attraction of using ARR as a method of investment appraisal lies in its simplicity and the ease with which it can be used to specify the impact of a project on a company's income statement. The measure is easily understood and can be directly linked to the use of ROCE as a performance measure. Nonetheless, ARR has been criticised for a number of major drawbacks, perhaps the most important of which is that it uses accounting profits after depreciation rather than cash flows in order to measure return. This means that the capital cost is over-stated in the calculation, via both the numerator and the denominator. In the numerator, the capital cost is taken into account via the depreciation charges used to derive accounting profit, but capital cost is also the denominator. The practical effect of this is to reduce the ARR and thus make projects appear less profitable. This might in turn result in some worthwhile projects being rejected. Note, however, that this problem does not arise where ARR is calculated as average annual profit as a percentage of average capital invested.

The most important criticism of ARR is that it takes no account of the time value of money. A second limitation of ARR, already suggested, is that its value is dependent on accounting policies and this can make comparison of ARR figures across different investments very difficult. A further difficulty with the use of ARR is that it does not give a clear decision rule. The ARR on any particular investment needs to be compared with the current returns being earned within a business, and so unlike NPV for example, it is impossible to say 'all investments with an ARR of x or below will always be rejected.

The payback method of investment appraisal is used widely in industry – generally in addition to other measures. Like ARR, it is easily calculated and understood. The payback approach simply measures the time required for cumulative cash flows from an investment to sum to the original capital invested.

Example

Original investment $100,000

Cash flow profile: Years 1–3 $25,000 p.a.

Years 4 – 5 $50,000 p.a.

Year 6 $5,000

The cumulative cash flows are therefore:

End Year 1	$25,000
End Year 2	$50,000
End Year 3	$75,000
End Year 4	$125,000
End Year 5	$175,000
End Year 6	$180,000

The original sum invested is returned via cash flows some time during the course of Year 4. If cash flows are assumed to be even throughout the year, the cumulative cash flow of $100,000 will have been earned halfway through year 4. The payback period for the investment is thus 3 years and 6 months.

The payback approach to investment appraisal is useful for companies which are seeking to claw back cash from investments as quickly as possible. At the same time, the concept is intuitively appealing as many businessmen will be concerned about how long they may have to wait to get their money back, because they believe that rapid repayment reduces risks. This means that the payback approach is commonly used for initial screening of investment alternatives.

The disadvantages of the payback approach are as follows:

(i)   Payback ignores the overall profitability of a project by ignoring cash flows after payback is reached. In the example above, the cash flows between 3–4 years and the end of the project total $80,000. To ignore such substantial cash flows would be naïve. As a consequence, the payback method is biased in favour of fast-return investments. This can result in rejecting investments that generate cash flows more slowly in the early years, but which are overall more profitable.

(ii) As with ARR, the payback method ignores the time value of money.

(iii) The payback method, in the same way as ARR, offers no objective measure of what is the desirable return, as measured by the length of the payback period.

(b)   (i)   Discounted cash flow analysis is a technique whereby the value of future cash flows is discounted back to a present value, so that the monetary values of all cash flows are equivalent, regardless of their timing. The logic for discounting is that the value of money declines over time because of individual time preferences and the impact of inflation in eroding spending power. People value money received sooner rather than later because as soon as cash is received they can increase consumption, or re-invest the capital.

NPV uses discounting to calculate the present value of all cash flows associated with a project. The present value of cash outflows is then compared with the present value of cash inflows, to obtain a net present value (NPV). If the present value (PV) of cash outflows exceeds the PV of cash inflows, then the NPV will be negative. If the present value (PV) of cash inflows exceeds the PV of cash outflows, then the NPV will be positive. The size of the NPV is dependent on the cash flow pattern and the rate of discount that is applied. The general rule is that a company will discount the forecast cash flows at a rate equal to its cost of capital. The reason for this is that if a company has an overall cost of capital of, for example, 12%, it is essential that the rate of return exceeds 12% or the funding costs will not be covered. Hence if the cash flows are discounted at the cost of capital and the project yields a positive NPV, this implies that the return exceeds the cost of capital. When using NPV for investment appraisal then a simple rule is applied: invest if NPV is positive, and do not invest if it is negative.

IRR uses discounting in a slightly different way to determine the profitability of an investment. The Internal Rate of Return is defined as the discount rate at which the net present value equals zero. For example, an investment may yield a forecast NPV of $15,000 when the cash flows are discounted at 10%. If the rate of discount is increased, the net present value will fall, and the IRR represents the effective, break-even discount rate for the investment. Suppose, for example, that the IRR is 15%, this figure can then be used to establish a decision rule for investments. An IRR of 15% means that if the cost of capital exceeds 15% then the investment would generate a negative NPV. If the company is currently having to pay 12% on its investment funds, then it knows that it can afford to see its cost of capital rise by 3% before the investment will become financially non-viable. As long as the IRR exceeds the cost of capital, then the company should invest and so, as a general rule, the higher the IRR the better.

NPV and IRR measures may sometimes contradict one another when used in relation to mutually exclusive investments. An example of the ambiguity which can occur when choosing between mutually exclusive decisions is when one of the investments has a higher NPV than the other, and so is preferable on that basis, but at the same time it has a lower IRR. When IRR and NPV give conflicting results, the preferred alternative is the project with the highest NPV.

In conclusion, although both NPV and IRR use discounted cash flows as a method of arriving at an investment decision, the results that they generate need to be interpreted with care, and they do not always yield the same investment decisions. NPV is the preferred criterion for selecting between two or more mutually exclusive investments, where the two approaches give differing recommendations.

(ii)   If the laptops are replaced every year:

NPV of one year replacement cycle

Year	Cash flow $	DF at 14%	PV $
0	(2,400)	1.000	(2,400.0)
1	1,200	0.877	1,052.4
			(1,347.6)

Equivalent annual cost = PV of cost of one replacement cycle/Cumulative discount factor

= $1,347.6/0.877 = $1,536.6

NPV of two-year replacement cycle

Year	Cash flow $	DF at 14%	PV $
0	(2,400)	1.000	(2,400.0)
1	(75)	0.877	(65.8)
2	800	0.769	615.2
			(1,850.6)

EAC = $1,850.6/1.647 = $1,123.6

NPV of three-year replacement cycle

Year	Cash flow	DF at 14%	PV
	$		$
0	(2,400)	1.000	(2,400.0)
1	(75)	0.877	(65.8)
2	(150)	0.769	(115.4)
3	300	0.675	202.5
			_____
			(2,378.7)
			_____

EAC = $2,378.7/2.322 = $1,024.4

Conclusion

The optimal cycle for replacement is every three years, because this has the lowest equivalent annual cost. Other factors which need to be taken into account are the non-financial aspects of the alternative cycle choices. For example, computer technology and the associated software is changing very rapidly and this could mean that failure to replace annually would leave the salesmen unable to utilise the most up to date systems for recording, monitoring and implementing their sales. This could have an impact on the company's competitive position. The company needs to consider also the compatibility of the software used by the laptops with that used by the in-house computers and mainframe. If system upgrades are made within the main business that render the two computers incompatible, then rapid replacement of the laptops to regain compatibility is essential.

23 PV CO

Key answer tips

Part (a) offers some relatively easy marks and should therefore be attempted first. When dealing with inflation in investment appraisal questions, it is very often easier to work with the money method, inflating the cash flows before discounting using the money cost of capital. This is particularly true here since the money cost of capital has been provided and different cash flows are expected to inflate at different rates. The highlighted words are key phrases that markers are looking for.

(a) The key stages in the capital investment decision-making process are identifying investment opportunities, screening investment proposals, analysing and evaluating investment proposals, approving investment proposals, and implementing, monitoring and reviewing investments.

Identifying investment opportunities

Investment opportunities or proposals could arise from analysis of strategic choices, analysis of the business environment, research and development, or legal requirements. The key requirement is that investment proposals should support the achievement of organisational objectives.

Screening investment proposals

In the real world, capital markets are imperfect, so it is usual for companies to be restricted in the amount of finance available for capital investment. Companies therefore need to choose between competing investment proposals and select those with the best strategic fit and the most appropriate use of economic resources.

Analysing and evaluating investment proposals

Candidate investment proposals need to be analysed in depth and evaluated to determine which offer the most attractive opportunities to achieve organisational objectives, for example to increase shareholder wealth. This is the stage where investment appraisal plays a key role, indicating for example which investment proposals have the highest net present value.

Approving investment proposals

The most suitable investment proposals are passed to the relevant level of authority for consideration and approval. Very large proposals may require approval by the board of directors, while smaller proposals may be approved at divisional level, and so on. Once approval has been given, implementation can begin.

Implementing, monitoring and reviewing investments

The time required to implement the investment proposal or project will depend on its size and complexity, and is likely to be several months. Following implementation, the investment project must be monitored to ensure that the expected results are being achieved and the performance is as expected. The whole of the investment decision-making process should also be reviewed in order to facilitate organisational learning and to improve future investment decisions.

(b) (i) **Calculation of NPV**

Year	0	1	2	3	4
	$	$	$	$	$
Investment	(2,000,000)				
Income		1,236,000	1,485,400	2,622,000	1,012,950
Operating costs		676,000	789.371	1,271,227	620,076
Net cash flow	(2,000,000)	560,000	696,028	1,350,773	392,874
Discount at 10%	1.000	0.909	0.826	0.751	0.683
Present values	(2,000,000)	509,040	574,919	1,014,430	268,333

Net present value $366,722

Workings

Calculation of income

Year	0	1	2	3	4
Inflated selling price ($/unit)		20.60	21.22	21.85	22.51
Demand (units/year)		60,000	70,000	120,000	45,000
Income ($/year)		1,236,000	1,485,400	2,622,000	1,012,950

Calculation of operating costs

Year	0	1	2	3	4
Inflated variable cost ($/unit)		8.32	8.65	9.00	9.36
Demand (units/year)		60,000	70,000	120,000	45,000
Variable costs ($/year)		499,200	605,500	1,080,000	421,000
Inflated fixed costs ($/year)		176,800	183,872	191,227	198,876
Operating costs ($ / year)		676,000	789,371	1,271,227	620,076

Alternative calculation of operating costs

Year	0	1	2	3	4
Variable cost ($/unit)		8.00	8.00	8.00	8.00
Demand (units/year)		60,000	70,000	120,000	45,000
Variable costs ($/year)		480,000	560,000	960,000	360,000
Fixed costs ($/year)		170,000	170,000	170,000	170,000
Operating costs ($ / year)		650,000	730,000	1,130,000	530,000
		676,000	789,568	1,271,096	620,025

(ii) **Calculation of internal rate of return**

Year	0	1	2	3	4
	$	$	$	$	$
Net cash flow	(2,000,000)	560,000	696,028	1,350,773	392,874
Discount at 20%	1.000	0.833	0.694	0.579	0.482
Present values	(2,000,000)	466,480	483,043	782,098	189,365

Net present value ($79,014)

Internal rate of return = 10 + ((20 − 10) × 366,722)/(366,722 + 79,014) = 10 + 8.2 = 18.2%

(iii) **Calculation of return on capital employed**

Total cash inflow = 560,000 + 696,028 + 1,350,773 + 392,874 = $2,999,675

Total depreciation and initial investment are same, as there is no scrap value

Total accounting profit = 2,999,675 − 2,000,000 = $999,675

Average annual accounting profit = 999,675/4 = $249,919

Average investment = 2,000,000/2 = $1,000,000

Return on capital employed = 100 × 249,919/1,000,000 = 25%

(iv) **Calculation of discounted payback**

Year	0	1	2	3	4
	$	$	$	$	$
Present values	(2,000,000)	509,040	574,919	1,014,430	268,333
Cumulative PV	(2,000,000)	(1,490,960)	(916,041)	98,389	366,722

Discounted payback period = 2 + (916,041/1,014,430) = 2 + 0.9 = 2.9 years

(c) The investment proposal has a positive net present value (NPV) of $366,722 and is therefore financially acceptable. The results of the other investment appraisal methods do not alter this financial acceptability, as the NPV decision rule will always offer the correct investment advice.

The internal rate of return (IRR) method also recommends accepting the investment proposal, since the IRR of 18.2% is greater than the 10% return required by PV Co. If the advice offered by the IRR method differed from that offered by the NPV method, the advice offered by the NPV method would be preferred.

The calculated return on capital employed of 25% is less than the target return of 30%, but as indicated earlier, the investment proposal is financially acceptable as it has a positive NPV. The reason why PV Co has a target return on capital employed of 30% should be investigated. This may be an out-of-date hurdle rate that has not been updated for changed economic circumstances.

The discounted payback period of 2.9 years is a significant proportion of the forecast life of the investment proposal of four years, a time period which the information provided suggests is limited by technological change. The sensitivity of the investment proposal to changes in demand and life-cycle period should be analysed, since an earlier onset of technological obsolescence may have a significant impact on its financial acceptability.

	ACCA marking scheme		
			Marks
(a)	Identification of decision-making stages	1 – 2	
	Explanation of decision-making stages	4 – 6	
	Role of investment appraisal	1 – 2	
		Maximum	7
(b)	Inflated income	2	
	Inflated operating costs	2	
	Discount factors	1	
	Net present value	1	
	Internal rate of return	3	
	Return on capital employed	2	
	Discounted payback	2	
			13
(c)	Discussion of investment appraisal findings	4	
	Advice on acceptability of project	1	
			5
Total			25

Examiner's comments

Part (a) of this question asked for an identification and explanation of the stages of the capital investment decision-making process, and the role of investment appraisal in this process. Better answers identified and discussed identification: screening; analysis and evaluation; approving; implementation and monitoring. Poorer answers looked at different aspects of the analysis and evaluation stage, or went off track by discussing the relative merits of the investment appraisal methods required in part (b) of this question.

Part (b) required the evaluation of an investment project using net present value (NPV), internal rate of return (IRR), return on capital employed (ROCE) and discounted payback, incorporating inflation.

Some candidates introduced capital allowances and taxation into their answers, but this was not required by the question. There is no point in doing unnecessary work in the examination, as marks will be lost elsewhere due to time pressure.

Most candidates calculated correctly the NPV of the investment project, although some answers did not handle inflation correctly, or omitted the fixed costs, or calculated and used (unnecessarily) a real discount rate.

Many candidates calculated correctly the IRR of the investment project, although there was a tendency for some candidates to use a second discount rate that led to unnecessary inaccuracy. For example, if the NPV is positive at a 10% discount rate, there is little point in calculating the NPV at a 5% discount rate and extrapolating to find the IRR. A more accurate result would arise by using the NPV calculated at a higher rate than 10%, for example 20%, as in the suggested answers to the exam.

Most candidates were not able to calculate correctly the ROCE of the investment project. The most common error was using average annual net cash flow, rather than average annual accounting profit.

Although a depreciation method was not given in the question, total depreciation could be subtracted from total net cash flow in order to give total accounting profit. Some candidates were unable to calculate the average investment.

Many candidates were able to calculate discounted payback, although some used an unnecessary amount of rounding, e.g. giving 3 years rather than 2.9 years.

Part (c) asked for a discussion of the findings from part (b) and a recommendation as to the acceptability of the investment project. Many candidates failed, either explicitly or implicitly, to recognise the superiority of the NPV method.

Most candidates stated correctly that the investment project was acceptable because it had a positive NPV and because the IRR was greater than the nominal discount rate used by the company. Some answers suggested that the project was acceptable because the ROCE was higher than the target ROCE, but this investment appraisal method cannot be relied upon to give correct investment advice. Better answers gave reasons why ROCE cannot be relied upon. Some candidates said the investment project was acceptable because the discounted payback period was less than the life of the project. This is almost the same as saying that the project has a positive NPV (it might not be true for a non-conventional project), but few candidates recognised this. Without a target payback period, payback cannot say whether a project is acceptable or not.

24 BFD CO

Key answer tips

Part (a) asks for a NPV calculation. The first consideration is how to set out your answer as there are cash flows for the first four years and annuities for t=5-∞ and t=1-10. These can be incorporated as separate calculations or you could have had columns for flows 0,1,2,3,4,5-10 and 11-∞. Either way you needed to be particularly careful when calculating the tax flows given the lack of a delay.

In part (b) it is vital that issues are applied to the scenario, making reference to specific figures where possible. The highlighted words are key phrases that markers are looking for.

(a)   **Net present value evaluation of proposed investment**

	20X5/6 $000	20X6/7 $000	20X7/8 $000	20X8/9 $000
Sales revenue	1,800	2,160	2,340	2,520
Variable costs	850	1,020	1,105	1,190
Contribution	950	1,140	1,235	1,330
Fixed costs	450	450	450	450
Net cash flow	500	690	785	880
Taxation @ 25%	125	173	196	220
After-tax cash flow	375	517	589	660
12% discount factors	0.893	0.797	0.712	0.636
Present values	335	412	419	419

	$
Sum of present values	1,585,000
PV of writing down allowances	423,750
PV of cash flows after Year 4 =	3,498,000
	5,506,750
Less initial investment	3,200,000
Net present value	2,306,750

Workings

	20X5/6	20X6/7	20X7/8	20X8/9
Sales volume (units)	100,000	120,000	130,000	140,000
Selling price ($/unit)	18.00	18.00	18.00	18.00
Sales revenue ($)	1,800,000	2,160,000	2,340,000	2,520,000
Variable costs ($/unit)	8.50	8.50	8.50	8.50
Variable costs ($)	850,000	1,020,000	1,105,000	1,190,000

Fixed costs = $4.50 \times 100,000 = \$450,000$ per year

Annual writing down allowance = $3,000,000/10 = \$300,000$

Annual writing down allowance tax benefits = $25\% \times 300,000 = \$75,000$

Ten-year annuity factor at 12% = 5.650

Present value of writing down allowance tax benefits = $75,000 \times 5.650 = \$423,750$

Year 4 value of year 5 after-tax cash flows in perpetuity = $660,000/0.12 = \$5,500,000$

Present value of these cash flows = $5,500,000 \times 0.636 = \$3,498,000$

(b)   From a net present value perspective the proposed investment is acceptable, since the net present value (NPV) is large and positive. However, a large part of the present value of benefits (63%) derives from the assumption that cash flows will continue indefinitely after Year 4. This is very unlikely to occur in practice and excluding these cash flows will result in a negative net present value of approximately $1.2m. In fact the proposed investment will not show a positive NPV until more than seven years have passed.

Before rejecting the proposal, steps should be taken to address some of the limitations of the analysis performed.

Inflation

Forecasts of future inflation of sales prices and variable costs should be prepared, so that a nominal NPV evaluation can be undertaken. This evaluation should employ a nominal after-tax cost of capital: it is not stated whether the 12% after-tax cost of capital is in nominal or real terms. Sales price is assumed to be constant in real terms, but in practice substitute products are likely to arise, leading to downward pressure on sales price and sales volumes.

Constant fixed costs

The assumption of constant fixed costs should be verified as being acceptable. Sales volumes are forecast to increase by 40% and this increase may result in an increase in incremental fixed costs.

Constant working capital

The assumption of constant working capital should be investigated. Net working capital is likely to increase in line with sales and so additional investment in working capital may be needed in future years. Inflation will increase required incremental working capital investment.

Taxation and capital allowances

The assumptions made regarding taxation should be investigated. The tax rate has been assumed to be constant, when there may be different rates of profit tax applied to companies of different size. The method available for claiming capital allowances should be confirmed, since it is usual to find a different method being applied to buildings compared to that applied to machinery, whereas here they are the same.

Machine replacement

The purchase of replacement machinery has been ignored, which seems unreasonable. Future reinvestment in new machinery will be needed and this will reduce the net present value of the proposed investment. Technological change is also possible, bringing perhaps new manufacturing methods and improved or substitute products, and these may affect the size of future cash flows.

Changes in technology

Technological change is also possible, bringing perhaps new manufacturing methods and improved or substitute products, and these may affect the size of future cash flows.

Financing

The method of financing the proposed investment should be considered. It may be that leasing will be cheaper than borrowing to buy, increasing the net present value and making the project more attractive.

25   TRECOR

Key answer tips

This is a fairly straightforward question that gives an opportunity to cover three of the four main investment appraisal techniques. It does however include both taxation and inflation in the scenario meaning you have to feel confident with the advanced elements of discounted cash flows in order to score well. The highlighted words are key phrases that markers are looking for.

(a)   **Calculation of NPV**

Nominal discount rate using Fisher effect: 1.057 × 1.05 = 1.1098 i.e. 11%

	1	2	3	4	5
	$000	$000	$000	$000	$000
Sales revenue(W1)	433	509	656	338	
Variable cost (W2)	284	338	439	228	
Contribution	149	171	217	110	
Fixed production overheads	27	28	30	32	
Net cash flow	122	143	187	78	
Tax		(37)	(43)	(56)	(23)
CA tax benefits (W3)		19	14	11	30
After-tax cash flow	122	125	158	33	7
Disposal				5	
After-tax cash flow	122	125	158	38	7
Discount factors	0.901	0.812	0.731	0.659	0.593
Present values	110	102	115	25	4

	$
PV of benefits	356,000
Investment	250,000
NPV	106,000

Since the NPV is positive, the purchase of the machine is acceptable on financial grounds.

Workings

(W1)

Year	1	2	3	4
Demand (units)	35,000	40,000	50,000	25,000
Selling price ($/unit)	12.36	12.73	13.11	13.51
Sales revenue ($/year)	432,600	509,200	655,500	337,750

(W2)

Year	1	2	3	4
Demand (units)	35,000	40,000	50,000	25,000
Variable cost ($/unit)	8.11	8.44	8.77	9.12
Variable cost ($/year)	283,850	337,600	438,500	228,000

(W3)

Year	Capital allowances		Tax benefits	
1	250,000 × 0.25 =	62,500	62,500 × 0.3 =	18,750
2	62,500 × 0.75 =	46,875	46,875 × 0.3 =	14,063
3	46,875 × 0.75 =	35,156	25,156 × 0.3 =	10,547
4	By difference	100,469	100,469 × 0.3 =	30,141
	250,000 − 5.000 =	245,000		73,501

(b)   Calculation of before-tax return on capital employed

Total net before-tax cash flow = 122 + 143 + 187 + 78 = $530,000

Total depreciation = 250,000 – 5,000 = $245,000

Average annual accounting profit = (530 – 245)/ 4 = $71,250

Average investment = (250,000 + 5,000)/ 2 = $127,500

Return on capital employed = 100 × 71,250/ 127,500 = 56%

Given the target return on capital employed of Trecor Co is 20% and the ROCE of the investment is 56%, the purchase of the machine is recommended.

(c)   One of the strengths of internal rate of return (IRR) as a method of appraising capital investments is that it is a discounted cash flow (DCF) method and so takes account of the time value of money. It also considers cash flows over the whole of the project life and is sensitive to both the amount and the timing of cash flows. It is preferred by some as it offers a relative measure of the value of a proposed investment, i.e. the method calculates a percentage that can be compared with the company's cost of capital, and with economic variables such as inflation rates and interest rates.

IRR has several weaknesses as a method of appraising capital investments. Since it is a relative measurement of investment worth, it does not measure the absolute increase in company value (and therefore shareholder wealth), which can be found using the net present value (NPV) method. A further problem arises when evaluating non-conventional projects (where cash flows change from positive to negative during the life of the project). IRR may offer as many IRR values as there are changes in the value of cash flows, giving rise to evaluation difficulties. There is a potential conflict between IRR and NPV in the evaluation of mutually exclusive projects, where the two methods can offer conflicting advice as which of two projects is preferable. Where there is conflict, NPV always offers the correct investment advice: IRR does not, although the advice offered can be amended by considering the IRR of the incremental project. There are therefore a number of reasons why IRR can be seen as an inferior investment appraisal method compared to its DCF alternative, NPV.

ACCA marking scheme		
		Marks
(a)	Discount rate	1 mark	
	Inflated sales revenue	2 marks	
	Inflated variable cost	1 mark	
	Inflated fixed production overheads	1 mark	
	Taxation	2 marks	
	Capital allowance tax benefits	3 marks	
	Discount factors	1 mark	
	Net present value	1 mark	
	Comment	1 mark	
			13
(b)	Calculation of average annual accounting profit	2 marks	
	Calculation of average investment	2 marks	
	Calculation of return on capital employed	1 mark	
			5
(c)	Strengths of IRR	2–3 marks	
	Weaknesses of IRR	5–6 marks	
	Maximum		7
Total			25

26   CHARM INC

Key answer tips

In part (a) the NPV calculation is reasonably straightforward provided you read the information carefully. The calculation of fixed costs is an easy number to get wrong if you didn't carefully read that the financial information presented on 'Fingo' was for the first year of production.

In part (c) ensure you compare with NPV with other appraisal methods rather than just stating the benefits of NPV. The highlighted words are key phrases that markers are looking for.

(a)   **Calculation of NPV of 'Fingo' investment project**

Year	1	2	3	4
	$000	$000	$000	$000
Sales revenue	3,750	1,680	1,380	1,320
Direct materials	(810)	(378)	(324)	(324)
Variable production	(900)	(420)	(360)	(360)
Advertising	(650)	(100)		
Fixed costs (W1)	(600)	(600)	(600)	(600)
Taxable cash flow	790	182	96	36
Taxation	(237)	(55)	(29)	(11)
	553	127	67	25
CA tax benefits (W2)	60	45	34	101
Net cash flow	613	172	101	126
Discount at 10%	0.909	0.826	0.751	0.683
Present values	557.2	142.1	75.9	86.1

	$000
Present value of future benefits	861.3
Initial investment	800.0
Net present value	61.3

Workings

(W1) Fixed costs in year 1 = $150,000 × 4 = $600,000 and since these represent a one-off increase in fixed production overheads, these are the fixed costs in subsequent years as well.

(W2) **Capital allowance (CA) tax benefits**

Year	Capital allowance ($)		Tax benefit ($)	
1	200,000	(800,000 × 0.25)	60,000	(0.3 × 200,000)
2	150,000	(600,000 × 0.25)	45,000	(0.3 × 150,000)
3	112,500	(450,000 × 0.25)	33,750	(0.3 × 112,500)
	462,500			
	nil	(scrap value)		
	462,500			
4	337,500	(by difference)	101,250	(0.3 × 337,500)
	800,000			

Comment

The net present value of $61,300 is positive and the investment can therefore be recommended on financial grounds. However, it should be noted that the positive net present value depends heavily on sales in the first year. In fact, sensitivity analysis shows that a decrease of 5% in first year sales will result in a zero net present value. (Note: you are not expected to conduct a sensitivity analysis)

(b) **Calculation of IRR of 'Fingo' investment project**

Year	1	2	3	4
	$000	$000	$000	$000
Net cash flow	613	172	101	126
Discount at 20%	0.833	0.694	0.579	0.482
Present values	510.6	119.4	58.5	60.7

	$000
Present value of future benefits	749.2
Initial investment	800.0
Net present value	(50.8)

Internal rate of return = 10 + [(20 -10) × (61.3 / (61.3 + 50.8))] = 15.5%

Since the internal rate of return is greater than the discount rate used to appraise new investments, the proposed investment is financially acceptable.

(c)   There are many reasons that could be discussed in support of the view that net present value (NPV) is superior to other investment appraisal methods.

NPV considers cash flows

This is the reason why NPV is preferred to return on capital employed (ROCE), since ROCE compares average annual accounting profit with initial or average capital invested. Financial management always prefers cash flows to accounting profit, since profit is seen as being open to manipulation. Furthermore, only cash flows are capable of adding to the wealth of shareholders in the form of increased dividends. Both internal rate of return (IRR) and Payback also consider cash flows.

NPV considers the whole of an investment project

In this respect NPV is superior to Payback, which measures the time it takes for an investment project to repay the initial capital invested. Payback therefore considers cash flows within the payback period and ignores cash flows outside of the payback period. If Payback is used as an investment appraisal method, projects yielding high returns outside of the payback period will be wrongly rejected. In practice, however, it is unlikely that Payback will be used alone as an investment appraisal method.

NPV considers the time value of money

NPV and IRR are both discounted cash flow (DCF) models which consider the time value of money, whereas ROCE and Payback do not. Although Discounted Payback can be used to appraise investment projects, this method still suffers from the criticism that it ignores cash flows outside of the payback period. Considering the time value of money is essential, since otherwise cash flows occurring at different times cannot be distinguished from each other in terms of value from the perspective of the present time.

NPV is an absolute measure of return

NPV is seen as being superior to investment appraisal methods that offer a relative measure of return, such as IRR and ROCE, and which therefore fail to reflect the amount of the initial investment or the absolute increase in corporate value. Defenders of IRR and ROCE respond that these methods offer a measure of return that is understandable by managers and which can be intuitively compared with economic variables such as interest rates and inflation rates.

NPV links directly to the objective of maximising shareholders' wealth

The NPV of an investment project represents the change in total market value that will occur if the investment project is accepted. The increase in wealth of each shareholder can therefore be measured by the increase in the value of their shareholding as a percentage of the overall issued share capital of the company. Other investment appraisal methods do not have this direct link with the primary financial management objective of the company.

NPV always offers the correct investment advice

With respect to mutually exclusive projects, NPV always indicates which project should be selected in order to achieve the maximum increase on corporate value. This is not true of IRR, which offers incorrect advice at discount rates which are less than the internal rate of return of the incremental cash flows. This problem can be overcome by using the incremental yield approach.

NPV can accommodate changes in the discount rate

While NPV can easily accommodate changes in the discount rate, IRR simply ignores them, since the calculated internal rate of return is independent of the cost of capital in all time periods.

NPV has a sensible re-investment assumption

NPV assumes that intermediate cash flows are re-invested at the company's cost of capital, which is a reasonable assumption as the company's cost of capital represents the average opportunity cost of the company's providers of finance, i.e. it represents a rate of return which exists in the real world. By contrast, IRR assumes that intermediate cash flows are reinvested at the internal rate of return, which is not an investment rate available in practice,

NPV can accommodate non-conventional cash flows

Non-conventional cash flows exist when negative cash flows arise during the life of the project. For each change in sign there is potentially one additional internal rate of return. With non-conventional cash flows, therefore, IRR can suffer from the technical problem of giving multiple internal rates of return.

27   PLAY CO

Key answer tips

This is a fairly typical NPV with tax and inflation question. The key to picking up the easy marks in the calculative part (a) is to take a methodical approach that you show clearly in a series of workings.

Parts (b) & (c) are more discursive and require you to demonstrate your knowledge in the context of this scenario. Try to think broadly and ensure you go into sufficient depth in your answer to score highly.

The highlighted words in the written sections are key phrases that markers are looking for.

(a)

Year	1	2	3	4	5
	$000	$000	$000	$000	$000
Costs saved (W1)	350	385	455	560	
Variable costs (W2)	(82)	(94)	(113)	(144)	
Maintenance costs	(42)	(44)	(46)	(49)	
Fixed costs (W3)	(66)	(68)	(69)	(70)	
	——	——	——	——	
Taxable cash flow	160	180	227	297	
Taxation		(48)	(54)	(68)	(89)
CA tax benefits (W4)		30	23	17	36
Scrap value				50	
	——	——	——	——	——
After-tax cash flows	160	162	196	296	(53)
Discount at 15%	0.870	0.756	0.658	0.572	0.497
	——	——	——	——	——
Present values	139	122	129	169	(26)

	$000
Present value of benefits	533
Initial investment	400
Early termination fine	150
Net present value	(18)

The net present value is negative and so the investment is not financially acceptable.

Workings

(W1) **Costs saved**

Year	1	2	3	4
Demand (tonnes/yr)	100,000	110,000	130,000	160,000
Cost ($/tonne)	3.50	3.50	3.50	3.50
Contribution ($/yr)	350,000	385,000	455,000	560,000

(W2) **Variable costs incurred**

Year	1	2	3	4
Demand (tonnes/yr)	100,000	110,000	130,000	160,000
Cost ($/tonne) – 3% inflation	0.82	0.85	0.87	0.90
Contribution ($/yr)	82,000	93,500	113,100	144,000

(W3) **Fixed costs incurred**

Annual depreciation = ($400,000 – $50,000) ÷ 4 = $87,500

Other fixed costs = $192,500 – $87,500 – $40,000 = $65,000

Inflating at 2% per annum

(W4) **Capital allowance (CA) tax benefits**

Year	Capital allowance ($)		Tax benefit ($)	
1	100,000	(400,000 × 0.25)	30,000	(0.3 × 100,000)
2	75,000	(300,000 × 0.25)	22,500	(0.3 × 75,000)
3	56,250	(225,000 × 0.25)	16,875	(0.3 × 56,250)
	231,250			
	50,000	(scrap value)		
	281,250			
4	118,750	(by difference)	35,625	(0.3 × 118,750)
	400,000			

(b)

Tutorial note:

There are more points noted below than would be needed to earn full marks, however, they do reflect the full range of limitations that could be discussed.

NPV is a commonly used technique employed in investment appraisal, but it is subject to a number of restrictive assumptions and limitations which call into question its general relevance. Nonetheless, if the assumptions and limitations are understood then its application is less likely to be undertaken in error.

Some of the difficulties with NPV are listed below:

(i) NPV assumes that firms pursue an objective of maximising the wealth of their shareholders. This is questionable given the wider range of stakeholders who might have conflicting interests to those of the shareholders. NPV is largely redundant if organisations are not wealth maximising. For example, public sector organisations may wish to invest in capital assets but will use non-profit objectives as part of their assessment.

(ii) NPV is potentially a difficult method to apply in the context of having to estimate what is the correct discount rate to use. This is particularly so when questions arise as to the incorporation of risk premia in the discount rate, since an evaluation of the riskiness of the business, or of the project in particular, will have to be made but may be difficult to discern. In this instance, the additional fixed costs will increase the risk profile of the business and this will need to be factored in.

(iii) NPV can most easily cope with cash flows arising at period ends and is not a technique that is used easily when complicated, mid-period cash flows are present.

(iv) NPV is not universally employed, especially in a small business environment. The available evidence suggests that businesses assess projects in a variety of ways (payback, IRR, accounting rate of return). The fact that such methods are used which are theoretically inferior to NPV calls into question the practical benefits of NPV, and therefore hints at certain practical limitations.

(v) The conclusion from NPV analysis is the present value of the surplus cash generated from a project. If reported profits are important to businesses, then it is possible that there may be a conflict between undertaking a positive NPV project and potentially adverse consequences on reported profits. This will particularly be the case for projects with long time horizons, large initial investment and very delayed cash inflows. In such circumstances, businesses may prefer to use accounting measures of investment appraisal.

(vi) Managerial incentive schemes may not be consistent with NPV, particularly when long time horizons are involved. Thus managers may be rewarded on the basis of accounting profits in the short term and may be incentivised to act in accordance with these objectives, and thus ignore positive NPV projects. This may be a problem of the incentive schemes and not of NPV; nonetheless, a potential conflict exists and represents a difficulty for NPV.

(vii)   NPV treats all time periods equally, with the exception of discounting far cash flows more than near cash flows. In other words, NPV only accounts for the time value of money. To many businesses, distant horizons are less important than near horizons, if only because that is the environment in which they work. Other factors besides applying higher discount rates may work to reduce the impact of distant years. For example, in the long term, nearly all aspects of the business may change and hence a too-narrow focus on discounting means that NPV is of limited value and more so the further the time horizon considered.

(viii) NPV is of limited use in the face of non-quantifiable benefits or costs. NPV does not take account of non-financial information which may even be relevant to shareholders who want their wealth maximised. For example, issues of strategic or environmental benefit may arise against which it is difficult to immediately quantify the benefits but for which there are immediate costs. NPV would treat such a situation as an additional cost since it could not incorporate the indiscernible benefit.

(c)

Tutor's top tips:

Start by identifying the range of stakeholders affected before considering the impact this proposal will have on them. Make sure you include the details given in the scenario to ensure you give a tailored answer.

The project should affect the different stakeholders of Play Co as follows:

Stakeholder	Impact
Shareholders	• Wealth would decrease by the negative NPV of the project – i.e. $18,000 • Risks will increase due the higher fixed costs (increased operational gearing)
Society	• More tyres will be recycled, protecting the environment
Customers	• Customers may perceive the quality of the product to increase because it is more environmentally friendly
Suppliers	• Existing suppliers of particles will lose business (although they will receive the $150,000 early termination fine)
Potential investors	• Play Co will become more attractive to "green chip" investors, possibly making future financing easier.

28 DUO CO *Walk in the footsteps of a top tutor*

Key answer tips

Given the generic nature of part (c) and the significant number of marks available (32% of the total), it would be sensible to tackle this part of the requirement first. You can then follow on with the calculations in part (a) and (b).

The key learning point from this question is the importance of being efficient when reading the scenario to cut down on the amount of time wasted trying to locate information. By forming an expectation of what you'll be given and considering the significance of information that you read, you can easily complete the question in the time allocated. The highlighted words are key phrases that markers are looking for.

(a) Net present value evaluation of investment

Tutor's top tips:

An NPV calculation in part (a) followed by an IRR calculation in part (b) is a fairly common exam question. Clearly it is more logical to tackle part (a) first. One important aspect to note from the requirement is to work to the nearest $1,000. This can help to save a significant amount of time when performing the calculations and noting your workings.

Knowing that you must calculate an NPV, you should carefully read the scenario, looking for details on:

— *Relevant cash flows*

— *Tax payments (1 year time lag or not)*

— *Capital expenditure and scrap values*

— *Timescales and length of the project*

— *Working capital*

— *Inflation*

— *Discount rate*

Whenever you read any details, make a note in the margin on what that section provides you information on. This will help prevent you having to re-read the scenario several times to find the bit of information you require.

From reading this scenario, you should have noted that:

— *Relevant cash flows will be the incremental contribution and fixed costs only*

— *Incremental contribution will be calculated based on the excess of demand over current production capacity (one million kilograms)*

— *The maximum output of the new machine is 600,000 kg meaning that even with the new machine, Duo will be unable to produce more that 1.6 million kg.*

— *The tax rate is 30% and there is a one year time lag*

- The cost of the machine is $800,000 and it will be scrapped in four years time for $30,000

- The length of the project is four years

- You are not given any information on working capital requirements or inflation. These can therefore be ignored.

- You have not been told what discount rate to use. Instead you've been given information on the cost of equity and the cost of debt, together with the capital structure (ratio of equity to debt) in the company

Having gleaned this information, you should start by setting up your proforma NPV calculation based on 5 periods (4 years of the project + 1 year time lag for tax). Next you should enter in any easy numbers that require little or no calculation. This would include the asset purchase and scrap and the incremental fixed costs.

Now you can move on to calculating some of the more complex numbers. All of these calculations should be performed using workings that should be clearly cross referenced to your main NPV calculation. You should end up with workings for contribution (make sure you clearly show how many extra units will be sold), the tax effect of capital allowances and the weighted average cost of capital / discount factors. As you complete each working, transfer the numbers into your main calculation and add anything extra that you can now complete (for example, once you have calculated contribution, you can enter the tax charge at 30%). When all of your workings are complete, discount the cash flow in each year and work out the net present value. Don't forget that the requirement is to calculate and advise. There will always be marks available for reaching a conclusion and stating whether the project should be accepted or not. Note the examiner's comment (below) about explaining your decision.

After-tax weighted average cost of capital = $(11 \times 0.8) + (8.6 \times (1 - 0.3) \times 0.2) = 10\%$

Year	1	2	3	4	5
	$000	$000	$000	$000	$000
Contribution	440	550	660	660	
Fixed costs	(240)	(260)	(280)	(300)	
Taxable cash flow	200	290	380	360	
Taxation		(60)	(87)	(114)	(108)
CA tax benefits		60	45	34	92
Scrap value				30	
After-tax cash flows	200	290	338	310	(16)
Discount at 10%	0.909	0.826	0.751	0.683	0.621
Present values	182	240	254	212	(10)

	$000
Present value of benefits	878
Initial investment	800
Net present value	78

The net present value is positive and so the investment is financially acceptable. However, demand becomes greater than production capacity in the fourth year of operation and so further investment in new machinery may be needed after three years. The new machine will itself need replacing after four years if production capacity is to be maintained at an increased level. It may be necessary to include these expansion and replacement considerations for a more complete appraisal of the proposed investment.

A more complete appraisal of the investment could address issues such as the assumption of constant selling price and variable cost per kilogram and the absence of any consideration of inflation, the linear increase in fixed costs of production over time and the linear increase in demand over time. If these issues are not addressed, the appraisal of investing in the new machine is likely to possess a significant degree of uncertainty.

Workings

Annual contribution

Year	1	2	3	4
Excess demand (kg/yr)	400,000	500,000	600,000	700,000
New machine output (kg/yr)	400,000	500,000	600,000	600,000
Contribution ($/kg)	1.1	1.1	1.1	1.1
Contribution ($/yr)	440,000	550,000	660,000	660,000

Capital allowance (CA) tax benefits

Year	Capital allowance ($)	Tax benefit ($)		
1	200,000	$(800,000 \times 0.25)$	60,000	$(0.3 \times 200,000)$
2	150,000	$(600,000 \times 0.25)$	45,000	$(0.3 \times 150,000)$
3	112,500	$(450,000 \times 0.25)$	33,750	$(0.3 \times 112,500)$
	462,500			
	30,000	(scrap value)		
	492,500			
4	307,500	(by difference)	92,250	$(0.3 \times 307,500)$
	800,000			

(b) **Internal rate of return evaluation of investment**

Tutor's top tips:

Finally, for part (b) you will need to quickly calculate a second NPV, using the cash flows you've worked out for part (a). Try to choose you second discount rate sensibly. For example, if your answer to part (a) was a positive NPV, you should select a second discount rate that is higher than the one you originally used.

If you are running out of time, a useful shortcut is to add up the undiscounted cash flows and treat that as an NPV at 0%. Your resulting answer will not be as accurate and you may not pick up all of the marks available but it will allow you to access the marks for advising on the acceptability of the proposal.

Year	1	2	3	4	5
	$000	$000	$000	$000	$000
After-tax cash flows	200	290	338	310	(16)
Discount at 20%	0.833	0.694	0.579	0.482	0.402
Present values	167	201	196	149	(6)

	$000
Present value of benefits	707
Initial investment	800
Net present value	(93)

Internal rate of return = $10 + [((20 − 10) \times 78)/(78 + 93)] = 10 + 4.6 = 14.6\%$

The investment is financially acceptable since the internal rate of return is greater than the cost of capital used for investment appraisal purposes. However, the appraisal suffers from the limitations discussed in connection with net present value appraisal in part (a).

Tutor's top tips:

A careful read of the requirement shows that part (c) is essentially three requirements rolled into one:

(i)   Explain the difference between risk and uncertainty

(ii)   Describe how sensitivity analysis can be used to incorporate risk into investment appraisal

(iii) Describe how probability analysis can be used to incorporate risk into investment appraisal

Given the verbs being used (both 'explain' and 'describe' imply much more that merely 'stating') we can expect between 2 & 3 marks for each section, with 2 or 3 relevant comments picking up those marks.

Don't forget, there are often marks available for defining terms. So in part (i), a definition should be given of both risk and uncertainty before the differences between the two are explained. Similarly, in parts (ii) & (iii), you could define both sensitivity analysis and probability analysis before describing how they incorporate risk into the appraisal process.

Finally, you could touch on the common problems with the two techniques although be careful not to spend too much time on this as it wasn't specifically mentioned in the requirement. Now you can move on to the numerical aspects of the question.

(c)   Risk refers to the situation where probabilities can be assigned to a range of expected outcomes arising from an investment project and the likelihood of each outcome occurring can therefore be quantified. Uncertainty refers to the situation where probabilities cannot be assigned to expected outcomes. Investment project risk therefore increases with increasing variability of returns, while uncertainty increases with increasing project life. The two terms are often used interchangeably in financial management, but the distinction between them is a useful one.

Sensitivity analysis assesses how the net present value of an investment project is affected by changes in project variables. Considering each project variable in turn, the change in the variable required to make the net present value zero is determined, or alternatively the change in net present value arising from a fixed change in the given project variable. In this way the key or critical project variables are determined. However, sensitivity analysis does not assess the probability of changes in project variables and so is often dismissed as a way of incorporating risk into the investment appraisal process.

Probability analysis refers to the assessment of the separate probabilities of a number of specified outcomes of an investment project. For example, a range of expected market conditions could be formulated and the probability of each market condition arising in each of several future years could be assessed. The net present values arising from combinations of future economic conditions could then be assessed and linked to the joint probabilities of those combinations. The expected net present value (ENPV) could be calculated, together with the probability of the worst-case scenario and the probability of a negative net present value. In this way, the downside risk of the investment could be determined and incorporated into the investment decision.

ACCA marking scheme		
		Marks
(a)	After-tax weighted average cost of capital	2
	Annual contribution	2
	Fixed costs	1
	Taxation	1
	Capital allowance tax benefits	3
	Scrap value	1
	Discount factors	1
	Net present value	1
	Comment	1–2
		13
(b)	Net present value calculation	1
	Internal rate of return calculation	2
	Comment	1–2
		4
(c)	Risk and uncertainty	2–3
	Discussion of sensitivity analysis	2–3
	Discussion of probability analysis	2–3
		8
Total		25

Examiner's comments

Part (a) of this question asked candidates to calculate the net present value (NPV) of buying a new machine and to advise on its acceptability. Many candidates gained very high marks here.

Common errors (where there were errors) included failing to calculate correctly the weighted average cost of capital of the investing company (for example using the before-tax rather than the after-tax cost of debt in the calculation): failing to use incremental demand as the production volume of the new machine; failing to recognise the cap on production in Year 4 compared to demand; failing to lag tax liability by one year; including scrap value or tax benefits of capital allowances with taxable income; incorrect calculation of balancing allowance; treating initial investment as a Year 1 rather than a Year 0 cash flow; and using annuity factors rather than discount factors in calculating NPV.

A number of candidates lost straightforward marks by failing to comment on the calculated NPV, or by simply saying 'accept' without referring to the NPV decision rule. The reason for accepting an investment project must be clearly explained.

In part (b) candidates were asked to calculate the internal rate of return (IRR) of buying the new machine and to advise on its acceptability. Many candidates gained full marks here. Some candidates lost marks through the incorrect application of linear interpolation in calculating IRR (for example adding instead of subtracting values, or multiplying instead of adding). Some candidates said that both a positive NPV and a negative NPV were needed in order to calculate IRR, when in fact two positive values can be used (resulting in extrapolation, but the extrapolation calculation is identical in structure to an interpolation calculation). A number of candidates lost a straightforward mark by not commenting on their calculated IRR.

Some candidates confused IRR with accounting rate of return (ARR) and as a result gained no credit.

Candidates were asked in part (c) to explain the difference between risk and uncertainty in the context of investment appraisal, and to describe how sensitivity analysis and probability analysis could be used to incorporate risk and uncertainty into investment appraisal. Answers here tended to be weaker than answers to parts (a) and (b).

Many candidates were not able to explain the difference between risk and uncertainty in investment appraisal, offering answers that were founded on interpretations of the words 'risk' and 'uncertainty', or which discussed the various kinds of risk to be found in financial management. The key point is to recognise that risk can be quantified (probabilities can be assigned and outcomes can be predicted) while uncertainty cannot be quantified. Answers that offered numerical examples of sensitivity analysis or probability analysis gained credit, although candidates should note that sensitivity analysis is not a method of measuring or predicting risk.

29 OKM CO

Key answer tips

The style of this question is not something we've seen regularly from the examiner. Based on the core topic of investment appraisal, students should easily be able to spot the mistakes in the appraisal presented and, having done that, should not encountered many problems preparing a revised calculation. The highlighted words are key phrases that markers are looking for.

(a)   **Errors in the original investment appraisal**

Inflation was incorrectly applied to selling prices and variable costs in calculating contribution, since only one year's inflation was allowed for in each year of operation.

The fixed costs were correctly inflated, but included $200,000 per year before inflation that was not a relevant cost. Only relevant costs should be included in investment appraisal.

Straight-line accounting depreciation had been used in the calculation, but this depreciation method is not acceptable to the tax authorities. The approved method using 25% reducing balance capital allowances should be used.

Interest payments have been included in the investment appraisal, but these are allowed for by the discount rate used in calculating the net present value.

The interest rate on the debt finance has been used as the discount rate, when the nominal weighted average cost of capital should have been used to discount the calculated nominal after-tax cash flows.

(b)   Nominal weighted average cost of capital = 1.07 × 1.047 = 1.12, i.e. 12% per year

Year	1	2	3	4	5
	$000	$000	$000	$000	$000
Contribution	1,330	2,264	3,010	1,600	
Fixed costs	(318)	(337)	(357)	(379)	
Taxable cash flow	1,012	1,927	2,653	1,221	
Taxation		(304)	(578)	(796)	(366)
CA tax benefits		150	112	84	178
After-tax cash flow	1,012	1,773	2,187	509	(188)
Scrap value				250	
After-tax cash flows	1,012	1,773	2,187	759	(188)
Discount at 12%	0.893	0.797	0.712	0.635	0.567
Present values	904	1,413	1,557	482	(107)

	$000
Present value of future cash flows	4,249
Initial investment	2,000
Net present value	2,249

The net present value is positive and so the investment is financially acceptable.

Alternative NPV calculation using taxable profit calculation

Year	1	2	3	4	5
	$000	$000	$000	$000	$000
Contribution	1,330	2,264	3,010	1,600	
Fixed costs	(318)	(337)	(357)	(379)	
Taxable cash flow	1,012	1,927	2,653	1,221	
Capital allowances	(500)	(375)	(281)	(594)	
Taxable profit	512	1,552	2,372	627	
Taxation	(154)	(466)	(712)	(188)	
Profit after tax	512	1,398	1,906	(85)	(188)
Capital allowances	500	375	281	594	
After-tax cash flow	1,012	1,773	2,187	509	(188)
Scrap value		250			
After-tax cash flows	1,012	1,773	2,187	759	(188)
Discount at 12%	0.893	0.797	0.712	0.635	0.567
Present values	904	1,413	1,557	482	(107)

	$000
Present value of future cash flows	4,249
Initial investment	2,000
Net present value	2,249

Workings

Annual contribution

Year	1	2	3	4
Sales volume (units/yr)	250,000	400,000	500,000	250,000
Selling price ($/unit)	12.60	13.23	13.89	14.59
Variable cost ($/unit)	7.28	7.57	7.87	8.19
Contribution ($/unit)	5.32	5.66	6.02	6.40
Contribution ($/yr)	1,330,000	2,264,000	3,010,000	1,600,000

Capital allowance (CA) tax benefits

Year	Capital allowance ($)	Tax benefit ($)
1	500,000	150,000
2	375,000	112,500
3	281,250	84,375
4	593,750	178,125
Scrap value	250,000	
	2,000,000	

(c) (i) **Asset replacement decisions**

The problem here is that the net present value investment appraisal method may offer incorrect advice about when an asset should be replaced. The lowest present value of costs may not indicate the optimum replacement period.

The most straightforward solution to this problem is to use the equivalent annual cost method. The equivalent annual cost of a replacement period is found by dividing the present value of costs by the annuity factor or cumulative present value factor for the replacement period under consideration. The optimum replacement period is then the one that has the lowest equivalent annual cost.

Tutorial note:

Other solutions that could be discussed are the lowest common multiple method and the limited time horizon method.

(ii) **Multiple internal rates of return**

An investment project may have multiple internal rates of return if it has unconventional cash flows, that is, cash flows that change sign over the life of the project. A mining operation, for example, may have initial investment (cash outflow) followed by many years of successful operation (cash inflow) before decommissioning and environmental repair (cash outflow). This technical difficulty makes it difficult to use the internal rate of return (IRR) investment appraisal method to offer investment advice.

One solution is to use the net present value (NPV) investment appraisal method instead of IRR, since the non-conventional cash flows are easily accommodated by NPV. This is one area where NPV is considered to be superior to IRR.

(iii) **Projects with significantly different business risk to current operations**

Where a proposed investment project has business risk that is significantly different from current operations, it is no longer appropriate to use the weighted average cost of capital (WACC) as the discount rate in calculating the net present value of the project. WACC can only be used as a discount rate where business risk and financial risk are not significantly affected by undertaking an investment project.

Where business risk changes significantly, the capital asset pricing model should be used to calculate a project-specific discount rate which takes account of the systematic risk of a proposed investment project.

ACCA marking scheme			Marks
(a)	Identification of errors in the evaluation		
		Maximum	5
(b)	Nominal weighted average cost of capital		1
	Inflated selling prices		1
	Inflated variable costs		1
	Inflated contribution		1
	Inflated fixed costs		1
	Capital allowances and/or related tax benefits		3
	Scrap value		1
	Discount factors		1
	Net present value		1
	Comment		1–2
		Maximum	12
(c)	Discussion of asset replacement decisions		2–3
	Discussion of projects with several IRR		2–3
	Discussion of projects with different business risk		3–4
		Maximum	8
Total			25

Examiner's comments

Many students did well on parts (a) and (b) of this question, while finding part (c) to be more challenging.

In part (a), candidates were asked to identify and comment on any errors in an investment appraisal prepared by a trainee accountant. Candidates who did not gain full marks failed to identify clearly the errors they had identified, or did not comment on these errors, or identified errors that did not exist.

Part (b) required candidates to prepare a revised calculation of the NPV of an investment project and to comment on its acceptability.

Many candidates did well here, using the template of the NPV calculation provided in the question to prepare a corrected calculation. The contribution had to be inflated correctly, the fixed costs had to be calculated correctly, the depreciation and interest payments had to be stripped out, the tax effect of capital allowances needed to be calculated and included, and the correct discount rate had to be used.

Candidates who did not amend the provided contribution figures were not aware that inflation must be applied every year and not just in the first year. The development costs had to be excluded from the fixed costs in the investment appraisal because they had already been incurred, i.e. they were not relevant costs. Depreciation had to be stripped out because it is not a cash flow, and NPV is an investment appraisal method that uses cash flows. Interest payments had to be excluded because they would be taken account of by the discount rate.

The tax effect of capital allowances (tax allowable depreciation) could be included by any one of three methods: by using the correctly timed tax benefits of each capital allowance; by subtracting the capital allowances from taxable cash flow to give taxable profit and then adding them back after calculating the tax liability; and by carrying out a separate tax calculation.

Within the investment appraisal, cash flows had been inflated by specific inflation rates and so the evaluation was a nominal terms (or money terms) evaluation, requiring a nominal discount rate. The real discount rate was provided in the question, together with the general rate of inflation, and the nominal discount rate could be calculated from these two pieces of information using the Fisher equation.

Part (c) tested candidates' understanding of different aspects of investment appraisal by asking what problems were faced, and how these problems could be overcome, in three different investment appraisal areas.

The first investment appraisal area related to assets with replacement cycles of different lengths. Many candidates stated correctly that the NPV method may not choose the optimum asset, and that this problem could be overcome by adopting an equivalent annual cost approach.

The second investment appraisal area related to multiple internal rates of return, a technical problem associated with non-conventional cash flows that is not experienced by NPV.

The third investment appraisal area related to investments with a different level of business risk than the investing company. Many candidates identified correctly here that the capital asset pricing model could be used to calculate a project-specific discount rate that reflected project risk.

30 UMUNAT INC

Key answer tips

The calculations in this question are quite straightforward although you would not be able to pass the question if you focussed on the numbers alone. Don't neglect the discussional element of parts of the requirement that might at first appear to be numerical. Virtually half of the marks available in parts (b), (c), & (d) will be for the commentary that accompanies your calculations. The highlighted words are key phrases that markers are looking for.

(a) The investment appraisal process is concerned with assessing the value of future cash flows compared to the cost of investment.

Since future cash flows cannot be predicted with certainty, managers must consider how much confidence can be placed in the results of the investment appraisal process. They must therefore be concerned with the risk and uncertainty of a project. Uncertainty refers to the situation where probabilities cannot be assigned to future cash flows. Uncertainty cannot therefore be quantified and increases with project life: it is usually true to say that the more distant is a cash flow, the more uncertain is its value. Risk refers to the situation where probabilities can be assigned to future cash flows, for example as a result of managerial experience and judgement or scenario analysis. Where such probabilities can be assigned, it is possible to quantify the risk associated with project variables and hence of the project as a whole.

If risk and uncertainty were not considered in the investment appraisal process, managers might make the mistake of placing too much confidence in the results of investment appraisal, or they may fail to monitor investment projects in order to ensure that expected results are in fact being achieved. Assessment of project risk can also indicate projects that might be rejected as being too risky compared with existing business operations, or projects that might be worthy of reconsideration if ways of reducing project risk could be found in order to make project outcomes more acceptable.

(b) Contribution per unit   = 3.00 – 1.65 = $1.35 per unit

   Total annual contribution   = 20,000 × 1.35 = $27,000 per year

   Annual cash flow after fixed costs = 27,000 – 10,000 = $17,000 per year

   Payback period   = 50,000/17,000 = 2.9 years

   (assuming that cash flows occur evenly throughout the year)

   The payback period calculated is greater than the maximum payback period used by Umunat Inc of two years and on this basis should be rejected. Use of payback period as an investment appraisal method cannot be recommended, however, because payback period does not consider all the cash flows arising from an investment project, as it ignores cash flows outside of the payback period. Furthermore, payback period ignores the time value of money.

   The fact that the payback period is 2.9 years should not therefore be a reason for rejecting the project. The project should be assessed using a discounted cash flow method such as net present value or internal rate of return, since the project as a whole may generate an acceptable return on investment.

(c) **Calculation of project net present value**

Annual cash flow = ((20,000 × (3 − 1.65)) − 10,000 = $17,000 per year

Net present value = (17,000 × 3.605) − 50,000 = 61,285 − 50,000 = $11,285

	PV ($)
Alternatively:	
Sales revenue: 20,000 × 3.00 × 3.605 =	216,300
Variable costs: 20,000 × 1.65 × 3.605 =	(118,965)
Contribution	97,335
Initial investment	(50,000)
Fixed costs: 10,000 × 3.605 =	(36,050)
Net present value:	11,285

Sensitivity of NPV to sales volume

Sales volume giving zero NPV = ((50,000/3.605) + 10,000)/1.35 = 17,681 units.

This is a decrease of 2,319 units or 11.6%.

Alternatively, sales volume decrease = 100 × 11,285/97,335= 11.6%.

Tutorial note:

The second method presented above is probably the method most people will feel comfortable with. This uses the generic formula of:

$$\frac{NPV}{PV \text{ of affected cashflow}} \times 100\%$$

Sensitivity of NPV to sales price

Sales price for zero NPV = (((50,000/3.605) + 10,000)/20,000) + 1.65 = $2.843.

This is a decrease of 15.7¢ or 5.2%.

Alternatively, sales price decrease = 100 × 11,285/216,300 = 5.2%.

Sensitivity of NPV to variable cost

Variable cost must increase by 15.7¢ or 9.5% to make the NPV zero.

Alternatively, variable cost increase = 100 × 11,285/118,965 = 9.5%.

Sensitivity analysis evaluates the effect on project net present value of changes in project variables. The objective is to determine the key or critical project variables, which are those where the smallest change produces the biggest change in project NPV. It is limited in that only one project variable at a time may be changed, whereas in reality several project variables may change simultaneously. For example, an increase in inflation could result in increases in sales price, variable costs and fixed costs. Sensitivity analysis is not a way of evaluating project risk, since although it may identify the key or critical variables, it cannot assess the likelihood of a change in these variables. In other words, sensitivity analysis does not assign probabilities to project variables. Where sensitivity analysis is useful is in drawing the attention of management to project variables that need careful monitoring if a particular investment project is to meet expectations. Sensitivity analysis can also highlight the need to check the assumptions underlying the key or critical variables.

(d)   **Expected value of sales volume**

(17,500 × 0.3) + (20,000 × 0.6) + (22,500 × 0.1) = 19,500 units

Expected NPV = (((19,500 × 1.35) − 10,000) × 3.605) − 50,000 = $8,852

Since the expected net present value is positive, the project appears to be acceptable. From earlier analysis we know that the NPV is positive at 20,000 per year, and the NPV will therefore also be positive at 22,500 units per year. The NPV of the worst case is:

(((17,500 × 1.35) − 10,000) × 3.605) − 50,000 = ($882)

The NPV of the best case is:

(((22,500 × 1.35) − 10,000) × 3.605) − 50,000 = $23,452

There is thus a 30% chance that the project will produce a negative NPV, a fact not revealed by considering the expected net present value alone.

The expected net present value is not a value that is likely to occur in practice: it is perhaps more useful to know that there is a 30% chance that the project will produce a negative NPV (or a 70% chance of a positive NPV), since this may represent an unacceptable level of risk as far as the managers of Umunat Inc are concerned. It can therefore be argued that assigning probabilities to expected economic states or sales volumes has produced useful information that can help the managers of Umunat Inc to make better investment decisions. The difficulty with this approach is that probability estimates of project variables or future economic states are likely to carry a high degree of uncertainty and subjectivity.

31   VICTORY

Key answer tips

Parts (a) and (c) offer some good opportunities to pick up some relatively easy marks. Both require you to apply a sound knowledge base to the scenario given. Part (c) should be attempted first in order to manage time more effectively for the required calculations.

Part (b) is slightly more challenging although those who keep going and apply some of the basic principles should be able to comfortably achieve a pass mark.

(a) **NPV**

$000	T0	T1	T2	T3
Sales (60,000 × $40)		2,400	2,400	2,400
Variable costs (60,000 × $25)		(1,500)	(1,500)	(1,500)
Fixed costs (W1)		(355)	(355)	(355)
Rent	(80)	(80)	(80)	
Net operating cash flows	(80)	465	465	545
Tax	24	(140)	(140)	(164)
Initial cost	(1,200)			
Capital allowances (W2)		90	68	22
Residual value				600
WC	(340)	(60)	(50)	450
Totals	**(1,596)**	**355**	**343**	**1,453**
10% DF	1	0.909	0.826	0.751
PV	**(1,596)**	**323**	**283**	**1,091**

Hence the NPV is about $101,000, which would suggest that the equipment is purchased.

Tutorial note:

Remember, relevant cash flows are those which are in the future, incremental to the project and that correspond to actual cash flows and not notional charges. You must also remember that any cash flows relating to the financing of a project should be excluded from your NPV calculation. The discounting process takes account of these so, if you included them, you would effectively be double counting them.

Workings

(W1) **Relevant fixed costs**

	$000
Amount charged to project	715
Bank interest (not relevant – covered by discount rate)	(86)
Head office overheads (not incremental)	(74)
Depreciation (non-cash – $1.2m – £600k ÷ 3)	(200)
Relevant fixed costs	355

(W2) **Capital allowances**

Year	TWDV – $000	Tax saving at 30%	Timing
1	1,200		
WDA	(300)	90	T1
	——		
2	900		
WDA	(225)	68	T2
	——		
3	675		
Balancing allowance	(75)	22	T3
	——		
RV	600		

It has been assumed that the asset is bought on the first day of an accounting period and that the first capital allowance will be received 12 months later.

(b)

Tutorial note:

When calculating sensitivity you must remember to include the tax effects relating to each of the cash flows.

Sensitivity of annual sales volume

Total current annual contribution	
([$40 – $25] × 60,000	$900,000
Less tax @ 30%	($270,000)
	————
	$630,000
Annuity factors (years 1 – 3)	× 2.487
	————
	$1,566,810
	————
Net present value of scheme	$101,000
Sensitivity of annual sales	
($101,000 ÷ $1,566,810)	6.45%
(6.45% × 60,000 units)	3,870 units
Break-even level of annual sales	
(60,000 – 3,870)	56,130 units

Annual sales volume is fairly sensitive – a 6.45% overestimation of the expected volume increase would mean that the investment is no longer worthwhile. This would therefore be of concern to the management of Victory. Further research to ensure the validity of these estimates should be performed before the equipment is purchased.

Sensitivity of sales proceeds

Let A be the fall in the resale value (and therefore, the rise in the balancing allowance)

$$(A \times 0.751) - (A \times 0.3 \times 0.751) = \$101,000$$

$$0.751A - 0.2253A = \$101,000$$

$$0.5257A = \$101,000$$

$$A = \$192,125$$

The resale value can fall to ($600,000 – $192,125) $407,875 before the project is no longer worthwhile. At a fall of approximately 32%, the sales proceeds of the equipment is not very sensitive. No further action would be advised in this area.

(c) Risk refers to the situation where probabilities can be assigned to a range of expected outcomes arising from an investment project and the likelihood of each outcome occurring can therefore be quantified. Uncertainty refers to the situation where probabilities cannot be assigned to expected outcomes. Investment project risk therefore increases with increasing variability of returns, while uncertainty increases with increasing project life. The two terms are often used interchangeably in financial management, but the distinction between them is a useful one.

One way of incorporating risk into investment decision making is using probability analysis. A probability distribution of expected cash flows may be determined and the expected net present value (ENPV) could be calculated, together with the probability of the worst-case scenario and the probability of a negative net present value. In this way, the downside risk of the investment could be determined and incorporated into the investment decision.

A second way of incorporating risk into the decision is to add an additional premium to the discount rate. This will provide a safety margin meaning that marginally profitable projects (perhaps the riskiest) are less likely to have a positive NPV. The premium applied can vary from project to project to reflect the different levels of risk.

32 SPRINGBANK INC

Key answer tips

Part (a) gives an opportunity to gain some easy marks provided you read the scenario carefully. Part (b) is much harder, especially for the low marks available and a thorough understanding of sensitivity analysis is needed to produce some sensible numbers. Be careful you don't spend too much time trying to answer this part of the question. For 10 marks, part (c) requires you to demonstrate your knowledge of both investment appraisal and sources of finance. The highlighted words are key phrases that markers are looking for.

(a)   **Working W1**

Calculation of tax benefits of capital allowances

Year	Tax written-down value of asset	Writing down allowance – WDA (25%)	Tax saving due to WDA (30%)
	$	$	$
1	3,000,000	750,000	225,000
2	2,250,000	562,500	168,750
3	1,687,500	421,875	126,563
4	1,265,625	316,406	94,922
5	949,219		284,766

(balancing allowance in Year 5)

These figures for tax savings will be rounded to the nearest $1,000.

Calculation of net present value of proposed investment

Year	0	1	2	3	4	5
	$000	$000	$000	$000	$000	$000
Sales		2,750	2,750	2,750	2,750	2,750
Production costs		(1,100)	(1,100)	(1,100)	(1,100)	(1,100)
Admin/dist'n expenses		(220)	(220)	(220)	(220)	(220)
Net revenue		1,430	1,430	1,430	1,430	1,430
Tax payable at 30%		(429)	(429)	(429)	(429)	(429)
Tax benefits from WDAs (W1)		225	169	127	95	285
Working capital	(400)					400
Machinery	(3,000)					
Project cash flows	(3,400)	1,226	1,170	1,128	1,096	1,686
Discount factor at 12%	1.000	0.893	0.797	0.712	0.636	0.567
Present value	(3,400)	1,095	932	803	697	956

The net present value is approximately $1,083,000.

This analysis makes the following assumptions:

(1)   The first tax benefit occurs in Year 1, the last tax benefit occurs in Year 5

(2)   Cash flows occur at the end of each year.

(3)   Inflation can be ignored.

(4)   The increase in capacity does not lead to any increase in fixed production overheads.

(5)   Working capital is all released at the end of Year 5

(b)   **Solution**

Some costs and benefits would be fixed amounts. These are the cost of the investment and the tax benefits from the writing down allowances. The present value of these tax benefits is as follows:

Year	Tax benefit (see (W1)) $000	Discount factor at 12%	Present value $000
1	225	0.893	200.9
2	169	0.797	134.7
3	127	0.712	90.4
4	95	0.636	60.4
5	285	0.567	161.6
			———
			648.0
			———

After-tax profit from units sold

Variable administration and distribution expenses per unit = 220,000/5,500 = $40 per unit

Net revenue from additional units sold, before tax = $500 – $200 – $40 = $260 per unit.

Net revenue from additional units sold, after tax = 70% of $260 = $182.

Let the volume of annual sales be V units.

The present value of after-tax profits from selling V units each year for 5 years (years 1 – 5) = $182V × 3.605 (at a discount rate of 12%).

Working capital

Tutorial note:

The method of reaching a solution depends on whether it is assumed that the working capital investment varies with the volume of sales, or whether it is a fixed amount at $400,000. The solution here makes the assumption, preferred by the examiner, that the investment in working capital varies with the volume of sales. If you failed to take this into account you would only lose one or two marks.

It is assumed that the amount of working capital investment varies with the volume of annual sales.

Incremental working capital per unit = 400,000/5,500 = $72.73 per unit.

The net present value of the working capital investment is therefore:

Year	Cash flow	Discount factor at 12%	Present value
	$000		$000
0	(72.73V)	1.000	(72.73V)
5	72.73V	0.567	41.24V
Net PV of cost			31.49V

The NPV of the project is zero when:

(3,000,000) + 648,000 + 656.11V – 31.49V = 0

624.62V = 2,352,000

V = 3,765 units.

To achieve breakeven will therefore require an increase in annual sales of 3,765 units.

This is about 32% (1,735/5,500) less than the expected increase in sales volume.

(c) Since the investment has a positive NPV it is acceptable in financial terms. Sensitivity analysis shows the proposed expansion is robust in terms of sales volume, since a 32% reduction below the forecast increase in sales is needed to eliminate the positive NPV. The proposed expansion is therefore acceptable, but the choice of financing is critical.

Springbank should be able to meet future interest payments if the cash flow forecasts for the increase in capacity are sound. However, no account has been taken of expected **inflation**, and both sales prices and costs will be expected to change. There is also an underlying **assumption of constant sales volumes**, when changing economic circumstances and the actions of competitors make this assumption unlikely to be true. More detailed financial forecasts are needed to give a clearer indication of whether Springbank can meet the additional interest payments arising from the new loan stock. There is also a danger that managers may focus more on the short-term need to meet the increased interest payments, or on the longer-term need to replace the machinery and redeem the loan stock, rather than on increasing the wealth of shareholders.

Financial risk will increase from a balance sheet (statement of financial position) point of view and this is likely to have a negative effect on how financial markets view the company. The cost of raising additional finance is likely to rise, while the increased financial risk may lead to downward pressure on the company's share price. The assets available for offering as security against new debt issues will decrease, and continue to decrease as non-current assets depreciate.

No information has been offered as to the **maturity of the new loan stock issue**. If the matching principle is applied, a medium term maturity of five to six years would be suggested.

On the basis of the above discussion, careful thought needs to be given to the maturity of any new issue of loan stock and it may be advisable to use debt finance to meet only part of the financing need of the proposed capacity expansion. Alternative sources of finance such as equity and leasing should be considered.

33 CJ CO

Key answer tips

Part (a) is a fairly typical exam requirement on the frequently visited topic of investment appraisal with inflation and tax.

To score well on the discursive element in part (b), you need to go beyond a simple critique of payback v ROCE. There are a number of different factors presented within the section containing the directors' views, and all must be commented on in order to pick up the full range of marks on offer.

Part (c) covers the more difficult topic of calculating a risk-adjusted cost of equity by de-gearing and re-gearing betas. This is an area that typically students tend not to like. However, the formulas are provided in the exam so, once you've practised the calculation a few times, this should represent some fairly easy marks. The highlighted words are key phrases that markers are looking for.

(a) **Net present value evaluation**

Year	1	2	3	4	5
	$000	$000	$000	$000	$000
Sales revenue (W)	1,575	1,654	1,736	1,823	
Selling costs (W)	(32)	(33)	(35)	(37)	
Variable costs (W)	(624)	(649)	(675)	(702)	
Before-tax cash flows	919	972	1,026	1,084	
Taxation at 30%		(276)	(292)	(308)	(325)
Tax benefits		263	197	148	443
After-tax cash flows	919	959	931	924	118
Working capital	(11)	(12)	(12)	(13)	
Project cash flows	908	947	919	911	118
Discount at 10%	0.909	0.826	0.751	0.683	0.621
Present values	825	782	690	622	73

	$000
PV of cash flows:	2,992
Working capital:	(250)
Initial investment:	(3,500)
Net present value:	(758)

The NPV is negative, with a value of minus $758,000, and Project A is therefore not financially acceptable.

Tutor's top tips:

The term 'nominal' weighted average cost of capital means this already includes the effects of inflation.

Workings

Year	1	2	3	4
Selling price ($/unit)	2.100	2.205	2.315	2.431
Sales volume (units/year)	750,000	750,000	750,000	750,000
Sales revenue ($/years)	1,575,000	1,653,750	1,736,250	1,823,250

Year	1	2	3	4
Selling cost ($/unit)	0.042	0.044	0.046	0.049
Sales volume (units/year)	750,000	750,000	750,000	750,000
Selling cost ($/years)	31,500	33,000	34,500	36,750

Year	1	2	3	4
Variable cost ($/unit)	0.832	0.865	0.900	0.936
Sales volume (units/year)	750,000	750,000	750,000	750,000
Variable cost ($/years)	624,000	648,750	675,000	702,000

Year	Capital allowance ($)	30% Tax benefit ($)	Year taken
1	875,000	262,500	2
2	656,250	196,875	3
3	492,188	147,656	4
4	1,476,562*	442,969	5

*This figure includes the balancing allowance

Tutorial note:

Even though the volume of business remains constant, the presence of inflation will mean the investment in working capital will increase over time. This is therefore a relevant cash flow that must be included.

Year	Working capital ($)	Incremental investment ($)
0	250,000	
1	261,250	11,250
2	273,006	11,756
3	285,292	12,286
4	298,130	12,838

Alternative NPV evaluation

An alternative approach to evaluating the NPV of Project A is to subtract and add back the capital allowances, which are not cash flows.

Year	1	2	3	4	5
	$000	$000	$000	$000	$000
Before-tax cash flows	919	972	1,026	1,084	
Capital allowances	(875)	(656)	(492)	(1,477)	
Taxable profit	44	316	534	(393)	
Taxation		(13)	(95)	(160)	118
After-tax profit	44	303	439	(553)	118
Add capital allowances	875	656	492	1,477	
After-tax cash flows	919	959	931	924	118

The evaluation will then proceed as earlier.

(b)

Tutor's top tips:

Always make sure you read the requirement and the relevant part of the scenario carefully before answering the question.

The directors' views on investment appraisal are discussed in turn.

Evaluation using either payback or return on capital employed

Both payback period and return on capital employed (ROCE) are inferior to discounted cash flow (DCF) methods such as net present value (NPV) and internal rate of return (IRR). Payback ignores the time value of money and cash flows outside of the payback period. ROCE uses profit instead of cash flow. Both payback and ROCE have difficulty in justifying the target value used to determine acceptability. Why, for example, use a maximum payback period of two years? DCF methods use the weighted average cost of capital of an investing company as the basis of evaluation, or a project-specific cost of capital, and both can be justified on academic grounds.

The company should also clarify why either method can be used, since they assess different aspects of an investment project.

Evaluation over a four-year planning period

Using a planning period or a specified investment appraisal time horizon is a way of reducing the uncertainty associated with investment appraisal, since this increases with project life. However, it is important to determine the expected life of an investment project if at all possible, since evaluation over the whole life of a project may help a company avoid sub-optimal investment decisions. In the case of CJ Co, for example, a further year of operation may lead to Project A generating a positive NPV.

Scrap value is ignored

Scrap value, salvage value or terminal value must be included in the evaluation of a project since it is a cash inflow. Ignoring scrap value will reduce the NPV and may lead to rejection of an otherwise acceptable investment project.

Working capital recovery is ignored

If an investment project ends, then working capital can be recovered and it must be included in the evaluation of an investment project, since it is a cash inflow. In the case of CJ Co, the directors' decision to ignore working capital recovery means ignoring a fourth year cash inflow of $298,130.

A balancing allowance is claimed at the end of the fourth year of operation

Introducing a balancing allowance which can only be claimed when allowed by the taxation authorities will distort the taxation aspects of the investment appraisal. If it is anticipated that a project will continue beyond the fourth year, including a balancing allowance in the evaluation will overstate cash inflows and hence the NPV, potentially leading to incorrect investment decisions being made.

(c)   The first step is to ungear the equity beta of GZ Co. This removes the effect of the financial risk of the company on the value of its equity beta. It is usual to assume that the beta of debt is zero and hence the ungearing formula is as follows:

$$\beta_a = \beta_e (V_e / (V_e + V_d(1-T)))$$

Substituting, the asset beta = β_a = 1.5 × 90/(90 + (0.7 × 30)) = 1.216

Using percentages: asset beta = β_a = 1.5 × 75/(75 + (0.7 × 25)) = 1.216

The asset beta of GZ Co reflects only the business risk of the new business area.

The next stage is to regear the asset beta into an equity beta that reflects the financial risk of the investing company. Rearranging the ungearing formula used earlier gives:

$$\beta_a = \beta_e (V_e + V_d(1-T))V_e$$

Substituting, the equity beta = β_a = 1.216 × (180 + (0.7 × 45))/180 = 1.429

This regeared equity beta can be inserted in the capital asset pricing model equation to give a project-specific cost of equity:

$$k_e = E(r_i) = R_f + \beta_e (E(r_m) - R_f)$$

Substituting, the cost of equity = k_e = 4 + (1.429 × 6) = 12.6%

			Marks
	ACCA marking scheme		
(a)	Sales revenue		1
	Selling costs		1
	Variable costs		1
	Capital allowances, years 1 to 3		1
	Capital allowance/balancing allowance, year 4		1
	Tax liabilities		1
	Timing of taxation		1
	Incremental working capital		2
	Discount factors		1
	NPV calculation		1
	Decision as to financial acceptability		1
		Maximum	12
(b)	Discussion of payback and ROCE		2–3
	Discussion of planning period		1–2
	Discussion of scrap value		1–2
	Discussion of working capital recovery		1–2
	Discussion of balancing allowance		1–2
		Maximum	7
(c)	Ungearing equity beta		1
	Regearing equity beta		1
	Calculating project-specific cost of equity		1
	Explaining stages of calculation		3
			6
Total			**25**

Examiner's comments

Most candidates gained good marks in parts (a) and (c), while part (b) was rarely answered well.

Part (a) asked candidates to calculate the net present value (NPV) of Project A, allowing for inflation and taxation.

Most candidates inflated correctly selling price, selling cost and variable cost in order to find the before-tax cash flows over the four year appraisal period required by the directors of the company. Some candidates did not defer tax liability by one year, although the question required this. Some candidates calculated correctly the tax benefit arising from capital allowances (tax-allowable depreciation), but did not provide a balancing allowance in the final year, as the directors required. The directors also required that scrap value be excluded from the evaluation.

The treatment of working capital was a problem for some candidates. Three elements of working capital can be relevant in investment appraisal, namely initial investment, incremental investment and recovery at the end of the investment project. The first two elements were needed here, with incremental investment arising from general inflation. Working capital recovery was excluded by the directors' views on investment appraisal. Even though working capital investment was specified in the question as an initial investment, some candidates inflated the initial investment and placed it at the end of year one.

The inflated after-tax cash flows were nominal (money terms) cash flows and the question provided a nominal weighted average after-tax cost of capital. This was the discount rate needed for Project A, although some candidates calculated another incorrect discount rate by either inflating or deflating the discount rate provided.

The calculated NPV of Project A was negative and so the investment project was not financially acceptable.

In part (b), candidates were asked to critically discuss the directors' views on investment appraisal. These views were requirements to use either payback period or return on capital employed (ROCE), to evaluate over a four year planning period, to ignore any scrap value or working capital recovery, and to claim a balancing allowance at the end of the four-year evaluation period.

Although part (b) asked for a critical discussion, a significant number of candidates calculated and commented on the payback period and the ROCE of Project A. This was not what the question asked for and gained no credit. Many candidates limited their discussion to payback and ROCE, and therefore lost marks because they did not discuss the four-year planning period, ignoring any scrap value or working capital recovery, and claiming a balancing allowance at the end of four years.

The directors' views were not consistent with a theoretically sound evaluation of Project A using relevant cash flows, A critical discussion should have focused on this.

Part (c) required candidates to calculate a project-specific cost of equity for Project B, which was a diversification into a new business area, and to explain the stages of their calculation.

Answers that calculated a project specific weighted average cost of capital (WACC) in addition to a project specific cost of equity did not gain any additional credit, since this was not required. In fact, the WACC could not be calculated, since the question did not include a cost of debt.

Better answers ungeared the equity beta of the proxy company to give an asset beta, regeared the asset beta to give a project-specific equity beta, and then used this equity beta and the capital asset pricing model (CAPM) to calculate a project-specific cost of equity, explaining the stages of the calculation in terms of systematic risk, business risk and financial risk.

34   BASRIL

Key answer tips

With 15 of the 25 marks available being for discussing various elements relating to capital rationing and relevant cash flows, this question should be a good opportunity to pick up some easy marks. Students who score badly on this question do so because they get bogged down in the numerical calculations in part (a). The best way to avoid this trap is to tackle the wordy parts of the requirement first. The highlighted words are key phrases that markers are looking for.

(a)   (i)   **Analysis of projects assuming they are divisible**

	Discount factor at 12%	Project 1 Cash flow	PV	Project 3 Cash flow	PV
		$	$	$	$
Initial investment	1.000	(300,000)	(300,000)	(400,000)	(400,000)
Year 1	0.893	85,000	75,905	124,320	111,018
Year 2	0.797	90,000	71,730	128,795	102,650
Year 3	0.712	95,000	67,640	133,432	95,004
Year 4	0.636	100,000	63,600	138,236	87,918
Year 5	0.567	95,000	53,865	143,212	81,201
			———		———
PV of savings			332,740		477,791
			———		———
NPV			32,740		77,791
Profitability index			332,740/300,000 = 1.11		477,791/400,000 = 1.19

	Discount factor at 12%	Project 2 Cash flow	PV
		$	$
Initial investment	1.000	(450,000)	(450,000)
Annual cash flows, years 1 – 5	3.605	140,800	507,584
			———
Net present value			57,584
			———
Profitability index	507,584/450,000		= 1.13

Order of preference (in order of profitability index) = Project 3 then Project 2 then Project 1.

Project	Profitability index	Ranking	Investment	NPV	
			$	$	
3	1.19	1st	400,000	77,791	
2	1.13	2nd	400,000	51,186	(= 57,584 × 400/450)
			800,000	128,977	

(ii) **Analysis of projects assuming they are indivisible**

If the projects are assumed to be indivisible, the total NPV of combinations of projects must be considered.

Projects	Investment	NPV	
	$	$	
1 and 2	750,000	90,324	£(32,740 + 57,584)
1 and 3	700,000	110,531	£(32,740 + 77,791)
2 and 3	850,000	not feasible, too much investment	

The optimum combination is now projects 1 and 3.

(b) The NPV decision rule requires that a company invest in all projects that have a positive net present value. This assumes that sufficient funds are available for all incremental projects, which is only true in a perfect capital market. When insufficient funds are available, that is when capital is rationed, projects cannot be selected by ranking by absolute NPV. Choosing a project with a large NPV may mean not choosing smaller projects that, in combination, give a higher NPV. Instead, if projects are divisible, they can be ranked using the profitability index in order make the optimum selection. If projects are not divisible, different combinations of available projects must be evaluated to select the combination with the highest NPV.

(c) The NPV decision rule, to accept all projects with a positive net present value, requires the existence of a perfect capital market where access to funds for capital investment is not restricted. In practice, companies are likely to find that funds available for capital investment are restricted or rationed.

Hard capital rationing is the term applied when the restrictions on raising funds are due to causes external to the company. For example, potential providers of debt finance may refuse to provide further funding because they regard a company as too risky. This may be in terms of financial risk, for example if the company's gearing is too high or its interest cover is too low, or in terms of business risk if they see the company's business prospects as poor or its operating cash flows as too variable. In practice, large established companies seeking long-term finance for capital investment are usually able to find it, but small and medium-sized enterprises will find raising such funds more difficult.

Soft capital rationing refers to restrictions on the availability of funds that arise within a company and are imposed by managers. There are several reasons why managers might restrict available funds for capital investment. Managers may prefer slower organic growth to a sudden increase in size arising from accepting several large investment projects. This reason might apply in a family-owned business that wishes to avoid hiring new managers. Managers may wish to avoid raising further equity finance if this will dilute the control of existing shareholders. Managers may wish to avoid issuing new debt if their expectations of future economic conditions are such as to suggest that an increased commitment to fixed interest payments would be unwise.

One of the main reasons suggested for soft capital rationing is that managers wish to create an internal market for investment funds. It is suggested that requiring investment projects to compete for funds means that weaker or marginal projects, with only a small chance of success, are avoided. This allows a company to focus on more robust investment projects where the chance of success is higher. This cause of soft capital rationing can be seen as a way of reducing the risk and uncertainty associated with investment projects, as it leads to accepting projects with greater margins of safety.

(d) When undertaking the appraisal of an investment project, it is essential that **only relevant cash flows** are included in the analysis. If non-relevant cash flows are included, the result of the appraisal will be misleading and incorrect decisions will be made. A relevant cash flow is a differential (incremental) cash flow, one that changes as a direct result of an investment decision.

If current fixed production overheads are expected to increase, for example, the additional fixed production overheads are a relevant cost and should be included in the investment appraisal. Existing fixed production overheads should not be included.

A new cash flow arising as the result of an investment decision is a relevant cash flow. For example, the purchase of raw materials for a new production process and the net cash flows arising from the production process are both relevant cash flows.

The incremental tax effects arising from an investment decision are also relevant cash flows, providing that a company is in a tax-paying position. Direct labour costs, for example, are an allowable deduction in calculating taxable profit and so give rise to tax benefits: tax liabilities arising on incremental taxable profits are also a relevant cash flow.

One area where caution is required is interest payments on new debt used to finance an investment project. They are a differential cash flow and hence relevant, but the effect of the cost of the debt is incorporated into the discount rate used to determine the net present value. Interest payments should not therefore be included as a cash flow in an investment appraisal.

Market research undertaken to determine whether a new product will sell is often undertaken prior to the investment decision on whether to proceed with production of the new product. This is an example of a **sunk cost**. These are costs already incurred as a result of past decisions, and so are not relevant cash flows.

35   ASOP CO

Key answer tips

This question encompasses three of the more fringe topics within the investment appraisal part of the syllabus; lease v buy, equivalent annual costs and capital rationing. It is a fair question, which well prepared students (those who have studied the syllabus in detail) should handle well.

The highlighted words are key phrases that markers are looking for.

(a)   After-tax cost of borrowing = 8.6 × (1 – 0.3) = 6% per year

Evaluation of leasing

Year	Cash flow	Amount ($)	6% Discount factors	Present value ($)
0–3	Lease rentals	(380,000)	1.000 + 2.673 = 3.673	(1,395,740)
2–5	Tax savings	114,000	4.212 – 0.943 = 3.269	372,666
				—————
				(1,023,074)
				—————

Present value of cost of leasing = $1,023,074

Evaluation of borrowing to buy

Year	Capital	Licence fee	Tax benefits	Net cash flow	6% discount factors	Present value
	$	$	$	$	$	$
0	(1,000,000)			(1,000,000)	1.000	(1,000,000)
1		(104,000)		(104,000)	0.943	(98,072)
2		(108,160)	106,200	(1,960)	0.890	(1,744)
3		(112,486)	88,698	(23,788)	0.840	(19,982)
4	100,000	(116,986)	75,934	58,948	0.792	46,687
5			131,659	131,659	0.747	98,349
						—————
						(974,762)
						—————

Present value of cost of borrowing to buy = $974,762

Workings

Year	Capital allowance	Tax benefits	Licence fee tax benefits	Total
	$	$	$	$
2	1,000,000 × 0.25 = 250,000	75,000	31,200	106,200
3	750,000 × 0.25 = 187,500	56,250	32,448	88,698
4	562,500 × 0.25 =140,625	42,188	33,746	75,934
5	421,875 – 100,000 = 321,875	96,563	35,096	131,659

ASOP Co should buy the new technology, since the present cost of borrowing to buy is lower than the present cost of leasing.

(b) **Nominal terms net present value analysis**

Year	1	2	3	4	5
	$	$	$	$	$
Cost savings	365,400	479,250	637,450	564,000	
Tax liabilities		(109,620)	(143,775)	(191,235)	(169,200)
Net cash flow	365,400	369,630	493,675	372,765	(169,200)
Discount at 11%	0.901	0.812	0.731	0.659	0.593
Present values	329,225	300,140	360,876	245,652	(100,336)

Present value of benefits	1,135,557
Present cost of financing	(974,762)
Net present value	160,795

The investment in new technology is acceptable on financial grounds, as it has a positive net present value of $160,795.

Workings

Year	1	2	3	4
	$	$	$	$
Operating cost saving ($/unit)	6.09	6.39	6.71	7.05
Production (units/year)	60,000	75,000	95,000	80,000
Operating cost savings ($/year)	365,400	479,250	637,450	564,000
Tax liabilities at 30% ($/year)	109,620	143,775	191,235	169,200

(Examiner's note: Including the financing cash flows in the NPV evaluation and discounting them by the WACC of 11% is also acceptable)

(c)   The equivalent annual cost or benefit method can be used to calculate the equal annual amount of cost or benefit which, when discounted at the appropriate cost of capital, produces the same present value of cost or net present value as a set of varying annual costs or benefits.

For example, the net present value (NPV) of investing in the new technology of $160,795 in part (b) was calculated using a weighted average cost of capital (WACC) of 11% over an expected life of four years. The annuity factor for 11% and four years is 3.102. The equivalent annual benefit (EAB) is therefore 160,795/3.102 = $51,835.9 per year. This can be checked by multiplying the EAB by the annuity factor, i.e. 51,835.9 × 3.102 = $160,795.

If an alternative investment in similar technology over five years had a lower EAB, the four-year investment would be preferred as it has the higher EAB.

(d)   When capital is rationed, the optimal investment schedule is the one that maximises the return per dollar invested. The capital rationing problem is therefore concerned with limiting factor analysis, but the approach adopted is slightly different depending on whether the investment projects being evaluated are divisible or indivisible.

With divisible projects, the assumption is made that a proportion rather than the whole investment can be undertaken, with the net present value (NPV) being proportional to the amount of capital invested. If 70% of a project is undertaken, for example, the resulting NPV is assumed to be 70% of the NPV of investing in the whole project.

For each divisible project, a profitability index can be calculated, defined either as the net present value of the project divided by its initial investment, or as the present value of the future cash flows of the project divided by its initial investment. The profitability index represents the return per dollar invested and can be used to rank the investment projects. The limited investment funds can then be invested in the projects in the order of their profitability indexes, with the final investment selection being a proportionate one if there is insufficient finance for the whole project. This represents the optimum investment schedule when capital is rationed and projects are divisible.

With indivisible projects, ranking by profitability index will not necessarily indicate the optimum investment schedule, since it will not be possible to invest in part of a project. In this situation, the NPV of possible combinations of projects must be calculated. The most likely combinations are often indicated by the profitability index ranking. The combination of projects with the highest aggregate NPV will then be the optimum investment schedule.

			Marks
(a)	Present value of lease rentals	2	
	Present value of lease rental tax benefits	1	
	Present value of cost of leasing	1	
	Investment and scrap values	1	
	Licence fee	1	
	Capital allowance tax benefits	2	
	Licence fee tax benefits	1	
	Present value of cost of borrowing to buy	1	
	Appropriate decision on leasing versus buying	1	
			11
(b)	Inflated cost savings	2	
	Tax liabilities	1	
	Present values of net cash flows	1	
	Net present value	1	
	Advice on acceptability of investment	1	
			6
(c)	Definition of equivalent cost or benefit	1	
	Relevant discussion	1	
	Appropriate illustration	1	
			3
(d)	Capital rationing	1–2	
	Divisible projects and profitability index	2–3	
	Indivisible projects and combinations	1–2	
		Maximum	5
Total			25

ACCA marking scheme

Examiner's comments

Many students were able to do well in this question, especially in parts (b) and (d).

In part (a), candidates were asked to calculate and determine whether a company should lease or buy new technology. Since this was a financing decision, candidates were instructed to use only financing cash flows. The lease versus borrowing to buy decision is covered in the Study Texts that support students studying Paper F9.

From a leasing perspective, candidates needed to calculate the present value of correctly-timed annual lease rental payments and their tax benefits, discounted by the after-tax cost of debt.

From a buying perspective, candidates needed to calculate the present value of the purchase price of the new technology and related capital allowance tax benefits, and the annual licence fees and their associated tax benefits, discounted by the after-tax cost of debt.

Many candidates did not follow the instruction to use financing cash flows only and included in their evaluation the reduced operating costs arising from using the new technology.

Common errors were splitting the licence fee out of the lease rental payments: using the weighted average cost of capital of the company as the discount rate, rather than the after-tax cost of debt; including interest payments in the evaluation, when these are taken account of by the discount rate: omitting the tax benefit arising on lease rental payments; incorrect timing of lease rental payments or tax benefits; including loan repayments or repayment of principal; and not using a present value approach to comparing the two financing choices. The correct approach can be found in the suggested answers to this examination.

Part (b) required calculating the net present value of buying the new technology using a nominal terms approach, and offering advice on the acceptability of the investment.

The net present value calculation included the nominal value of the operating cost reductions and their associated tax benefits, discounted by the weighted average cost of capital of the company, less the present value of the financing cash flows. Some candidates used the Fisher equation and the inflation rate of the costs savings to calculate a 'nominal' discount rate, but specific inflation cannot be used in this way and no other inflation rate was given in the question. The weighted average cost of capital could therefore be assumed to be in nominal terms.

While some answers included the net present value calculation with the financing evaluation by combining parts (a) and (b) of the question, many answers to this part of question one were of a good standard.

Part (c) asked candidates to discuss and illustrate how equivalent annual cost or equivalent annual benefit could be used to choose between technologies with different expected lives. Candidates who had studied the equivalent annual cost method were able to gain full marks on this part of question one.

Weaker answers discussed new technology or the need for cost-benefit analysis rather than meeting the requirement of the question.

While many answers gave a suitable illustration, such as dividing the net present value calculated in part (b) by a suitable annuity factor, some answers provided illustrations that were much longer than necessary and therefore wasted valuable time, given that this part of question 1 was worth only three marks.

Part (d) asked how an optimal investment schedule could be formulated when capital was rationed and investment projects were either divisible or non-divisible.

Some students discussed hard and soft capital rationing and the reasons for capital rationing, but the question did not ask for this.

Good answers focused on the need to maximise the return per dollar invested by using the profitability index as a way of ranking divisible projects. The optimal investment schedule could then be formulated by working down the rankings. Where investment projects were non-divisible, the procedure would be to determine by trial and error which combination of projects would give the highest net present value. While the profitability index could be helpful here, there was no guarantee it would provide the correct answer in every case.

Weaker answers suggested that ranking by net present value would lead to the optimum investment schedule, which is not true when capital is rationed. Some answers discussed mutually exclusive projects, which was not required.

36   CAVIC

Key answer tips

This question is a good balance between discussional aspects (in parts (b) & (c)) and calculations (in part (a)).   The numerical aspects are uncomplicated and a basic understanding of replacement analysis should be enough to gain most of the marks available.   The highlighted words are key phrases that markers are looking for.

(a)   **Calculation of annual equivalent cost**

Year	1	2	3
Servicing costs	10,000	14,000	19,600
Cleaning costs	5,000	6,250	7,813
Total costs	15,000	20,250	27,413
Discount factors	0.909	0.826	0.751
Present values of costs	13,635	16,727	20,587
Replacement cycle (years)	1	2	3
Cost on new vehicles	150,000	150,000	150,000
PV of Year 1 costs	13,635	13,635	13,635
PV of Year 2 costs		16,727	16,727
PV of Year 3 costs			20,587
Sum of PV of costs	163,635	180,362	200,949
Less PV of trade-in value	102,263	74,340	46,562
Net PV of cost of cycle	61,372	106,022	154,387
Annuity factor	0.909	1.736	2.487
Equivalent annual cost	67,516	61,073	62,078

Replacement after two years is recommended, since this replacement cycle has the lowest equivalent annual cost.

Tutorial note:

The above evaluation could have been carried out on a per car basis rather than on a fleet basis with the same conclusion being made.

Workings

Servicing costs

Year 1: 1,000 × 10	= $10,000
Year 2: 10,000 × 1.4	= $14,000
Year 3: 14,000 × 1.4	= $19,600

Cleaning costs

Year 1: 500 × 10	= $5,000
Year 2: 5,000 × 1.25	= $6,250
Year 3: 6,250 × 1.25	= $7,813

PV of trade-in values

Year 1: 11,250 × 10 × 0.909	= $102,263
Year 2 9,000 × 10 × 0.826	= $74,340
Year 3: 6,200 × 10 × 0.751	= $46,562

(b)   In order to invest in all projects with a positive net present value a company must be able to raise funds as and when it needs them: this is only possible in a perfect capital market. In practice capital markets are not perfect and the capital available for investment is likely to be limited or rationed. The causes of capital rationing may be external (hard capital rationing) or internal (soft capital rationing). Soft capital rationing is more common than hard capital rationing.

When a company cannot raise external finance even though it wishes to do so, this may be because providers of debt finance see the company as being too risky. In terms of financial risk, the company's gearing may be seen as too high, or its interest cover may be seen as too low. From a business risk point of view, lenders may be uncertain whether a company's future profits will be sufficient to meet increased future interest payments because its trading prospects are poor, or because they are seen as too variable.

When managers impose restrictions on the funds they are prepared to make available for capital investment, soft capital rationing is said to occur. One reason for soft capital rationing is that managers may not want to raise new external finance. For example, they may not wish to raise new debt finance because they believe it would be unwise to commit the company to meeting future interest payments given the current economic outlook. They may not wish to issue new equity because the finance needed is insufficient to justify the transaction costs of a new issue, or because they wish to avoid dilution of control. Another reason for soft capital rationing is that managers may prefer slower organic growth, where they can remain in control of the growth process, to the sudden growth arising from taking on one or more large investment projects.

A key reason for soft capital rationing is the desire by managers to make capital investments compete for funds, i.e. to create an internal market for investment funds. This competition for funds is likely to weed out weaker or marginal projects, thereby channelling funds to more robust investment projects with better chances of success and larger margins of safety, and reducing the risk and uncertainty associated with capital investment.

(c)   The net present value decision rule is to invest in all projects that have a positive net present value. By following this decision rule, managers will maximise the value of a company and therefore maximise the wealth of ordinary shareholders, which is a primary objective of financial management. Even when capital is rationed, it is still essential to be able to offer advice on which capital investment projects should be selected in order to secure the maximum return for the investing company, i.e. the maximum overall net present value.

Single-period and multi-period capital rationing

Capital may be rationed in more than one period, i.e. not only in the current period at the start of an investment project (single-period rationing), but in future periods as well (multi-period capital rationing). Selecting the best projects for investment in order to maximise overall net present value when faced with multi-period capital rationing calls for the use of linear programming. Here, the available capital investments are expressed as an objective function, subject to a series of constraints. Only simple linear programming problems can be solved by hand, for example using the simplex method. More complex linear programming problems require the use of computers.

Project divisibility

The approach to solving single-period capital rationing problems depends on whether projects are divisible or not. A divisible project is one where a partial investment can be made in order to gain a pro rata net present value. For example, investing in a forest is a divisible project, since the amount of land purchased can be varied according to the funds available for investment (providing the seller agrees to a partial sale, of course). A non-divisible project is one where it is not possible to invest less than the full amount of capital. When building an oil refinery, for example, it is not possible to build only one part of the overall facility.

Where projects are divisible, the objective of maximising the net present value arising from invested funds can be achieved by ranking projects according to their profitability index and investing sequentially in order of decreasing profitability index, beginning with the highest, assuming that each project can be invested in only once, i.e. is non-repeatable. The profitability index can be defined as net present value divided by initial investment. Ranking projects by profitability index is an example of limiting factor analysis. Because projects are divisible, there will be no investment funds left over: when investment funds are insufficient to for the next ranked project, part of the project can be taken on because it is divisible.

When projects are non-divisible, the objective of maximising the net present value arising from invested funds can be achieved by calculating the net present value arising from different combinations of projects. With this approach, there will usually be some surplus funds remaining from the funds initially available.

The investment of surplus funds

When investigating combinations of non-divisible projects in order to find the combination giving rise to the highest net present value, any return from investing surplus funds is ignored. The net present value analysis has been based on the company's average cost of capital and it is unlikely that surplus funds can be invested in order to earn a return as high as this. Investment of surplus funds in, for example, the money markets would therefore be an investment project that would be rejected as having a negative net present value, or an internal rate of return less than the company's average cost of capital if using IRR to assess investments projects. However, it is good working capital management to ensure that liquid funds are invested to earn the highest available return, subject to any risk constraints, in order to increase overall profitability.

BUSINESS FINANCE

37 FMY

Key answer tips

The requirement in part (a) is fairly general so to provide a comprehensive answer you will need to think through the different theories of business valuation and what influences it.

Parts (b) and (c) offer an opportunity to pick up some easier marks provided you tailor your comments to the scenario presented.

The highlighted words in the written sections are key phrases that markers are looking for.

(a)   **The effect of method of financing on company value**

Tutor's top tips

Before starting to answer this section you should think about what factors you know that will influence business valuation. Don't confine yourself to just the business valuation part of the syllabus; try to think more broadly and consider how different elements of the syllabus inter-relate. The sorts of things you should identify are:

– *TERP calculations (rights issues only)*

– *P/E ratio method (with a focus on changes in earnings and the market forces that will influence the P/E ratio)*

– *Discounted future cash flows (and the as capital structure changes so to may the WACC leading to changes in business valuation)*

– *Market efficiency*

Rights issue

If the funds were raised via a rights issue, the theoretical ex-rights price (TERP) can be calculated as:

Current share price = $2.20 per share

Current number of shares = 10 million shares

Finance to be raised = $5m

Number of shares issued = 10m ÷ 4 = 2.5 million shares

Theoretical ex rights price per share = ((10m × 2.20) + $5m) / (10m + 2.5m) = $2.16 per share

The share price would theoretically fall from $2.20 to $2.16 per share although there would be no effect on overall shareholder wealth and total market capitalisation would only increase by the proceeds raised.

However, this does not take account of the benefits of the project. The investment made would result in an overall increase in shareholder wealth equal to the NPV of the project. This could be expected to increase the value of each share by a further 10 cents ($1.2m ÷ 12.5m shares).

Tutorial note

You would never be expected to include the NPV of a project in a TERP calculation but, as we see here, you may be required to recognise that investing in a project will lead to an increase in shareholder wealth equal to the value of the positive NPV.

Effect of rights issue on earnings per share

Current EPS = $4.5m ÷ 10m = 45 cents per share

Revised EPS = ($4.5m + $1.0m) ÷ 12.5m = 44 cents per share

The EPS would fall from 45 cents per share to 44 cents per share. As mentioned earlier, there would be no effect on shareholder wealth in the short term, although in the longer term, a fall in this key investor ratio could lead to some investors disposing of their shares, which would cause the share price to fall.

FMY would therefore have to persuade investors of the benefits of the project and of management's ability to deliver these on schedule. This is really an issue of investors' faith in management competence. If investors are convinced then the current P/E ratio of 4.9 ($0.45 ÷ $2.20) might be expected to increase to reflect the expectation of higher growth rates in the future.

Effect of rights issue on the debt/equity ratio

The company is currently 100% finance by equity. A rights issue would preserve this meaning there would be no change in the company's cost of capital, and therefore no additional movements in the valuation of the business other than those noted above.

Issue of debt

Effect of debt issue on earnings per share

Tutorial note

The trick with this calculation is to recognise the impact of the additional interest on the post-tax earnings of the business.

Interest payments on debt finance = $5m × 8.6% = $0.43m

Post tax fall in earnings = $0.43m × (1 − 0.3) = $0.3m

Revised EPS = ($4.5m + $1.0m − $0.3m) ÷ 10m = 52 cents per share

The EPS would increase from 45 cents per share to 52 cents per share. As mentioned earlier, there would be no effect on shareholder wealth in the short term, although in the longer term, an increase in this key investor ratio could attract investors and cause the share price to rise.

Effect of debt issue on the debt/equity ratio

In theory, the value of the firm is found by discounting all post-tax operating cash flows available for investors at the company's WACC. The method of financing has an impact as if it is possible to reduce the WACC, the value of the company will be increased.

The company is currently ungeared (100% equity financed).

Assuming the market value of equity remained unchanged, the revised debt/equity ratio would be: $5m ÷ (10m × $2.20) = 23%

Capital structure theories provide a useful guide to assessing the impact of methods of financing on the value of the firm.

The traditional view

The traditional view is that as a company first introduces debt into its capital structure, the impact of the cheap debt exceeds the impact of any increase in the cost of equity or debt due to the increased financial risk. Hence, the final impact is that WACC will fall.

As FMY is currently all equity financed, raising more equity is likely to maintain the current WACC and company value. If debt was raised, WACC is likely to fall and company value will be raised.

Modigliani & Miller (M&M)

M&M originally claimed that company value was independent of capital structure. However, once they considered the impact of tax relief that is available when debt interest is paid, they concluded that the WACC of a company would be minimized and its value maximised if debt made up 99.9% of a company's capital. Whilst real world factors such as bankruptcy risk preclude such high levels of gearing, FMY currently has no gearing. Hence, M&M's theory would also support the idea that raising more equity is likely to maintain the current WACC and company value, but that if debt was raised WACC is likely to fall and company value will be raised.

Conclusion

The company should investigate further the use of debt finance as this could enhance the value of the company.

(b)   **Additional factors to consider when raising new equity through a rights issue**

The terms of the issue

Rights issue price = $5m ÷ 2.5m shares = $2.00 per share

Based on the terms suggested the subscription price of $2 represents only a 9% discount to the current share price, and may not provide sufficient an incentive to motivate shareholders to invest further funds. There is also a risk that the share price could fall to this level in the period between announcing the rights issue and the closure of the offer.

Ability of owners to invest

Some shareholders may be unwilling or unable to provide funds to the extent required. The take-up of the new shares is thus by no means guaranteed. The issue could be underwritten by financial institutions, but this would be expensive.

Failure to sell the target amount of shares might spell inability to invest as planned, or having to fill the gap with borrowing.

Implications for control

To the extent that shares are offered to new investors and at a discount, the equity of existing owners could be diluted and this may alter the balance of control

Legal aspects

We must check that the firm's Articles of Association allow finance to be raised in this quantity and for these purposes.

Cost

Equity is usually more costly than debt finance and so it should be considered whether or not the debt finance might be cheaper and more appropriate.

Risk

The company should aim to keep total risk at a level acceptable to both management and shareholders. Equity finance is low risk to the company and it should be considered whether the risk of the company as a whole is too low and the company could benefit from some riskier but cheaper debt finance.

Costs of issue

Issuing equity is costly. There are legal and administrative costs involved in drawing up the necessary documents and circularising shareholders. For instance, an Extraordinary General Meeting, with its associated costs, might be necessary.

(c) **Islamic finance**

Islamic finance rests on the application of Islamic, or Shariah, law.

The main principles of Islamic finance are that:

- Wealth must be generated from legitimate trade and asset-based investment. The use of money for the purposes of making money is forbidden.

- Investment should also have a social and an ethical benefit to wider society beyond pure return.

- Risk should be shared.

- Harmful activities (such as gambling, alcohol and the sale of certain foods) should be avoided.

The issue of debt finance as proposed by FMY Co (where the lender would make a straight interest charge, irrespective of how the underlying assets fare) would violate the principle of sharing risk and of not using money for the purposes of making money. Under Islamic finance, the charging and receiving of interest (riba) is strictly prohibited. This is in stark contrast to more conventional, western forms of finance.

One alternative form of finance would be Murabaha, a form of trade credit for asset acquisition. Here the provider of finance would buy the item and then sell it on to FMY Co at a price that includes an agreed mark-up for profit. The mark-up is fixed in advance and cannot be increased and the payment is made by instalments.

Another form of finance would be Islamic bonds, known as sukuk. To be Shariah-compliant, the sukuk holders must have a proprietary interest in the assets which are being financed. The sukuk holders' return for providing finance is a share of the income generated by the assets. The key distinction between sukuk and murabaha is that sukuk holders have ownership of the cash flows but not the assets themselves.

38 NUGFER

Key answer tips

This question combines business finance with financial ratios, interest rates and market efficiency. It is an excellent example of the current examiner's style, especially part (a) where the requirement is deliberately left fairly open. The highlighted words are key phrases that markers are looking for.

(a)

Tutor's top tips

Before starting to answer this section you should think about what sources of finance you can think of, and what might be the deciding factors regarding whether they would be suitable or not. Key to this will be the current financial position of the company (existing gearing levels in particular) and how the company has performed recently. Take your steer from the information provided in the scenario – for every item consider why the examiner might have told you that, and how you can use this in your answer.

Nugfer Co is looking to raise $200m in cash in order to acquire a competitor. Any recommendation as to the source of finance to be used by the company must take account of the recent financial performance of the company, its current financial position and its expected financial performance in the future, presumably after the acquisition has occurred.

Recent financial performance

The recent financial performance of Nugfer Co will be taken into account by potential providers of finance because it will help them to form an opinion as to the quality of the management running the company and the financial problems the company may be facing. Analysis of the recent performance of Nugfer Co gives the following information:

Year	2007	2008	2009	2010
Operating profit	$41.7m	$43.3m	$50.1m	$56.7m
Net profit margin	34%	34%	32%	30%
Interest coverage ratio	7 times	7 times	4 times	3 times
Revenue growth		3.8%	23.0%	20.9%
Operating profit growth		3.8%	15.7%	13.2%
Finance charges growth		3.3%	101.6%	50.4%
Profit after tax growth		4.0%	1.2%	0.8%

Geometric average growth in turnover = $(189.3/122.6)^{0.33} - 1 = 15.6\%$

Geometric average operating profit growth = $(56.7/41.7)^{0.33} - 1 = 10.8\%$

One positive feature indicated by this analysis is the growth in revenue, which grew by 23% in 2009 and by 21% in 2010. Slightly less positive is the growth in operating profit, which was 16% in 2009 and 13% in 2010. Both years were significantly better in revenue growth and operating profit growth than 2008. One query here is why growth in operating profit is so much lower than growth in revenue. Better control of operating and other costs might improve operating profit substantially and decrease the financial risk of Nugfer Co.

The growing financial risk of the company is a clear cause for concern. The interest coverage ratio has declined each year in the period under review and has reached a dangerous level in 2010. The increase in operating profit each year has clearly been less than the increase in finance charges, which have tripled over the period under review. The reason for the large increase in debt is not known, but the high level of financial risk must be considered in selecting an appropriate source of finance to provide the $200m in cash that is needed.

Current financial position

The current financial position of Nugfer Co will be considered by potential providers of finance in their assessment of the financial risk of the company. Analysis of the current financial position of Nugfer Co shows the following:

Debt/equity ratio = long-term debt/total equity = 100 × (100/221) = 45%

Debt equity/ratio including short-term borrowings = 100 × ((100 + 160)/221) = 118%

The debt/equity ratio based on long-term debt is not particularly high. However, the interest coverage ratio indicated a high level of financial risk and it is clear from the financial position statement that the short-term borrowings of $160m are greater than the long-term borrowings of $100m. In fact, short-term borrowings account for 62% of the debt burden of Nugfer Co. If we include the short-term borrowings, the debt/equity ratio increases to 118%, which is certainly high enough to be a cause for concern. The short-term borrowings are also at a higher interest rate (8%) than the long-term borrowings (6%) and as a result, interest on short-term borrowings account for 68% of the finance charges in the income statement.

It should also be noted that the long-term borrowings are bonds that are repayable in 2012. Nugfer Co needs therefore to plan for the redemption and refinancing of $100m of debt in two years' time, a factor that cannot be ignored when selecting a suitable source of finance to provide the $200m of cash needed.

Recommendation of suitable financing method

There are strong indications that it would be unwise for Nugfer Co to raise the $200m of cash required by means of debt finance, for example the low interest coverage ratio and the high level of gearing.

If no further debt is raised, the interest coverage ratio would improve after the acquisition due to the increased level of operating profit, i.e. (56.7m + 28m)/18.8 = 4.5 times. Assuming that $200m of 8% debt is raised, the interest coverage ratio would fall to ((84.7/(18.8 + 16)) = 2.4 times and the debt/equity ratio would increase to 100 × (260 + 200)/221 = 208%.

If convertible debt were used, the increase in gearing and the decrease in interest coverage would continue only until conversion occurred, assuming that the company's share price increased sufficiently for conversion to be attractive to bondholders. Once conversion occurred, the debt capacity of the company would increase due both to the liquidation of the convertible debt and to the issuing of new ordinary shares to bond holders. In the period until conversion, however, the financial risk of the company as measured by gearing and interest coverage would remain at a very high level.

If Nugfer Co were able to use equity finance, the interest coverage ratio would increase to 4.5 times and the debt/equity ratio would fall to 100 × (260/(221 + 200)) = 62%. Although the debt/equity ratio is still on the high side, this would fall if some of the short-term borrowings were able to be paid off, although the recent financial performance of Nugfer Co indicates that this may not be easy to do. The problem of redeeming the current long-term bonds in two years also remains to be solved.

However, since the company has not paid any dividend for at least four years, it is unlikely that current shareholders would be receptive to a rights issue, unless they were persuaded that dividends would be forthcoming in the near future. Acquisition of the competitor may be the only way of generating the cash flows needed to support dividend payments.

A similar negative view could be taken by new shareholders if Nugfer Co were to seek to raise equity finance via a placing or a public issue.

Sale and leaseback of non-current assets could be considered, although the nature and quality of the non-current assets is not known. The financial position statement indicates that Nugfer Co has $300m of non-current assets, $100m of long-term borrowings and $160m of short-term borrowings. Since its borrowings are likely to be secured on some of the existing non-current assets, there appears to be limited scope for sale and leaseback.

Venture capital could also be considered, but it is unlikely that such finance would be available for an acquisition and no business case has been provided for the proposed acquisition.

While combinations of finance could also be proposed, the overall impression is that Nugfer Co is in poor financial health and, despite its best efforts, it may not be able to raise the $200m in cash that it needs to acquire its competitor.

(b)   When a new issue of bonds is made by a company, the interest rate on the bonds will be influenced by factors that are specific to the company, and by factors that relate to the economic environment as a whole.

Company-specific factors

The interest rate charged on a new issue of bonds will depend upon such factors as the risk associated with the company and any security offered.

The risk associated with the company will be assessed by considering the ability of the company to meet interest payments in the future, and hence its future cash flows and profitability, as well as its ability to redeem the bond issue on maturity.

Where an issue of new bonds is backed by security, the interest rate charged on the issue will be lower than for an unsecured bond issue. A bond issue will be secured on specific non-current assets such as land or buildings, and as such is referred to as a fixed-charge security.

Economic environment factors

As far as the duration of a new issue of bonds is concerned, the term structure of interest rates suggests that short-term debt is usually cheaper than long-term debt, so that the yield curve slopes upwards with increasing term to maturity. The longer the duration of an issue of new bonds, therefore, the higher will be the interest rate charged. The shape of the yield curve, which can be explained by reference to liquidity preference theory, expectations theory and market segmentation theory, will be independent of any specific company.

The rate of interest charged on a new issue of bonds will also depend on the general level of interest rates in the financial system. This is influenced by the general level of economic activity in a given country, such as whether the economy is in recession (when interest rates tend to fall) or experiencing rapid economic growth (when interest rates are rising as capital availability is decreasing). The general level of interest rates is also influenced by monetary policy decisions taken by the government or the central bank. For example, interest rates may be increased in order to exert downward pressure on demand and hence decrease inflationary pressures in an economy.

Tutorial note

The above answer is longer than would be expected from a candidate under examination conditions.

(c) The three forms of capital market efficiency are weak form, semi-strong form and strong form efficiency. The three forms of efficiency can be distinguished by considering the different kinds of information that are reflected in security prices.

Weak form efficiency

This refers to a situation where securities trading on a capital market (e.g. shares and bonds) are shown to reflect all relevant past information. If a capital market is weak form efficient, it is not possible to predict security prices by studying share price movements in the past. There is no correlation between share price movements in successive periods and, in fact, share prices appear to be following a random walk.

Semi-strong form efficiency

This refers to a situation where securities trading on a capital market are shown to reflect all past and public information. If a capital market is semi-strong form efficient, it is not possible to make above-average (abnormal) returns by studying information in the public domain (this includes past information), because the prices of securities move quickly and accurately to reflect new information as it becomes available.

Strong form efficiency

If a capital market is described as strong form efficient, the prices of securities trading on the market reflect all information, whether past, public or private. It is not possible for this form of capital market efficiency to exist in the real world, since it is always possible for an individual with access to relevant information which is not public to benefit from it by buying and selling securities.

	ACCA marking scheme		Marks
(a)	Analysis of recent financial performance		1–3
	Discussion of recent financial performance		1–3
	Analysis of current financial position		1–3
	Discussion of current financial position		1–2
	Consideration of suitable sources of finance		4–6
	Recommendation of suitable source of finance		1
		Maximum	15
(b)	Company-specific factors		2–3
	Economic environment factors		2–3
		Maximum	4
(c)	Weak form efficiency		2
	Semi-strong form efficiency		2
	Strong form efficiency		2
		Maximum	6
Total			25

Examiner's comments

Many students gained good marks on parts (b) and (c) of this question, while not doing very well on part (a).

In part (a) of this question, candidates were provided with financial information for a company and asked to evaluate suitable methods for it to raise $200 million, using both analysis and critical discussion. Many answers struggled to gain good marks for reasons such as poor understanding of sources of finance, a lack of analysis or errors in analysis, misunderstanding of the financial position and performance of the company, and a shortage of discussion.

The question said that the current assets of the company did not include any cash, but many answers suggested that $121 million of the $200 million needed could be provided from $121 million of retained earnings in the balance sheet. As the company had no cash, this was of course not possible and shows a misunderstanding of the nature of retained earnings.

Some answers suggested asking the bank to increase the $160 million overdraft to $360 million in order to provide the finance for the $200 million acquisition. Since the acquisition was a long-term investment, short term finance could not be used under the matching principle. Suggestions of using lease finance were also not appropriate, although discussion of the sale and leaseback of the company's non-current assets was relevant. Some answers discussed business angels, government grants and venture capital, but these sources of finance are not relevant to a $200 million acquisition.

Analysis of the financial information given in the question was needed to support any critical discussion of ways of raising the $200 million required. Some answers gave no analysis or very little analysis and so were quite general in nature, outlining for example the differences between equity finance and debt finance. Errors in ratio calculations were common, highlighting the need for candidates to understand accounting ratio definitions. Four years of profitability information was provided, allowing trends and growth rates to be calculated, although some answers considered only information from the first year and the last year. The information, when analysed, gave a very gloomy picture and indicated that the company would have difficulty raising the cash it needed, whether from debt finance or equity finance. Taking on more debt would cause gearing, interest cover and financial risk to rise to dangerous levels, while existing and potential shareholders would not look favourably on a company that had not paid dividends for four years, especially one whose growth in profitability was on a downward trend.

Part (b) asked candidates to briefly explain the factors that influence the interest rate charged on a new issue of bonds, i.e. traded debt. Good answers discussed such factors as the period to redemption, the risk of the issuing company, the general level of interest rates in the economy, expectations of future inflation, redemption value and so on, and easily gained full marks. Poorer answers did not show understanding of the relationship for a bond between market value, interest rate, period to redemption, redemption value and cost of debt.

Part (c) asked candidates to identify and describe the three forms of efficiency that can be found in a capital market and many answers correctly identified and described weak form efficiency, semi-strong form efficiency and strong form efficiency. Some answers incorrectly stated that capital market efficiency was about the information available in the market, when in fact capital market efficiency is concerned with pricing efficiency, i.e. the nature of the information reflected in the market prices of traded securities, something which is investigated by carrying out empirical tests. From this point of view, it is theoretically possible for a capital market to be simultaneously weak form, semi-strong form and strong form efficient.

39   ECHO CO   *Walk in the footsteps of a top tutor*

Key answer tips

The key learning points from this question are the benefits of answering requirements in an order that best suits you as well as the need to take guidance from the specific words used in both the scenario and the requirement itself. The highlighted words are key phrases that markers are looking for.

Tutor's top tips:

Start by reading the requirement. Having a good understanding of what is expected from you will allow you to read the scenario more effectively, processing the information as you go. Scribble you thoughts in the margins on what each piece of information could be used for in relation to the requirements.

The first thing that should strike you is this question has 4, very independent requirements. This means you can pick the order in which to tackle them to suit your strengths. For the majority, part (d) should be attempted first. The question is very generic and requires little more than regurgitation of knowledge from the syllabus.

Of the remaining three parts, part (c) has the most guidance on the structure and content of your answer. These therefore represent the easiest of the remaining marks. The layout of the scenario means you can immediately re-read the information on proposal C and then consider what additional information you will need.

Tutor's top tips:

The slightly different requirements in part (a) and part (b) is reflected in the mark allocation. In part (a) the requirement is to 'analyse' and 'discuss' compared to 'evaluate' and 'discuss' in part (b). Part (b) will therefore require some further calculations.

In part (a) you need to link back to the scenario where we're told the aim of proposal A is to make the company more attractive to equity investors. A sensible approach is to consider what makes a share attractive. You should immediately highlight the dividend payment, discussion of which would lead on to Modigliani & Miller's theories on dividend policy and efficient markets hypothesis.

(a)   Echo Co paid a total dividend of $2 million or 20c per share according to the income statement information. An increase of 20% would make this $2.4 million or 24c per share and would reduce dividend cover from 3 times to 2.5 times. It is debatable whether this increase in the current dividend would make the company more attractive to equity investors, who use a variety of factors to inform their investment decisions, not expected dividends alone. For example, they will consider the business and financial risk associated with a company when deciding on their required rate of return.

It is also unclear what objective the finance director had in mind when suggesting a dividend increase. The primary financial management objective is the maximisation of shareholder wealth and if Echo Co is following this objective, the dividend will already be set at an optimal level. From this perspective, a dividend increase should arise from increased maintainable profitability, not from a desire to 'make the company more attractive'. Increasing the dividend will not generate any additional capital for Echo Co, since existing shares are traded on the secondary market.

Furthermore, Miller and Modigliani have shown that, in a perfect capital market, share prices are independent of the level of dividend paid. The value of the company depends upon its income from operations and not on the amount of this income which is paid out as dividends. Increasing the dividend would not make the company more attractive to equity investors, but would attract equity investors who desired the new level of dividend being offered. Current shareholders who were satisfied by the current dividend policy could transfer their investment to a different company if their utility had been decreased.

The proposal to increase the dividend should therefore be rejected, perhaps in favour of a dividend increase in line with current dividend policy.

Tutor's top tips:

In part (b), the scenario directs us towards the differences between short term and long term interest rates. As in part (c) the impact on gearing and interest cover can be highlighted and the lack of any investment opportunity should by highlighted as a problem.

(b) The proposal to raise $15 million of additional debt finance does not appear to be a sensible one, given the current financial position of Echo Co. The company is very highly geared if financial gearing measured on a book value basis is considered. The debt/equity ratio of 150% is almost twice the average of companies similar to Echo Co. This negative view of the financial risk of the company is reinforced by the interest coverage ratio, which at only four times is half that of companies similar to Echo Co.

Raising additional debt would only worsen these indicators of financial risk. The debt/equity ratio would rise to 225% on a book value basis and the interest coverage ratio would fall to 2.7 times, suggesting that Echo Co would experience difficulty in making interest payments.

The proposed use to which the newly-raised funds would be put merits further investigation. Additional finance should be raised when it is needed, rather than being held for speculative purposes. Until a suitable investment opportunity comes along, Echo Co will be paying an opportunity cost on the new finance equal to the difference between the interest rate on the new debt (10%) and the interest paid on short-term investments. This opportunity cost would decrease shareholder wealth. Even if an investment opportunity arises, it is very unlikely that the funds needed would be exactly equal to $15m.

The interest charge in the income statement information is $3m while the interest payable on the 8% loan notes is $2.4m (30 × 0.08). It is reasonable to assume that $0.6m of interest is due to an overdraft. Assuming a short-term interest rate lower than the 8% loan note rate – say 6% – implies an overdraft of approximately $10m (0.6/0.06), which is one-third of the amount of the long-term debt. The debt/equity ratio calculated did not include this significant amount of short-term debt and therefore underestimates the financial risk of Echo Co.

The bond issue would be repayable in eight years' time, which is five years after the redemption date of the current loan note issue. The need to redeem the current $30m loan note issue cannot be ignored in the financial planning of the company. The proposal to raise £15m of long-term debt finance should arise from a considered strategic review of the long-term and short-term financing needs of Echo Co, which must also consider redemption or refinancing of the current loan note issue and, perhaps, reduction of the sizeable overdraft, which may be close to, or in excess of, its agreed limit.

In light of the concerns and considerations discussed, the proposal to raise additional debt finance cannot be recommended.

Analysis

Current gearing (debt/equity ratio using book values) = 30/20 = 150%

Revised gearing (debt/equity ratio using book values) = (30 + 15)/20 = 225%

Current interest coverage ratio = 12/3 = 4 times

Additional interest following debt issue = 14m × 0.1 = $1.5m

Revised interest coverage ratio = 12/(3 + 1.5) = 2.7 times

Tutorial note:

The industry gearing has been calculated as debt / equity. You must ensure your calculation is consistent with this otherwise an effective comparison could not be made.

Tutor's top tips:

To calculate the theoretical ex-rights price (TERP), you will need the current share price, the subscription price and the basis of the issue. All are contained in the paragraph labelled 'Proposal C'. To calculate the amount of finance that would be raised, you also need to know the number of shares to be issued. This can be worked out based on the current number of shares in issue given in the Statement of financial position information. Be careful to read this carefully. There is $5m of share capital but as the nominal value of each share is 50c, this means there are 10m in issue.

Both of these are simple calculations and will most likely attract 1 mark each. This therefore leaves 5 marks for your evaluation and discussion of the proposal.

A requirement to 'evaluate' implies some further calculations will be needed, this time relating to gearing and financial risk. Start by reviewing the information given in the scenario and consider what calculations would be both possible and useful. You should identify:

— *Gearing calculations. Whilst you have market values for equity, you only have the book value of debt. To be consistent you should therefore use book values of both to calculate gearing. In order to discuss the proposal, you will need to know the existing gearing and the new gearing under the proposal. Both can be usefully compared to the industry average.*

> – You have also been provided with average data on interest cover. This signals that calculation of current and projected interest cover will be a source of further marks. Some further calculations need to be done by assuming the proceeds from the rights issue are able to earn the same rate of return as existing funds. This will therefore give an estimate of the new level of profitability. These calculations might not seem obvious and are not essential to passing the question.
>
> When discussing the impact of the proposal on gearing and financial risk it is essential to highlight that there doesn't appear to be a need to raise this finance as there is no plan on how it will be spent.

(c) **Analysis**

Rights issue price = $2.30 \times 0.8 = \$1.84$

Theoretical ex rights price = $(1.84 + (2.30 \times 4))/5 = \$2.21$ per share

Number of new shares issued = $(5/0.5)/4 = 2.5$ million

Cash raised = $1.84 \times 2.5m = \$4.6$ million

Number of shares in issue after rights issue = $10 + 2.5 = 12.5$ million

Current gearing (debt/equity ratio using book values) = $30/20 = 150\%$

Revised gearing (debt/equity ratio using book values) = $30/24.6 = 122\%$

Current interest coverage ratio = $12/3 = 4$ times

Current return on equity (ROE) = $6/20 = 30\%$

In the absence of any indication as to the return expected on the new funds, we can assume the rate of return will be the same as on existing equity, an assumption consistent with the calculated theoretical ex rights price. After-tax return on the new funds = $4.6m \times 0.3 = \$1.38$ million Before-tax return on new funds = $1.38m \times (9/6) = \$2.07$ million Revised interest coverage ratio = $(12 + 2.07)/3 = 4.7$ times

The current debt/equity and interest coverage ratios suggest that there is a need to reduce the financial risk of Echo Co. A rights issue would reduce the debt/equity ratio of the company from 150% to 122% on a book value basis, which is 50% higher than the average debt/equity ratio of similar companies. After the rights issue, financial gearing is still therefore high enough to be a cause for concern.

The interest coverage ratio would increase from 4 times to 4.7 times, again assuming that the new funds will earn the same return as existing equity funds. This is still much lower than the average interest coverage ratio of similar companies, which is 8 times. While 4.7 times is a safer level of interest coverage, it is still somewhat on the low side.

No explanation has been offered for the amount to be raised by the rights issue. Why has the Finance Director proposed that $4.6m be raised? If the proposal is to reduce financial risk, what level of financial gearing and interest coverage would be seen as safe by shareholders and other stakeholders? What use would be made of the funds raised? If they are used to redeem debt they will not have a great impact on the financial position of the company, in fact it appears likely that the overdraft is twice as big as the amount proposed to be raised by the rights issue. The refinancing need therefore appears to be much greater than $4.6m. If the funds are to be used for investment purposes, further details of the investment project, its expected return and its level of risk should be considered.

There seems to be no convincing rationale for the proposed rights issue and it cannot therefore be recommended, at least on financial grounds.

(d)   Operating leasing is a popular source of finance for companies of all sizes and many reasons have been advanced to explain this popularity. For example, an operating lease is seen as protection against obsolescence, since it can be cancelled at short notice without financial penalty. The lessor will replace the leased asset with a more up-to-date model in exchange for continuing leasing business. This flexibility is seen as valuable in the current era of rapid technological change, and can also extend to contract terms and servicing cover.

Operating leasing is often compared to borrowing as a source of finance and offers several attractive features in this area. There is no need to arrange a loan in order to acquire an asset and so the commitment to interest payments can be avoided, existing assets need not be tied up as security and negative effects on return on capital employed can be avoided. Since legal title does not pass from lessor to lessee, the leased asset can be recovered by the lessor in the event of default on lease rentals. Operating leasing can therefore be attractive to small companies or to companies who may find it difficult to raise debt.

Operating leasing can also be cheaper than borrowing to buy. There are several reasons why the lessor may be able to acquire the leased asset more cheaply than the lessee, for example by taking advantage of bulk buying, or by having access to lower cost finance by virtue of being a much larger company. The lessor may also be able use tax benefits more effectively than the lessee. A portion of these benefits can be made available to the lessee in the form of lower lease rentals, making operating leasing a more attractive proposition that borrowing. Operating leases also have the attraction of being off-balance sheet financing, in that the finance used to acquire use of the leased asset does not appear in the balance sheet.

ACCA marking scheme		Marks
(a)	Discussion of proposal to increase dividend	
		5
(b)	Evaluation of debt finance proposal	3–4
	Discussion of debt finance proposal	4–5
		7
(c)	Theoretical ex rights price per share	1
	Amount of finance raised	1
	Evaluation of rights issue proposal	2–3
	Discussion of rights issue proposal	3–4
		7
(d)	Discussion of attractions of leasing	6
Total		25

Examiner's comments

Part (a) asked candidates to analyse and discuss a proposal to increase dividend per share. Many candidates calculated correctly the increased dividend per share and then offered very little by way of discussion in order to gain any further marks.

There were a number of points that could have been discussed, including the finance director's view that the dividend per share 'should be increased by 20% in order to make the company more attractive to equity investors'. Increases in dividends usually lag behind increases in earnings and depend on the dividend policy of a company. It is debatable whether increasing the dividend per share makes a company more attractive to investors. It could be argued, for example, that its existing dividend clientele are satisfied by its current dividend policy. It could also be argued that making a dividend decision without also considering investment and financing needs is foolish: paying an increased dividend and then borrowing to meet investment plans is not advisable for a company as highly geared as the one under consideration here. Other points are discussed in the suggested answer to this question.

Part (b) asked for evaluation and discussion of a proposal to make a $15m bond issue and to invest the funds raised on a short-term basis until a suitable investment opportunity arose.

Candidates were expected to be aware that finance should be raised in order to meet a specific need and that investing long-term funds on a short-term basis would incur an unnecessary net interest cost. In this case, a highly-geared company would be choosing to increase its gearing and financial risk, without the prospect of investing the funds in a project offering returns greater than the increased financing cost.

The sector average debt/equity ratio (D/E) was provided, but many candidates chose to calculate capital gearing (D/(D + E)) in the mistaken belief that this was the debt to equity ratio. Comparison with the sector average gearing was therefore pointless, since the gearing ratios were on a different basis. Some candidates also calculated incorrectly the interest coverage, dividing interest into profit before tax or profit after tax, rather than into profit before interest and tax.

There were some lucid discussions of the dangers attached to the proposal to make a bond issue and these gained high marks.

It was surprising to see many candidates attempting to calculate the cost of debt (internal rate of return) of the bond issue. The bonds were to be issued and redeemed at par and so their cost of debt was the same as their interest rate, as these unnecessary calculations confirmed (where they were made correctly).

In part (c), candidates were asked to calculate the theoretical ex rights price per share and the amount of finance to be raised by a proposed rights issue, which was intended to reduce gearing and financial risk.

Many candidates were able to calculate the theoretical ex rights price and the finance raised, and went on to calculate the effect of the rights issue on the gearing of the company. Some candidates mistakenly assumed that the proceeds of the right issue would be used to redeem some of the existing debt, but the question did not specify this and in practice this might not be possible. Very few candidates recognised that, just as with the proposal to make a bond issue, there had been no evaluation of the funding needs of the company. Why raise $4.6m? Why not $10m? What were the rights issue funds going to be used for? A more concrete plan than raising cash to reduce gearing was needed if shareholder wealth was going to be maximised.

Part (d) asked candidates to discuss the attractions of operating leasing as a source of finance. Many answers offered an explanation of operating leasing, but very little discussion of its attractions as a source of finance to a company. Common points made included the tax deductibility of lease rental payments (although interest payments on debt are also tax-deductible), the flexibility of operating leases, and the way in which operating leases helped to overcome the obsolescence problem. Many answers did not compare leasing as a source of finance with borrowing to buy.

40   PAVLON

Key answer tips

This is a difficult question that requires some imaginative thinking in order to tackle efficiently. The idea of calculating the dividend payout ratio for part (a) is one which seems logical when you review the answer but might not necessarily have occurred to you when attempting the question under timed conditions.

Part (b) is a more clear cut application of the dividend valuation model with the change in growth rate being the only complication. The highlighted words are key phrases that markers are looking for.

(a)   (i)   The first step is to try to determine exactly what is Pavlon's current dividend policy.

Year prior to listing	Number of shares	EPS	Growth over previous year	Dividend per share	Payout ratio
5	21,333,333	8.44¢	–	3.6¢	42.7%
4	21,333,333 (Note 2)	11.25¢	33%	4.8¢	42.7%
3	26,666,667	14.44¢	28%	6.16¢	42.7%
2	26,666,667	15.38¢	6%	6.56¢	42.7%
1	26,666,667 (Note 1)	16.69¢	8.5%	7.12¢	42.7%
Current	40,000,000	13.75¢ (est)	-18%	5.5¢ (proposed)	40%

Note 1 $\dfrac{40,000,000}{1.5} = 26,666,667$

Note 2 $\dfrac{26,666,667}{1.25} = 21,333,333$

Pavlon appears to be adopting a policy of a fixed payout ratio of 42.7% pa over the five year period. In general such a policy can lead to wide variations in dividends per share. In Pavlon's case over the last five years earnings have been rising and a continual (though declining) growth in dividend has resulted.

If it is believed that share price is affected by dividend policy then these fluctuations in dividends and the decline in growth could depress equity value.

Most listed companies attempt to adopt a stable or rising level of dividend per share even in the face of fluctuating earnings. This approach is taken in order to maintain investor confidence. If Pavlon were to continue with its present policy and earnings were to decline the resultant dividend could have serious repercussions for share price.

(ii)   The proposed final dividend gives a total for the year of 5.5¢. This is a significant fall in dividend per share and a small decline in the dividend payout ratio. In the absence of market imperfections such as taxation and transaction costs, it could be argued that dividend policy has no impact on shareholder wealth. It is the firm's future earnings stream that is of importance, not the way in which it is split between dividend and retentions.

However, once market imperfections are introduced dividend policy can be shown to have an impact on investor wealth.

Private individuals may pay income tax at a higher rate than capital gains tax due to available CGT annual exemptions. They would therefore prefer retentions to distributions. Any income required could be generated by selling shares to manufacture 'home made' dividends (note however the problem of transaction costs).

If the reduction in dividend payout were carefully explained it might therefore be acceptable to wealthy individuals.

The tax position of institutional shareholders varies and so therefore will their attitude to dividend policy. Most, however, require a steady flow of income to meet their day-to-day obligations (pensions, insurance claims etc) and may not wish (or be able) to generate home made dividends.

It could be argued that new investors have bought shares in Pavlon with full knowledge of its dividend policy and should therefore not be surprised if it sticks to a policy of a 40% payout. However, many shareholders might expect it to change its policy now that it has obtained a listing.

A further factor to consider is the informational content of dividends. The proposed dividend cut might be seen as a signal of poor earnings in the future and lead to investors of either group selling shares.

Overall there is no conclusive evidence on what makes for an optimal dividend policy. Pavlon should however consider the tax position of its investors and the potential reaction of the market to a cut in dividend.

(b)   If the company's profits and dividends are expected to increase initially by 15% pa then investors will expect this year's dividend to be 7.12¢ × 1.15 = 8.188¢

(i)   **Value of first three years' dividend**

Year	Dividend			PV factor 12%	Present value
Current	7.12 × 1.15	=	8.188	0.893	7.312
2	8.188 × 1.15	=	9.416	0.797	7.505
3	9.416 × 1.15	=	10.829	0.712	7.710
					22.527

Note for simplicity we assume that the current dividend is one year hence.

Value of dividends years 4 − ∞

$$= \frac{d(1+g)}{i-g} = \frac{10.829(1.08)}{0.12-0.08} = 292.383$$

This gives the value of the perpetuity as at year 3. To obtain year 0 values we must discount back.

$292.383 \times 0.712 = 208.2$

Value of share at time 0 = 22.527 + 208.2 = 231¢

Since the current market value of Pavlon's shares is $78m/40m = $1.95 the share appears to be under valued.

(ii)   **Weaknesses of the dividend valuation model**

In principle there is little wrong with the dividend valuation model. Its basic premise that the value of a share is the present value of all future dividends is difficult to challenge. Its major weakness is the volume of data it requires.

Specifically:

(a)   the need to forecast all future dividends is a major obstacle to its use. Simplifying assumptions of constant growth make it easy to work with but their practical validity can be questioned.

(b)   if it is to be used in share valuation the problem of determining the correct discount rate is substantial.

(c)   if it is to be used to determine the cost of equity the selection of the appropriate share price free from short-term influences is difficult.

(d)   it assumes that investors are indifferent between tax and capital gains.

41   ARWIN

Key answer tips

Part (a) should be straightforward, except that you need to be careful with the calculation of the fixed costs in the cost of sales. These are not expected to rise next year, and so should be calculated using the current year figures. For part (b), the question does not state how financial gearing or operational gearing should be measured: there are different methods of calculation. Make clear the method of calculation you are using. (The solution here gives two methods of measuring financial gearing and three methods of measuring operational gearing, but your answer only needs one of each.) For part (c), you need to discuss the problems of high gearing, and you need to spot that 'gearing' in this question refers to both financial gearing and operational gearing. The question hints at this strongly, by referring to both business risk and financial risk. Unfortunately, an unwary student will overlook operational gearing and business risk entirely. The highlighted words are key phrases that markers are looking for.

(a)   The forecast income statements are as follows:

	Debt finance $000	Equity finance $000
Sales revenue (50,000 × 1.12)	56,000	56,000
Variable cost of sales (85% × sales)	28,560	28,560
Fixed cost of sales (15% × 30,000)	4,500	4,500
Gross profit	22,940	22,940
Administration costs (14,000 × 1.05)	14,700	14,700
Profit before interest and tax	8,240	8,240
Interest (see working)	800	300
Profit before tax	7,440	7,940
Taxation at 30%	2,232	2,382
Profit after tax	5,208	5,558
Note: Dividends paid (60%)	3,125	3,335
Net change in equity (retained profit)	2,083	2,223

Working

Interest under debt financing = $300,000 + ($5,000,000 × 0.10) = $800,000.

(b)   **Financial gearing**

If financial gearing is measured as the debt: equity ratio:

Using debt/equity ratio:	Current	Debt finance	Equity finance
Debt	2,500	7,500	2,500
Share capital and reserves	22,560	24,643	29,783
Debt/equity ratio (%)	11.1	30.4	8.4

Workings:

Share capital and reserves (debt finance) = 22,560 + 2,083 = $24,643

Share capital and reserves (equity finance) = 22,560 + 5,000 + 2,223 = $29,783.

If financial gearing is measured as the ratio of debt capital to total capital:

Using capital (total) gearing:	Current	Debt finance	Equity finance
Debt	2,500	7,500	2,500
Total long-term capital	25,060	32,143	32,283
Capital (total) gearing (%)	10.0	23.3	7.7

Operational gearing:

If operational gearing is measured as the ratio of fixed costs to total costs:

Using fixed costs/total costs:	Current	Debt finance	Equity finance
Fixed costs	18,500	19,200	19,200
Total costs	44,000	47,760	47,760
Operational gearing (%)	42.0%	40.2%	40.2%

Total costs are assumed to consist of cost of sales plus administration costs.

If operational gearing is measured as the ratio of fixed costs to variable costs:

Using fixed costs/variable costs:	Current	Debt finance	Equity finance
Fixed costs	18,500	19,200	19,200
Variable costs	25,500	29,560	28,560
Operational gearing (%)	0.73	3.3	3.3

If operational gearing is measured as the ratio of contribution to profit before interest and tax (PBIT):

Using contribution/PBIT	Current	Debt finance	Equity finance
Contribution	24,500	27,440	27,440
PBIT	6,000	8,240	8,240
Operational gearing	4.1	3.3	3.3

Contribution is sales revenue minus the variable cost of sales.

Interest cover:

	Current	Debt finance	Equity finance
Profit before interest and tax	6,000	8,240	8,240
Debt interest	300	800	300
Interest cover	20	10.3	27.5

Earnings per share:

	Current	Debt finance	Equity finance
Profit after tax	3,990	5,208	5,558
Number of shares	10,000	10,000	11,250
Earnings per share (cents)	39.9	52.1	49.4

Comment:

The debt finance proposal leads to the largest increase in earnings per share, but results in an increase in financial gearing and a decrease in interest cover. Whether these changes in financial gearing and interest cover are acceptable depends on the attitude of both investors and managers to the new level of financial risk; a comparison with sector averages would be helpful in this context. The equity finance proposal leads to a decrease in financial gearing and an increase in interest cover. The expansion leads to a decrease in operational gearing, whichever measure of operational gearing is used, indicating that fixed costs have decreased as a proportion of total costs.

(c) Business risk could be described as the possibility of a company experiencing changes in the level of its profit before interest as a result of changes in sales revenue or operating costs. For this reason it is also referred to as operating risk. Business risk relates to the nature of the business operations undertaken by a company. For example, we would expect profit before interest to be more volatile for a luxury goods manufacturer than for a food retailer, since sales of luxury goods will be more closely linked to varying economic activity than sales of a necessity good such as food.

The nature of business operations influences the proportion of fixed costs to total costs. Capital intensive business operations, for example, will have a high proportion of fixed costs to total costs. From this perspective, operational gearing is a measure of business risk. As operational gearing increases, a business becomes more sensitive to changes in sales revenue and the general level of economic activity, and profit before interest becomes more volatile. A rise in operational gearing may therefore lead to a business experiencing difficulty in meeting interest payments. Managers of businesses with high operational risk will therefore be keen to keep fixed costs under control.

Financial risk in the context of this question can be described as the possibility of a company experiencing changes in the level of its distributable earnings as a result of the need to make interest payments on debt finance. The earnings volatility of companies in the same business will therefore depend not only on business risk, but also on the proportion of debt finance each company has in its capital structure. Since the relative amount of debt finance employed by a company is measured by gearing, financial risk is also referred to as gearing risk.

As financial gearing increases, the burden of interest payments increases and earnings become more volatile. Since interest payments must be met, shareholders may be faced with a reduction in dividends; at very high levels of gearing, a company may cease to pay dividends altogether as it struggles to find the cash to meet interest payments.

The pressure to meet interest payments at high levels of gearing can lead to a liquidity crisis, where the company experiences difficulty in meeting operating liabilities as they fall due. In severe cases, liquidation may occur.

The focus on meeting interest payments at high levels of financial gearing can cause managers to lose sight of the primary objective of maximizing shareholder wealth. Their main objective becomes survival and their decisions become focused on this, rather than on the longer-term prosperity of the company. Necessary investment in fixed asset renewal may be deferred or neglected.

A further danger of high financial gearing is that a company may move into a loss-making position as a result of high interest payments. It will therefore become difficult to raise additional finance, whether debt or equity, and the company may need to undertake a capital reconstruction.

It is likely that a business with high operational gearing will have low financial gearing, and a business with high financial gearing will have low operational gearing. This is because managers will be concerned to avoid excessive levels of total risk, i.e. the sum of business risk and financial risk. A business with a combination of high operational gearing and high financial gearing clearly runs an increased risk of experiencing liquidity problems, making losses and becoming insolvent.

42   SPENDER CONSTUCTION INC

Key answer tips

In part (a) you will need to apply your knowledge to the specifics of the scenario. Do the calculations and comment on the implications for equity investors. A good approach is to illustrate your answer with some numerical examples.

In part (b) you are specifically told to look at EPS. You will therefore need to forecast this under both scenarios. Link this part of your answer to what you've written in part (a) and financial risk to score highly. Finally, part (c) builds on part (b) and should be an opportunity to score some easy marks. The highlighted words are key phrases that markers are looking for.

(a)   (i)   **Operational gearing** may be defined as a measure of the impact of a change in sales on Earnings Before Interest and Taxation (EBIT). For any given level of output:

Operational gearing = Contribution/EBIT

(*Note:* Other definitions of operational gearing such as fixed costs as a percentage of total costs are also acceptable)

A company's level of operational gearing is dependent on the ratio of fixed to variable costs and the current level of profit. If a company has a high level of fixed costs, then beyond the break-even point, an increase in the volume of sales will lead to a high percentage increase in profit. However, the percentage increase declines as the size of the profit continues to grow. Applying the formula shown above to the 20X7 financial statements for Spender Construction Inc, we can compute the current level of operational gearing within the company:

Operational gearing = Contribution/EBIT

For 20X7:

Variable selling and distribution costs = $348,000 − $100,000= $0.248 million.

Variable administration costs = $8.250m − $7m (fixed) = $1.250 million

Contribution = Sales − Variable costs

= $55.258m − (41.827m + 0.248m + 1.250m)

= $11.933m

EBIT = $4.833m

Operational gearing = 11,933/4.833= 2.47

(ii) **Financial gearing** is measured by comparing a company's use of long-term debt finance relative to equity. The higher the proportion of debt finance, the higher the level of gearing. Financial gearing affects the sensitivity of the profit attributable to equity (profit after interest and tax) to changes in EBIT. Using debt as a source of finance commits a company to the payment of debt interest which, for any given level of operating profit, erodes the amount of profit attributable to equity investors. However, once operating profits are sufficient to cover the interest payments due, all additions to operating profit will be fully attributable to equity investors.

Textbooks contain a number of different formulae for financial gearing. They include the following alternatives:

(1) $\dfrac{\text{Long - term interest bearing debt} + \text{preference share capital}}{\text{Equity plus reserves}}$

(2) $\dfrac{\text{Long - term interest bearing debt} + \text{preference share capital}}{\text{Total long - term capital}}$

(3) $\dfrac{\text{Profit before interest}}{\text{Profit after interest}}$

A further variation on the formula might be applied which includes short-term interest bearing debt in the numerator. In this way financial gearing is then measuring the proportion of total borrowing relative to total capital, rather than just the proportion of long-term loans in the total capital base.

It is useful to note the differences between the formulae. The first two differ only in relation to the denominator, but this has the effect of altering the resulting figure for financial gearing. This can be illustrated by reference to Spender Construction Inc.

Using formula (1) in respect of the 20X7 financial statements.

$$\text{Financial gearing} = \frac{1{,}200}{12{,}452} = 0.0964 \text{ or } 9.64\%$$

Using formula (2):

$$\text{Financial gearing} = \frac{1{,}200}{13{,}652} = 0.0879 \text{ or } 8.799\%$$

The second figure is lower because the denominator is larger. This means that care must be taken in interpreting figures for financial gearing to ensure that there is consistency in the formula chosen for the calculation. Finally, applying formula (3), which uses figures from the income statement (as opposed to the balance sheet (statement of financial position)), and so is more consistent with the operational gearing calculation done earlier, we get:

$$\text{Financial gearing} = \frac{\text{Profit before interest}}{\text{Profit after interest}} = \frac{4{,}833}{4{,}506} = 1.07$$

Formula (3) yields a very different result to the other two, and so serves to underline further the need for caution in interpretation of gearing figures.

Financial gearing is sometimes referred to as 'second tier' gearing because it affects the profit going to equity but not until the impact of operational gearing has already affected the level of EBIT. This means that if a company trades with a high level of operational gearing, EBIT is already highly sensitive to changes in sales revenue. If this is then combined with the potential for further erosion of the returns to equity as a result of large debt interest payments (caused by high financial gearing) then the overall risk to equity investors is high. This overall effect is most important to investors, and means that attention needs to be given to a company's level of operational and financial gearing in combination.

Spender's fixed costs (which are $7,100,000 excluding interest payments) equal over 12.5 % of sales, compared with the industry average of just 7%. The potential risk of this high operational gearing level lies in the sales volatility that is often associated with construction firms. The industry is very sensitive to the state of the economy, and an economic downturn can hit sales quite dramatically. Under such circumstances, and with an operational gearing level of 2.47, Spender Construction Inc could find that a 10% fall in sales from current levels would cause a drop of almost 25% in operating profit. It is worth noting, however, that this gearing level will come down next year as a result of increased sales and reduced fixed costs. It is probably in recognition of this sensitivity of profits to changes in sales that the company has chosen to keep its level of financial gearing relatively low at 1.07.

Spender's financial gearing cannot be compared with that of the industry because the relevant information is not available. The lower level helps to limit the potential impact of sales changes on the profit available to equity, and so limits the overall risk to equity investors. Nonetheless, Spender Construction Inc must be regarded as a somewhat risky choice for equity investors and the example clearly demonstrates how a company needs to think about how it mixes its levels of financial and operating gearing in such a way as to limit the risk to equity shareholders.

(b)   Number of shares currently in issue = 8 million (i.e. $4m/$0.50).

EPS in 20X7 = 39.4 cents (i.e. $3.154m/8m).

Dividend per share in 20X7 = 19 cents (i.e. $1.520 million/8 million).

In comparing a rights issue and a loan stock issue as alternative funding sources, it is important to take account of the effect of each alternative on the returns to ordinary shareholders, and the level of risk to those shareholders. It is reasonable to assume that if we are asking shareholders to accept a higher level of risk (operational or financial) then they will expect to receive an increase in their returns in compensation. The two alternative methods of funding affect only the level of financial risk in the company. The loan stock issue will increase the level of financial gearing whilst the rights issue will reduce the level of financial gearing. As at December 20X7 the financial gearing of Spender Construction Inc was 1.07. In selecting the most appropriate source of funding, therefore, consideration must be given as to whether such changes would be acceptable to the equity shareholders. A comparison of the forecast EPS under both types of funding is useful in assessing the likely shareholder response. Care must be taken, however, in interpreting the forecast, because only one year's data is available.

Forecast income statement, Spender Construction,

Year ending 31 December 20X8

		With loan stock issue $000	With rights issue $000
Sales revenue	($55,258 × 1.15)	63,547	63,547
Cost of sales	0.98 × ($41,827 × 1.15)	47,139	47,139
Gross profit		16,408	16,408
Selling and dist'n costs	($248 × 1.15) + 100	385	385
Administration costs	(1,250 × 1.15) + (7,000 − 500)	7,938	7,938
Operating profit		8,085	8,085
Interest charges	(10% of 1,200) + 280 + (10% of 7,000)	1,100	400
Profit before tax		6,985	7,685
Corporation tax (30%)		2,096	2,306
Profit after tax		4,889	5,379
Dividend		2,000	2,333
Retained profit		2,889	3,046

Assuming loan stock is issued:
Forecast EPS,
Year ending 31 December 20X8
EPS = 4,889/8,000 = 61.1 cents
Change in EPS = 55.1% growth

Assuming rights issue
Forecast EPS,
Year ending 31 December 20X8
EPS = 5,379/9,333 = 57.6 cents
Change in EPS = 46.2% growth

The figures show that if the sales targets are achieved, the **EPS will grow faster if loan stock financing is selected**, but in both instances the growth is substantial. This is largely because profits are already sufficiently high to meet the interest payments required and so, helped substantially by other changes, such as the fixed cost savings, all increases in profit (net of tax) can accrue to equity investors. The rights issue generates a smaller EPS because the number of shares in issue has been increased by 1.33 million, and so the equity earnings are shared more widely. In either case the shareholders benefit from a growth of EPS which exceeds the rate of growth of sales. However, if sales were to fall, then EPS would fall at a rate greater than the drop in sales, again because of the leverage effect. This risk from additional borrowing must be acknowledged and explained to shareholders.

If shareholders are looking for rapid growth of earnings, it is marginally preferable to fund the investment with the loan stock issue. However the **effect** of this choice **on shareholder risk** needs to be taken into account, because Spender's financial gearing will be increased by the loan stock issue. Whether shareholders will accept the higher risk or not depends to some extent on industry and economic forecasts. If the outlook for the construction industry is good, then shareholders are likely to accept such a proposal; conversely if the future prospects look poor then the rights issue is the safer choice. The attractiveness of the higher returns from using loan stock finance needs to compensate for the marginal additional risk created by the issue, and given that the use of loan stock yields an EPS 6% greater than if the rights issue is made then it is likely that this is the case.

In addition to financial considerations, Spender Construction Inc should also take into account the **organisational aspects of the two financing alternatives**, including the speed of issue, issue costs, and prevailing stock market conditions. Rights issues will tend to be slower to arrange and complete than a loan stock issue, but rights do offer the advantage that the issue costs may be kept low as it is not a requirement (though it is usual practice) for them to be underwritten. At the same time, loan stock may be easier to sell if the stock market is volatile or on a bear run.

In conclusion, the loan stock issue should be the chosen source of funding if market forecasts indicate rising future sales and earnings. The rights issue should be the chosen source of finance if the directors believe that shareholders are highly risk averse, and would prefer to avoid any additional financial gearing, and that stock market conditions are favourable to such an issue.

(c) **Dividend cover** is calculated by dividing the profit available to equity by the total dividend payable, and it measures the extent to which equity investors can view their dividend as being 'secure'. As the level of cover rises, so does the security of the dividend, inasmuch as equity investors can still expect there to be sufficient profit available to pay the dividend. A high dividend cover offers a reasonable certainty that dividend levels can be maintained, but it should also lead investors to question how the retained profits are being utilised. By definition, a high dividend cover implies that a large proportion of profits are being retained within the business, and unless these funds are being invested wisely, the equity investor may be better off if the cash is paid out to shareholders, who can then re-invest it elsewhere to earn a better rate of return.

For Spender Construction Inc, the forecast profit available to equity (from (d)) if the loan stock issued equals $4.889m and the dividend forecast for the year is $2m. This gives a dividend cover of:

4.889/2 = 2.44 times.

This means that over half of the profit is being retained for re-investment. If the re-investment can be expected to maintain the profit growth achieved between 20X7 and 20X8, then investors have little to worry about. If, however, Spender Construction Inc gives little indication of how it intends to use this money, then shareholders should be concerned that dividend cover is perhaps a little high.

43   ASSOCIATED INTERNATIONAL SUPPLIES CO

Key answer tips

The best starting point for part (a) is to prepare the appendix to your report. You will need to calculate all the main groups of ratios; be led by the scenario and consider why each piece of information has been provided. You can use the requirement to help structure your report. In this instance you have been asked to comment on growth, liquidity and the capacity to continue trading. These would therefore make excellent sub-headings.

Part (b) is very generic and should have been tackled before part (a). The requirement is to 'explain' and 'evaluate' so make sure you draw out the advantages and disadvantages of each source of finance as well as just identifying them should. For 8 marks you have aimed for at least four sources of finance. The highlighted words are key phrases that markers are looking for.

(a)   **Analysis of company position**

Associated International Supplies Co

Circulation: Associated International Supplies Co (AIS Co)

Author:

Date: xx/xx/xx

General appraisal

The first point to note is that, by most standards, the company would be regarded as small, and is therefore likely to exhibit many of the problems typical of the small company sector. Generally, small companies which are characterised by strong growth also usually exhibit substantial borrowings in relation to equity funds. It is likely, therefore, that the appropriate mix of financing for the business becomes a critical issue in the appraisal of AIS Co.

Growth and liquidity

In the five year period from 20X4 to 20X9 sales for AIS have grown by 151%. In terms of supporting the business with adequate working capital, the pressures of such growth can be substantial. Thus, in the same period we see that current assets have expanded by 54% and current liabilities by 91%. Whilst this aspect of the business will be dealt-with in more detail below, it is worthwhile questioning at this stage whether sufficient funding for working capital is available to support the growth in sales.

Whilst there has been significant growth in sales during the period, profit before tax (PBT) as a percentage of sales has actually declined from 8% to about 5%. This must call into question either the management of costs (operational or financial) or whether the company is unable to force price increases on to customers. Given the information available, the most likely source of this problem appears to relate to interest costs. Both current and non-current liabilities have increased substantially (91% and 276%, respectively) against a background of barely increased equity funding. Debt funding (both long and short term) looks to have increased (see detail below) and this will have an associated interest burden. This has an importance in relation to the sustainability of the business.

Earnings retentions do not appear sufficient to fund business growth, and hence it is clear that borrowings have been increased to deal with this problem. However, a balance must be kept in the business between its earnings capability and its capacity to service its debt commitments. Whilst PBT has increased by 53% over the period, retentions have declined by about 74%. This may be partly explained by an increased tax burden, but is obviously due mainly to excessive distributions. In other words, not enough funds are being retained in the business to support its growth or funded from increased equity issues.

The impact of excessive growth in relation to its funding base might have a severe impact on liquidity. Net current assets are not seriously out of line if a ratio of current assets to current liabilities of 1.0 (unity) is considered acceptable. However, when current assets are looked at in relation to sales a different picture emerges. The ratio was 54% in 20X4 and only 33% in 20X9. This suggests, in combination with the other information, that inventories, receivables and cash resources might be insufficient to support the volume of sales. It might be argued that this reflects greater efficiency in current asset management. This is indeed the case when receivables days are compared over the period (they declined from 99 to 61), but it is not in relation to payables days which also declined (from 88 to 67 during the period). When working capital is measured as a proportion of sales, we observe a decline from 11.4% in 20X4 to 0.5% in 20X9. This appears to be a reflection of reduced current asset investment and overdraft increases.

Because it is debt rather than equity funding that has grown, the business faces a potentially critical situation. We know that current assets consist mainly of inventory and receivables (because the business has substantial borrowings, it is unlikely to simultaneously have large cash balances) and that this is being funded by borrowing rather than retained earnings. The reason why this is the case is because the business is not generating adequate profits and it is distributing too much of post tax earnings. The outlook is for greater borrowing. The poor profit figures suggest that a critical point has been reached in terms of liquidity and solvency. This is reflected in debt/equity ratios which have increased from 2.19 in 20X4 to 4.22 in 20X9 (current and non-current liabilities used as debt and capital and reserves used as equity). Unless a capital reorganisation can take place quickly, either through injected funds or conversion of debt into equity, the business is likely to become insolvent.

Company capacity to continue trading

Given the points made above, it is unlikely that the business can continue in its current form. The trading performance is obviously very strong when measured in terms of its sales capacity and growth. This indicates a good customer base and the ability to service customer needs. The markets the company serves suggest a long-term future for its product or service.

However, it is likely that the company's cost base will be overwhelmed by interest charges, which is resulting in reduced PBT/Sales ratios over the period in spite of significant sales growth. If that is the case, it may well be that the underlying trading profitability is good. If it is not found to be good after further investigation then additional action may need to be taken. For example if low profitability is due to aggressive pricing, an investigation into alternative marketing strategies may be appropriate. In addition, given the significant growth, it may now be an appropriate time to look at the customer base and withdraw service from those customers who are either unprofitable or otherwise difficult (late payers, for example). Product mix might be usefully assessed to focus on higher-margin sales activities and to decrease effort on lower-margin activities. A business plan describing the customer base and the strategy for greater profitability will underpin any bid for a reorganisation of AIS Co's finances.

Bank support is crucial to long term survival if the debt is in the form of bank related lending. Alternative sources of finance should also be considered, particularly in the form of equity which is required to re-balance the business.

Other factors

(i) Venture capitalists might be interested in the business because of its significant growth but poorly structured finance. An equity injection would stabilise the business' finances.

(ii) Future projections of growth might provide a clearer picture of how to respond to the situation the business is now in.

(iii) The maturity of the debt obligations would indicate any critical repayments that may be due.

(iv) Comparisons with other businesses in the sector may provide some assurance as to the debt levels if high debt is a characteristic of the sector.

(v) Investigation of possible renegotiation of the debt to ease the interest burden.

(vi) Investigation of potential sale of the business or merger with a large partner with a view to securing a realistic equity base.

(vii) Information on detailed trading results would enable an accurate assessment of the profitability of AIS Co.

(viii) Working capital management needs to be investigated to assess if it is being efficiently organised.

Appendix to report: Ratio calculations

Sales growth:	(3,010 – 1,200)/1,200 = 151%
Current asset growth:	(1,000 – 650)/650 = 54%
Current liability growth:	(982 – 513)/513 = 91%
Non-current liabilities growth:	(158 – 42)/42 = 276%
PBT growth:	(150 – 98)/98 = 53%
Retained earnings decline:	(65 – 17)/65 = 74%

	20X4	20X9
PBT/Sales	98/1,200 = 8%	150/3,010 = 5%
Current assets/Current liabilities	650/513 = 1.3	1,000/982 = 1.0
Current assets/Sales	650/1,200 = 54%	1,000/3,010 = 33%
Working capital/Sales	(650–513)/1,200 = 11.4%	(1,000–982)/3,010 = 0.5%
Debt/Equity	(513 + 42)/210 = 2.64	(982 + 158)/270 = 4.22
Receivables at 50% of current assets	$325,000	$500,000
Sales per day (365 days)	$3,288	$8,247
Receivables days	325,000/3,288 = 99	500,000/8,247 = 61
Payables at 25% of current liabilities	$128,000	$245,500
Cost of sales per day (365 days)	$1,452	$3,643
Payables days	128,000/1,452 = 88	245,500/3,643 = 67

(b) **General**

Funds for non-current assets would normally be long term in nature in order to match asset use with funding maturity. Moreover, if the asset is a building or other major asset which has a secondary market value, then secured lending may be arranged where lower rates of interest are accessible. In particular, specific asset financing may be available (such as for fleet cars) which may represent an efficient source of funds. In general, the finance leasing option is available and represents a significant source of flexibility to the business. Non-current assets with secondary market values may also be subject to sale and leaseback arrangements.

Long-term sources of finance would typically be either equity funds (either injections or dividend retentions), bank debt or possibly venture capital equity interests for small businesses. What would not be appropriate are loan stock, convertibles, warrants, equity public issues, and listings (with the potential exception of a small company stock market like AIM in the UK).

The most significant barrier to secure external equity funding for small firms is the lack of liquidity, or the inability to either find a market or buyer for the shares when the time arrives when the investor wishes to sell. There is evidence that small companies tend to have low gearing ratios when long-term debt finance to long-term finance plus equity is used as the measure of gearing. Moreover, a large proportion of the debt finance, in general, comes from overdrafts and short-term loans.

Sources of finance

No details are given concerning the nature of a business to comment on, and hence only general recommendations can be made. Given that non-current asset finance is required, long-term finance that is likely to be the most appropriate. Below are listed some ideas of what might be most suitable:

(i) If the non-current asset is substantial, such as a new building, or tooling for a new product, then a smaller stock market, such as the Alternative Investment Market in the UK, may be suitable. AIM is directed largely at small and growing companies who do not qualify for the main stock market. The restrictions for admission are not that binding and may suit a company such as AIS Co.

(ii) Venture capital may also be suitable. This would be desirable from the point of view that, whilst venture capitalists may take an equity participation, they are likely to liquidate their shareholders to the owners of the business and hence ownership dilution would not occur.

(iii) Cash or dividend retentions. This would clearly take time for major asset purchases and may not be suitable for companies that face a funding shortfall in any case (the costs required in asset purchase may simply be too big for any realistic retention timescale).

(iv) Entering a merger or partnership, or accessing 'Business Angel' funding.

(v) Leasing the asset or arranging secured loans at lower interest rates.

(vi) Possible mortgages for buildings, or specialist financing for cars (for example hire purchase, leasing).

(vii) Sale and leaseback of existing non-current assets such as land and buildings.

(viii) Availability of government grants, European funding or other agency assistance.

44   GTK INC *Walk in the footsteps of a top tutor*

Key answer tip

Both parts (a) & (b) are relatively straightforward investment appraisal calculations which shouldn't pose many problems. In part (c) it is essential that you read the requirement carefully. As you have to make a recommendation you must ensure any advantages or disadvantages you note are relevant to the scenario given. The highlighted words are key phrases that markers are looking for.

(a)   **Expected net present value of Proposed 1**

Tutor's top tips:

It's worthwhile giving some quick consideration to the best way to layout your answer to this part of the requirement. A columnar format, like that presented here, will often be the most efficient and will reduce the amount of information you need to write more than once. This is particularly important here since your answer to part (i) will naturally lead into your answer to part (ii).

Don't forget the requirement to comment on your findings. In situation involving expected values, your comments should generally focus on the reliability of the probability estimates and the risk involved (look at the variability between the best result and the worst).

	Scenario 1	Scenario 2	Scenario 3
Number of sunny days	100	125	150
Saving ($/day)	700	700	700
Annual saving ($)	70,000	87,500	105,000
Costs	(24,000)	(24,000)	(24,000)
Net annual savings	46,000	63,500	81,000
Present value of net savings at 10%	460,000	635,000	810,000
Investment	500,000	500,000	500,000
Net present value	(40,000)	135,000	310,000
Probability	30%	60%	10%

Expected net present value = (−40,000 × 0.3) + (135,000 × 0.6) + (310,000 × 0.1) = $100,000

The ENPV is $100,000 so if the investment is evaluated on this basis, it is financially acceptable. In reaching a decision, however, the company should consider that there is a 30% chance of making a loss. This may be seen as an unacceptably high risk. Furthermore, the number of sunny days each year will not be constant, as assumed here, and may or may not be exactly 100, 125 or 150 days. It is possible the net present values of Scenarios 1 and 3 represent extremes in terms of expectations, and that the net present value of Scenario 2 may be most useful as representing the most likely outcome, even on a joint probability basis. It is also worth noting that inflation has not been taken into account and that the ever-increasing cost of energy may make the proposed investment much more financially attractive if it were factored into the analysis.

Workings

Present values must be calculated with the before-tax cost of capital of 10%, since before-tax cash flows are being evaluated here. The present value of a perpetuity is found by dividing the constant annual cash flow by the cost of capital.

Present value of net savings, Scenario 1 = 46,000/0.10 = $460,000

Present value of net savings, Scenario 2 = 63,500/0.10 = $635,000

Present value of net savings, Scenario 3 = 81,000/0.10 = $810,000

(b)   **Before-tax return on capital employed of Project 2**

Tutor's top tips:

The key to this part is remembering that ROCE is the only investment appraisal method that links back to profits rather than cash flows.

To do the calculation you will need to work out both the average annual profits as the average investment. You should work out each of these in turn, being careful to adjust for things like depreciation and sunk costs.

Total cash flow over five years before advertising and depreciation = $500,000

Total depreciation over five years = 300,000 – 30,000 = $270,000

Total accounting profit over five years = 500,000 – 100,000 – 270,000 = $130,000

Average annual accounting profit = 130,000/5 = $26,000 per year

Average investment = (initial investment + scrap value)/2 = (300,000 + 30,000)/2 = $165,000

ROCE = 100 × (26,000/165,000) = 15.8%

The ROCE of Proposal 3 is marginally greater than the target level of 15%. ROCE cannot be recommended as an investment appraisal method, however, and the NPV of Proposal 3 should be calculated in order to determine whether it is financially acceptable.

Tutor's top tips:

You are asked how equity finance or traded debt might be raised and will therefore need to discuss the different methods of issuing shares (rights issue, and placing being the most suitable here) and different things to consider when issuing debt.

(c)   GTK Inc is a company with a small overdraft and no long-term debt. The $1.1 million could be raised as follows:

Equity finance

The equity financing choices available to GTK Inc are a rights issue or a placing.

Rights issue

In this method of raising new equity finance, new shares are offered to existing shareholders pro rata to their existing shareholdings, meeting the requirements of company law in terms of shareholders' pre-emptive rights. Since GTK Inc has several million dollars of shareholders' funds, it may be able to raise $1.1 million through a rights issue, but further investigation will be needed to determine if this is possible. Factors to consider in reaching a decision will include

- the number of shareholders, the type of shareholders (institutional shareholders may be more willing to subscribe than small shareholders),

- whether a recent rights issue has been made,

- the recent and expected financial performance of GTK Inc, and

- the effect of a rights issue on the company's cost of capital.

A rights issue would not necessarily disturb the existing balance of ownership and control between shareholders. Approximately half of the finance needed is for a permanent investment and the permanent nature of equity finance would match this.

Placing

This way of raising equity finance involves allocating large amounts of ordinary shares with a small number of institutional investors. Existing shareholders will need to agree to waive their pre-emptive rights for a placing to occur, as it entails issuing new shares to new shareholders. The existing balance of ownership and control will therefore be changed by a placing. Since GTK Inc is a listed company, it is likely that a significant percentage of its issued ordinary share capital will be in public hands and the effect of a placing on this fraction will need to be considered. There may be a change in shareholder expectations after the placing, depending on the extent to which institutional investors are currently represented among existing shareholders, but since the company is listed there is likely to be a significant institutional representation.

Traded debt

A new issue of traded debt could be redeemable or irredeemable, secured or unsecured, fixed rate or floating rate, and may perhaps be convertible. Deep discount bonds and zero coupon bond are also a possibility, but much rarer. The effect of an issue of debt on the company's cost of capital should also be considered.

Security

Bonds may be secured on assets in order to reduce the risk of the bond from an investor point of view. Fixed charge debt is secured on specified non-current assets, such as land or buildings, while floating charge debt is secured on all assets or on a particular class of assets. In the event of default, holders of secured debt can take action to recover their investment, for example by appointing a receiver or by enforcing the sale of particular assets.

Redemption

Irredeemable corporate debt is very rare and a new issue of traded debt by GTK Inc would be redeemable, i.e. repayable on a specified future date. The project life of two of the proposed capital investments suggests that medium-term debt would be appropriate.

Fixed rate and floating rate

Fixed rate debt gives a predictable annual interest payment and, in terms of financial risk, makes the company immune to changes in the general level of interest rates. If interest rates are currently low, GTK Inc could lock into these low rates until its new debt issue needs to be redeemed. Conversely, if interest rates are currently high and expected to fall in the future, GTK Inc could issue floating rate debt rather than fixed rate debt, in the expectation that its interest payments would decrease as interest rates fell.

Cost of capital

GTK Inc has no long-term debt and only a small overdraft. Since debt is cheaper than equity in cost of capital terms, the company could reduce its overall cost of capital by issuing traded debt. A decrease in the overall cost of capital could benefit the company and its shareholders in terms of an increase in the market value of the company, and an increase in the number of financially acceptable investment projects.

45 TFR

Key answer tips

Provided you have carefully read the details of the scenario, the calculations in part (a) should be relatively uncomplicated. Parts (b) & (c) require you to be more practical. The key element in part (b) is the implications for cash flow. An estimate of this would therefore be useful. In part (c) you must ensure you draw out the difficulties of raising additional finance rather than just going through the different sources. The highlighted words are key phrases that markers are looking for.

(a)   **Income statements for TFR for the four-year period**

Year	Current	Year 1	Year 2	Year 3	Year 4
	$	$	$	$	$
Sales revenue	210,000	255,000	300,000	345,000	390,000
Expenses	168,000	204,000	240,000	276,000	312,000
Net profit	42,000	51,000	60,000	69,000	78,000
Interest	2,000	11,000	8,750	6,500	4,250
Profit before tax	40,000	40,000	51,250	62,500	73,750
Tax	10,000	10,000	12,813	15,625	18,438
Profit after tax	30,000	30,000	38,438	46,875	55,313
Finance					
Dividend	15,000	15,000	19,219	23,438	27,656
Retained profit	15,000	15,000	19,219	23,438	27,656
Equity finance	200,000	215,000	234,219	257,656	285,313
Debt finance	Nil	75,000	50,000	25,000	Nil
Ratios					
Interest cover (times)	21.0	4.6	6.9	10.6	18.4
Debt/equity (%)	Nil	35	21	10	Nil
Return on equity (%)	15	14	16	18	19
ROCE (%)	21	18	21	24	27
ROCE (%)*	19	16	20	23	26

*Including the existing and continuing overdraft in capital employed.

Workings

Annual interest (assuming the continuing overdraft is maintained at the current level)

Year 1 interest payment = 100,000 × 0.09 = 9,000 + 2,000 = $11,000

Year 2 interest payment = 75,000 × 0.09 = 6,750 + 2,000 = $8,750

Year 3 interest payment = 50,000 × 0.09 = 4,500 + 2,000 = $5,500

Year 4 interest payment = 25,000 × 0.09 = 2,250 + 2,000 = $4,250

(b)   **Financial implications for TFR of accepting bank loan**

A key consideration is whether TFR will be able to meet the annual payments of interest and capital. It is assumed, in preparing a cash flow forecast, that there is no difference between profit and cash, and that inflation can be ignored. The annual cash surplus after meeting interest and tax payments is therefore assumed to be equal to retained profit.

Year	1	2	3	4
Net change in equity (retained profit)	15,000	19,219	23,438	27,656
Capital repayment	25,000	25,000	25,000	25,000
Net cash flow	(10,000)	(5,781)	(1,563)	2,656

TFR is clearly not able to meet the annual capital repayments. In order to do so, it will need to change the dividend policy it appears to have maintained for several years of paying out a constant proportion of profit after tax as dividends. One possible course of action is to cut its dividend now and then increase it in the future as profitability allows. Since TFR is owner-managed, a change in dividend policy may be possible, depending of course on the extent to which the owner or owners rely on dividend income. The annual cash flow shortfall is less than the annual dividend payment, so a change in dividend policy would probably allow the loan to be accepted.

Year	1	2	3	4
Profit after tax	30,000	38,438	46,875	55,313
Capital repayment	25,000	25,000	25,000	25,000
Available funds	5,000	13,438	21,875	30,313

It is useful to consider key financial information after the loan has been paid off, i.e. in year 5, assuming that no further growth in sales revenue occurs after the fourth year:

Year	Year 5
Sales revenue	390,000
Expenses	312,000
Net profit	78,000
Interest	2,000
Profit before tax	76,000
Tax	19,000
Profit after tax	57,000
Dividend	28,500
Retained profit	28,500
Equity finance	313,813
Debt finance	Nil
Interest cover (times)	39
Debt/equity (%)	Nil
Return on equity (%)	18
ROCE (%)	25
ROCE (%)*	23

*Including the existing and continuing overdraft in capital employed.

The effect on financial risk of taking on the loan can be examined. If the interest and capital payments are kept up, financial risk will be lower than its current level at the end of four years, all things being equal. Interest cover increases from its current level after five years, from 21 times to 39 times, but is on the low side at the end of the first year (4.6 times), although an improved level is reached at the end of the second year (6.9 times), with further increases in subsequent years. The debt/equity ratio peaks at 35% at the end of the first year and falls rapidly thereafter, at no time looking dangerous, and TFR returns to its current ungeared position after five years. The bank, as provider of debt finance, would be interested in the trend in these ratios, as well as in the ongoing cash flow position.

Both return on equity (ROE) and return on capital employed (ROCE) improve with growth in sales revenue, but are lower than current levels in the first and second years following taking on the loan. At the end of five years ROE has improved to 18% from 15% and ROCE from 19% to 23%. Interest and capital payments would not increase with inflation.

Provided TFR can meet the interest and capital repayments, business expansion using debt finance may be financially feasible. However, this analysis has ignored any potential pressure for reduction or repayment of the overdraft. An average overdraft of $20,000 is quite large for a company with an annual sales revenue of $210,000 and therefore cannot be ignored in any assessment of financial risk. TFR may therefore consider asking for a longer repayment period, with lower annual capital repayments, if it plans to reduce the size of the overdraft or if it is concerned about future cash flow problems.

(c)   TFR is owner-managed and profitable, and financed by equity apart from its large overdraft. It is currently seeking a bank loan in order to finance an expansion of business.

Equity finance

The owner could inject new equity finance himself but his personal financial situation may make this impossible. There are unlikely to be any wealthy individuals willing to invest in his company because there are likely to be more attractive investments elsewhere. Investing in a UK pension fund, for example, carries a tax incentive in that the UK government increases any contributions by the amount of income tax paid. There is therefore a disincentive to invest in the shares of a small company which may be difficult to sell in the future unless another investor can be found who wishes to buy the shares.

However, there is in the UK a Business Angel network which can bring potential investors and small companies together, with the added bonus that the Business Angel may have expertise and experience to offer that could be useful in a small company situation. The owner of TFR may wish to look into this possibility.

There is also a UK government initiative called the Enterprise Investment Scheme, which is of potential benefit to trading companies rather than service companies. The government offers tax advantages in terms of income tax and capital gains tax in order to encourage investment by individuals in the ordinary shares of small companies.

A further UK government scheme offers tax advantages to Venture Capital Trusts, who are required to invest a large part of their funds in the ordinary shares of small companies.

Other government assistance schemes

A range of other UK and EU government assistance schemes exist but almost all of these are targeted towards companies in particular geographic locations, or within particular ranges in terms of number of employees, or with particular funding requirements, for example training.

Debt finance

Small companies are faced with a risk-averse attitude from banks when they seek to raise debt finance. Banks tend to ask for personal guarantees from owners and will set interest rates at higher levels than those charged to larger companies. TFR has non-current assets which are much greater in terms of value than the amount of its overdraft and so the company may be able to offer these as security for a loan. In fact, it is almost certain that the loan under consideration would be secured in some way. Many small companies, particularly service companies, may not be in a position to offer other than personal guarantees.

Examiner's note: Candidates will be given credit for providing local examples of financial assistance available to small firms seeking additional finance.

COST OF CAPITAL

46   DROXFOL

Key answer tips

This is a nice, relatively simple weighted average cost of capital question. As is often the case, the calculation has been teamed with a discussion on capital structure and the impact on ratios to complete the 25 mark question The highlighted words are key phrases that markers are looking for.

(a)   **Calculation of weighted average cost of capital (WACC)**

Market values

Market value of equity = 5m × 4.50 = $22.5 million

Market value of preference shares = 2.5m × 0.762 = $1.905 million

Market value of 10% loan notes = 5m × (105/100) = $5.25 million

Total market value = 22.5m + 1.905m + 5.25m = $29.655 million

Cost of equity using dividend growth model = [(35 × 1.04)/ 450] + 0.04 = **12.08%**

Cost of preference shares = 100 × 9/ 76.2 = 11.81%

Annual after-tax interest payment = 10 × 0.7 = $7

Year	Cash flow	$	10% DF	PV ($)	5% DF	PV ($)
0	Market value	(105)	1.000	(105)	1.000	(105)
1–8	Interest	7	5.335	37.34	6.463	45.24
8	Redemption	100	0.467	46.70	0.677	67.70
				(20.96)		7.94

Using interpolation, after-tax cost of loan notes = 5 + [(5 × 7.94)/ (7.94 + 20.96)] = 6.37%

WACC = [(12.08 × 22.5) + (11.81 × 1.905) + (6.37 × 5.25)]/29.655 = 11.05%

(b)   Droxfol Co has long-term finance provided by ordinary shares, preference shares and loan notes. The rate of return required by each source of finance depends on its risk from an investor point of view, with equity (ordinary shares) being seen as the most risky and debt (in this case loan notes) seen as the least risky. Ignoring taxation, the weighted average cost of capital (WACC) would therefore be expected to decrease as equity is replaced by debt, since debt is cheaper than equity, i.e. the cost of debt is less than the cost of equity.

However, financial risk increases as equity is replaced by debt and so the cost of equity will increase as a company gears up, offsetting the effect of cheaper debt. At low and moderate levels of gearing, the before-tax cost of debt will be constant, but it will increase at high levels of gearing due to the possibility of bankruptcy. At high levels of gearing, the cost of equity will increase to reflect bankruptcy risk in addition to financial risk.

In the traditional view of capital structure, ordinary shareholders are relatively indifferent to the addition of small amounts of debt in terms of increasing financial risk and so the WACC falls as a company gears up. As gearing up continues, the cost of equity increases to include a financial risk premium and the WACC reaches a minimum value. Beyond this minimum point, the WACC increases due to the effect of increasing financial risk on the cost of equity and, at higher levels of gearing, due to the effect of increasing bankruptcy risk on both the cost of equity and the cost of debt. On this traditional view, therefore, Droxfol Co can gear up using debt and reduce its WACC to a minimum, at which point its market value (the present value of future corporate cash flows) will be maximised.

In contrast to the traditional view, continuing to ignore taxation but assuming a perfect capital market, Miller and Modigliani demonstrated that the WACC remained constant as a company geared up, with the increase in the cost of equity due to financial risk exactly balancing the decrease in the WACC caused by the lower before-tax cost of debt. Since in a perfect capital market the possibility of bankruptcy risk does not arise, the WACC is constant at all gearing levels and the market value of the company is also constant. Miller and Modigliani showed, therefore, that the market value of a company depends on its business risk alone, and not on its financial risk. On this view, therefore, Droxfol Co cannot reduce its WACC to a minimum.

When corporate tax was admitted into the analysis of Miller and Modigliani, a different picture emerged. The interest payments on debt reduced tax liability, which meant that the WACC fell as gearing increased, due to the tax shield given to profits. On this view, Droxfol Co could reduce its WACC to a minimum by taking on as much debt as possible.

However, a perfect capital market is not available in the real world and at high levels of gearing the tax shield offered by interest payments is more than offset by the effects of bankruptcy risk and other costs associated with the need to service large amounts of debt. Droxfol Co should therefore be able to reduce its WACC by gearing up, although it may be difficult to determine whether it has reached a capital structure giving a minimum WACC.

(c) (i) **Interest coverage ratio**

Current interest coverage ratio = 7,000/500 = 14 times

Increased profit before interest and tax = 7,000 × 1.12 = $7.84m

Increased interest payment = (10m × 0.09) + 0.5m = $1.4m

Interest coverage ratio after one year = 7.84/1.4 = 5.6 times

The current interest coverage of Droxfol Co is higher than the sector average and can be regarded as quite safe. Following the new loan note issue, however, interest coverage is less than half of the sector average, perhaps indicating that Droxfol Co may not find it easy to meet its interest payments.

(ii) **Financial gearing**

This ratio is defined here as prior charge capital (debt)/equity share capital on a book value basis

Current financial gearing = 100 × (5,000 + 2,500)/(5,000 + 22,500) = 27%

Ordinary dividend after one year = 0.35 × 5m × 1.04 = $1.82 million

Total preference dividend = 2,500 × 0.09 = $225,000

Income statement after one year:

	$000	$000
Profit before interest and tax		7,840
Interest		(1,400)
Profit before tax		6,440
Income tax expense		(1,932)
Profit for the period		4,508
Preference dividends	225	
Ordinary dividends	1,820	
		(2,045)
Retained earnings		2,463

Financial gearing after one year = 100 × (15,000 + 2,500)/ (5,000 + 22,500 + 2,463) = 58%

The current financial gearing of Droxfol Co is 40% less (in relative terms) than the sector average and after the new loan note issue it is 29% more (in relative terms). This level of financial gearing may be a cause of concern for investors and the stock market. Continued annual growth of 12%, however, will reduce financial gearing over time.

(iii) **Earnings per share**

Current earnings per share = 100 × (4,550 − 225)/5,000 = 86.5 cents

Earnings per share after one year = 100 × (4,508 − 225)/5,000 = 85.7 cents

Earnings per share is seen as a key accounting ratio by investors and the stock market, and the decrease will not be welcomed. However, the decrease is quiet small and future growth in earnings should quickly eliminate it.

The analysis indicates that an issue of new debt has a negative effect on the company's financial position, at least initially. There are further difficulties in considering a new issue of debt. The existing non-current assets are security for the existing 10% loan notes and may not available for securing new debt, which would then need to be secured on any new non-current assets purchased. These are likely to be lower in value than the new debt and so there may be insufficient security for a new loan note issue. Redemption or refinancing would also pose a problem, with Droxfol Co needing to redeem or refinance $10 million of debt after both eight years and ten years. Ten years may therefore be too short a maturity for the new debt issue.

An equity issue should be considered and compared to an issue of debt. This could be in the form of a rights issue or an issue to new equity investors.

ACCA marking scheme			
			Marks
(a)	Calculation of market values	2 marks	
	Calculation of cost of equity	2 marks	
	Calculation of cost of preference shares	1 mark	
	Calculation of cost of debt	2 marks	
	Calculation of WACC	2 marks	
			9
(b)	Relative costs of equity and debt	1 mark	
	Discussion of theories of capital structure	7–8 marks	
	Conclusion	1 mark	
	Maximum		8
(c)	Analysis of interest coverage ratio	2–3 marks	
	Analysis of financial gearing	2–3 marks	
	Analysis of earnings per share	2–3 marks	
	Comment	2–3 marks	
	Maximum		8
Total			25

47   ILL COLLEAGUE

Key answer tips

A solid understanding of the basics of calculating the weighted average cost of capital will be sufficient to answer part (a). Part (b) represents more of a challenge and requires you to be competent in gearing and ungearing betas. Part (c) could have been attempted first as it gave an opportunity to gain some easy marks.

(a)   (i)   **Dividend valuation model**

If we assume a constant growth in dividends, we may estimate the cost of equity by using:

$$K(e) = \frac{Do(1+g)}{Po} + g$$

where: D_0 = $2.14m/10m shares = 21.4c

P_0 = 321c

g   = 11%

Therefore:

K(e)   = (21.4c × 1.11 / 321c) + 0.11 = 0.184, or 18.4%

Kd(1-t)

As the question tells us to assume that 'corporate debt is risk-free', we can therefore assume that the cost of debt equals the risk free rate:

Kd (1-t)   = 12% × (1 − 0.35) = 7.8%

The weighted average cost of capital (WACC) is therefore:

WACC   = 18.4% × $\frac{2}{3}$ + 7.8% × $\frac{1}{3}$

= 14.87%

(ii)   **Capital asset pricing model**

R SHARES   = R_f + βSHARES × [R_m − R_f]

Beta   = 1.4

R_f = 12%

R_m = 16%

Therefore:

R SHARES   = 12% + [16% − 12%] × 1.40 = 17.6%

Kd   = 7.8% as in part (i)

WACC   = 17.6% × $\frac{2}{3}$ + 7.8% × $\frac{1}{3}$

= 14.33%

The cost of equity may be estimated using either the dividend valuation model or the capital asset pricing model. In theory the two models should provide the same estimate of the cost of equity. In many instances, because of market imperfections and problems in the estimation of an appropriate growth rate in the dividend valuation model, the two models often give different results. CAPM is normally considered to be the better alternative. However, this model also has theoretical weaknesses and there may be problems in obtaining data to input into the model.

(b) A major diversification into a new industry is likely to involve a different level of systematic risk from that of the company's existing investment portfolio. In these circumstances a project specific discount rate should be estimated, and the company's weighted average cost of capital is not appropriate. The project specific discount rate will need to reflect both the systematic risk (business risk) of operating cash flows and the financial gearing (financial risk) of the company as a whole.

A pragmatic way of identifying the systematic business risk is to use the published equity beta coefficients of other companies within the industry. These equity betas are considered to reflect the systematic risk of our company's major investment in the industry. However, if the average gearing level of the companies in the industry differs from our company's gearing, the beta will need to be adjusted (degeared and regeared) to reflect the gearing level (financial risk) of our company.

The β equity of the industry is 1.50.

Using β asset $= \beta$ equity $\dfrac{E}{E+D(1-t)} + \beta$ debt $\dfrac{D(1-t)}{E+D(1-t)}$

As β debt is 0.

β asset $= 1.50 \times \dfrac{3}{3+1(1-0.35)} + 0$

β asset (= β equity for an ungeared project) = 1.23

Adjustment for the company's gearing level may be achieved by 're-gearing' the β asset.

Asset beta $=$ Equity beta $\times \dfrac{E}{E+D(1-t)}$

$1.23 =$ Equity beta $\times \dfrac{2}{2+1(1-0.35)}$

Equity beta $= 1.23/0.75 = 1.64$

Project E(r equity) $= 12 + (16 - 12) \times 1.64$

$= 18.56\%$

Project weighted average cost of capital is $18.56\% \times \frac{2}{3} + 7.8\% \times \frac{1}{3} = 14.97\%$

14.97% or approximately 15% is the suggested discount rate for the project.

This discount rate must only be regarded as a rough approximation.

(c)   **Practical problems of the CAPM**

(i)   The CAPM is an ex-ante model. It is difficult, if not impossible, to forecast accurate future returns of the company, project, or market. For practical purposes, ex-post data is normally used in the CAPM.

(ii)   Even if the use of ex-post data is considered to be acceptable, it is difficult to estimate the appropriate data inputs:

R_f – What is the appropriate risk-free rate? A short-term government bill? A long-term government stock?

R_m – What is the market return? Do returns on companies comprising the FTSE All Share Index (or similar) provide a satisfactory estimate of returns on the market as a whole?

Beta – The use of an historical beta assumes that future risk is the same as past risk. Evidence for individual companies suggests that this is not the case.

Timescale – Over what period should historic data be considered? How frequently should returns be calculated?

(iii)   CAPM only considers systematic risk. This may not be satisfactory to the management of a company that is not fully diversified.

(iv)   CAPM is a one-period model; investment appraisal is multi-period. However, attempts have been made to produce multi-period extensions of the basic CAPM.

(v)   CAPM considers only the level of return, not how the return is received by the providers of finance, and the significance to shareholders of whether the return is in the form of dividends, interest or capital gains.

48   KFP CO

Key answer tips

This is an excellent example of the examiner's style and in particular the way he combines two or more areas of the syllabus into one question.   Part (c) should be fairly straightforward, just drawing on the basic theories of gearing. Don't forget to address the final sentence though – what will these theories mean if KFP were to issue further debt finance.

(a)   **Weighted average cost of capital (WACC) calculation**

Cost of equity of KFP Co = 4.0 + (1.2 × (10.5 – 4.0)) = 4.0 + 7.8 = 11.8% using the capital asset pricing model

To calculate the after-tax cost of debt, linear interpolation is needed

After-tax interest payment = 100 × 0.07 × (1 – 0.3) = \$4.90

Year	Cash flow	$	10% discount	PV ($)	5% discount	PV ($)
0	Market value	(94.74)	1.000	(94.74)	1.000	(94.74)
1 to 7	Interest	4.9	4.868	23.85	5.786	28.35
7	Redemption	100	0.513	51.30	0.711	71.10
				(19.59)		4.71

After-tax cost of debt = 5 + ((10 − 5) × 4.71)/(4.71 + 19.59) = 5 + 1.0 = 6.0%

Number of shares issued by KFP Co = $15m/0.5 = 30 million shares

Market value of equity = 30m × 4.2 = $126 million

Market value of bonds issued by KFP Co = 15m × 94.74/100 = $14.211 million

Total value of company = 126 + 14.211 = $140.211 million

WACC = ((11.8 × 126) + (6.0 × 14.211))/140.211 = 11.2%

(b) (i) **Price/earnings ratio method**

Earnings per share of NGN = 80c per share

Price/earnings ratio of KFP Co = 8

Share price of NGN = 80 × 8 = 640c or $6.40

Number of ordinary shares of NGN = 5/0.5 = 10 million shares

Value of NGN = 6.40 × 10m = $64 million

However, it can be argued that a reduction in the applied price/earnings ratio is needed as NGN is unlisted and therefore its shares are more difficult to buy and sell than those of a listed company such as KFP Co. If we reduce the applied price/earnings ratio by 10% (other similar percentage reductions would be acceptable), it becomes 7.2 times and the value of NGN would be (80/100) × 7.2 × 10m = $57.6 million

(ii) **Dividend growth model**

Dividend per share of NGN = 80c × 0.45 = 36c per share

Since the payout ratio has been maintained for several years, recent earnings growth is the same as recent dividend growth, i.e. 4.5%. Assuming that this dividend growth continues in the future, the future dividend growth rate will be 4.5%.

Share price from dividend growth model = (36 × 1.045)/ (0.12 − 0.045) = 502c or $5.02 Value of NGN = 5.02 × 10m = $50.2 million

(c) A discussion of capital structure could start from recognising that equity is more expensive than debt because of the relative risk of the two sources of finance. Equity is riskier than debt and so equity is more expensive than debt. This does not depend on the tax efficiency of debt, since we can assume that no taxes exist. We can also assume that as a company gears up, it replaces equity with debt. This means that the company's capital base remains constant and its weighted average cost of capital (WACC) is not affected by increasing investment.

The traditional view of capital structure assumes a non-linear relationship between the cost of equity and financial risk. As a company gears up, there is initially very little increase in the cost of equity and the WACC decreases because the cost of debt is less than the cost of equity. A point is reached, however, where the cost of equity rises at a rate that exceeds the reduction effect of cheaper debt and the WACC starts to increase. In the traditional view, therefore, a minimum WACC exists and, as a result, a maximum value of the company arises.

Modigliani and Miller assumed a perfect capital market and a linear relationship between the cost of equity and financial risk. They argued that, as a company geared up, the cost of equity increased at a rate that exactly cancelled out the reduction effect of cheaper debt. WACC was therefore constant at all levels of gearing and no optimal capital structure, where the value of the company was at a maximum, could be found.

It was argued that the no-tax assumption made by Modigliani and Miller was unrealistic, since in the real world interest payments were an allowable expense in calculating taxable profit and so the effective cost of debt was reduced by its tax efficiency. They revised their model to include this tax effect and showed that, as a result, the WACC decreased in a linear fashion as a company geared up. The value of the company increased by the value of the 'tax shield' and an optimal capital structure would result by gearing up as much as possible.

It was pointed out that market imperfections associated with high levels of gearing, such as bankruptcy risk and agency costs, would limit the extent to which a company could gear up. In practice, therefore, it appears that companies can reduce their WACC by increasing gearing, while avoiding the financial distress that can arise at high levels of gearing.

It has further been suggested that companies choose the source of finance which, for one reason or another, is easiest for them to access (pecking order theory). This results in an initial preference for retained earnings, followed by a preference for debt before turning to equity. The view suggests that companies may not in practice seek to minimise their WACC (and consequently maximise company value and shareholder wealth).

Turning to the suggestion that debt could be used to finance a cash bid for NGN, the current and post acquisition capital structures and their relative gearing levels should be considered, as well as the amount of debt finance that would be needed. Earlier calculations suggest that at least $58m would be needed, ignoring any premium paid to persuade target company shareholders to sell their shares. The current debt/equity ratio of KFP Co is 60% (15m/25m). The debt of the company would increase by $58m in order to finance the bid and by a further $20m after the acquisition, due to taking on the existing debt of NGN, giving a total of $93m. Ignoring other factors, the gearing would increase to 372% (93m/25m). KFP Co would need to consider how it could service this dangerously high level of gearing and deal with the significant risk of bankruptcy that it might create. It would also need to consider whether the benefits arising from the acquisition of NGN would compensate for the significant increase in financial risk and bankruptcy risk resulting from using debt finance.

			Marks
ACCA marking scheme			
(a)	Cost of equity calculation	2	
	Correct use of taxation rate	1	
	Cost of debt calculation	3	
	Market value of equity	1	
	Market value of debt	1	
	WACC calculation	2	
			10
(b)	Price/earnings value of company	2	
	Current dividend per share	1	
	Dividend growth model value of company	3	
			6
(c)	Traditional view of capital structure	1 - 2	
	Miller & Modigliani and capital structure	2 - 3	
	Market imperfections	1 - 2	
	Other relevant discussion	1 - 2	
	Comment on debt finance for cash offer	2 - 3	
		Maximum	9
Total			25

Examiner's comments

In part (a), candidates were asked to calculate the weighted average cost of capital (WACC) of a company. Many candidates gained full marks for their calculations. Some answers lost marks because they included the debt of the target company in their calculation. The WACC of one company is clearly independent of the debt of another company.

Information provided in the question enabled the cost of equity to be found using the CAPM formula. Some candidates ignored this information and attempted to use the dividend growth model instead. Other candidates un-geared and re-geared the equity beta of the company, even though this was unnecessary since the equity beta was not from a proxy company. Most candidates calculated the cost of equity correctly.

The cost of debt had to be calculated using linear interpolation and most answers did this more or less successfully. Where errors arose, these involved using a shorter bond maturity

than that in the question (7 years), exchanging the market value and the par value in the interpolation calculation, omitting to make the interest payment after-tax, and mixing total values and per share values in the same calculation.

Most candidates correctly used market values as weights.

Part (b) called for the calculation of the value of the target company using the PER (price/earnings ratio) method and the dividend growth model (DGM). These were not complicated calculations, although it was necessary to assume with the DGM that the dividend growth rate was the same as the earnings per share growth rate given in the question. This was a reasonable assumption, as the earnings per share growth rate and the dividend payout ratio had both been constant for several years.

Even though the question gave both the earnings per share (EPS) of the target company and an instruction to use the PER provided, some candidates made life difficult for themselves by doing something other than multiplying the earnings per share by the PER. The most common error was using the retained earnings of the target company instead of the EPS provided. Another common error was trying to calculate a PER value, rather than using the one given.

Many candidates had difficulty in calculating the dividend per share for using in the DGM. Since the target company EPS and payout ratio were provided in the question, this can only be explained by a lack of understanding of the payout ratio.

Part (c) called for a discussion of the relationship between WACC and the capital structure of a company. Some candidates incorrectly discussed the circumstances under which WACC could be used in investment appraisal, when in fact the question was asking for a discussion of optimal capital structure theory. Better answers looked at the traditional view, the views of Miller and Modigliani, and the effect on their views of market imperfections such as bankruptcy risk and the costs of financial distress. An optimal capital structure is one that gives a minimum WACC.

This part of the question asked candidates to comment on the use of debt to finance the acquisition. Some answers were very general in nature, discussing the attractions of debt as a source of finance. Better answers calculated the current gearing of the bidding company and then considered the effect on that gearing of adding debt equal to the value of the target company calculated earlier.

49 BURSE CO *Walk in the footsteps of a top tutor*

Key answer tips

The layout of this question is very straightforward with all facts being clearly presented. Parts (b) & (c) are both discussional and between them, account for 52% of the available marks. As they do not rely on the calculations in part (a), they should be attempted first.

The key learning point from this question is the importance of being organised. By utilising a summary table and noting assumptions as you go along, you save precious time not having to search for information or rack your brain for something when it just won't come to you. The highlighted words are key phrases that markers are looking for.

Tutor's top tips:

In part (a) you are required to calculated the weighted average cost of capital and state any assumptions you make, don't forget to do the latter. It's easiest if you jot down any thoughts you have as you go along.

You should start by drawing out a table listing all the different sources of finance down the left hand side. Your table should have two further columns for you to enter the cost and market value of each type of finance as you calculate it.

> *A quick read of the scenario should therefore give you a table as follows:*
>
> | | Cost (%) | Market value |
> |---|---|---|
> | Equity | | |
> | 7% convertible debt | | |
> | 8% bank loan | | |
> | Total | | |
>
> *Now you must work through each source of finance in turn, working out both the cost and market value in order to populate your table.*
>
> *The bank loan is probably the easiest to start with. The cost is simply the bank's interest rate adjusted for tax. Since the bank loan is not traded, the market value is the same as the book value. Fill these results into your table.*
>
> *Now move on to equity. To work out the cost of equity you will either need to apply the dividend valuation model or alternatively, use CAPM. Given the information supplied in the question, it is clear that CAPM is the appropriate method here. The scenario informs you of an equity risk premium of 6.5%. This is a term that you may not have seen before but don't let that throw you. Think about the different elements of a CAPM calculation and consider what information you have and what you don't have. This should reveal that you don't have the average market return and will therefore need to use the information on the risk premium to calculate it. When you have an answer for cost and market value, fill in your table.*
>
> *The convertible loan stock is slightly trickier although don't let this worry you. The key is to remember that the cost of convertible debt is calculated just like the cost of redeemable debt but with an extra step. Before you can work out the cost, you must first calculate whether the debt is likely to be converted or not.*
>
> *When you've looked at all of the different sources, your table should be fully populated. You now have all the information you need to be able to calculate the overall WACC.*
>
> *Hopefully, you've remembered to jot down any ideas on assumptions implicit in your work. Note these down underneath, and add a few more by considering the general assumptions of both WACC calculations and the CAPM. Make sure you don't overlap with the points you've made in parts (b) or (c).*

(a) **Calculation of weighted average cost of capital (WACC)**

  Cost of equity

  Cost of equity using capital asset pricing model = 4.7 + (1.2 × 6.5) = 12.5%

  Cost of convertible debt

  Annual after-tax interest payment = 7 × (1 − 0.3) = $4.90 per bond
  Share price in six years' time = 5.50 × 1.066 = $7.80
  Conversion value = 7.80 × 15 = $117.00 per bond
  Conversion appears likely, since the conversion value is much greater than par value.

  The future cash flows to be discounted are therefore six years of after-tax interest payments and the conversion value received in year 6:

Year	Cash flow	$	10% DF	PV ($)	5% DF	PV ($)
0	market value	(107.11)	1.000	(107.11)	1.000	(107.11)
1–6	interest	4.9	4.355	21.34	5.076	24.87
6	conversion	117.00	0.564	66.00	0.746	87.28
				(19.77)		5.04

Using linear interpolation, after-tax cost of debt = 5 + [(5 × 5.04)/(5.04 + 19.77)] = 6.0%.

(Note that other after-tax costs of debt will arise if different discount rates are used in the linear interpolation calculation.)

We can confirm that conversion is likely and implied by the current market price of $107.11 by noting that the floor value of the convertible debt at an after-tax cost of debt of 6% is $93.13 (4.9 × 6.210 + 100 × 0.627).

Cost of bank loan

After-tax interest rate = 8 × (1 − 0.3) = 5.6%

This can be used as the cost of debt for the bank loan.

An alternative would be to use the after-tax cost of debt of ordinary (e.g. not convertible) traded debt, but that is not available here.

Market values

Market value of equity = 20m × 5.50 = $110 million
Market value of convertible debt = 29m × 107.11/100 = $31.06 million
Book value of bank loan = $2m
Total market value = 110 + 31.06 + 2 = $143.06 million

WACC = [(12.5 × 110) + (6.0 × 31.06) + (5.6 × 2)]/143.06 = 11.0%

Tutor's top tips:

The specific requirement in both parts (b) & (c) is to 'discuss'. This would imply a mark allocation of around 2 marks per relevant point discussed. You should therefore aim for between 3 or 4 points in each part.

(b)   The weighted average cost of capital (WACC) can be used as a discount rate in investment appraisal provided that the risks of the investment project being evaluated are similar to the current risks of the investing company. The WACC would then reflect these risks and represent the average return required as compensation for these risks.

WACC can be used in investment appraisal provided that the business risk of the proposed investment is similar to the business risk of existing operations. Essentially this means that WACC can be used to evaluate an expansion of existing business. If the business risk of the investment project is different from the business risk of existing operations, a project specific discount rate that reflects the business risk of the investment project should be considered. The capital asset pricing model (CAPM) can be used to derive such a project-specific discount rate.

WACC can be used in investment appraisal provided that the financial risk of the proposed investment is similar to the financial risk of existing operations. This means that financing for the project should be raised in proportions that broadly preserve the capital structure of the investing company. If this is not the case, an investment appraisal method called adjusted present value (APV) should be used. Alternatively, the CAPM-derived project-specific cost of capital can be adjusted to reflect the financial risk of the project financing.

A third constraint on using WACC in investment appraisal is that the proposed investment should be small in comparison with the size of the company. If this were not the case, the scale of the investment project could cause a change to occur in the perceived risk of the investing company, making the existing WACC an inappropriate discount rate.

(c) The dividend growth model has several difficulties attendant on its use as a way of estimating the cost of equity. For example, the model assumes that the future dividend growth rate is constant in perpetuity, an assumption that is not supported by the way that dividends change in practice. Each dividend paid by a company is the result of a dividend decision by managers, who will consider, but not be bound by, the dividends paid in previous periods. Estimating the future dividend growth rate is also very difficult. Historical dividend trends are usually analysed and on the somewhat risky assumption that the future will repeat the past, the historic dividend growth rate is used as a substitute for the future dividend growth rate. The model also assumes that business risk, and hence business operations and the cost of equity, are constant in future periods, but reality shows us that companies, their business operations and their economic environment are subject to constant change. Perhaps the one certain thing about the future is its uncertainty.

It is sometimes said that the dividend growth model does not consider risk, but risk is implicit in the share price used by the model to calculate the cost of equity. A moment's thought will indicate that share prices fall as risk increases, indicating that increasing risk will lead to an increasing cost of equity. What is certainly true is that the dividend growth model does not consider risk explicitly in the same way as the capital asset pricing model (CAPM). Here, all investors are assumed to hold diversified portfolios and as a result only seek compensation (return) for the systematic risk of an investment. The CAPM represent the required rate of return (i.e. the cost of equity) as the sum of the risk-free rate of return and a risk premium reflecting the systematic risk of an individual company relative to the systematic risk of the stock market as a whole. This risk premium is the product of the company's equity beta and the equity risk premium. The CAPM therefore tells us what the cost of equity should be, given an individual company's level of systematic risk.

The individual components of the CAPM (the risk-free rate of return, the equity risk premium and the equity beta) are found by empirical research and so the CAPM gives rise to a much smaller degree of uncertainty than that attached to the future dividend growth rate in the dividend growth model. For this reason, it is usually suggested that the CAPM offers a better estimate of the cost of equity than the dividend growth model.

ACCA marking scheme			
			Marks
(a)		Calculation of cost of equity	2
		Calculation of cost of convertible debt	5
		Calculation of cost of bank loan	1
		Calculation of market values	2
		Calculation of WACC	2
			12
(b)		Discussion of business risk	2–3
		Discussion of financial risk	1–2
		Discussion of other relevant factors	1–2
		Maximum	6
(c)		Discussion of dividend growth model	2–3
		Discussion of capital asset pricing model	2–3
		Conclusion	1–2
		Maximum	7
Total			25

Examiner's comments

In part (a), candidates were asked to calculate the weighted average cost of capital (WACC) of a company which was financed by equity (ordinary shares), a bank loan and convertible bonds. Answers to this part of the question were of variable quality.

The cost of equity had to be calculated using the capital asset pricing model (CAPM) because there was insufficient data in the question to use the dividend growth model. The risk-free rate of return, the equity beta and the equity risk premium were given, and so the cost of equity could be calculated from the CAPM formula (provided in the formulae sheet). A common error was to confuse the equity risk premium with the return on the market, resulting in a cost of equity less than the cost of debt. Such a result is inconsistent with the risk-return hierarchy.

Many candidates ignored the bank loan, or assumed that it was not relevant, and lost credit as a result.

Finding the cost of debt of the convertible bonds proved to be a challenge for many candidates. Some candidates stated simply that they assumed the bonds were to be redeemed rather than converted and lost marks as a result, even if they calculated correctly the cost of debt of the bond with redemption after eight years. The correct approach was to calculate that conversion was likely to occur, and then calculate the cost of debt using the current market value, the after-tax interest rate, the conversion value after six years and linear interpolation. Students gained credit for any parts of this evaluation that were carried out correctly

The costs of the individual sources of finance were then weighted on a market value basis and added to give the WACC. Many candidates were able to calculate market weights correctly, although some chose to ignore the current bond market price and calculate a market price based on the present value of the conversion value. The WACC is, of course, a percentage value and not a monetary amount.

Credit was given where method was correct but calculation errors were made.

Part (b) asked candidates to discuss the circumstances under which WACC can be used in investment appraisal. Some candidates discussed correctly the dependence of the WACC on the current capital structure and business operations, and therefore on the current financial risk and business risk, of the company, linking this with using the WACC as a discount rate in appraisal of investments that did not affect materially the current financial risk and business risk.

Candidates who were not aware of these restrictions on the use of the WACC in investment appraisal tended to discuss how the WACC is calculated, or to suggest that WACC could be used if a company had debt in its capital structure. Credit could also have been gained here through discussing risk-adjusted discount rates and the link between project-specific discount rates and the WACC.

Part (c) required candidates to discuss whether the CAPM or the dividend growth model (DGM) offered the better estimate of cost of equity. In order to answer this question, candidates had to have an understanding of the assumptions underlying the two models and the extent to which these assumptions could be challenged as being unrealistic or inappropriate. Weaker answers simply outlined the two models and their constituent variables. Better answers compared and contrasted the two models, and argued for the superiority of the CAPM.

50   YGV CO

Key answer tips

This question contains some fairly straightforward calculations relating to the impact of a proposed new issue of debt finance on a company. The discursive aspects of the question are harder and, although fairly typical in style, will leave many students wondering how best to approach it. The highlighted words are key phrases that markers are looking for.

(a)   **Calculation of cost of debt**

After-tax interest payment = 9 × 0.7 = $6.30 per bond

Year	Cash flow	$	8% discount factor	Present value ($)
0	Issue price	(100)	1.000	(100.00)
1–10	After-tax interest	6.30	6.710	42.27
10	Redemption	110	0.463	50.93
				(6.80)

Year	Cash flow	$	6% discount factor	Present value ($)
0	Issue price	(100)	1.000	(100.00)
1–10	After-tax interest	6.30	7.360	46.37
10	Redemption	110	0.558	61.38
				7.75

After-tax cost of debt = 6 + [(8 − 6) × 7.75/(7.75 + 6.8)] = 6 + 1.1 = 7.1%

(b)   YGV Co does not currently have any long-term debt and so the current weighted average cost of capital (WACC) is the same as the current cost of equity, which is 12%.

Current market capitalisation = 10m × $4.10 = $41 million

If the company issues $4m of bonds at par with an after-tax cost of debt of 7.1%, the WACC will be [(41m × 12) + (4m × 7.1)]/45m = 11.6%

The effect of the bond issue is therefore to reduce the WACC from 12% to 11.6% per year.

This calculation assumes that the current share price does not change as a result of the bond issue. In reality, the share price might change as a result of the change in financial risk. This calculation also assumes that the overdraft is not relevant in calculating the WACC, when in reality the size of the overdraft might make it a significant factor.

Tutorial note:

WACC calculations that include the overdraft are also acceptable.

(c)   (i)   **Interest coverage ratio**

Current interest = $4.5m × 5% = $225,000 per year

Current interest coverage ratio = 1m/0.225 = 4.4 times

Interest from bond issue = $4m × 9% = $360,000 per year

Interest on remaining overdraft = $0.5m × 5% = $25,000 per year

Total interest = 360,000 + 25,000 = $385,000 per year

Revised interest coverage ratio = 1m/0.385 = 2.6 times

(ii)   **Gearing**

Market capitalisation of YGV plc = 10m shares × $4.10 = $41 million

Current gearing using market values, excluding overdraft = zero

Revised gearing using market values, excluding overdraft = 100 × (4,000/ 41,000) = 9.8%

Current gearing using market values, including overdraft = 100 × (4,500/ 41,000) = 11.0%

Revised gearing using market values, including overdraft = 100 × (4,500/ 41,000) = 11.0%

Tutorial note:

Full credit could have been obtained whether or not the overdraft had been included in the gearing calculations..

(d)

Tutor's top tips:

Don't forget to read the requirement carefully to ensure you pick up on all aspects. Here you were asked to not only evaluate the proposal to use the bond issue to finance the reduction in the overdraft but ALSO to discuss alternative sources of finance that could be considered.

Interest coverage ratio

The current interest coverage ratio of 4·4 times is just over half of the sector average value of 8 times, although before the fall in profit it was 22 times. As a result of the bond issue, the interest coverage ratio would fall to 2·6 times, which is a dangerously low level of cover.

Gearing

Whether the bond issue has an effect on gearing depends on whether the gearing calculation includes the overdraft. If the overdraft is excluded, gearing measured by the debt/equity ratio on a market value basis increases from zero to 9·8%. If the overdraft is included, there is no change in gearing, since the bond issue replaces an equal amount of the overdraft. Given the sector average debt/equity of 10%, there does not appear to be any concerns about gearing as a result of the bond issue.

Security

It is very likely that the bond issue would need to be secured against the tangible non-current assets of YGV Co, especially in light of the recent decline in profitability. However, the bond issue is for $4 million while the tangible non-current assets of YGV Co have a value of only $3 million. It is not known whether the intangible non-current assets can be used as security, since their nature has not been disclosed.

Advisability of using the bond issue to reduce the overdraft

Considering the significant decrease in the interest coverage ratio as a result of the bond issue and the lack of tangible non-current assets to offer as security, it appears that the proposed bond issue cannot be recommended and would probably be unsuccessful. YGV Co should therefore consider alternative sources of finance in order to reduce the overdraft.

Alternative sources of finance

Given the recent fall in profit before interest and tax from $5 million to $1 million, any potential investor would initially seek reassurances that YGV Co would continue to be a viable business. The reason for the decline in profitability needs to be determined and the longer-term sustainability of the company needs to be confirmed before further financing is considered.

If longer-term viability is assured, the need for further finance could be reduced by taking measures to reduce costs and increase income, for example through improved working capital management.

If the company pays dividends, consideration could be given to reducing or passing the dividend in order to increase the flow of retained earnings in the company.

Given the problems with interest coverage and security, and the lack of availability of further overdraft finance, equity finance is the first alternative choice that could be considered. While no information has been provided on recent share price changes or on the dividend policy of YGV Co, existing shareholders could be consulted about a rights issue. Using a discount to the current market price of 20% gives a rights issue price of $3·28. A 1 for 8 rights issue at this price would raise $4·1 million, increasing the interest coverage ratio to 50 (1m/0·02m) if the proceeds were used to reduce the overdraft to $400,000.

If shares were offered to new shareholders, the dilution of existing ownership and control would be small, given that $4 million is only 9% of $45 million (41 + 4). New shareholders would be unlikely to invest, however, if no dividend were on offer.

Sale and leaseback would not raise sufficient finance, given that tangible non-current assets are only $3 million, but this avenue could be explored in conjunction with another source of finance.

Other finance sources that could be considered include convertible bonds or bonds with warrants attached. Improved working capital management could also decrease the amount of finance required.

ACCA marking scheme			
			Marks
(a)	Calculation of after-tax interest payment		1
	Calculation of after-tax cost of debt		3
		Maximum	4
(b)	Current WACC		1
	Calculation of WACC after bond issue		2
	Comment on effect of bond issue		1
	Comment on assumptions		1
		Maximum	5
(c)	Current interest coverage ratio		1
	Revised interest coverage ratio		1
	Current gearing		1
	Revised gearing		1
		Maximum	4
(d)	Comment on interest coverage ratio		1–2
	Comment on gearing		1–2
	Comment on need for security		2–3
	Comment on advisability of bond issue		1–2
	Discussion of alternative sources of finance		4–5
	Other relevant discussion		1–2
		Maximum	12
Total			25

Examiner's comments

Many students gained good marks on parts (a) and (b) of this question, while not doing as well on parts (c) and (d).

In part (a) of this question, candidates were asked to calculate the after-tax cost of debt of a redeemable bond.

Many candidates gained full marks here by using linear interpolation to calculate the after-tax cost of debt.

Some candidates calculated a bond issue price, but this was unnecessary, as the question stated that the bond was issued at par, i.e. the bond was issued at $100 per bond. Other candidates wrongly used the redemption value of $110 as the issue price, or wrongly used a redemption value of $100, when the question said that redemption was at a 10% premium to par. Occasionally, an answer used the annual before-tax interest payment of $9 per year, but the correct calculation of the after-tax cost of debt uses the after-tax annual interest payment of $6.30.

Weaker answers offered a monetary value for the after-tax cost of debt, rather than a percentage figure, or offered the annual after-tax interest rate as the cost of debt, or divided the annual interest by the market value of the bond, as though the bond was irredeemable rather than redeemable.

Part (b) asked candidates to calculate and comment on the effect of the bond issue on the weighted average cost of capital (WACC), clearly stating any assumptions made.

Since candidates were asked to calculate the effect on the WACC, answers needed to offer two values for the WACC, one before the bond issue and one after the bond issue. Many answers calculated the post-issue WACC, and then implied rather than calculated the pre-issue WACC. Some answers discussed, occasionally at length, optimal capital structure theory in support of a claim that issuing the bonds would cause the WACC to fall, since debt is cheaper than equity. This was much more than the question, which was worth 5 marks, was asking candidates to do.

In fact there were two possible answers about the effect of the bond issue on the WACC. If an answer assumed that the current overdraft was not included in the WACC calculation (even though the bond issue was replacing the overdraft), the bond issue caused a decrease in the WACC. However, if an answer assumed that the overdraft was included in the WACC calculation, the bond issue led to an increase in WACC, since the more expensive bond issue (after-tax cost of debt of 7.2%) was replacing a cheaper overdraft (after-tax cost of debt of 3.5%).

Many candidates did not state any of the assumptions underlying their calculations. The most obvious ones, perhaps, were the assumptions that the cost of equity was not affected by the bond issue, and that the share price was unchanged.

In part (c) candidates were asked to calculate the effect of using the bond issue to finance the reduction in the overdraft on the interest coverage ratio and on gearing.

Although the question said 'calculate', many answers chose to discuss their findings, sometimes at length. This discussion was not asked for in this part of the question and students must learn to follow the question requirement.

Since the question asked candidates to calculate the effect of the bond issue on the two ratios, values before and after the issue were required. Interest cover fell from 4.4 times to 2.6 times, compared with a sector average of 8 times indicating a substantial increase in financial risk. Gearing increased from zero to 9.8%, compared to a sector average of 10%. Many people ignored the definition of the sector average gearing given in the question (debt/equity, market value basis), and calculated gearing using their own definition. The calculated gearing values could not then, of course, be compared with the sector average gearing. The golden rule with ratios, remember, is to compare like with like.

Part (d) required candidates to evaluate the proposal to use the bond issue to finance the reduction in the overdraft, and to discuss alternative sources of finance, given the company's current position. Many answers were very brief, given the marks on offer.

Better answers recognised that the company had severe problems. Its profit before interest and tax had fallen from $5 million to $1 million over the last year, its interest cover was dangerously low, its bank had given it two months to reduce its overdraft by $4 million and no other bank had been found that was willing to offer an overdraft. This was the situation forced on some companies by the credit crunch.

Recognising these problems and using the calculated ratios from part (c), better answers suggested that using a bond issue to reduce the overdraft was unlikely to be in the best interests of the company. The company would be committing to paying additional interest each year, at a time when its profitability had fallen dramatically. Better answers then went on to discuss alternative sources of finance that might be suitable, while recognising that the company's circumstances meant that the search for sources of finance might be fruitless.

Weaker answers, in contrast, ignored the company's current position, or failed to recognise the danger of taking on more debt, or discussed the relative merits of an overdraft and a bond issue (when the overdraft was being largely withdrawn), or suggested paying off the overdraft from the company's $7 million of reserves (when the company had no cash in its statement of financial position), or proposed asking a venture capitalist or a business angel to pay of the company's overdraft.

51   GM CO

Key answer tips

Both parts (a) & (c) should be relatively straightforward. Part (b) is slightly more challenging although a basic knowledge of gearing and ungearing betas, together with the formula provided in the exam, will be sufficient to gain most of the marks available. The highlighted words are key phrases that markers are looking for.

(a)   **Calculation of weighted average cost of capital**

Market values

Market value of equity = $\dfrac{\$225m}{\$0.50}$ × $3.76 = $1,692 million

Market value of 14% loan notes = 75m (110/100) = $82.5 million

Market value of 9% bank loan = book value = $250 million

Total market value = 1,692m + 82.5 + 250 = $2,024.5 million

Cost of equity

Using CAPM = 0.07 + 1.2(0.135 − 0.07) = 0.148 (14.8%)

Cost of loan notes

Annual after tax interest payments = 14 × (1 − 0.3) = 9.80

Time	Description	Cash flow	DF 5%	PV	DF 10%	PV
T0	Market value	(110)	1	(110)	1	(110)
T1–5	Interest (1–T)	9.80	4.329	42.42	3.791	37.15
T5	Redemption	100	0.784	78.40	0.621	62.10
				10.82		(10.75)

$$\text{IRR} = 5\% + \frac{10.82}{10.82 + 10.75}(10\% - 5\%) = 7.5\%$$

Cost of bank loan

9% (1 − 0.3) = 6.3%

$$\text{WACC} = \frac{1{,}692}{2{,}024.5}\ 14.8\% + \frac{82.5}{2{,}024.5}\ 7.5\% + \frac{250}{2{,}024.5}\ 6.3\% = 13.5\%$$

(b) The cost of capital should take account of the systematic risk of the new investment, and therefore it is not appropriate to us GM Co's existing equity beta. Since the systematic risk of debt can be assumed to be zero, the competitor's equity beta can be ungeared using the following formula:

$$\beta a = \beta e \times \frac{E}{E + D(1 - T)}$$

Where: β_a = asset beta
β_e = equity beta
E = proportion of equity in capital structure
D = proportion of debt in capital structure
T = tax rate

For the competitors:

$$\beta a = 1.8 \times \frac{60}{60 + 40(1 - 0.3)} = 1.23$$

We can now apply GM Co's gearing level (using the market values calculated in part (a) to the asset beta to calculate the relevant equity beta.

$$\beta e = \beta a \times \frac{E + D(1 - T)}{E}$$

$$\beta e = 1.23 \times \frac{1{,}692 + 332.5(1 - 0.3)}{1{,}692} = 1.4$$

Using this risk adjusted equity beta, we can calculate a new, risk adjusted cost of equity:

Using CAPM = 0.07 + 1.4(0.135 − 0.07) = 0.161 (16.1%)

Assumptions taken include:

- Debt is risk free

- The competitor operates in an industry which has the same level of business risk as GM faces on its new project.

(c)   The main advantages of the CAPM are:

–   It only considers systematic risk as it assumes that investors have a diversified portfolio meaning all unsystematic risk has been eliminated. This reflects what is often seen in reality

–   The relationship between required return and systematic risk has been supported by empirical research and testing

–   It is seen as a better method of calculating the cost of equity than the dividend growth model and it takes into account a company's level of systematic risk relative to the stock market as a whole.

The main disadvantages are:

–   In order to use CAPM, it is necessary to assign values to the risk free rate of return, the average return on the market and the equity beta. In reality, it can be difficult to assign these values since:

•   The risk free rate is often taken as the yield on short term government debt. This is not a fixed rate and can change on a daily basis

•   In the short term, falling share prices could mean the stock market provides a negative return rather than a positive one. It is therefore usual to use long term average values but even these are not stable over time.

•   In a similar way, the value of the beta also changes over time

–   When using CAPM to calculate a project-specific discount rate, it is necessary to find a suitable proxy beta. This can be difficult since it is rare to find another company that only operates in the one market sector you are looking to evaluate. There is also an added difficulty in ungearing proxy betas as the calculation uses capital structure information that may not be readily available.

–   Finally, the assumption within CAPM of a single period time horizon is at odds with the multi-period nature of investment appraisal.

51   IRQ CO

Key answer tips

Part (a) represents a fairly straightforward WACC calculation and should give an early opportunity to pick up some easy marks.

Parts (b) and (c) both focus on the interest rate risk management section of the syllabus. As a less frequently examined area, this is one that can often cause difficulties for students due to lack of knowledge. Make sure you're able to handle these requirements in case something comes up in your exam.

To score well in part (d) you must talk about the key principles underpinning Islamic finance and give some examples that would be suitable given the scenario.

The highlighted words in the written sections are key phrases that markers are looking for.

(a)   Cost of equity:

Cost = 4% + (1.1 × 7%) = 4% + 7.7% = 11.7%

Cost of irredeemable loan notes:

Post tax cost = $100 × 6% × (1 − 0.28) ÷ $107 = 4.0%

Cost of the variable rate bank loan:

Cost = 5% × (1 − 0.28) = 3.6%

Total market values:

Equity − $400m ÷ 0.5 × $2.30 = $1,840m

Irredeemable loan notes − $600m × $107 ÷ $100 = $642m

Variable rate bank loan − use book value − $100m

Total market value of finance − $2,582m (1,840 + 642 + 100)

WACC = (11.7% × 1,840/2,582) + (4.0% × 642/2,582) + (3.6% × 100/2,582) = 9.5%

(b)   The theoretical factors which determine the term structure of interest rates or yield curve are as follows:

Liquidity preference theory − this states that investors will prefer their funds returned sooner rather than later and hence if they are to invest in the longer term they will require a higher return/will charge a higher interest rate. This explains the normal upward sloping yield curve.

Expectations theory − this states that the yield curve will reflect the markets expectation of future interest rates. Hence if interest rates in the future are likely to rise the yield curve will become steeper and vice versa.

Market segmentation theory − this states that the market for lending and borrowing is segmented. Due to the fact that the markets are not perfect the different segments have differing information and hence different views on interest rates. Hence the yield curve is not smooth as effectively each segment develops its own separate yield curve and indeed these separate yield curves will often overlap.

(c)   The over-the-counter methods of interest rate hedging include:

A forward rate agreement (FRA) − this effectively fixes the amount of interest to be paid by a borrower such as IRQ Co.

An interest rate guarantee (IRG) − this is effectively an option on a forward rate agreement. Hence if an adverse interest rate movement arises the IRG will be exercised and will fix the maximum amount a borrower will pay. However if a favourable interest rate movement arises the IRG will be allowed to lapse and a borrower will be able to benefit from the fall in interest rates.

The exchange traded methods of interest rate hedging include:

Futures − like an FRA this effectively fixes the interest rate.

Options on futures − like an IRG this lets a company take advantage of a favourable move in interest rates but provides protection against adverse interest rate moves.

As both the IRG and options on futures provide flexibility they are costly and a premium will be payable.

The exchange traded methods use the standardised contracts available on the futures market and hence it may not be possible to hedge exactly the amount you want to hedge.

Tutorial note:

Any sensible illustration will be given credit if it shows the workings of an FRA.

FRA illustration:

Assume that IRQ Co identifies the need to borrow an additional $40m in 5 months time for a period of 6 months.

Assume a 5v11 FRA at 5.20 – 5.30 is available.

If IRQ Co takes up this FRA they are effectively fixed into paying a rate of 5.3% on the borrowings.

If the commercial rate in 5 months is 5.7% then the following cash flows will arise:

Interest paid on commercial borrowings – $40m × 5.7% × 6/12 = $1.14m

Compensation received from the FRA provider – $40m × 0.4% × 6/12 = $0.08m

(0.4% is the difference between the commercial rate and the rate agreed in the FRA)

Net cost – $1.06m (1.14 – 0.08) – this is $40m × 5.3% × 6/12

If the interest is lower than 5.3% in 5 months time the cash flows will be calculated in a similar way but compensation will be paid to the FRA provider.

(d) The key principles of Islamic Finance are that the risk and reward should be shared between the investor and the user of the funds. Making money with money is deemed immoral and hence interest (riba) is forbidden. As a result, the profitability of a bank is more closely tied to that of its clients than is the case with conventional banking.

As interest is forbidden a conventional variable rate bank loan would not be allowed. Instead a murabaha contract could be used. Under such a contract the bank buys the assets and then sells them to the company. The company then pays the bank by way of a deferred payment or makes payments by instalments. The assets involved could be both non-current assets such as machinery or current assets such as raw materials. However the assets must actually exist/be tangible. Hence the company can use the assets to generate a profit and use this profit to repay the bank. Hence Murabaha is similar in nature to a loan.

Tutorial note:

Marks would also be awarded for discussing a sukuk contract.

53   DD CO

Key answer tips

Parts (a) and (b) both relate to the cost of debt before part (c) expands the calculations to the full cost of capital. Finally, part (d) is a discursive requirement on the impact of dividend policy on the share price of the company. There is a lot of structure to this question (especially in part (c) where there are four sub-requirements) and this helps students to score well on this question.

The highlighted words are key phrases that markers are looking for.

(a)   The cost of debt of Bond A can be found by linear interpolation.

Using 11%, the difference between the present value of future cash flows and the ex interest market value = (9 × 5.889) + (100 × 0.352) − 95.08 = 53.00 + 35.20 − 95.08 = ($6.88)

As the net present value is negative, 11% is higher than the cost of debt.

Using 9%, the difference between the present value of future cash flows and the ex interest market value = (9 × 6.418) + (100 × 0.22) − 95.08 = 57.76 + 42.20 − 95.08 = $4.88

As the net present value is positive, 9% is lower than the cost of debt.

Cost of debt = 9 + ((11 − 9) × 4.88)/(4.88 + 6.88) = 9 + 0.83 = 9.83%

Using estimates other than 11% and 9% will give slightly different values of the cost of debt.

(b)   A key factor here could be the duration of the bond issues, linked to the term structure of interest rates. Normally, the longer the time to maturity of a debt, the higher will be the interest rate and the cost of debt. Bond A has the greater time to maturity and therefore would be expected to have a higher interest rate and a higher cost of debt than Bond B, which is the case here.

Liquidity preference theory suggests that investors require compensation for deferring consumption, i.e. for not having access to their cash in the current period, and so providers of debt finance require higher compensation for lending for longer periods. The premium for lending for longer periods also reflects the way that default risk increases with time.

Expectations theory suggests that the shape of the yield curve depends on expectations as to future interest rates. If the expectation is that future interest rates will be higher than current interest rates, the yield curve will slope upwards. If the expectation is that future interest rates will be lower than at present, the yield curve will slope downwards.

Market segmentation theory suggests that future interest rates depend on conditions in different debt markets, e.g. the short-term market, the medium-term market and the long-term market. The shape of the yield curve therefore depends on the supply of, and demand for, funds in the market segments.

Since the two bonds were issued at the same time by the same company, the business risk of DD Co can be discounted as a reason for the difference between the two costs of debt. If the two bonds had been issued by different companies, a different business risk might have been a reason for the difference in the costs of debt.

The size of the debt could be a contributory factor, since the Bond A issue is twice the size of the Bond B issue. The greater size of the Bond A issue could be one of the reasons it has the higher cost of debt.

(c) (i) Cost of equity = 4 + (1.2 × (11 − 4)) = 4 + 8.4 = 12.4%

(ii) Dividend growth rate = 100 × ((52/50) − 1) = 100 × (1.04 − 1) = 4% per year

Share price using DGM = (50 × 1.04)/(0.124 − 0.04) = 52/0.84 = 619c or $6.19

(iii) Number of ordinary shares = 25 million

Market value of equity = 25m × 6.19 = $154.75 million

Market value of Bond A issue = 20m × 95.08/100 = $19.016m

Market value of Bond B issue = 10m × 102.01/100 = $10.201m

Market value of debt = $29.217m

Market value of capital employed = 154.75m + 29.217m = $183.967m

Capital gearing = 100 × 29.217/183.967 = 15.9%

(iv) WACC = ((12.4 × 154.75) + (9.83 × 19.016) + (7.82 × 10.201))/183.967 = 11.9%

(d) Miller and Modigliani showed that, in a perfect capital market, the value of a company depended on its investment decision alone, and not on its dividend or financing decisions. In such a market, a change in dividend policy by DD Co would not affect its share price or its market capitalisation. They showed that the value of a company was maximised if it invested in all projects with a positive net present value (its optimal investment schedule). The company could pay any level of dividend and if it had insufficient finance, make up the shortfall by issuing new equity. Since investors had perfect information, they were indifferent between dividends and capital gains. Shareholders who were unhappy with the level of dividend declared by a company could gain a 'home-made dividend' by selling some of their shares. This was possible since there are no transaction costs in a perfect capital market.

Against this view are several arguments for a link between dividend policy and share prices. For example, it has been argued that investors prefer certain dividends now rather than uncertain capital gains in the future (the 'bird-in-the-hand' argument). It has also been argued that real-world capital markets are not perfect, but semi-strong form efficient. Since perfect information is therefore not available, it is possible for information asymmetry to exist between shareholders and the managers of a company. Dividend announcements may give new information to shareholders and as a result, in a semi-strong form efficient market, share prices may change. The size and direction of the share price change will depend on the difference between the dividend announcement and the expectations of shareholders. This is referred to as the 'signalling properties of dividends'.

It has been found that shareholders are attracted to particular companies as a result of being satisfied by their dividend policies. This is referred to as the 'clientele effect'. A company with an established dividend policy is therefore likely to have an established dividend clientele. The existence of this dividend clientele implies that the share price may change if there is a change in the dividend policy of the company, as shareholders sell their shares in order to reinvest in another company with a more satisfactory dividend policy. In a perfect capital market, the existence of dividend clienteles is irrelevant, since substituting one company for another will not incur any transaction costs. Since real-world capital markets are not perfect, however, the existence of dividend clienteles suggests that if DD Co changes its dividend policy, its share price could be affected.

ACCA marking scheme			
			Marks
(a)	Calculation of cost of debt of Bond A		3.0
		Maximum	3.0
(b)	Term structure of interest rates		1–2
	Liquidity preference theory		1–2
	Expectations theory		1–2
	Market segmentation theory		1–2
	Other relevant discussion		1–2
		Maximum	6.0
(c)	Cost of equity		2.0
	Dividend growth rate		1.0
	Share price using dividend growth model		2.0
	Capital gearing		2.0
	Weighted average cost of capital		2.0
		Maximum	9.0
(d)	Dividend irrelevance		3–4
	Dividend relevance		3–4
		Maximum	7.0
Total			25

Examiner's comments

Many students gained good marks on parts (a) and (b) of this question, while not performing as well on parts (b) and (d).

Part (a) of this question asked candidates to calculate the cost of debt of a redeemable bond.

Many candidates gained full marks here by using linear interpolation to find the internal rate of return (cost of debt) that produced an equilibrium between the present value of future cash flows (interest payments and redemption value) and the given market value.

Weaker answers treated the debt as irredeemable by dividing the annual interest by the market value of the bond. Some candidates calculated the after-tax cost of debt, even though the question said to ignore taxation and did not provide a tax rate. It is clearly essential to follow the instructions given in the question.

Part (b) asked students to discuss the reasons why different bonds of the same company might have different costs of debt. Many students failed to gain full marks here because they did not appear to understand the link between risk and return.

Candidates who discussed reasons that related to the company, rather than to the bonds, failed to recognise that reasons had to relate specifically to differences between the bonds.

One such difference was the duration of each bond, linking to a discussion of the term structure of interest rates and the theories that can be used to explain it (liquidity preference theory, expectations theory and market segmentation theory). Other differences could relate to the relative features of each bond, such as convertibility, currency or security. Risk was therefore an underlying theme here.

Part (c) required candidates to calculate the weighted average cost of capital of a company following preliminary calculations of the cost of equity (using the capital asset pricing model), the ex div share price (using the dividend growth model), and the market value-based capital gearing (defined as debt divided by debt plus equity).

Most candidates calculated correctly the cost of equity using the capital asset pricing model, although occasional arithmetical errors were made.

In order to use the dividend growth model, candidates had to calculate a dividend growth rate. The question gave next year's dividend and this year's dividend: simply dividing the former by the latter gave a growth rate of 4% per year. Using the dividend growth model then gave an ex div share price of $6.19. Common errors found here were taking the square root of the ratio of the two dividends, leading to a growth rate of 2% per year: using next year's dividend as the current dividend; multiplying the dividend per share by the dividend payout ratio to give the dividend per share; and re-arranging the dividend growth model to calculate the cost of equity, but calling the result of the calculation the ex div share price.

Many students had difficulty in calculating the capital gearing on a market value basis. Some students calculated capital gearing using book values: others calculated the market values of the two bonds, but used the book value of equity; some students incorrectly added the value of reserves to the equity market value of the company.

Many students made a good attempt at calculating the market value weighted average cost of capital (WACC) of the company. Even though the cost of debt of the second bond was given in the question, some students wasted time by calculating it again using linear interpolation. Other students calculated a WACC that was higher than the highest cost of capital, or used an average cost of debt by adding together the costs of debt of the two bonds and dividing by two.

Part (d) asked for a discussion of whether a change in dividend policy would affect the share price of the company. A significant number of students showed that they had not studied well this part of the syllabus as they were simply stating that if the dividend went up, the share price went up, and vice versa. Answers that gained higher credit referred to a number of key issues in the debate on dividend relevance and dividend irrelevance, such as the clientele effect, the bird-in-the-hand theory, the signalling properties of dividends and the perfect capital market-based view of Miller and Modigliani.

BUSINESS VALUATIONS

54   QSX CO

Key answer tips

Many students will find this a hard question, both in terms of calculations and the discursive elements. A number of different syllabus areas are drawn together including business valuations, financial ratios, and risk and return. Those candidates who 'do what they can' will likely do enough to pick up over 50% of the marks. The highlighted words are key phrases that markers are looking for.

(a)   Dividend yield is calculated as the dividend divided by the share price at the start of the year.

2008: dividend yield = 100 × 38.5/740 = 5.2% 2009: dividend yield = 100 × 40.0/835 = 4.8%

The capital gain is the difference between the opening and closing share prices, and may be expressed as a monetary amount or as a percentage of the opening share price.

2008: capital gain = 835 – 740 = 95c or 12.8% (100 × 95/740)

2009: capital gain = 648 – 835 = (187c) or (22.4%) (100 × –187/835)

The total shareholder return is the sum of the percentage capital gain and the dividend yield, or the sum of the dividend paid and the monetary capital gain, expressed as a percentage of the opening share price.

2008: total shareholder return = 100 × (95 + 38.5)/740 = 18.0% (5.2% + 12.8%) 2009: total shareholder return = 100 × (–187 + 40)/835 = –17.6% (4.8% – 22.4%)

(i)   **The return on equity predicted by the CAPM**

The actual return for a shareholder of QSX Co, calculated as total shareholder return, is very different from the return on equity predicted by the CAPM. In 2008 the company provided a better return than predicted and in 2009 the company gave a negative return while the CAPM predicted a positive return.

Year	2009	2008
Total shareholder return	(17.6%)	18.0%
Return on equity predicted by CAPM	8%	12%

Because the risk-free rate of return is positive and the equity risk premium is either zero or positive, and because negative equity betas are very rare, the return on equity predicted by the CAPM is invariably positive. This reflects the reality that shareholders will always want a return to compensate for taking on risk. In practice, companies sometimes give negative returns, as is the case here. The return in 2008 was greater than the cost of equity, but the figure of 10% quoted here is the current cost of equity; the cost of equity may have been different in 2008.

(ii)   **Other comments**

QSX Co had turnover growth of 3% in 2008, but did not generate any growth in turnover in 2009. Earnings per share grew by 4.1% in 2008, but fell by 8.3% in 2009. Dividends per share also grew by 4.1% in 2008, but unlike earnings per share, dividend per share growth was maintained in 2009. It is common for dividends to be maintained when a company suffers a setback, often in an attempt to give reassurance to shareholders.

There are other negative signs apart from stagnant turnover and falling earnings per share. The shareholder will be concerned about experiencing a capital loss in 2009. He will also be concerned that the decline in the price/earnings ratio in 2009 might be a sign that the market is losing confidence in the future of QSX Co. If the shareholder was aware of the proposal by the finance director to suspend dividends, he would be even more concerned. It might be argued that, in a semi-strong form-efficient market, the information would remain private. If QSX Co desires to conserve cash because the company is experiencing liquidity problems, however, these problems are likely to become public knowledge fairly quickly, for example through the investigations of capital market analysts.

Workings:

Year	2009	2008	2007
Closing share price	$6.48	$8.35	
Earnings per share	58.9c	64.2c	61.7c
PER	11 times	13 times	
Earnings per share	58.9c	64.2c	61.7c
Dividend per share	40.0c	38.5c	37.0c
Dividend cover	1.5 times	1.7 times	1.7 times
Earnings per share growth	(8.3%)	4.1%	
Dividend per share growth	3.9%	4.1%	
Turnover growth	nil	3%	

(b)   Historical dividend growth rate = $(40/37)^{0.5} - 1 = 0.04$ or 4% per year

Share price using dividend growth model = $(40 \times 1.04)/(0.1 - 0.04) = 693c$ or $6.93

Tutor's top tips:

The key to calculating the share price under the proposed policy is to recognise that the dividend growth model simply calculates the value of a growing perpetuity. Therefore, to reflect the fact that this growing perpetuity won't begin for three years, we can treat this like any other delayed perpetuity, and discount the answer back to its present value To make sure you get the timings right, consider drawing out a quick time line, marking off the periods and what cash flows will occur in each.

In three years' time, the present value of the dividends received from the fourth year onwards can be calculated by treating the fourth-year dividend as D1 in the dividend growth model and assuming that the cost of equity remains unchanged at 10% per year. Applying the dividend growth model in this way gives the share price in three years' time: Share price = $70/(0.1 - 0.03) = 1,000c$ or $10.00.

For comparison purposes this share price must be discounted back for three years: Share price = $0.751 \times 10.00 = 7.51$.

Tutor's top tips:

Don't forget the requirement to comment on the outcome of your calculations.

The current share price of $6.48 is less than the share price of $6.93 calculated by the dividend growth model, indicating perhaps that the capital market believes that future dividend growth will be less than historic dividend growth.

The share price resulting from the proposed three-year suspension of dividends is higher than the current share price and the share price predicted by the dividend growth model. However, this share price is based on information that is not public and it also relies on future dividends and dividend growth being as predicted. It is very unlikely that a prediction as tentative as this will prove to be accurate.

(c) Investment decisions, dividend decisions and financing decisions have often been called the decision triangle of financial management. The study of financial management is often divided up in accordance with these three decision areas. However, they are not independent decisions, but closely connected.

For example, a decision to increase dividends might lead to a reduction in retained earnings and hence a greater need for external finance in order to meet the requirements of proposed capital investment projects. Similarly, a decision to increase capital investment spending will increase the need for financing, which could be met in part by reducing dividends.

The question of the relationship between the three decision areas was investigated by Miller and Modigliani. They showed that, if a perfect capital market was assumed, the market value of a company and its weighted average cost of capital (WACC) were independent of its capital structure. The market value therefore depended on the business risk of the company and not on its financial risk. The investment decision, which determined the operating income of a company, was therefore shown to be important in determining its market value, while the financing decision, given their assumptions, was shown to be not relevant in this context. In practice, it is recognised that capital structure can affect WACC and hence the market value of the company.

Miller and Modigliani also investigated the relationship between dividend policy and the share price of a company, i.e. the market value of a company. They showed that, if a perfect capital market was assumed, the share price of a company did not depend on its dividend policy, i.e. the dividend decision was irrelevant to value of the share. The market value of the company and therefore the wealth of shareholders were shown to be maximised when the company implemented its optimum investment policy, which was to invest in all projects with a positive NPV. The investment decision was therefore shown to be theoretically important with respect to the market value of the company, while the dividend decision was not relevant.

In practice, capital markets are not perfect and a number of other factors become important in discussing the relationship between the three decision areas. Pecking order theory, for example, suggests that managers do not in practice make financing decisions with the objective of obtaining an optimal capital structure, but on the basis of the convenience and relative cost of different sources of finance. Retained earnings are the preferred source of finance from this perspective, with a resulting pressure for annual dividends to be lower rather than higher.

	ACCA marking scheme	
		Marks
(a)	Calculation of dividend yields	2
	Calculation of capital gains	2
	Calculation of total shareholder returns	2
	Discussion of returns relative to the CAPM	1–3
	General discussion of returns	1–3
	Maximum	10
(b)	Calculation of historic dividend growth rate	1
	Calculation of share price using DGM	2
	Calculation of share price after policy change	3
	Comment on shares prices	1–2
	Maximum	7
(c)	Practical links between the decision areas	1–2
	Relevant illustrations	1–2
	Miller and Modigliani and dividend decisions	2–3
	Miller and Modigliani and financing decisions	2–3
	Other relevant discussion	1–3
	Maximum	8
Total		25

Examiner's comments

Candidates in general tended to find parts of this question heavy going, but well-prepared candidates picked up some straightforward marks in parts (a) and (b). Many answers to parts (c) did not focus on the question that was asked.

In part (a) candidates were required to calculate dividend yield, capital gain and total shareholder wealth, and to discuss their findings with respect to returns predicted by the capital asset pricing model (CAPM), and with respect to other financial information provided.

Many candidates were not able to calculate the capital gain (the increase in ordinary share price over a year), and did not know that the sum of the dividend yield and the capital gain is total shareholder return. Shareholder wealth is increased by capital gains and dividends, and this increase is measured by total shareholder return. Here, this was the actual return that shareholders had received (a positive return in the prior year and a negative return in the current year), while the CAPM-predicted returns were given in the question (positive in both years, but higher in the prior year than the current year). The discussion of the differences between the actual and predicted returns was generally quite weak.

The standard of the discussion with respect to the other financial information tended to be stronger. With regards to the negative return in the current year, candidates could have commented on static turnover, falling earnings per share, increasing dividends per share and, in particular, the falling share price. There was general agreement that the company was increasing its dividend per share in a situation where the market had, perhaps, doubts about its future performance.

Part (b) required candidates to calculate and comment on the share price using the dividend growth model (DGM), using firstly historical information and, secondly, information relating to a proposed change in dividend payments.

Most students calculated the historical dividend growth rate and the current share price using the DGM, although some students used the CAPM-predicted return rather than the cost of equity provided in the question. Comment on why this share price was different to the current market price was not strong. One possible explanation was that the market felt that future dividend growth would be less than historical dividend growth. It is worth remembering that analysing historical dividends is only one of several ways of estimating the future dividend growth rate, and that using this approach to estimating the future dividend growth rate depends on the (questionable) assumption that the future will repeat the past.

Fewer candidates were able to apply the DGM in the situation where no dividends would be paid for three years and then a higher dividend would be paid, with a lower expected dividend growth rate than had historically been the case. Some candidates wrongly said that the DGM could not be used if no dividends were paid: the suggested answer shows how to calculate the current share price in this situation. Many candidates calculated the share price in three years' time, but did not discount this share price to give the current share price, thereby weakening any comparative discussion of the two share prices.

Part (c) asked for a discussion of the relationship between investment decisions, dividend decisions and financing decisions, with illustrations where appropriate.

Many answers did not gain good marks because they did not focus on the key word 'relationship', and instead discussed at length a range of features of each decision area, with little or no attempt to relate the decision areas to each other.

Candidates could have gained higher marks by discussing the many practical ways in which these decision areas interact, or by discussing the theoretical views of Miller and Modigliani on the relationship between investment decisions, financing decisions and dividend decisions.

55 OCT

Key answer tips

Parts (a) to (c) require a series of calculations that will test your underlying knowledge on this key topic.

Part (d) gives an opportunity to pick up some easy marks but don't forget to tailor your comments to the scenario presented and include some calculations as directed.

The highlighted words in the written sections are key phrases that markers are looking for.

(a) In order to use the dividend growth model, the expected future dividend growth rate is needed.

Here, it may be assumed that the historical trend of dividend per share payments will continue into the future.

The geometric average historical dividend growth rate = $100 \times ((20.0/17.77)^{\frac{1}{3}} - 1)$ = 4% per year.

Tutorial note:

Alternatively, the arithmetical average of annual dividend growth rates could be used. This will be (4.2 + 4.2 + 3.6)/3 = 4.0%.

Using the formula for the dividend growth model from the formula sheet, the ex dividend share price = $(0.20 \times 1.04)/(0.11 - 0.04)$ = $2.97

(b) Net proceeds from the sale must be $12 million to allow the expansion to proceed.

If issue costs are 4% of the gross proceeds, the net proceeds must equal 96% (100% - 4%).

The gross proceeds can therefore be calculated as $12 million ÷ 0.96 = $12.5 million.

The directors are interested in a 1 for 5 rights issue. With 25 million shares currently in issue, this implies a further 5 million (25 ÷ 5) shares must be issued.

Each new share will therefore need to be sold for $2.50 ($12.5 million ÷ 5 million shares)

(c)

Tutor's top tips:

This part of the requirement draws upon calculations you've done in parts (a) and (b). If you haven't been able to complete these, you could make some assumptions here to allow you to complete this part of the question.

(i) Current share price (from part (a)) $2.97

New shares issued = 25m/5 = 5 million

Cash raised = $12.5 million (5 million × $2.50 per share)

Theoretical ex rights price = $[(5 \times \$2.97) + \$2.50]/6$ = $2.89 per share

> **Tutorial note:**
>
> *Alternatively, this could be calculated by looking at the company as a whole:*
>
> [(25 million × $2.97) + $12.5m]/ (25 million + 5 million) = $2.89 per share

(ii)   Market capitalisation after rights issue = (25 million × $2.97) + $12.5m = $86.75m – $0.5m = $86.25m

This is equivalent to a share price of $86.25m/30 million = $2.875 per share

The issue costs result in a decrease in the market value of the company and therefore a decrease in the wealth of shareholders equivalent to 1.67c per share.

(d)   The efficient market hypothesis describes an efficient market as one where security prices fully and speedily (strictly, instantaneously) reflect available information. This result is the product of the actions of market participants actively competing with each other. The content of any new information becoming available will be quickly digested by market participants and, if the information causes them to change their opinion of the security's intrinsic value, their subsequent actions will rapidly cause an equivalent change in the security's market price.

The hypothesis takes three forms depending upon the extent of the information deemed available to market participants:

(i)   **Weak form**

Information available is restricted to details of past share prices, returns and trading volumes. Hence future prices cannot be predicted from historic price data and trading rules based only on such price and volume data i.e., the chartists approach, cannot consistently produce excess returns if the hypothesis holds true.

If this form of efficiency was seen, OCT Co would be valued based on its historic earnings performance alone.

(ii)   **Semi-strong form**

Share prices reflect all publicly available information. Reaction to public announcements, published accounting information, etc will not produce excess returns as the information content of such announcements is reflected in share prices.

If the market was semi-strong form efficient, the market capitalisation of OCT Co would depend on whether the market had been informed of the expected increase in earnings.

- If no announcement had been made, the market capitalisation would be the same as for weak form efficiency.

- If an announcement was made the share price would react immediately to this new information.

To calculate the expected movement in the share price, we need to calculate the company's P/E and its expected future earnings.

Tutorial note:

In order to do this calculation, you must read the information presented carefully. We're told the EPS will increase by 5 cents above the 2010 level. Usually when a company undertakes a rights issue, the EPS will fall. What we're being told here is that sufficient additional returns will be earned from the expansion to offset this reduction and still deliver an increase of 5 cents per share.

DPS in 2010 = $0.20

Based on a 50% dividend payout ratio, EPS (pre rights issue) = $0.40

Share price pre rights issue was $2.97.

P/E = $2.97 ÷ $0.40 = 7.425

We're told that the P/E has remained fairly constant in recent years and that the future growth rates are expected to be consistent with what has been seen in the past. We can therefore assume that this P/E will remain in the future (all other things being equal)

New earnings per share (post rights issue and expansion) is expected to be ($0.40 + $0.05) = $0.45

Therefore, upon announcing the expected increase in earnings to the market, the share price might be expected to increase from $2.875 (part c) to $3.34 ($0.45 × 7.425).

(iii) **Strong form**

Share prices reflect all information whether publicly available or not. The implication of this for OCT Co is that regardless of whether the additional returns expected from the expansion had been announced to the market, the share price following the expansion would immediately have increased to $3.34.

The efficient market hypothesis has far-reaching implications for the study of finance and hence for the financial management of a publicly quoted company.

If the stock market is fully efficient it should quickly and accurately reflect the real financial position of the company in share prices. In this situation financial managers can confidently employ rational decision rules and know that good decisions will lead to increases in shareholder wealth. If on the other hand the market is not considered to be fully efficient other considerations have to be made. The way in which shareholders interpret information will be of great importance as will the short term picture of the company revealed in its financial statements. Also if the market misprices securities it could mean that one source of finance is significantly cheaper than another.

In general it is normally considered that the majority of developed countries' markets for leading equities are at least semi-strong efficient. Financial managers should therefore be able to rely on the decision rules developed in our study of financial management.

56   HENDIL (PART II)

Key answer tips

This is a reasonable straightforward question that is more about application of models than detailed calculations. You will need to think of practical implications to score highly on the discussional aspects. The highlighted words are key phrases that markers are looking for.

(a)   (i)   Number of ordinary shares = 1,000,000/0.5 = 2 million

Current dividend per share = 100 × (300,000/2,000,000) = 15¢

Share price predicted by dividend growth model = (15 × 1.05)/(0.12 − 0.05) = 225¢

(ii)   Market efficiency is usually taken to refer to the way in which ordinary share prices reflect information. Fama defined an efficient market as one in which share prices fully and fairly reflect all available information.

A semi-strong form efficient market is one where share prices reflect all publicly available information, such as past share price movements, published company annual reports and analysts' reports in the financial press.

A strong form market is one where share prices reflect all information, whether publicly available or not. Share prices would reflect, for example, takeover decisions made at private board meetings.

(iii)   The share price predicted by the dividend growth model is 45¢ greater than the current share price of the company. However, the dividend growth model has used the proposed dividend of the company (15¢), which may not yet have been made public. If the stock market is semi-strong form efficient and therefore unaware of the proposed dividend, the company's ordinary share price could be different to that predicted by the dividend growth model because the market expects a dividend which is different from the proposed dividend used in the model. Working backwards using the dividend growth model suggests that the market expects a dividend of 12¢ per share (180 x (0.12 − 0.05)/1.05).

In a strong form efficient market, the information about the proposed dividend will already be reflected in the share price. The difference between the share price predicted by the dividend growth model and the current share price of the company may therefore be explained by different views of the expected dividend growth rate or the return required by ordinary shareholders. The market might expect a lower growth rate than the 5% expected by the directors, for example, or the return required by ordinary shareholders might have increased due to economic expectations or changing perceptions of risk. An increase in the required return to 13.75% would give a share price of $1.80 (15 × 1.05/(0.1375 − 0.05)). Another explanation is that the market may not be fully efficient.

(b)   **Interest cover**

Average interest cover of similar companies = 6 times

Current interest cover = 624/156 = 4 times

Annual interest on new loan stock = $1m × 0.08 = $80,000

Assuming no change to existing interest, increased annual interest = 80 + 156 = $236,000

Interest cover after new loan stock issue = 624/236 = 2.6 times

This would not change significantly if profit before interest and tax were increased by the profit (after accounting depreciation) from the first year's sales of the proposed investment.

The current interest cover of Hendil Inc (four times) is less than the average interest cover of similar companies (six times), suggesting that the financial risk of the company is higher than that of similar companies even before the new debt is issued. After the new issue, interest cover would fall to 2.6 times, a level that would be regarded with concern by both lenders and investors. Although the interest on the new debt might be overstated in our interest cover calculation (debt in the balance sheet accounts for only part of the interest in the income statement, implying that the overdraft may have decreased substantially in the last year), it is likely that a new debt issue might be unwise.

Gearing (long-term debt/equity)

Average gearing (book value basis) of similar companies = 50%

Current gearing (book value basis) = 29%

Revised gearing (book value basis) = 54%

Average gearing (market value basis) of similar companies = 25%

Current gearing (market value basis) = 38%

Revised gearing (market value basis) = 65%

Two conclusions can be drawn from these gearing values. Firstly, the current gearing of Hendil Inc is below the average gearing of similar companies on a book value basis, but higher than the average gearing of similar companies on a market value basis. Secondly, the revised gearing of Hendil Inc after the new issue is slightly above the average gearing of similar companies on a book value basis, and more than double the average gearing of similar companies on a market value basis. Gearing based on market values is preferred in financial management.

Workings

Current gearing (book value basis) = 100 × (1,200/4,100) = 29%

Revised book value of long-term debt = 1.2m + 1m = $2.2 million

Revised gearing (book value basis) = 100 × (2,200/4,100) = 54%

Market value of debt = $1.2m × 113/ 100 = $1,356,000

Number of ordinary shares = 1,000,000/0.5 = 2 million

Market value of ordinary shares = 2m × 1.80 = $3.6 million

Current gearing (market value basis) = 100 × (1,356/3,600) = 38%

Market value of new debt issue = $1 million

Total market value of debt = 1,356 + 1,000 = $2,356,000

Market value of ordinary shares = 2m × 1.80 = $3.6 million

Revised gearing (market value basis) = 100 × (2,356/3,600) = 65%

The calculation of the revised gearing (market value basis) assumes that the ordinary share price and the market value of existing debt are unchanged. An alternative calculation could use a revised share price, for example $2.22 per share (see below), giving a lower gearing on a market value basis of 100 × (2,356/(2m × 2.22)) = 53%.

Ordinary share price

Current ordinary share price = $1.80 per share

Current market value of company = 1.80 × 2m = $3.6 million

Net present value of investment = $832,000

If the market is efficient, the value of the company will increase by the NPV of the investment, although this assumes that the current average cost of capital of Hendil Inc, which was used as the discount rate in the NPV analysis, would remain unchanged by the new loan stock issue. This may not be true.

Revised market value = 3,600 + 832 = $4,432 million

Revised ordinary share price = 4,432,000/2,000,000 = $2.22 per share

Maturity

The proposed loan stock has a maturity of 15 years but the life of the proposed investment is not clear. We know that it is more than four years, but we do not know how much more. We also do not know whether the new machinery can be used to produce other products, whether at the same time as the new product range or when the new product range is in the decline phase of its product life-cycle. The matching principle holds that maturity of finance should match the expected life of the assets financed.

Security

It has been suggested that the new loan stock could be secured on existing assets of Hendil Inc. This would be on non-current rather than current assets. Since the existing $1.2 million loan stock is already secured on non-current assets of the company, the most that might be available is $1.05 million of non-current assets. However, since loan stock is usually secured on particular assets rather than on a given value of assets, there may be insufficient existing assets to offer as security for the new loan stock issue. The new machinery may be suitable to offer as security in order to make up the deficit.

57   NN CO

Key answer tips

A fairly straightforward question for this key syllabus area. The calculations in parts (a) to (c) shouldn't present many problems and the discursive part (d) showcases how dividend policy is most frequently examined. The highlighted words are key phrases that markers are looking for.

(a)   Using the dividend growth model, the share price of NN Co will be the present value of its expected future dividends, i.e. (66 × 1.03)/(0.12 − 0.03) = 755 cents per share or $7.55 per share

Number of ordinary shares = 50/0.5 = 100m shares

Value of NN Co = 100m × 7.55 = $755m

Net asset value of NN Co = total assets less total liabilities = 143 − 29 − 20 − 25 = $69m

In calculating net asset value, preference share capital is included with long-term liabilities, as it considered to be prior charge capital.

Tutorial note:

Don't forget that you're trying to get back to the value of the company for the owners – meaning the ordinary shareholders. This is why you need to also deduct the value of preference shares, even though they are not shown as liabilities on the statement of financial position.

(b)   The after-tax cost of debt of NN Co can be found by linear interpolation

The annual after-tax interest payment = 7 × (1 − 0.25) = 7 × 0.75 = $5.25 per year

Year	Cash flow ($)	5% Discount factor	Present value ($)
0	(103.50)	1.000	(103.50)
1–6	5.25	5.076	26.65
6	100	0.746	74.60
			─────
			(2.25)
			─────

Year	Cash flow ($)	4% Discount factor	Present value ($)
0	(103.50)	1.000	(103.50)
1–6	5.25	5.242	27.52
6	100	0.790	79.00
			─────
			3.02
			─────

After-tax cost of debt = 4 + [(1 × 3.02)/(3.02 + 2.25)] = 4 + 0.57 = 4.6%

Tutorial note:

The calculated value of the after-tax cost of debt will be influenced by the choice of discount rates used in the linear interpolation calculation and so other values would also gain credit here.

(c) Annual preference dividend = 8% × 50 cents = 4 cents per share

Cost of preference shares = 100 × (4/67) = 6%

Number of ordinary shares = 50/0.5 = 100m shares

Market value of equity = V_e = 100m shares × 8.30 = $830m

Number of preference shares = 25/0.5 = 50m shares

Market value of preference shares = V_p = 0.67 × 50m = $33.5m

Market value of long-term borrowings = V_d = 20 × 103.50/100 = $20.7m

Total market value of company = $(V_e + V_d + V_p)$ = (830 + 33.5 + 20.7) = $884.2m

WACC = $(k_eV_e + k_pV_p + k_d(1 - T)V_d)/ (V_e + V_p + V_d)$ = (12 × 830 + 6 × 33.5 + 4.6 × 20.7)/884.2 = 11.6%

(d) A number of factors should be considered in formulating the dividend policy of a stock-exchange listed company, as follows.

Profitability

Companies need to remain profitable and dividends are a distribution of after-tax profit. A company cannot consistently pay dividends higher than its profit after tax. A healthy level of retained earnings is needed to finance the continuing business needs of the company.

Liquidity

Although a dividend is a distribution of profit, it is a cash payment by the company to its shareholders. A company must therefore ensure it has sufficient cash to pay a proposed dividend and that paying a dividend will not compromise day-to-day cash financing needs.

Legal and other restrictions

A dividend can only be paid out in accordance with statutory requirements, such as the requirement in the United Kingdom for dividends to be paid out of accumulated net realised profits. There may also be restrictions on dividend payments imposed by, for example, restrictive covenants in bond issue documents.

The need for finance

There is a close relationship between investment, financing and dividend decisions, and the dividend decision must consider the investment plans and financing needs of the company. A large investment programme, for example, will require a large amount of finance, and the need for external finance can be reduced if dividend increases are kept in check. Similarly, the decision to increase dividends may reduce retained earnings to the extent where external finance is needed in order to meet investment needs.

The level of financial risk

If financial risk is high, for example due to a high level of gearing arising from a substantial level of debt finance, maintaining a low level of dividend payments can result in a high level of retained earnings, which will reduce gearing by increasing the level of reserves. The cash flow from a higher level of retained earnings can also be used to decrease the amount of debt being carried by a company.

The signalling effect of dividends

In a semi-strong form efficient market, information available to directors is more substantial than that available to shareholders, so that information asymmetry exists. This is one of the causes of the agency problem. If dividend decisions convey new information to the market, they can have a signalling effect concerning the current position of the company and its future prospects. The signalling effect also depends on the dividend expectations in the market. A company should therefore consider the likely effect on share prices of the announcement of a proposed dividend.

ACCA marking scheme		
		Marks
(a)	Share price using dividend growth model	2
	Value of company using dividend growth model	1
	Net asset value of company	2
		———
	Maximum	5
(b)	Correct use of taxation	1
	Calculation of after-tax cost of debt	3
		———
	Maximum	4
(c)	Cost of preference shares	1
	Market value of equity	1
	Market value of preference shares	1
	Market value of debt	1
	Weighted average cost of capital	2
		———
	Maximum	6
(d)	Profitability	1–2
	Liquidity	1–2
	Legal and other restrictions	1–2
	The need for finance	1–2
	The level of financial risk	1–2
	The signalling effect of dividends	1–2
		———
	Maximum	10
		———
Total		25
		———

Examiner's comments

Many candidates did well in parts (a)(i), (b) and (c), while doing poorly in part (a)(ii) and struggling to remain focused on the question asked in part (d).

In part (a) candidates were required to calculate the equity value of a company using the dividend growth model (DGM) and then the net asset value.

Many candidates calculated correctly the share price of the company using the DGM, although some candidates failed to multiply this share price by the number of shares to give the equity value of the company. Poorer answers re-arranged the DGM in order to calculate a cost of equity using the current share price, but this was unnecessary, as the cost of equity was given in the question.

The net asset value calculated by many candidates showed that they were uncertain as to the meaning of 'net asset value'. Some candidates gave a net asset value of $94 million, a figure which fails to treat preference share capital as prior charge capital and hence include it with long-term liabilities.

Part (b) asked candidates to calculate the after-tax cost of debt of a company. Many candidates gained full marks by calculating the after-tax interest payment, using two discount rates to calculate two net present values for investing in the bond, and using linear interpolation to calculate the after-tax cost of debt. Answers that did not gain full marks contained errors such as using the wrong tax rate (it was 25%), addition or multiplication errors, using the before-tax interest payment, or putting incorrect values to variables in the linear interpolation calculation.

Some answers calculated the cost of capital of preference shares in addition to calculating the after-tax cost of debt, and then attempted to average the two costs of capital. While preference shares are classed as prior charge capital, they pay a dividend, not interest, and preference shares are not debt.

In part (c), candidates were required to calculate the weighted average cost of capital (WACC) of a company. Candidates therefore needed to calculate the market values of ordinary shares, preference shares and bonds, and the preference share cost of capital, having already calculated the after-tax cost of debt and being given the cost of equity by the question.

The most common reason for not gaining full marks was calculating incorrectly the cost of capital of the preference shares. This can be found by dividing the preference dividend by the market price of the preference share, but many candidates used the dividend rate of the preference shares (8% per year) as the dividend, instead of calculating the preference dividend from the nominal value (par value), i.e. 8% of 50 cents giving a dividend of 4 cents per share.

Other reasons for losing marks included aggregating the market values of ordinary shares and preference shares, before applying the cost of equity to both: omitting the preference share capital from the WACC calculation; multiplying the after-tax cost of debt by (1 − t) (one minus the tax rate); and calculating a new cost of equity, even though the cost of equity was given in the question.

Part (d) asked for a discussion of the factors to be considered in formulating the dividend policy of a stock exchange listed company. The requirement was worded carefully to encourage candidates to consider the dividend policy of a company faced by the demanding business environment of the real world. Little credit was therefore given to discussions of the dividend irrelevance theory of Miler and Modigliani, which is based on the assumption of a perfect capital market, since capital markets in the real world are no more than semi-strong form efficient.

While a discussion of dividend relevance theory compared to dividend irrelevance theory was not asked for, some credit was given to answers that discussed dividend relevance theory where points were made that had real world relevance. These points included the signalling effect of dividends, shareholder preference for certain dividends rather uncertain capital gains, and the importance of the clientele effect in imperfect capital markets.

Better answers focused on some of the factors covered in the suggested answer, including the need to consider liquidity, the importance of relating dividend decisions to investment and financing decisions, and the need to consider financial risk.

58   MAT CO

Key answer tips

To answer part (a) effectively you need a logical approach and an awareness of the calculations behind the valuation methods. A look down the formulae sheet will help to reveal the correct path for part (a) (i).

This question is an excellent example of how calculations alone will not get you through this paper. Part (b) requires you to understand the meaning of the calculations so you can comment sensibly on your results. Finally, part (c) gives you an opportunity to demonstrate your knowledge about raising finance. If you are to score well on this section you must apply your comments to the specific scenario presented.

(a)   (i)   **Dividend growth model**

From the formulae sheet - $P_0 = \dfrac{Do(1+g)}{(r_e - g)}$

Tutorial note:

From the formulae sheet you can directly see that to calculate the share price (P_0) using the growth model, you will need three pieces of information: the dividend (D_0), the growth rate in dividends (g) and the cost of equity (r_e). Now you can look into the scenario and see how this information can be obtained.

1   You're told the dividend about to be paid is 5.0 cents.

2   You've been provided with information on the dividends paid in recent years. This means you can calculate the historic growth rate and assume this will continue in the future. Since we don't have any information on profitability, this will be only method of estimating dividend growth in this question.

3   You've been told that the return on government bonds (i.e. the risk free rate of return) is 5% and that the equity risk premium ($R_m - R_f$) is 8%. These pieces of information should trigger you to realise that CAPM can be used to calculate the cost of equity. In the formulae sheet you're given the correct formula to use.

To calculate the cost of equity (r_e) using CAPM, we have the formula (from the sheet)

$E(r)_j = R_f + \beta_j (E(r_m) - R_f)$

$r_e = 5\% + (1.15 \times 8\%) = 14.2\%$

Annual dividend growth (g) = $\sqrt[n]{\dfrac{\text{current dividend}}{\text{dividend n years ago}}} - 1$

$g = \sqrt[3]{\dfrac{5.0}{4.1}} - 1 = 0.0684$

Value per share = $\dfrac{5.0 \times 1.0684}{0.142 - 0.0684}$ = 72.6c

Total number of shares – $40m ÷ 0.25 = 160 million

Total equity value (ex div) – 160m × $0.726 = $116.16m

(ii) **Net asset value**

Tutorial note:

In order to be comparable with the valuation above (which is based on the ex-div share price), you must deduct the value of the dividend about to paid. This is in addition to the adjustments relating to the valuation of property and the write down of inventories.

	$m
Total equity value per the statement of financial position	67
Adjustments:	
Revaluation of property ($65m–$52m)	13
Write down of inventories	(2)
Dividend due to be paid (160m × $0.05)	(8)
Total equity value (ex div)	$70m

(b)

Summary of equity values:	
Dividend growth model (from (a)(i) above)	$116.16m
Net asset value (from (a) (ii) above)	$70m
Total market value of equity (ex div) (from the scenario):	
160m × ($0.66 – $0.05) =	$97.6m

Tutor's top tips:

To score well on this sort of requirement you must look at each number in turn and outline the arguments for and against the value as a basis. Remember, business valuation is not a precise science and many of the theories presented can be challenged when faced with reality.

Comments:

Dividend growth model value:

The dividend growth model value is just under $20m higher than the current market value.

A market value is often considered a highly relevant value but the current market value of MAT Co could be understated because the market is a secondary market and hence may not be so efficient and may not properly reflect the value of MAT Co. The market value may also be understated because the shares in the company are only traded infrequently and hence are not very liquid.

The dividend growth model could be incorrect and hence less relevant as it is very sensitive to changes in the inputs. For instance the forecast dividend growth rate is just based on recent growth and could prove wrong. The growth rate forecast of 6.84% does seem high given recent economic circumstances and could well prove unsustainable. Equally the cost of equity used is based on an estimate of the equity beta. This estimate could be incorrect.

Net asset value:

The net asset value is $27.6m less than the current market value.

A net asset value will often produce a low value as it is not the assets of a company which drives its value but the ability of that company to generate earnings and cash flows. Equally a net asset value often ignores the intangible assets of the company such as goodwill or highly effective staff. These assets can have considerable value as they are key to creating the earnings and cash flows for the company.

Hence net asset values are often considered less relevant. However they can often be used to set a minimum value for a company.

(c)

Tutor's top tips:

Key to scoring well on this requirement is to relate your comments back to the scenario given. Simply writing a list of generic factors that any company should consider will not score highly.

The directors of MAT Co should take the following factors into account when considering how to raise additional finance:

Cost – Debt finance is cheaper and hence if the company has the capacity to raise more debt it could be advantageous. Indeed given the property value in the company of $65m and the long term debt of only $18m the company would seem capable of raising more debt.

Cash flows – Prior to raising more debt the company must forecast future cash flows to ensure sufficient cash will be generated to service any debt raised. Given the current cash balances the company does seem to be cash generative.

Risk – Prior to raising finance the directors must consider the risk of the company. For instance if future expansion is going to increase the business risk of the company they may be more wary of taking on more debt and increasing the financial risk. Equally the directors should consider the gearing/financial risk of similar companies and the appetite for risk of the shareholders.

Availability – The directors must consider the likely availability of finance.

As the shares do not seem very liquid raising new equity from new investors may be difficult. Equally they should question whether the existing shareholders have the ability to support a rights issue. Given the recent dividend growth and dividend yield they may be happy to invest more in the company.

More debt finance is likely to be available if the company can show good cash flow forecasts as plenty of security seems available.

Security & Covenants – The directors must be aware that additional debt finance is likely to require security and may require covenants. The directors must ensure they are happy to give any such guarantees before raising additional debt.

Control – The directors must consider that raising equity from new investors could have an impact upon the control of the company.

Duration – The directors must consider the term of any proposed finance and make sure it is appropriate given the nature of what it is to be invested in. Furthermore the investors should ensure that any new debt finance does not become repayable at the same time as the existing long term liability as this could put a large cash flow strain on the company.

Economic outlook – Prior to raising finance the directors should ensure that they have considered the outlook for the economy and the impact this could have on the trade of the company and the cost of finance. In particular the outlook for interest rates should be considered if debt finance is to be raised.

59 THP CO *Walk in the footsteps of a top tutor*

Key answer tips

The key learning point from this question is the importance of making sure your marker can follow your answer. This will often involve explaining your thought process, including commenting on why the calculation you've performed is the right approach. The highlighted words are key phrases that markers are looking for.

Tutor's top tips:

In the 15 minutes reading time you should aim to have skim read the scenario, getting a feeling for the information you've been provided with and paying particular attention to names and dates. You should also have skim read the requirement, underlining the models referred to and noted the calculations that are being asked for. Look for any part of the question that relies purely on knowledge of the syllabus (i.e. no calculations) and flag these as a good place to start. Part (e) of this question falls into this category.

Once you've completed part (e) you should look at the other requirements. Is there a specific order you will need to do them in or can you choose your strongest area to do first. Here we'll need to tackle the requirements in order as you need the output of part (a) to answer part (b).

Tutor's top tips:

Part (a) specifically asks for you to use the dividend growth (or valuation) model. Start by writing down the formula and then search the scenario for the information you need. For this calculation you need the dividend, dividend growth and the cost of equity. 2 of the 3 are clearly stated. The dividend is a bit harder to find but as you're told THP has a payout ratio of 50% and you know EPS is currently 64c, the dividend per share can be quickly worked out. Don't forget to read the requirement carefully. You are not just asked for the share price but also the current market capitalisation. You would have lost a very easy mark if you didn't spot this.

(a) **Calculation of share price**

THP Co dividend per share = 64 × 0.5 = 32c per share

Share price of THP Co = (32 × 1.05)/(0.12 – 0.05) = $4.80

Market capitalisation of THP Co = 4.80 × 3m = $14.4m

Tutor's top tips:

In part (b) you should follow the order presented in the requirement. It is leading you through the process. All the information is stated in the scenario or can be calculated without many complications. Part (iv) is the area most likely to cause problems (although you might not realise it at the time). The majority of situations the market capitalisation after an issue would be the TERP × new number of shares in issue. However, in this scenario, we've been told of some issue costs which must be deducted. Don't worry if you didn't spot this, it will only have been worth 2 marks (maximum). However, this does show the benefits of querying every piece of information provided by the examiner and asking "why has he told me that?"

(b) **Rights issue price**

This is at a 20% discount to the current share price = 4.80 × 0.8 = $3.84 per share

New shares issued = 3m/3 = 1m

Cash raised = 1m × 3.84 = $3,840,000

Theoretical ex rights price = [(3 × 4.80) + 3.84]/4 = $4.56 per share

Market capitalisation after rights issue = 14.4m + 3.84m = $18.24 – 0.32m = $17.92m

This is equivalent to a share price of 17.92/4 = $4.48 per share

The issue costs result in a decrease in the market value of the company and therefore a decrease in the wealth of shareholders equivalent to 8c per share.

Tutor's top tips:

The key to part (c) is recognising that since CRX is in the same business sector as THP, you can use THP's P/E ratio as a proxy for CRX. Whilst you're not specifically told this, you do have the information to work it out. Make sure your answer explains what you're doing and why this is an acceptable approach.

(c) **Price/earnings ratio valuation**

Price/earnings ratio of THP Co = 480/64 = 7.5

Earnings per share of CRX Co = 44.8c per share

Using the price earnings ratio method, share price of CRX Co = (44.8 × 7.5)/100 = $3.36

Market capitalisation of CRX Co = 3.36 × 1m = $3,360,000

(Alternatively, earnings of CRX Co = 1m × 0.448 = $448,000 × 7.5 = $3,360,000)

Tutor's top tips:

Part (d) starts by asking you to assume a semi-strong form efficient market. Your first thought should be to consider the implications of this, which is that only publicly available information will be reflected in the share price. Again, you should note down your thought process. Next you will need to identify what will affect the market capitalisation post acquisition. You should conclude this will be the market capitalisation of THP plus the market capitalisation of CRX less the price paid for CRX (since this cash has left the business). All of this information is available, either as a result of your previous calculations or given in the scenario. Only in part (ii) will we need to factor in the additional savings since this information has now been made public.

(d) In a semi-strong form efficient capital market, share prices reflect past and public information. If the expected annual after-tax savings are not announced, this information will not therefore be reflected in the share price of THP Co. In this case, the post acquisition market capitalisation of THP Co will be the market capitalisation after the rights issue, plus the market capitalisation of the acquired company (CRX Co), less the price paid for the shares of CRX Co, since this cash has left the company in exchange for purchased shares. It is assumed that the market capitalisations calculated in earlier parts of this question are fair values, including the value of CRX Co calculated by the price/earnings ratio method.

Price paid for CRX Co = 3.84m − 0.32m = $3.52m

Market capitalisation = 17.92m + 3.36m − 3.52m = $17.76m

This is equivalent to a share price of 17.76/4 = $4.44 per share

The market capitalisation has decreased from the value following the rights issue because THP Co has paid $3.52m for a company apparently worth $3.36m. This is a further decrease in the wealth of shareholders, following on from the issue costs of the rights issue.

If the annual after-tax savings are announced, this information will be reflected quickly and accurately in the share price of THP Co since the capital market is semi-strong form efficient. The savings can be valued using the price/earnings ratio method as having a present value of $720,000 (7.5 × 96,000). The revised market capitalisation of THP Co is therefore $18.48m (17.76m + 0.72m), equivalent to a share price of $4.62 per share (18.48/4). This makes the acquisition of CRX Co attractive to the shareholders of THP Co, since it offers a higher market capitalisation than the one following the rights issue. Each shareholder of THP Co would experience a capital gain of 14c per share (4.62 – 4.48).

In practice, the capital market is likely to anticipate the annual after-tax savings before they are announced by THP Co.

Tutor's top tips:

Part (e) is an opportunity to score an easy 8 marks by discussing the relative things to consider when deciding between debt and equity. Be careful though, the requirement does specify that your points should be relevant to THP. So for example, don't just talk about the impact on gearing, work it out using the information provided. To ensure you don't spend too much time on this part of the question, you should think about the mark allocation. For 8 marks where you are being asked to 'discuss' you should be spend no more than 14 minutes (8 × 1.8 mins per mark) talking about 4 factors THP should consider. Contrast this with a requirement to 'state' or 'list' which is more likely to attract only 1 mark per relevant point.

(e)   There are a number of factors that should be considered by THP Co, including the following:

Gearing and financial risk

Equity finance will decrease gearing and financial risk, while debt finance will increase them. Gearing for THP Co is currently 68.5% and this will decrease to 45% if equity finance is used, or rise to 121% if debt finance is used. There may also be some acquired debt finance in the capital structure of CRX Co. THP Co needs to consider what level of financial risk is desirable, from both a corporate and a stakeholder perspective.

Target capital structure

THP Co needs to compare its capital structure after the acquisition with its target capital structure. If its primary financial objective is to maximise the wealth of shareholders, it should seek to minimise its weighted average cost of capital (WACC). In practical terms this can be achieved by having some debt in its capital structure, since debt is relatively cheaper than equity, while avoiding the extremes of too little gearing (WACC can be decreased further) or too much gearing (the company suffers from the costs of financial distress).

Availability of security

Debt will usually need to be secured on assets by either a fixed charge (on specific assets) or a floating charge (on a specified class of assets). The amount of finance needed to buy CRX CO would need to be secured by a fixed charge to specific fixed assets of THP Co. Information on these fixed assets and on the secured status of the existing 8% loan notes has not been provided.

Economic expectations

If THP Co expects buoyant economic conditions and increasing profitability in the future, it will be more prepared to take on fixed interest debt commitments than if it believes difficult trading conditions lie ahead.

Control issues

A rights issue will not dilute existing patterns of ownership and control, unlike an issue of shares to new investors. The choice between offering new shares to existing shareholders and to new shareholders will depend in part on the amount of finance that is needed, with rights issues being used for medium-sized issues and issues to new shareholders being used for large issues. Issuing traded debt also has control implications however, since restrictive or negative covenants are usually written into the bond issue documents.

Workings

Current gearing (debt/equity, book value basis) = 100 × 5,000/7,300 = 68.5%

Gearing if equity finance is used = 100 × 5,000/(7,300 + 3,840) = 45%

Gearing if debt finance is used = 100 × (5,000 + 3,840)/7,300 = 121%

	ACCA marking scheme	Marks
(a)	Dividend per share	1
	Ex dividend share price	2
	Market capitalisation	1
		4
(b)	Rights issue price	1
	Cash raised	1
	Theoretical ex rights price per share	1
	Market capitalisation	2
		5
(c)	Calculation of price/earnings ratio	1
	Price/earnings ratio valuation	2
		3
(d)	Calculations of market capitalisation	2–3
	Comment	3–4
	Maximum	5
(e)	Relevant discussion	6–7
	Links to scenario in question	2–3
	Maximum	8
Total		25

Examiner's comments

Part (a) asked candidates to calculate the current ex dividend share price and the current market capitalisation of a company using the dividend growth model (DGM).

The first step was to calculate the current dividend per share, which surprisingly many candidates found difficult. Only one calculation, multiplying the earnings per share of the company by its payout ratio, was needed, but some candidates used half a page of calculations to produce the same answer. This highlights the importance of being familiar with the accounting ratios included in the F9 syllabus.

The formula for the DGM is given in the formula sheet, and the cost of equity and dividend growth rate were given in the question. Calculating the current ex dividend share price by inserting these values in the formula should therefore have posed no problem. Candidates who ignored or rearranged this formula created unnecessary difficulties for themselves and wasted valuable time. For example, some candidates rearranged the DGM formula into a cost of equity calculation and then called the cost of equity the current share price. This emphasises that candidates must be familiar with the formulae provided in the examination paper.

Finally, the current ex div share price had to be multiplied by the number of shares issued by the company to give its market capitalisation, or total value on the capital market. Surprisingly, some candidates did not understand 'market capitalisation' and offered no answer here for what was a straightforward calculation.

In part (b) candidates were asked to calculate the rights issue price per share, the cash raised by the rights issue, the theoretical ex rights price per share and the market capitalisation after the rights issue.

A significant number of candidates showed that they were unfamiliar with this part of the syllabus and gave answers that gained little credit. Some answers ignored the share price they had calculated in part (a) and assumed a different market price prior to the rights issue, frequently the company's ordinary share par value. Candidates should be aware that rights issues will not be made at a discount to par value. Many 'own error' marks were awarded in marking this part of question 2, following on from an assumed share price. In calculating market capitalisation after the rights issue, many answers neglected to subtract the issue costs.

Part (c) required the use of the price/earnings ratio method to calculate a share price and market capitalisation. Answers to this part of question 2 were often incomplete or adopted an incorrect methodology, for example calculating the price/earnings ratio of the target company when the question did not give the information needed for this. The correct approach is to multiply an earnings per share figure (or total earnings) by a suitable price/earnings ratio (in this case that of the acquirer).

Part (d) asked candidates to calculate and comment on market capitalisation before and after an announcement of expected annual after-tax cost savings, assuming a semi-strong form efficient market. The key thing to remember here is that in such a market, share prices fully and fairly reflect all relevant past and public information. The market capitalisation after the announcement would include the present value of the expected savings, calculated for example by the price/earnings method or by the dividend growth model. Before the announcement, the market capitalisation would not include this information and would be the market capitalisation immediately after the rights issue had taken place, adjusted for issue costs and the market value of the company acquired. Many candidates did not offer any calculations to support their discussion here, or offered calculations that did not relate to the question asked. Please refer to the suggested answer to this question for more detailed information on appropriate discussion and calculations.

Part (e) asked for a discussion of the factors that should be considered in choosing between equity and debt, with the answer being related to the circumstances of the acquirer and its proposed cash offer. Good answers focused on the circumstances of the company, considered its current capital structure, and discussed such factors as financial risk, current and expected interest rates, security and servicing costs, while weak answers offered a brief list of points with no discussion.

60 PHOBIS

Key answer tips

This question has three discrete requirements which are of varying difficulty. To score well you must ensure you capture the easy marks quickly and don't get bogged down on one particular area meaning you run out of time, or worse still, run over time and limit your ability to get all marks on later questions. Part (b) is the most difficult of the three requirements. This should have been tackled last. The highlighted words are key phrases that markers are looking for.

(a) (i) **Price/earnings ratio method valuation**

Earnings per share of Danoca Co = 40c

Average sector price/earnings ratio = 10

Implied value of ordinary share of Danoca Co = 40 × 10 = $4.00

Number of ordinary shares = 5 million

Value of Danoca Co = 4.00 × 5m = $20 million

(ii) Dividend growth model

Earnings per share of Danoca Co = 40c

Proposed payout ratio = 60%

Proposed dividend of Danoca Co is therefore = 40 × 0.6 = 24c

If the future dividend growth rate is expected to continue the historical trend in dividends per share, the historic dividend growth rate can be used as a substitute for the expected future dividend growth rate in the dividend growth model. Average geometric dividend growth rate over the last two years = $(24/22)^{1/2}$ = 1.045 or 4.5% (Alternatively, dividend growth rates over the last two years were 3% (24/23.3) and 6% (23.3/22), with an arithmetic average of (6 + 3)/2 = 4.5%)

Cost of equity of Danoca Co using the capital asset pricing model (CAPM)

= 4.6 + 1.4 × (10.6 − 4.6) = 4.6 + (1.4 × 6) = 13%

Value of ordinary share from dividend growth model = (24 × 1.045)/(0.13 − 0.045) = $2.95

Value of Danoca Co = 2.95 × 5m = $14.75 million

The current market capitalisation of Danoca Co is $16.5m ($3.30 × 5m). The price/earnings ratio value of Danoca Co is higher than this at $20m, using the average price/earnings ratio used for the sector. Danoca's own price/earnings ratio is 8.25. The difference between the two price/earnings ratios may indicate that there is scope for improving the financial performance of Danoca Co following the acquisition. If Phobis Co has the managerial skills to effect this improvement, the company and its shareholders may be able to benefit as a result of the acquisition.

The dividend growth model value is lower than the current market capitalisation at $14.75m. This represents a minimum value that Danoca shareholders will accept if Phobis Co makes an offer to buy their shares. In reality they would want more than this as an inducement to sell. The current market capitalisation of Danoca Co of $16.5m may reflect the belief of the stock market that a takeover bid for the company is imminent and, depending on its efficiency, may indicate a fair price for Danoca's shares, at least on a marginal trading basis. Alternatively, either the cost of equity or the expected dividend growth rate used in the dividend growth model calculation could be inaccurate, or the difference between the two values may be due to a degree of inefficiency in the stock market.

(b)   **Calculation of market value of each convertible bond**

Expected share price in five years' time = $4.45 \times 1.065^5 = \$6.10$

Conversion value = $6.10 \times 20 = \$122$

Compared with redemption at par value of $100, conversion will be preferred

The current market value will be the present value of future interest payments, plus the present value of the conversion value, discounted at the cost of debt of 7% per year.

Market value of each convertible bond = $(9 \times 4.100) + (122 \times 0.713) = \$123.89$

Calculation of floor value of each convertible bond

The current floor value will be the present value of future interest payments, plus the present value of the redemption value, discounted at the cost of debt of 7% per year.

Floor value of each convertible bond = $(9 \times 4.100) + (100 \times 0.713) = \$108.20$

Calculation of conversion premium of each convertible bond

Current conversion value = $4.45 \times 20 = \$89.00$

Conversion premium = $\$123.89 - 89.00 = \$34.89$

This is often expressed on a per share basis, i.e. 34.89/20 = $1.75 per share

(c)   Stock market efficiency usually refers to the way in which the prices of traded financial securities reflect relevant information. When research indicates that share prices fully and fairly reflect past information, a stock market is described as weak-form efficient. Investors cannot generate abnormal returns by analysing past information, such as share price movements in previous time periods, in such a market, since research shows that there is no correlation between share price movements in successive periods of time. Share prices appear to follow a 'random walk' by responding to new information as it becomes available.

When research indicates that share prices fully and fairly reflect public information as well as past information, a stock market is described as semi-strong form efficient. Investors cannot generate abnormal returns by analysing either public information, such as published company reports, or past information, since research shows that share prices respond quickly and accurately to new information as it becomes publicly available.

If research indicates that share prices fully and fairly reflect not only public information and past information, but private information as well, a stock market is described as strong form efficient. Even investors with access to insider information cannot generate abnormal returns in such a market. Testing for strong form efficiency is indirect in nature, examining for example the performance of expert analysts such as fund managers. Stock markets are not held to be strong form efficient.

The significance to a listed company of its shares being traded on a stock market which is found to be semi-strong form efficient is that any information relating to the company is quickly and accurately reflected in its share price. Managers will not be able to deceive the market by the timing or presentation of new information, such as annual reports or analysts' briefings, since the market processes the information quickly and accurately to produce fair prices. Managers should therefore simply concentrate on making financial decisions which increase the wealth of shareholders.

ACCA marking scheme		
		Marks
(a)	Price/earnings ratio value of company	2
	Proposed dividend per share	1
	Average dividend growth rate	1
	Cost of equity using CAPM	1
	Dividend growth model value of company	2
	Discussion	4
		───
		11
		───
(b)	Conversion value	1
	Market value	2
	Floor value	2
	Conversion premium	1
		───
		6
		───
(c)	Weak form efficiency	1–2
	Semi-strong form efficiency	1–2
	Strong form efficiency	1–2
	Significance of semi-strong form efficiency	2–3
		───
		8
		───
Total		25
		───

Examiner's comments

In part (a), candidates were asked to calculate the value of a company using the price/earnings ratio method and the dividend growth model, and to discuss the significance of calculated values, in comparison to the current market value of the company, to a potential buyer. Answers to this part of question 1 often failed to gain many marks, mainly because candidates did not calculate company values.

The prices/earnings ratio method calculates the value of a company by multiplying an earnings per share figure by a price/earnings ratio, and then multiplying by the number of issued shares. Alternatively, total earnings can be multiplied by a price/earnings ratio. Although the question provided an average sector price/earnings ratio to use in this context, many candidates simply calculated the current price/earnings ratio of the company and compared this with the sector value. Calculating a price/earnings ratio is not the same as calculating the value of a company. Candidates should also note that the price/earnings ratio is a multiple and neither a percentage nor a monetary amount.

The dividend growth model (DGM) formula is given in the formulae sheet in the examination paper. Many candidates rearranged the DGM formula in order to calculate a cost of equity, even though what was needed was to calculate a share price by inserting values for the current dividend, the cost of equity and the dividend growth rate into the DGM formula provided. The cost of equity could be calculated from the capital asset pricing model, using the formula given in the formulae sheet. The current dividend could be calculated using the dividend payout ratio and the current earnings per share value provided in the question. The future dividend growth rate could be calculated on an historical average basis, although there were many errors in its calculation. A number of candidates were unable to distinguish between some of the variables given in the question, for example confusing dividend per share with earnings per share, return on the market with cost of equity, and equity beta with retention ratio.

Even though the current market value of the company (number of shares multiplied by share price) was needed, a number of candidates failed to calculate it. The level of discussion was often limited, although some candidates demonstrated that they were aware of the weaknesses of the valuation models used.

Part (b) asked candidates to calculate the market value, floor value and conversion value of a $100 convertible bond. Many candidates either failed to answer this part of question 1, or showed in their answers that they did not understand how to calculate the present value of a stream of future cash flows (which is what the market value of a bond is equivalent to).

Candidates needed to calculate the present value of future interest payments plus the present value of the future conversion value (the market value, since conversion was financially preferable to redemption), and the present value of future interest payments plus the present value of the future redemption at par value (the floor value, since this stream of future cash flows is guaranteed). Some candidates were able to calculate the floor value, but called it the market value. Some candidates were able to calculate the current conversion value, but were not aware that this was used in calculating the conversion premium.

A number of candidates were not aware of the difference between interest rate, cost of debt and share price growth rate and used their values interchangeably. Some candidates introduced an assumed tax rate, when the question made no reference to taxation at all. There were indications of candidates learning a computation method, without acquiring an understanding of the concepts underlying it. Candidates must understand the importance, in financial management, of discounting future values in order to obtain present values, since this is used in investment appraisal, bond valuation, share valuation and company valuation.

Part (c) required candidates to distinguish between weak form, semi-strong form and strong form stock market efficiency, and to discuss the significance to a listed company of its shares being traded on a semi-strong form efficient stock market.

A number of candidates did not understand and could not discuss market efficiency, and very few correctly discussed the significance of semi-strong market efficiency to a company. Some candidates simply picked up on the terms weak, semi-strong and strong and discussed a range of stock market trading conditions, including bull and bear markets and depressed markets. Some candidates were aware of the link between market efficiency and information, but in a very tenuous way, for example saying that only past information was available, rather than saying that share prices fully and fairly reflected past information (weak form efficiency), or saying that investors were aware of current information, rather than saying that share prices fully and fairly reflected all past and public information (semi-strong-form efficiency). Overall, many answers were not of a pass standard.

RISK MANAGEMENT

61   NG CO

Key answer tips

This is a fairly hard question on sources of finance and foreign exchange risk. To score well in parts (a) and (b) you need to be clear about which currency each piece of information has been given in and make sure you convert where necessary to ensure you're being consistent. Make sure you don't ignore the request for calculations to illustrate your suggestions in part (d). The highlighted words are key phrases that markers are looking for.

(a)   Amount of equity finance to be invested in Euros = 13m/2 = €6.5 million

Amount of equity to be invested in dollars = 6.5m/1.3000 = $5 million

The amount of equity finance to be raised in dollars = 5m + 0.312m = $5.312m

Rights issue price = 4.00 × 0.83 = $3.32 per share

Number of new shares issued = 5.312m/3.32 = 1.6 million shares

Current number of ordinary shares in issue = $100m/4.00 = 25 million shares

Total number of shares after the rights issue = 25m + 1.6m = 26.6 million shares

Theoretical ex rights price = ((25m × 4) + (1.6m × 3.32))/26.6 = 105.312/26.6 = $3.96 per share

(b)   (i)   **Effect on earnings per share**

Current EPS = 100 × 4.00/10 = 40 cents per share

(Alternatively, current profit after tax = 100m/10 = $10 million

Current EPS = 100 × 10m/25m = 40 cents per share)

Increase in profit before interest and tax = 13m × 0.2 = €2,600,000

Dollar increase in profit before interest and tax = 2,600,000/1.3000 = $2 million

	$000
Increase in profit before interest and tax	2,000
Increase in interest = 6.5m × 0.08 = 0.52m/1.3000 =	400
Increase in profit before tax	1,600
Taxation = 1.6m × 0.3 =	480
Increase in profit after tax	1,120
Current profit after tax = 100m/10 =	10,000
Revised profit after tax	11,120

Alternatively, using Euros:

	€000
Increase in profit before interest and tax = 13m × 0.2 =	2,600
Increase in interest = 6.5m × 0.08 =	520
Increase in profit before tax	2,080
Taxation = 2.08m × 0.3 =	624
Increase in profit after tax	1,456
	$000
Increase in dollar profit after tax = 1.456m/1.300 =	1,120
Current profit after tax = 100m/10 =	10,000
Revised profit after tax	11,120

Revised EPS = 100 × 11.12m/26.6m = 41.8 cents/share

(ii) **Effect on shareholder wealth**

Expected share price using PER method = (41.8 × 10)/100 = $4.18 per share

This should be compared to the theoretical ex rights price per share in order to evaluate any change in shareholder wealth.

The investment produces a capital gain of 22 cents per share ($4.18 – $3.96)

In the absence of any information about dividend payments, it appears that the investment will increase the wealth of shareholders.

(c) Transaction risk is exchange rate risk that arises as a result of short-term transactions. Because it is short term in nature, it has a direct effect on cash flows, which can either increase or decrease, depending on the movement in exchange rates before the settlement dates of individual short-term transactions.

NG Co is exposed to transaction risk on its euro-denominated European sales and interest payments. The dollar value of its euro-denominated sales, for example, would decrease if the dollar appreciated against the euro.

Translation risk is exchange rate risk that arises from the need to consolidate financial performance and financial position when preparing consolidated financial statements. For this reason, it is also referred to as accounting exposure.

NG Co is exposed to translation risk on its euro-denominated non-current assets. The dollar value of the non-current assets acquired by investing in the storage, packing and distribution network, for example, will change as the euro/dollar exchange rate changes.

(d) NG Co will receive euro-denominated income and will incur euro-denominated expenses as a result of its European operations. One hedging method is to maintain a euro-denominated bank account for all euro-denominated transactions. This natural hedge will minimise the need for cash to be exchanged from one currency to another.

Transactions that are deemed to have significant exchange-rate risk could be hedged using the forward market, i.e. using a forward exchange contract or FEC. This is a binding contract between a company and a bank for delivery or receipt of an agreed amount of foreign currency at an agreed exchange rate on an agreed future date.

The six-monthly interest payment of €260,000 can be used to illustrate an FEC. The current cost of the interest payment is $200,000. In six months and twelve months, as the euro is expected to strengthen against the dollar, the dollar cost of the interest payment is expected to rise. In order to protect against unexpected adverse exchange rate movements, NG Co can lock into the six-month and twelve-month forward rates of 1.2876 €/$ and 1.2752 €/$ using forward exchange contracts, thereby guaranteeing the dollar cost of its euro-denominated interest payments. The dollar cost of the six-month interest payment would be $201,926 (€260,000/1.2876) and the dollar cost of the twelve-month interest payment would be $203,890 (€260,000/1.2752).

An alternative to an FEC is a money market hedge. NG Co could borrow now in dollars in order to make a euro deposit which, with accrued interest, will be sufficient to pay the euro-denominated interest in six months' time.

The six-month euro deposit rate available to NG Co is 1.39% ($100 \times (1.028^{0.5} - 1)$) and the six-month dollar borrowing rate available to NG Co is 2.62% ($100 \times (1.053^{0.5} - 1)$). The amount of dollars to deposit now would be €256,436 (260,000/1.0139) and to make this payment NG Co would need to borrow $197,259 (256,436/1.3000). The six-month dollar cost of this debt would be $202,427 (197,259 × 1.0262). This is more expensive than using the six-month forward exchange contract.

Tutorial note:

An illustration using the interest payment due in twelve months would also be acceptable. It would also be acceptable to use six-monthly interest rates that are one half of the annual interest rates.

Other hedging methods that could be identified and briefly discussed are currency futures, currency options and currency swaps.

	ACCA marking scheme		
			Marks
(a)	Amount of equity finance to be raised in dollars		1.0
	Rights issue price		1.0
	Theoretical ex rights price		2.0
		Maximum	4.0
(b)	Current EPS		1.0
	Increase in PBIT from investment		1.0
	Interest on bond issue		1.0
	Revised dollar profit after tax		2.0
	Revised EPS		1.0
	Revised share price using PER method		1.0
	Comment on effect on shareholder wealth		1–3
		Maximum	9.0
(c)	Transaction risk		1–2
	Translation risk		1–2
	Link to question		1–2
		Maximum	4.0
(d)	Euro account		1.0
	Forward market hedge		1.0
	Illustration of forward market hedge		1–2
	Money-market hedge		1.0
	Illustration of money-market hedge		1–2
	Other hedging strategies, including derivatives		1–2
		Maximum	8.0
Total			25

Examiner's comments

Many students found parts (a) and (b) of question 3 to be challenging, while gaining high marks on parts (c) and (d).

Part (a) required candidates to calculate the theoretical ex rights price per share for a new equity issue.

The question stated that the rights issue needed to provide €6.5 million. Since the issue was in dollars and the exchange rate was 1.3000 €/$, the rights issue needed to raise $5 million. Since issue costs were $312,000 the rights issue needed to raise $5.312 million. The rights issue price was $3.32 per share meaning that 1.6 million shares needed to be issued.

The errors that candidates made here are instructive for students who are studying Paper F9, such as: not converting Euros into dollars: using the exchange rate incorrectly, so that the dollar amount was greater than the euro amount; being unable to calculate the number of new shares to be issued and assuming a form for the rights issue (such as a 1 for 1 issue); ignoring issue costs; and using a rights issue to raise all of the finance needed, even though the question said that 50% of funding was through debt.

Part (b) asked candidates to evaluate the effect of the European investment on the earnings per share of the company and on the wealth of its shareholders.

Many candidates ignored the 20% return on investment before interest and tax and discussed the position of the company after the rights issue; many were also unable to calculate the current earnings per share of the company, even though the question gave its current price earnings ratio and its current share price.

In order to make progress in answering the question, candidates needed to calculate the earnings per share after the new funds had been raised, taking into account the return on the new funds raised. This evaluation could be done in Euros or in dollars, provided that the revised earnings per share was expressed in the home currency of the company, which was dollars. Once the revised earnings per share had been calculated, multiplying by the price earnings ratio gave the revised share price.

The poor standard of answers here (in general) shows that candidates need to study the suggested answer with care and reflect on the areas where their own answers ran into difficulty.

Part (c) asked candidates to explain the difference between transaction risk and translation risk, illustrating their answers using the information given in the question. Many candidates gained full marks here and seemed to be well-prepared for this question and for the hedging question in part (d).

Candidates who lost marks were unable to distinguish clearly between the two forms of risk, or did not provide the illustrations required by the question.

Part (d) asked candidates to identify and briefly discuss hedging methods that could be used by the company, and provide illustrations of two of the hedging methods. In general answers were of an acceptable standard and many students gained good marks here. There were several reasons why marks were lost, such as confusing exchange rates with interest rates: discussing forward rate agreements, rather than forward exchange contracts; providing illustrations using calculations, but not giving an explanation of the calculations; and listing hedging methods (futures, options, swaps, leading and lagging, and so on) without explaining how these could help the company in question.

62   NEDWEN

Key answer tips

This is a fairly straightforward question that has a good balance of discursive and mathematical elements. Parts (a) and (b) offer a chance to pick up some easy marks for simple 'learn and churn' type answers. To score well in parts (c) and (d) you need to be clear on the spot and forward rates provided to ensure you select the right ones The highlighted words are key phrases that markers are looking for.

(a)   **Transaction risk**

This is the risk arising on short-term foreign currency transactions that the actual income or cost may be different from the income or cost expected when the transaction was agreed. For example, a sale worth $10,000 when the exchange rate is $1.79 per £ has an expected sterling value is $5,587. If the dollar has depreciated against sterling to $1.84 per £ when the transaction is settled, the sterling receipt will have fallen to $5,435. Transaction risk therefore affects cash flows and for this reason most companies choose to hedge or protect themselves against transaction risk.

Translation risk

This risk arises on consolidation of financial statements prior to reporting financial results and for this reason is also known as accounting exposure. Consider an asset worth €14 million, acquired when the exchange rate was €1.4 per $. One year later, when financial statements are being prepared, the exchange rate has moved to €1.5 per $ and the balance sheet value of the asset has changed from $10 million to $9.3 million, resulting an unrealised (paper) loss of $0.7 million. Translation risk does not involve cash flows and so does not directly affect shareholder wealth. However, investor perception may be affected by the changing values of assets and liabilities, and so a company may choose to hedge translation risk through, for example, matching the currency of assets and liabilities (e.g. a euro-denominated asset financed by a euro-denominated loan).

Economic risk

Transaction risk is seen as the short-term manifestation of economic risk, which could be defined as the risk of the present value of a company's expected future cash flows being affected by exchange rate movements over time. It is difficult to measure economic risk, although its effects can be described, and it is also difficult to hedge against it.

(a)   The law of one price suggests that identical goods selling in different countries should sell at the same price, and that exchange rates relate these identical values. This leads on to purchasing power parity theory, which suggests that changes in exchange rates over time must reflect relative changes in inflation between two countries. If purchasing power parity holds true, the expected spot rate (Sf) can be forecast from the current spot rate (S0) by multiplying by the ratio of expected inflation rates ((1 + if)/ (1 + iUK)) in the two counties being considered. In formula form: Sf = S0 (1 + if)/ (1 + iUK).

Tutorial note:

The formula you are supplied with in the exam uses S_1 to define the future spot rate, h_c to define the inflation rate in the overseas country (instead of i_f as given above) and h_b to define the inflation rate in the home country (instead of iUK given above).

This relationship has been found to hold in the longer-term rather than the shorter-term and so tends to be used for forecasting exchange rates several years in the future, rather than for periods of less than one year. For shorter periods, forward rates can be calculated using interest rate parity theory, which suggests that changes in exchange rates reflect differences between interest rates between countries.

(c)   **Forward market evaluation**

Net receipt in 1 month = $240,000 – $140,000 = $100,000

Nedwen Co needs to sell dollars at an exchange rate of 1.7829 + 0.003 = $1.7832 per £

Sterling value of net receipt = $100,000/1.7832 = £56,079

Receipt in 3 months = $300,000

Nedwen Co needs to sell dollars at an exchange rate of 1.7846 + 0.004 = $1.7850 per £

Sterling value of receipt in 3 months = $300,000/1.7850 = £168,067

(d) **Evaluation of money-market hedge**

Expected receipt after 3 months = $300,000

Dollar interest rate over three months = 5.4/4 = 1.35%

Dollars to borrow now to have $300,000 liability after 3 months = 300,000/1.0135 = $296,004

Spot rate for selling dollars = 1.7820 + 0.0002 = $1.7822 per £

Sterling deposit from borrowed dollars at spot = $296,004/1.7822 = £166,089

Sterling interest rate over three months = 4.6/ 4 = 1.15%

Value in 3 months of sterling deposit = £166,089 × 1.0115 = £167,999

The forward market is marginally preferable to the money market hedge for the dollar receipt expected after 3 months.

(e) A currency futures contract is a standardised contract for the buying or selling of a specified quantity of foreign currency. It is traded on a futures exchange and settlement takes place in three-monthly cycles ending in March, June, September and December, i.e. a company can buy or sell September futures, December futures and so on. The price of a currency futures contract is the exchange rate for the currencies specified in the contract.

When a currency futures contract is bought or sold, the buyer or seller is required to deposit a sum of money with the exchange, called initial margin. If losses are incurred as exchange rates and hence the prices of currency futures contracts change, the buyer or seller may be called on to deposit additional funds (variation margin) with the exchange. Equally, profits are credited to the margin account on a daily basis as the contract is 'marked to market'.

Most currency futures contracts are closed out before their settlement dates by undertaking the opposite transaction to the initial futures transaction, i.e. if buying currency futures was the initial transaction, it is closed out by selling currency futures. A gain made on the futures transactions will offset a loss made on the currency markets and vice versa.

Nedwen Co expects to receive $300,000 in three months' time and so is concerned that sterling may appreciate (strengthen) against the dollar, since this would result in a lower sterling receipt. The company can hedge the receipt by selling sterling futures contracts and since it is 1 April, would sell June futures contracts. In June, Nedwen Co would buy the same number of futures it sold in April and sell the $300,000 it received on the currency market.

ACCA marking scheme			
			Marks
(a)	Transaction risk	2 marks	
	Translation risk	2 marks	
	Economic risk	2 marks	
			6
(b)	Discussion of purchasing power parity	4–5 marks	
	Discussion of interest rate parity	1–2 marks	
	Maximum		6
(c)	Netting	1 mark	
	Sterling value of 3-month receipt	1 mark	
	Sterling value of 1-year receipt	1 mark	
			3
(d)	Evaluation of money market hedge	4 marks	
	Comment	1 mark	
			5
(e)	Definition of currency futures contract	1–2 marks	
	Initial margin and variation margin	1–2 marks	
	Buying and selling of contracts	1–2 marks	
	Hedging the three-month receipt	1–2 marks	
	Maximum		5
	Total		25

63 LAGRAG CO

Key answer tips

To ensure you capture all of the easy marks available in this question, you must read the requirement carefully and focus on the number of marks allocated to each part. Many students could write a lot to answer part (d) but it is only worth 4 marks. You must restrict your answer here and focus more on the earlier parts to the question. The highlighted words are key phrases that markers are looking for.

(a) The term structure of interest rates is revealed by the redemption yield data. As the term to maturity increases, the redemption yield also increases, producing what is known as the normal upward sloping yield curve. The shape of the yield curve can be explained as follows:

   (i) Liquidity preference theory states that as investors have a natural preference for more liquid investments, they will need to receive extra compensation in the form of an enhanced yield if they are to invest for the longer term

   (ii) Expectations theory suggests that the shape of the yield curve reflects the expectation of future interest rates. Hence if the yield curve becomes steeper, this indicates that interest rates are likely to rise, whereas if the yield curve becomes less steep, this indicates that interest rates are likely to decline.

     (iii)   Market segmentation theory suggests that the market for borrowing and lending is split into segments. For instance, some lenders specialise in shorter term lending. Supply and demand variations, the fact that the different segments will have different information and the operators in the different segments will have different views means that the yield curve may not be completely smooth.

Given the change in the redemption yields between the two years, it appears that the yield curve is becoming steeper and hence there is probably an expectation of a rise in interest rates.

(b)   The appropriate forward rate agreement is the 3 v 7 agreement and as a borrower the rate agreed will be 7.53%.

     (i)   If the actual interest rate payable is 7.76% in three months, then the cash flows will be as follows:

Actual interest paid	$10m × 4/12 × 7.76%	($258,667)
Compensation received	$10m × 4/12 × (7.76% − 7.53%)	$7,667
Net cost		($251,000)

     (ii)   If the actual interest rate payable is 7.42% in three months, then the cash flows will be as follows:

Actual interest paid	$10m × 4/12 × 7.42%	($247,333)
Compensation paid	$10m × 4/12 × (7.53% − 7.42%)	($3,667)
Net cost		($251,000)

Whatever the actual interest rate, the net cost remains the same.

(c)   **Futures**

As a borrower, a hedge with interest rate futures will protect Lagrag plc from higher borrowing costs. Should borrowing costs rise and our borrowings incur additional interest cost, then a compensating gain will be made as a result of the movement in the futures price. Unfortunately though, if our borrowing cost was to fall and we were to make a saving on our interest cost, an offsetting loss would be made as a result of the movement in the futures price.

Hence, the impact of a futures hedge would be to effectively fix our interest cost. The cost may not be completely fixed as the hedge may be imperfect due to basis risk.

Options on futures

As a borrower, a hedge with interest rate options on futures will protect Lagrag plc from higher borrowing costs. Should borrowing costs rise and our borrowings incur additional interest cost, then a compensating gain will be possible due to the movement in the futures price. To realise this gain the option would have to be exercised. If our borrowing costs were to fall and we were to make a saving on our interest cost, there would be no compensating loss as the option would not be exercised. Hence, a hedge using options on futures provides protection against a rise in interest rates, but will allow Lagrag plc to benefit if interest rates were to fall. Unfortunately though, as options are more flexible, they are more costly and there will be a premium to pay. This premium represents a sunk cost as is cannot be reclaimed in the option is not exercised.

Recommendation

As the yield curve is indicating that interest rates will rise, it is recommended that futures are used as it is unlikely to be worth paying for the flexibility of options on futures.

(d) If Lagrag plc were to sell to an overseas customer, the two major risks that are likely to arise would be the risk of non-collection and the transaction risk which arises as a result of potential exchange rate movements between the invoice date and the date the payment is received.

The risk of non-collection could be reduced by using, for instance, a factor who is willing to assist with collection and provide protection against bad debts.

Transaction risk could be hedged in a number of ways. The simplest of these would be the use of a forward contract if one is available. This is simple and cheap and fixes the exchange rate to be used.

64 BOLUJE CO

Key answer tips

Part (a) is a standard discussion on the benefits of debt finance. Part (b) may look complicated, dealing in foreign bonds denominated in pesos, but requires a straightforward application of the dividend valuation model using the base premise of the market value of an investment equalling the present value of the future cash flows.

Part (c) gives plenty of opportunity for students to cover familiar areas. The trick with the calculations (an illustration was requested) is to recognise that Boluje is hedging its interest payments only (and not the full amount of the foreign bonds).

Finally, for 8 marks part (d) should be a relatively easy discussion of other hedging methods primarily focussing on futures and options. The highlighted words are key phrases that markers are looking for.

(a) Pecking order theory suggests that companies have a preferred order in which they seek to raise finance, beginning with retained earnings. The advantages of using retained earnings are that issue costs are avoided by using them, the decision to use them can be made without reference to a third party, and using them does not bring additional obligations to consider the needs of finance providers.

Once available retained earnings have been allocated to appropriate uses within a company, its next preference will be for debt. One reason for choosing to finance a new investment by an issue of debt finance, therefore, is that insufficient retained earnings are available and the investing company prefers issuing debt finance to issuing equity finance.

Debt finance may also be preferred when a company has not yet reached its optimal capital structure and it is mainly financed by equity, which is expensive compared to debt. Issuing debt here will lead to a reduction in the WACC and hence an increase in the market value of the company. One reason why debt is cheaper than equity is that debt is higher in the creditor hierarchy than equity, since ordinary shareholders are paid out last in the event of liquidation. Debt is even cheaper if it is secured on assets of the company. The cost of debt is reduced even further by the tax efficiency of debt, since interest payments are an allowable deduction in arriving at taxable profit.

Debt finance may be preferred where the maturity of the debt can be matched to the expected life of the investment project. Equity finance is permanent finance and so may be preferred for investment projects with long lives.

(b) Annual interest paid per foreign bond = 500 × 0.061 = 30.5 pesos

Redemption value of each foreign bond = 500 pesos

Cost of debt of peso-denominated bonds = 7% per year

Market value of each foreign bond = (30.5 × 4.100) + (500 × 0.713) = 481.55 pesos

Current total market value of foreign bonds = 16m × (481.55/500) = 15,409,600 pesos

(c) (i) Interest payment in one year's time = 16m × 0.061 = 976,000 pesos

A money market hedge would involve placing on deposit an amount of pesos that, with added interest, would be sufficient to pay the peso-denominated interest in one year. Because the interest on the peso-denominated deposit is guaranteed, Boluje Co would be protected against any unexpected or adverse exchange rate movements prior to the interest payment being made.

Peso deposit required = 976,000/ 1.05 = 929,524 pesos

Dollar equivalent at spot = 929,524/ 6 = $154,921

Dollar cost in one year's time = 154,921 × 1.04 = $161,118

(ii) Cost of forward market hedge = 976,000/6.07 = $160,790

The forward market hedge is slightly cheaper

(d) Boluje receives peso income from its export sales and makes annual peso-denominated interest payments to bond-holders. It could consider opening a peso account in the overseas country and using this as a natural hedge against peso exchange rate risk.

Boluje Co could consider using lead payments to settle foreign currency liabilities. This would not be beneficial as far as peso-denominated liabilities are concerned, as the peso is depreciating against the dollar. It is inadvisable to lag payments to foreign suppliers, since this would breach sales agreements and lead to loss of goodwill.

Foreign currency derivatives available to Boluje Co could include currency futures, currency options and currency swaps.

Currency futures are standardised contracts for the purchase or sale of a specified quantity of a foreign currency. These contracts are settled on a quarterly cycle, but a futures position can be closed out any time by undertaking the opposite transaction to the one that opened the futures position. Currency futures provide a hedge that theoretically eliminates both upside and downside risk by effectively locking the holder into a given exchange rate, since any gains in the currency futures market are offset by exchange rate losses in the cash market, and vice versa. In practice however, movements in the two markets are not perfectly correlated and basis risk exists if maturities are not perfectly matched. Imperfect hedges can also arise if the standardised size of currency futures does not match the exchange rate exposure of the hedging company. Initial margin must be provided when a currency futures position is opened and variation margin may also be subsequently required. Boluje Co could use currency futures to hedge both its regular foreign currency receipts and its annual interest payment.

Currency options give holders the right, but not the obligation, to buy or sell foreign currency. Over-the-counter (OTC) currency options are tailored to individual client needs, while exchange-traded currency options are standardised in the same way as currency futures in terms of exchange rate, amount of currency, exercise date and settlement cycle. An advantage of currency options over currency futures is that currency options do not need to be exercised if it is disadvantageous for the holder to do so. Holders of currency options can take advantage of favourable exchange rate movements in the cash market and allow their options to lapse. The initial fee paid for the options will still have been incurred, however.

Currency swaps are appropriate for hedging exchange rate risk over a longer period of time than currency futures or currency options. A currency swap is an interest rate swap where the debt positions of the counterparties and the associated interest payments are in different currencies. A currency swap begins with an exchange of principal, although this may be a notional exchange rather than a physical exchange. During the life of the swap agreement, the counterparties undertake to service each others' foreign currency interest payments. At the end of the swap, the initial exchange of principal is reversed.

ACCA marking scheme			Marks
(a)	Relevant discussion		7
(b)	Market value of each foreign bond	3	
	Total market value of foreign bonds	1	
		——	4
(c)	(i) Explanation of money market hedge	2	
	Illustration of money market hedge	2	
		——	4
	(ii) Comparison with forward market hedge		2
(d)	Discussion of natural hedge	1 – 2	
	Description of other hedging methods	6 – 7	
		——	
			Max 8
Total			25

Examiner's comment

In part (a) of this question, candidates were asked to explain the reasons why a company might choose to finance a new investment by an issue of debt. Answers were of variable quality, with some candidates writing very little while others gained full marks.

Weaker answers discussed other sources of finance, such as leasing or preference shares, or focused on the disadvantages of equity finance, indicating perhaps that candidates had prepared for a question about equity, but were unprepared for a question about debt. Better answers covered such reasons as the lower cost of debt compared with other sources of finance, due to lower risk of debt finance and its tax efficiency: the relative ease with which debt finance could be raised; the potentially positive effect of the lower cost of debt on the weighted average cost of capital and the market value of the company; the place of debt finance in pecking order theory; and the matching of debt and asset maturity.

Part (b) required candidates to calculate the total market value (in pesos) of a foreign bond (denominated in pesos). The market value of a bond is the present value of future interest payments added to the present value of the future redemption value. Good answers calculated the interest payable in pesos on each bond, the market value of each bond as just described, and then the total market value by multiplying the market value per bond by the number of bonds issued. Weaker answers sought to calculate the internal rate of return of the bond, which was unnecessary as the cost of debt was given in the question. Internal rate of return is not equal to market value.

Part (c) asked for an explanation and an illustration of a money market hedge, and a comparison of the relative costs of a money market hedge and a forward market hedge. Answers were again of very variable quality.

Many candidates were unable to calculate the annual peso interest required by the illustration of the money market hedge. Both the interest rate and the par value of the bond issue were given in the question, and multiplying one by the other gives the amount of interest to be paid. Some candidates invented a cash flow to illustrate the money market hedge: candidates who invented a future peso receipt failed to notice that the interest rates given in the question could not then be used, since the peso rate was a deposit rate and the dollar rate was a borrowing rate. Weaker answers tried to hedge a future dollar payment, when the question stated that the dollar was the home currency.

Many candidates were able to calculate correctly the dollar value of a forward market hedge and indicate whether this hedge would be preferred to a money market hedge.

Many candidates gave good answers to part (d), even if some answers tended to be a list rather a description. The question was open-ended, asking for a description of methods (including derivatives) that could be used to hedge exchange rate risk. Many methods could be and were described, including netting, matching, invoicing in the home currency, leading and lagging, forward exchange contracts, futures, option and swaps.

65 EXPORTERS PLC *Walk in the footsteps of a top tutor*

Key answer tips

Another fairly standard question that combines knowledge with application. The highlighted words are key phrases that markers are looking for.

Tutor's top tips:

Don't feel you have to tackle the different parts of the requirement in order. Part (a) and part (b) (iii) give the best opportunities for some easy marks so are the best places to start.

(a) **Forward exchange contract**

- A firm and binding agreement for the future trading of a particular amount of currency at a given price.

- A fixed contract is one where the date on which the trade will take place has been specified. An option contract is one where the trade can take place within a specified period.

(b) **Exporters plc**

Tutor's top tips:

This first thing to appreciate about this part of the requirement is that it's asking a question that rarely gets asked in reality – what if we hadn't entered into that hedge? Remember, the purpose of hedging a transaction is to eliminate risk, and so it isn't often someone would bother looking back to calculate what would have happened if they hadn't bothered!

That said, to perform the calculation you need to keep in mind the following things:

1 Forward rates will be determined by interest differentials (the question doesn't specify the forward rate the company is locking in to. It does however, give you the interest differentials that will allow you to work the forward rate out.

2 What does happen to interest rates in the future will be determined by many different factors – the rate that does occur in the future is unlikely to be the same as the future rate that was contacted. This will give rise to a gain or loss on the transaction.

3 If the £ gains in value (appreciates), you will get more Northland dollars for each £. Equally, if it losses value (depreciates or weakens) it will buy less Northland dollars.

(i)   UK interest rates over 6 months are $\frac{1}{2} \times 12\% = 6\%$.

Northland interest rates over 6 months are $\frac{1}{2} \times 15\% = 7.5\%$

Implied forward rate for the £ after 6 months $= \frac{1.075}{1.06} \times 2.5 = 2.5354$.

Tutorial note:

If you calculated your forward rate using the annual interest rates, you would only lose one mark. All further calculations will be based on the 'own figure rule' which means that, provided you used the right technique, your answer would be marked as correct, even though you have a different answer to that shown here.

---

(1)   If the £ has gained 4%, N's actual rate is $2.5 \times 1.04 = 2.6$ to the £.

Hedged receipt $= \dfrac{\$500,000}{2.5354} = $ £197,208

Unhedged receipt $= \dfrac{\$500,000}{2.6} = $ £192,308

∴ Gain from hedging $= £197,208 - £192,308 = £4,900$.

(2)   If the £ has lost 2%, N's actual rate is $2.5 \times 0.98 = 2.45$ to the £

Unhedged receipt $= \dfrac{\$500,000}{2.45} = £204,082$

∴ Loss from hedging $= £204,082 - £197,208 = £6,874$.

(3)   If the £ has remained stable, N's actual rate is still 2.5 to the £.

Unhedged receipt $= \dfrac{\$500,000}{2.5} = £200,000$

∴ Loss from hedging $= £200,000 - £197,208 = £2,792$.

(ii)   The interest rate parity analysis of forward rates suggests that an equilibrium is reached when:

$$F_0 = S_0 \times \frac{(1 + i_c)}{(1 + i_b)}$$

If the above equation were not an equality, it would be possible to make riskless profits by buying a foreign currency and holding a deposit in that currency on which interest was earned before returning to sterling. The opportunity cost of holding the foreign currency must equal the real interest rate of that currency relative to sterling. Arbitrageurs would quickly move in to drive the relation back to equality if they identified the possibility of riskless profits.

The analysis holds true only in an efficient market, since it excludes practical factors such as transaction costs and illiquidity. However in markets such as the major currency Eurocurrency markets in the UK, there is sufficient efficiency for the analysis to hold very nearly true.

(iii)   **Forward market currency hedge**

A company can use the foreign exchange markets to hedge exactly as shown in the question. A company due to receive foreign currency in 6 months time can sell that currency forward, i.e. agree an exchange rate now at which that amount of foreign currency will be exchanged into sterling. The cost involved will be paid to the bank arranging the transaction and will usually be built into the contract's exchange rate so that the foreign currency is quoted net. The benefits are peace of mind to the company that they have laid off the risks of exchange rate movements between the contract date and the date when the foreign currency will be paid or received. Part (a) illustrates a range of possible gains and losses on a forward market currency hedge depending on the actual currency movements before the contract matures.

Currency futures hedge

Currency futures contracts are traded on separate exchanges such as the London International Financial Futures and Options Exchange (LIFFE). Each contract provides a simultaneous right and obligation to buy or sell on a specific future date a standard amount of a particular currency at a price that is known at the time of entering the contract. Since the contracts are sold in standard amounts and have a limited number of maturity dates each year, they are highly standardised and a liquid market has developed to trade them.

A UK exporting company due to receive 500,000 Northland dollars in six months' time could only hedge its currency exposure by means of currency futures if contracts are available between Northland dollars and sterling, and then only could it create an exact hedge if 500,000 dollars happened to be a multiple of the standard contract size.   But assuming that both these conditions are fulfilled, the company can buy contracts to sell Northland dollars into sterling at the required future time.

Currency options hedge

A call/put option gives the buyer of that option the right, but not the obligation, to buy/sell currency in the future at a particular exchange rate. A UK company which uses a forward or futures position avoids losing from adverse movements on currencies but also fails to gain from favourable movements. A currency option is suitable for a UK company which believes it knows the direction of future exchange rate movements, but is not sure and wishes to minimise the loss arising in the event of being proved incorrect.

The company in the question anticipates dollars receivable in six months' time. It can pay an option premium to buy sterling call options. These enable the company to benefit from the anticipated appreciating dollar while providing protection against the opposite movement.

66   ELECT CO

Key answer tips

This question is a good mixture of knowledge and application. Parts (d) and (e) offer a good opportunity to pick up some easy marks and so should be attempted first. The calculations within parts (a) and (b) are reasonably straightforward although those in part (c) will require you to make some assumptions in order to answer in full.

The highlighted words in the written sections are key phrases that markers are looking for.

(a)   The value of a $100 par value bond can be calculated as follows:

	Cash flow $	10% AF/DF	PV $
T1-6 – annual interest	8	4.355	34.84
T6 – conversion value	100	0.564	56.40
Value			91.24

Total market value of Bond A: $10m × 91.24/100 = $9.12m

(b)   Cost of equity shares = 15% (per question)

Cost of bank loan = (3% + 1%) × (1 − 0.3) = 2.8%

After-tax cost of Bond A:

	Cash flow	5% DF	PV	10% DF	PV
T0 – market value	(91.24)	1	(91.24)	1	(91.24)
T1-6 – post tax interest	5.6	5.076	28.43	4.355	24.39
T6 – conversion value	100	0.746	74.60	0.564	56.40
			11.79		−10.45

Cost = IRR = 5 + (11.79/(11.79 + 10.45)) × (10 − 5) = 7.65%

Total market values:

Equity – $1.70 × 10m/2 =	$34.00m
Bond A – as above	$9.12m
Bank loan –	$5.00m
Total MV –	$48.12m

$$\text{WACC} = \left[\frac{34}{48.12}\right]15\% + \left[\frac{9.12}{48.12}\right]7.65\% + \left[\frac{5}{48.12}\right]2.8\% = 12.3\%$$

(c)   (i)   Assuming that the new equity finance does not affect the market value of each existing share, the impact on the WACC can be estimated as:

$$\text{WACC} = \left[\frac{(34+5)}{(48.12+5)}\right]15\% + \left[\frac{9.12}{(48.12+5)}\right]7.65\% + \left[\frac{5}{(48.12+5)}\right]2.8\% = 12.6\%$$

(ii)   Assuming that the additional debt finance does not result in a change to the cost of equity, the impact on the WACC can be estimated as:

WACC =

$$\left[\frac{34}{(48.12+5)}\right]15\% + \left[\frac{9.12}{(48.12+5)}\right]7.65\% + \left[\frac{5}{(48.12+5)}\right]2.8\% + \left[\frac{5}{(48.12+5)}\right]7\% = 11.8\%$$

(d)

Tutorial note:

The answers given below for parts (d) and (e) contain a full range of factors that could be noted and are therefore more than you would need to write in the exam to score full marks.

The factors that Elect Co should consider when choosing between an issue of debt and issue of equity finance include the following:

Risk and return

Raising debt finance will increase the gearing and the financial risk of the company, while raising equity finance will lower gearing and financial risk.

Financial risk arises since raising debt brings a commitment to meet regular interest payments, whether fixed or variable. Failure to meet these interest payments gives debt holders the right to appoint a receiver to recover their investment. In contrast, there is no right to receive dividends on ordinary shares, only a right to participate in any dividend (share of profit) declared by the directors of a company. If profits are low, then dividends can be passed, but interest must be paid regardless of the level of profits. Furthermore, increasing the level of interest payments will increase the volatility of returns to shareholders, since only returns in excess of the cost of debt accrue to shareholders. Elect currently has a low level of financial gearing and so they should not be too concerned about the additional risk which would arise from a further $5m of debt finance.

Cost

Debt is cheaper than equity because debt is less risky from an investor point of view. This is because it is often secured by either a fixed or floating charge on company assets and ranks above equity on liquidation, and because of the statutory requirement to pay interest. Debt is also cheaper than equity because interest is an allowable deduction in calculating taxable profit. This is referred to as the tax efficiency of debt.

As can be seen from the calculations in part (c), raising the new funds via equity will increase the overall cost of capital to 12.6%, yet raising the funds via debt will reduce the cost of capital to 11.8%.

Ownership and control

Issuing equity can have ownership implications for a company, particularly if the finance is raised by means of a placing or offer for sale. Shareholders also have the right to appoint directors and auditors, and the right to attend general meetings of the company. While issuing debt has no such ownership implications, an issue of debt can place restrictions on the activities of a company by means of restrictive covenants included in the issue documents. For example, a restrictive covenant may specify a maximum level of gearing or a minimum level of interest cover which the borrowing company must not exceed, or a covenant may forbid the securing of further debt on particular assets.

Redemption

Equity finance is permanent capital that does not need to be redeemed, while debt finance will need to be redeemed at some future date. Redeeming a large amount of debt can place a severe strain on the cash flow of a company, although this can be addressed by refinancing or by using convertible debt.

This will be a particular consideration for Elect Co given that their current $5m bank loan must be repaid in two years.

Flexibility

Debt finance is more flexible than equity, in that various amounts can be borrowed, at a fixed or floating interest rate and for a range of maturities, to suit the financing need of a company. If debt finance is no longer required, it can more easily be repaid (depending on the issue terms).

Availability

A new issue of equity finance may not be readily available to a listed company or may be available on terms that are unacceptable with regards to issue price or issue quantity, if the stock market is depressed (a bear market). Current shareholders may be unwilling to subscribe to a rights issue, for example if they have made other investment plans or if they have urgent calls on their existing finances. A new issue of debt finance may not be available to a listed company, or available at a cost considered to be unacceptable, if it has a poor credit rating, or if it faces trading difficulties.

(e) **Factors affecting the choice between fixed and floating rate debt:**

Expected changes in interest rates

Obtaining a floating rate loan means a company will be affected by changes in interest rates. If rates increase, then the company will pay more interest on a loan; if rates fall, then the company pays less. If interest rates are expected to rise, then a fixed rate loan may be preferable as the company will not be affected by the rate increase; similarly, if rates are expected to fall, then a variable rate loan will be preferred to take advantage of falling rates of interest.

Amount of time the loan is required

Obtaining a fixed rate loan may be more risky if the loan is for a long period of time as the company will effectively be locked into this rate. Rate changes become more difficult to forecast in the long term. However, a fixed rate again provides certainty as to the amount of interest to be paid. If the loan is for a long period, then various hedging techniques will normally be considered.

Existing mix of fixed and variable loans

The finance director of Elect Co may require a portfolio of fixed and variable rates loans simply as a method of hedging risk. Given that the value of variable rate loans is currently lower than fixed loans then this may indicate a preference for variable rate loan.

Risk appetite

Elect Co will view the variable and fixed loans as having different levels of risk. If the company's risk appetite is low, then a lower risk alternative will be taken. However, treasurers will normally want a range of financial products to minimise risk for their company.

Methods of hedging interest rate risk

FRA

An FRA is an over-the-counter instrument that can be arranged with a bank, fixing the interest rate on a notional principal amount for a given period of time. FRAs are only available for quite large principal amounts (at least $1 million) and can be arranged up to about two years into the future.

A company wishing to fix an interest rate for borrowing should buy an FRA. The FRA is not an agreement to borrow the funds required. Elect Co must arrange to borrow the $5 million separately. Elect Co will borrow $5 million at the current market rate of interest, whatever this happens to be. The FRA would be settled by:

- a payment from the bank to Elect Co if the benchmark interest rate is higher than the FRA rate; or

- a payment from Elect Co to the bank if the benchmark rate is lower than the FRA rate.

The hedge works because the interest payment on the actual borrowing plus or minus the settlement amount for the FRA should fix the overall effective borrowing cost for Elect Co.

Interest rate futures

Short-term interest rate futures are exchange-traded instruments. A company wishing to fix a rate for borrowing should sell interest rate futures.

The interest rate is in the price of the future. Prices are quoted at 100 minus the interest rate, so if Elect Co were to sell futures, say, at 92.50, this would 'fix' its borrowing rate at 7.5%. As the future approaches settlement date, if the interest rate has risen (to say 9%), the market price of the futures should have moved to about 91.00. Elect Co could then close its position by buying futures, and making a profit of 1.50 (150 points) on each contract of its futures dealing. The net borrowing cost would be 9% less the value of the profit on futures trading (1.5%) giving a net effective interest cost of 7.5%.

Since interest rate futures are only available in standardised amounts and dates, they are less flexible than FRAs, and so possibly less attractive to Elect Co.

Interest rate guarantee

This is a type of borrower's option and unlike an FRA or futures which are binding contracts on both parties, it is not a binding commitment on the option holder. If Elect Co buys this instrument at a cap strike price of say 7%, it will exercise its option if the interest rate at expiry is higher than 7%. It will then receive the interest value of the difference between the actual interest rate and the cap rate of 7%.

However, if the interest rate was to fall, Elect Co would be able to walk away from the option.

The premiums payable on interest rate guarantees can be expensive and must be paid up-front.